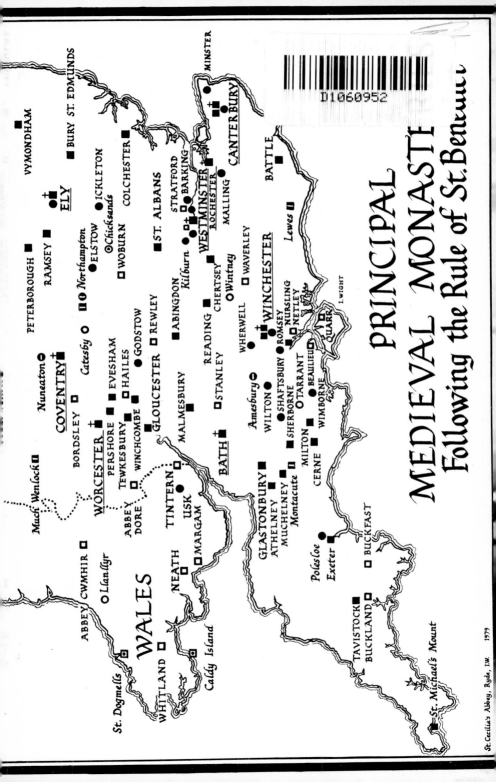

PRINCIPAL MEDIEVAL MONASTE...
Following the Rule of St. Benedict

MINSTER

VYMONDHAM

BURY ST. EDMUNDS

CANTERBURY

BATTLE

ELY

ICKLETON

COLCHESTER

Chicksands

WOBURN

STRATFORD

BARKING

WESTMINSTER

ROCHESTER

MALLING

Lewes

ST. ALBANS

PETERBOROUGH

RAMSEY

Northampton

ELSTOW

Kilburn

WINTNEY

WAVERLEY

Catesby

Nuneaton

COVENTRY

BORDSLEY

EVESHAM

HAILES

GODSTOW

REWLEY

ABINGDON

CHERTSEY

WHERWELL

WINCHESTER

Nursling

Netley

I. WIGHT

QUARR

Much Wenlock

WORCESTER

PERSHORE

TEWKESBURY

WINCHCOMBE

GLOUCESTER

MALMESBURY

READING

STANLEY

Amesbury

WILTON

ROMSEY

BEAULIEU

ABBEY DORE

TINTERN

USK

BATH

SHAFTSBURY

SHERBORNE

TARRANT

MILTON

WIMBORNE

CERNE

ABBEY CWMHIR

Llanllyr

NEATH

MARGAM

GLASTONBURY

ATHELNEY

MUCHELNEY

Montacute

Poleslee

Exeter

BUCKFAST

St. Dogmells

WHITLAND

Caldy Island

TAVISTOCK

BUCKLAND

St. Michael's Mount

WALES

St. Cecilia's Abbey, Ryde, I.W.   1979

Benedict's Disciples

Benedict's Disciples

Edited by

D. H. Farmer

FOWLER WRIGHT BOOKS LTD
LEOMINSTER, HEREFORDSHIRE

First published in Great Britain 1980
by Fowler Wright Books Ltd
Leominster, Herefordshire

Copyright © 1980

ISBN 0 85244 011 1

Cum permisso superiorum

Printed in Great Britain
by Ebenezer Baylis and Son Ltd
The Trinity Press, Worcester, and London

To all the men and women,
of each century from the sixth
to the twentieth, who have lived
under the Rule of St Benedict

Acknowledgements

The publishers and editor of this volume wish to acknowledge with thanks the help, encouragement and co-operation they have received from the superiors of the monasteries and the writers, who have contributed their articles to this volume; also to Cardinal Hume for his foreword; to Lady Mary Rennell, herself a Benedictine Oblate, for donating her illustrations; to the nuns of St Cecilia's Abbey, Ryde, for the maps; to the Abbot Primate, Rt Rev Victor Dammertz for the modern statistics of the Benedictines; above all to the abbot of Douai, Rt Rev Dom Gregory Freeman, who gave warm encouragement to the enterprise at a very early stage. Thanks are also due to the printers and especially Mr Tom Foy for his useful advice and constant help.

The views expressed in the articles are those of the writers concerned and not necessarily those of the community to which they belong.

Contents

Foreword

Through more than fourteen centuries St Benedict's disciples have been diverse in temperament, education and achievement. Yet they had common traits which linked them to their founder: without the influence of his Rule their lives would have been very different. In this book, offered to the general reader in celebration of the fifteenth centenary of Benedict's birth, the common theme is that each of the individuals and groups studied reveals in a greater or less degree this inspiration, which itself realizes that of the Gospel. This book is about people: about particular monks and nuns. It is not an assessment of the importance of the monastic Order in such fields as education, estate management, art, literature or architecture. It is concerned with individual spiritual witness and commitment.

The strength of the Benedictines has always been that they were not and are not a centralized body, but a series of scattered communities. Their response to their environment has varied in history, so has their interpretation of the spirituality and the discipline of the Rule. Wilfrid and Bede, Lanfranc and Anselm, Thomas de la Mare and Richard Whiting, Alban Roe and William Bernard Ullathorne were profoundly different from each other, yet their common inheritance was the influence of the Rule of St Benedict.

This was so widespread and so profound that it has earned for him the titles both of Monastic Patriarch of the West and Patron of Europe. His Rule and the monasteries which lived by it are part of our religious and cultural inheritance as Englishmen, as Europeans and as Christians. In these days when many Christians are examining afresh their own roots and traditional inheritance this present volume is both timely and appropriate.

The Rule's principal features are well known, but they do not grow stale with repetition. Externally it directs an organized community life, apart from the world, devoted to prayer, sacred reading and work. Internally it is a spiritual guide (although modestly called a little book for beginners), with profound passages on obedience, humility, silence and fraternal charity. It has directed many thousands of Christians in every age, throughout their lives, in the following of Christ. This is the deepest element in the Rule, realized by both communities and individuals. Christ is seen in the abbot who holds His place, who is obeyed ultimately for love of Christ. He is seen in the poor and in the guests, but above all in other members of the community, who through their different characters none the less share the same goal. Benedictine discretion, properly understood, mirrors the compassion of Christ: stability is constant commitment to Him in the community. Indeed Benedictine profession represents a total offering in and through the Cross of Christ.

On the firm basis of fidelity to prayer, both solitary and public, to poverty, which is community frugality and individual self-restraint, and to chastity, the voluntary renunciation of a natural family in order to follow Christ more fully in and through the monastic family, is built that radiation to the Church which has so often been beneficial.

This is fruitful insofar as the monks are faithful to their Rule and its initial inspiration. At the heart of this seeking of God are the liturgy, solitude and humble obedience. Where the Divine Office is appreciated and regularly performed by the whole community with prayerful reverence and intelligent devotion, that particular community will surely be blessed. Nothing, said St Benedict, is to be preferred to the work of God.

Secondary to this principal monastic task is work for men, for the Church. This may be scholarly or craft work, teaching or preaching; for many it is through the tasks of monastic officials. For some it is often outside the monastery, whether in the field of pioneer missionary activity, or the maintenance of existing Christian communities. The balance between these diverse elements, often difficult to achieve, is kept by *lectio divina*, the prayerful and studious reading of the Bible, as well as of the Fathers and other writers of wisdom and experience. This prevents the insidious erosion of monastic values and priorities.

Such erosion has been a danger in some circles as a partial result of the fundamental self-questioning which arose from the Second Vatican Council. Monks cannot and should not be exempted from such an exercise. Often it has been fruitful and rewarding. But sometimes false assumptions have been made, as though adaptation meant permissiveness or laxity. On the contrary, it should result in greater and deeper fidelity. Perhaps there has been too much emphasis on change and not enough on continuity. Neither the Church nor the monastic Order began its existence with this Council. Now that much turmoil and clamour have subsided, it seems time to stress once more the immense value of the monastic tradition as realized in the lives of its saints, who are, after all, its finest and most characteristic products. This should help to eliminate the loss of nerve, direction and conviction, sometimes more apparent than real, which some complain of today.

At the present time Benedictine communities are renewing themselves from the living sources of their own long and great tradition. This has not been uniform in the past, nor is it so now. Allowance must always be made for the particular development of individual communities. This is often irrevocably conditioned by their history and by the needs of the Church. But when all is said and done, there *is* a family likeness between different groups of monks, but this is more easily described than defined. Benedictines have more in common with each other and with Cistercians than either do with members of other Orders. Black and White monks are not cousins but brothers. Benedictine nuns are truly sisters of the monks, even though they remain in their cloisters while their brothers are often (perhaps too often) outside them.

This common ground of monastic life was described by Ralph, abbot of Battle and a disciple of Lanfranc in about 1100. If these points are well observed, he said, monks will be rightly regarded as fervent representatives of their Order. His points include fidelity to the Divine Office, exteriorly and interiorly, fraternal charity, enclosure, self-abnegation in preferring others to oneself, together with humble confession of one's faults. This list spells out the qualities of St Benedict's good zeal which monks should have: love of God in reverence, love of the brethren in sincerity and preferring nothing to Christ. Benedict's list of monastic qualities, like his reading-list (which includes St Basil and Cassian), has never gone out of date.

Today Benedictines are and should be conspicuous for their calm commitment to permanent values, often underrated. This includes constant reverence in public and private prayer, intelligent loyalty united with readiness to listen and a willingness to learn from the achievements, as well as the mistakes, of the past. These examples of personal and corporate failure should not be forgotten in the euphoria engendered by this centenary.

There will surely be a fruitful future, just as there has been a wonderful past, for the monastic Order. Some of its most significant developments are now taking place in the third world. There perhaps may one day be repeated some elements of the role of the Rule in early medieval Europe. But in countries like our own, where Christianity has been taught and practised, more or less well, for many centuries, there is nowadays a healthy curiosity about the religious life. At some of our universities there is constant interest by a sizeable minority in monastic topics. Monasteries too are of ecumenical interest and importance. The opportunity generously provided by Anglican cathedral authorities for Vespers to be sung again by monks in monastic cathedrals this year is a concrete example of their friendly interest. The roots of the monastic Order lie deep in the past before Christianity was divided in the West. Its emphasis on Scripture and the Fathers, its liturgy and hospitality enable it to provide centres of ecumenical understanding and exchange which may well be unique.

In different ways and in different places monasticism is evidently alive and the object of much interest. May this book foster this study, by recalling to our attention the past and present achievements of St Benedict's disciples, and through them of St Benedict himself.

Basil Hume

Cardinal Archbishop of Westminster

Introduction

St Benedict is the patron of Europe: 1980 marks the fifteenth
centenary of his birth. This volume of studies has been composed to
commemorate this centenary, especially that aspect of it which
concerns England. Benedict and his Rule are of European importance, they are also quite specially significant for Britain. The Rule
was introduced here in the seventh century; its oldest surviving
manuscript was written in England and is still in Oxford, while an
Englishman, Boniface, the thirteenth centenary of whose birth is
also celebrated in 1980, was an important influence in its diffusion
through western Europe.

It has often been said that Benedict never intended to found an
Order; instead, he wrote a Rule. This work has certainly been one
of the most influential documents of its length ever written. Its
origin and content will be described elsewhere; its influence was
fundamental in the making of Europe; its vitality is far from exhausted. At the present time, indeed, it is followed not only in many
European monasteries of monks and nuns, but also in those of every
continent of the world. It is, moreover, read with profit by bishops,
officers, fathers of families, industrial magnates and many others.
Its wisdom and its prudence are of permanent value.

Its sixth-century Latin text has been translated into very many
vernaculars. Although its full history has not yet been written, its
influence can readily be traced not only in other monastic rules, but
also in works of spirituality, in the development of Canon Law and
in the formation of bishops through St Gregory's *Pastoral Care*.
There are so many and such different forms of religious life in the
Church of today that it is difficult to realize the near-monopoly it
held during the early Middle Ages. This position was obtained
partly through its intrinsic qualities and partly through the extrinsic
direction given to monastic founders by a succession of emperors.

This situation did not however arise quickly or easily. Much is
still obscure in the early history of the Rule's diffusion. In Italy,
surprisingly, it seems to have been little known outside Monte
Cassino and its foundations for some centuries; there is better
evidence for its use in the seventh century from both France and
England. On another page will be discussed the question whether
Gregory and Augustine can still be considered strictly Benedictine.

In the seventh century the Benedictine Rule was by no means the
only one for monks. In the East that of St Basil had long been in

existence and in the West there were various derivatives of Eastern monasticism. One of these was from Ireland. In the same year that Augustine landed in Canterbury (597), St Columba died in Iona, an island monastery off the south-west coast of Scotland which he had founded long before. Irish monasticism, austere and in some ways individualistic, was the oldest known in Britain, but it was not destined to be the most influential in England. After the Synod of Whitby (663) and the episcopate of Theodore (d. 690), the future of English monasticism lay with the Rule of St Benedict and with the strongly Roman sympathies of Wilfrid (d. 709) and Benedict Biscop, the founder of Wearmouth and Jarrow (d. 689).

Hard evidence for the existence of the Rule in Northumbria through the influence of these two saints is stronger than that for the same period in southern England. About 700 was written, in uncial writing of a kind not identifiable as that of any other known scriptorium, the oldest surviving copy of the Rule. So solemn is the script, so large the margins, that it can only be compared with contemporary manuscripts of Holy Scripture. Both then and for centuries to come, books were very expensive objects: this one, written almost regardless of cost, may be connected with Wilfrid or possibly with the slightly later monasticism of Wessex.

About the inner life of Wilfrid's monasteries we know little for certain. But Wilfrid himself rightly regarded the introduction of the Rule of St Benedict as one of the most important achievements of his long and controversial life. We know much more about Benedict Biscop's monasteries through the work of Bede, his most learned and articulate disciple, who sketched in his Lives of the abbots of Wearmouth and Jarrow unforgettable portraits of these monks and precious details about their outlook and observance. The primacy of the Liturgy, whose details are in accord with that of the Rule, is evident; so is the diversity of manual work 'in the kitchen, the garden and the bakehouse' (another echo of the Rule), and in occupations such as winnowing and harvesting. Recent archaeological discoveries enable us to go further. Stained glass was certainly produced in the Jarrow workshops, while the discovery of animal bones under the guesthouse, but of fish-bones only under the monks' refectory enables us to assert that the abstinence enjoined by Benedict was better observed at Jarrow than in many later monasteries.

Also in Bede's abbey had taken place an important fusion of ideals, destined to have important future consequences. Cassiodorus was a Roman civil servant who founded two monasteries at Vivarium (Italy) about 550 in his retirement. He did not write a Rule, but did produce a commentary on the psalms, a compilation of Church History and the *Institutiones* which united sacred and profane knowledge in the scope of Christian education. The connexion between the libraries of Vivarium and Jarrow is certain. Some of Biscop's remarkable collection of books actually came from Vivarium. This made possible the literary achievement of Bede, which was to preserve and pass on to future generations the inherited wisdom of the past. This was particularly necessary both at the time of the barbarian invasions and in Bede's lifetime, when Christianity had been established in Northumbria only recently. One difference between them however was that there was more emphasis on preserving the classics at Vivarium than at Jarrow: the principal common element of their heritage was the wisdom of the Christian Fathers, especially their commentaries on the Bible. Indeed Jarrow, like Vivarium, was a very important centre for the production of manuscripts of the Latin Bible: pride of place is held by the *Codex Amiatinus* surviving at Florence, offered by Ceolfrith of Jarrow as a present to the pope in 716.

For his contemporaries Bede's principal achievement was to produce a useful 'digest' of the Fathers' scriptural works. Today he is better known for the work he produced towards the end of his life, the *Ecclesiastical History of the English People*. The nature, importance and accuracy of this pioneer work and its subsequent influence on generations of writers have given its author the name of Father of English History. Bede is also the patron of Benedictine scholars. His own words which describe his delight in the liturgy and in teaching and writing contributed to Newman's famous assessment of him as being as typical of Benedictine life as Thomas Aquinas is of the Dominican. But how Benedictine was Bede? The Rule was certainly known in his monastery; his own personality could hardly have developed as it did without the Rule; for the founder, initially, Benedict's Rule was one source among many which he used, but on his deathbed he clearly told his monks to follow its prescriptions in choosing his successor. In doing so, he not only made sure that his monastery would not be dominated by his own family, but also assured the future quality of monastic life. So fundamental is the role of the abbot in the Benedictine monastery that the choice of him according to the Rule is one of its greatest safeguards. Biscop's prescription then not only concerned legal procedure but also deeply influenced the choice of his successor, Ceolfrith, and hence the perpetuation of his ideals.

Meanwhile monastic life developed also in Wessex. Aldhelm of Malmesbury received his first training from an Irish monk but later, like others in the North, became more 'Roman' in his outlook. He became abbot, a writer and bishop of Sherborne. The most famous product of monastic Wessex in the eighth century however was Boniface, a Devon man who became apostle of both Germany and Holland. His foundation of Fulda, specially encouraged by the papacy, became a model of Benedictine life, while another Anglo-Saxon, Willibald, had helped to revive Monte Cassino itself. Boniface was nobly aided by other monks and nuns, mainly from Wessex, who chose voluntary exile for Christ like the Irish pioneers before them, but who accepted more organization and more discipline. Their influence in the field of learning through teaching and through the production and diffusion of manuscripts, was immense. Their monasteries were also notable centres of civilization and stability in a society at once warlike and illiterate.

Unfortunately this Anglo-Saxon monasticism did not survive in England itself. But England's loss was Germany's gain. In the Empire there was much consolidation under repeated imperial edicts that all new monasteries were to follow the Rule of St Benedict. Its earlier 'rival' had been that of the Irish St Columbanus, whose monks had flourished at Bobbio and Luxeuil. In the ninth century the most important monastic figure was St Benedict of Aniane (d. 821), whose *Capitula* of Aachen, strongly supported by the emperor, became the norm of most monasteries in the Empire. On the one hand these reasserted the basic importance of the Rule, both for the communities and for each monk within them; on the other, they regulated the internal regime of the monasteries by forbidding the teaching of external students, by declaring agriculture, as distinct from craft and garden work, an extraordinary occupation for monks, and by augmenting the monastic liturgy by the daily office of the dead, the *trina oratio* of extra psalms and prayers three times a day and ceremonial visits to various altars. These enactments marked the conviction that monks were primarily if not exclusively men of prayer; that they were expected to spend much of their day in intercession. Indeed feudal society regarded their intercession as in some way equivalent to military and civic duties and the just return for the generosity of the monasteries' founders. The extra elements henceforward present in the medieval Benedictine liturgy remained integral parts of the regimes of both Dunstan and Lanfranc as well as of the equivalent Continental revivals. They were also very influential later in forming late medieval piety: they provide the basic elements of innumerable surviving Books of Hours. But they were not mentioned in Benedict's Rule and they were abolished both by the early Cistercians and by the influential Solesmes revival of Benedictine life in the nineteenth century.

The role of founders and benefactors needs to be stressed. They were usually kings, emperors or secular magnates, occasionally bishops. What did they expect from the sometimes enormous benefactions which they made? In Germanic lands indeed a monastery or a church belonged always to an owner, usually a layman. Monasteries, like any other group of men and women, needed land, the principal item of wealth. They also needed protection in a violent age. For these benefits their prayers and penances were in some way the price.

In order to survive, the monasteries needed to be comparatively wealthy or to have powerful friends. Their permanence was often in jeopardy; they could so easily become victims of sequestration or secularization. Wilfrid on his deathbed bequeathed large sums of money so that the abbots of his monasteries could purchase the favour of kings and magnates, to avoid the danger of a secular takeover. Benedict Biscop, however, looked instead to the electoral procedure of the Rule of St Benedict to attain the same end. Even during Bede's lifetime, as his letter to Ecgbert testifies (734), there were some Northumbrian pseudo-monasteries in existence which were simply family fiefs. Their inmates, he says, led a corrupt life which was anything but monastic in character. Because they were called monasteries, they paid no taxes and they occupied lands which the king needed to give to his fighting-men. Such abuses are more understandable when we realize that in Anglo-Saxon law a family monastery possessed 'bookland' and enjoyed other privileges as long as a member of the particular family was also an inmate of the monastery.

The progressive hold of the local lords on the monasteries was one reason for their virtual extinction in England in the ninth and early tenth centuries. Another one, not mentioned by later reformers like Ethelwold, was the series of Viking raids from which Britain had suffered at the same time. These began as early as 793 with a raid on Lindisfarne, regarded through its association with Aidan and Cuthbert, as one of the holiest places in England. Wearmouth, Jarrow, Iona, Whitby, Peterborough and others all suffered in their turn. So did numerous Irish monasteries. They endured not only looting and destruction but also the culling of their monks and dependants for the flourishing, far-flung slave-trade.

Such external factors ensured the diminution or disappearance of monastic life. But so also, many times in monastic history, did internal factors such as weakness, corruption or lack of conviction. It is probable that all of these together were responsible for the virtual disappearance of monasteries in the strict sense in England in the ninth century. King Alfred (d. 899) attempted the restoration of Muchelney in Somerset, but the Anglo-Saxons of his time seemed unable to endure the regime. Possibly the nunneries founded by him or his son, Edward the Elder, could claim some kind of continuity.

The restoration of monastic life for men in England was primarily the work of Dunstan, powerfully aided by a succession of English kings. Glastonbury, of which he became abbot in 940, after a period as a priest-hermit there, practising metalwork and embroidery as well as pursuing the normal regime of eremitical life, had been a notable Christian sanctuary since before the Anglo-Saxons came to England. Its connexions with Ireland were strong, as is shown by the number of Irish saints who were claimed to rest in its church and by the presence there of Irish *peregrini*, i.e. those who had chosen exile for Christ as part of their ascetical programme. Their precise status and rule is impossible to determine; the change made by Dunstan certainly included the introduction (or restoration) of the Rule of St Benedict. This was a fundamental characteristic of his reform as it was of the near-contemporary revivals of Cluny and Gorze, of which news would have presumably come to Dunstan when he had been a young man at the court of King Athelstan. This was connected to those of Continental rulers through the repeated embassies in search of the hands of his marriageable sisters. His reform looked to royal protection as a safeguard against the excessive power of local lords.

Other fundamental elements of the reform were the observance of chastity and of a strict common life. This latter made the monastic community a very different entity from those communities of secular priests whose churches were often called *monasteria* or minsters in Anglo-Saxon sources. The acceptance of the common life was a significant element when houses, formerly secular, 'became monastic'. A considerable number of tenth-century foundations could be placed in this category such as Milton, Malmesbury and Abbotsbury.

Such transformations were not however confined to small churches of the second rank. A notable, but not primitive, feature of the reform in England was its adoption by cathedral churches and their clergy. In this matter St Ethelwold was the pioneer, when his monks from Abingdon took over Winchester cathedral in 963. This move, inspired by King Edgar (d. 975) in the most important town of Wessex, where the king had a palace within sight of the cathedral, was one without parallel in the contemporary Continental reforms. It was destined to influence the development of the Church in this country for centuries and affected the particular direction of the reform itself. Only England in the Middle Ages possessed such institutions as monastic cathedrals: before the Norman Conquest they were four in number, Winchester, Worcester, Sherborne and, from about the millennium, Canterbury. After the Conquest their number included also Rochester, Norwich, Durham, Chester, Coventry and Ely, or half the total number of English bishoprics. And so they remained until the Reformation.

This continuity of nearly six hundred years is one of the most important characteristics of many houses which were founded or refounded in the tenth century. Such famous centres as Glastonbury, Westminster, St Albans, Bury St Edmunds, Evesham, Ramsey, Peterborough and Crowland were all founded before the Norman Conquest and all continued right up to the Reformation. The number of monks inside them however was probably far smaller in the early than in the late eleventh century, as was the scale of their buildings. At Worcester, for example, when St Wulfstan became prior, there were but twelve monks in the house; the same number constituted the Evesham community early in the reign of Edward the Confessor. No doubt Winchester, Ely and Canterbury were larger communities, but Canterbury, according to so committed an Anglo-Saxon partisan as Eadmer, was far from perfect in its observance (the monks lived like lords and enjoyed hunting), while William of Malmesbury deplored the low standard of Latin education previously attained by the monks of his own and other monasteries. However this may be, these monasteries were important centres of vernacular culture. The writings of Ælfric and of Wulfstan of York provided for the different pastoral needs of the late Old English Church. The standard of artistic achievement, whether in the Winchester school or that of Canterbury in the field of illumination, or in the examples of ivory and metal work which have survived, was high, at least in the larger monasteries. But before the Norman Conquest their spiritual vitality seems to have been diminishing, and their libraries were very restricted in scope.

In part their very success had caused this decline. The principal leaders of the movement, Dunstan, Ethelwold and Oswald of Worcester, all became bishops. So did very many of their disciples. Indeed from the reign of Edgar to that of Canute nine-tenths of the English bishops were monks. Such a monopoly was unprecedented and ultimately undesirable. Only in the reign of Edward the Confessor was fresh blood introduced into the English episcopate. By then, perhaps, many of the monasteries had already been drained of their most able and promising members.

Another contribution they made in practice to the royal goodwill was their extensive involvement in local government. What little evidence there is for a 'pre-Conquest feudalism' comes from the Worcester estates. More generally there can be no doubt of the active participation of bishops and abbots in the Witan, in the shire-court, in the government of the country at one level or another.

Monasticism, which began as a flight from the world, had become in late Old English society a powerful force in the national life. The foundation charter of Winchester (966) emphasized that the monks' function was that of fighting the unseen enemies of the kingdom, namely the devils, on behalf of the king and clergy of the realm. Their purpose was here seen, not simply in terms of praying for benefactors, but of being an active spiritual force from whose prayers and penance the whole of society derived benefit. The *oratores* (those who pray), were as necessary for early medieval society as the *bellatores* (soldiers) or *laboratores* (workers).

In return for their lavish endowments, the monks in fact provided many services and much benefit to society. Hospitality, sometimes on a large scale, was expected from them. They were also distinguished for their 'welfare' work. Almsgiving was a willingly accepted, integral part of the monastic vocation. Provision was made for it both in monastic customaries and in the allocation of revenues. Dunstan's reform prescribed the daily maundy of three poor men chosen from those 'who are accustomed to receive their support from the monastery'. Æthelwig, the powerful abbot of Evesham before and after the Norman Conquest, distributed clothes, boots and money to the poor and pilgrims. At one time this distribution was on such a scale to victims of the Norman invasion that Evesham resembled a refugee camp. At this abbey the almoner claimed one loaf in every ten baked in the monastery and also allocated vegetables for the poor from the monks' kitchen garden. By the late twelfth century the almoner of Abingdon was important enough to have ten servants to help him in his duties. On St Cuthbert's day at Durham, later, a feast was regularly held for 300 poor men. Only large estates could cope with the supplies needed for generous hospitality and almsgiving of this kind. Another and neglected contribution they made was the provision of 'hospitals' either for the sick or for the aged.

In early medieval society most people were illiterate. The abbeys stood out as centres of learning, of book-production, of writing charters and composing books. This last activity was confined to comparatively few monks, but their contribution was significant. This was particularly so in the case of historical writing. Bede, Eadmer, William of Malmesbury, Ordericus Vitalis, Roger of Wendover, Matthew Paris, Thomas of Walsingham were all Benedictine monks: very much of what we know of medieval England comes from their writings. These were not without bias and need careful criticism. But their abbeys were also depositories of historical materials of immense significance. Land charters, legal documents, financial records, papal bulls, royal and episcopal privileges, bishops' registers and much more besides were kept in abbeys or in cathedral priories. This list does not include the books in the monastic libraries. Here were to be found, at least after the Norman Conquest, often marvellously written Bibles, patristic works, Lives of saints, copies of the Latin classics and grammars, besides other, sometimes surprising books. Standards of penmanship varied from one house to another and between scribes even of the same monasteries. The purpose of the particular book written frequently determined the quality of the workmanship. The later Anglo-Saxon scribes produced wonderful picture-books of high quality; the Anglo-Norman monks concentrated more on accurate, neatly written texts, illuminated by decorated initials; the skills and styles of both groups eventually fused.

The arrival of Lanfranc as archbishop of Canterbury in 1070 resulted in important and beneficial change. This was one of both quantity and quality. Norman abbots were appointed to English monasteries when these fell vacant; they brought with them better discipline, better organization and an ability to plan and execute new buildings on a scale hitherto unknown in England. Lanfranc's policy was to invigorate the old monasteries rather than found many new ones. How successful he was may be seen in the doubling of the number of monks in England by the time of his death and by his preservation and extension of the system of cathedral monasteries. Internally the monasteries gained from the better order that he brought and by the extension of the range, quality and quantity of books in the monastic libraries. How they gained externally may be glimpsed today in the spectacular grandeur of the cathedrals of Durham, Canterbury and Norwich or the abbey churches (now cathedrals) of Gloucester and St Albans. These however are a testimony to the quality also of the Englishmen who built them. Within most of such buildings were housed the shrines of Anglo-Saxon saints. The Normans had initially questioned or derided their cults, but eventually they accepted them and provided them with more magnificent shrines than ever before. These were greatly enriched through the centuries for and by the many pilgrims who visited them.

These pilgrims affected the monasteries in several ways. Their offerings were often substantial and increased the monastic revenues considerably. The presence of crowds, including the handicapped and the lame, the blind and the demented, provided the almoners with plenty of scope for their charitable work. The noise however must sometimes have been irksome to monks zealous for silence and solitude. Canterbury, Durham, Ely, Bury and Westminster all attracted large crowds of pilgrims to their shrines: at

least three of these claimed with some plausibility that the bodies of
the saints in question were incorrupt. The monks themselves were
enthusiastic devotees of these local saints: their cults were the
occasion of Lives being written, miracle stories collected and the
details of the saint's life celebrated in manuscript illumination, in
sculpture or stained glass or in the composition of liturgical anthems
and hymns.

In many ways the late eleventh and early twelfth century can be
regarded as the age of the finest achievements of the monastic Order
in England and elsewhere. With archbishops of the eminence of
Lanfranc and Anselm, both monks, both Italians, the one a lawyer
and organizer and the other a theologian and devotional writer,
there was certainly excellent example from the top. Many of the
Norman abbots were also men of exceptional ability such as Serlo
of Gloucester or Paul of St Albans. The foundation of Durham by a
predominantly English community originally from the Severn
valley marked a new departure in the north, an area virtually
untouched by the Dunstan revival. In Durham cathedral rest the
bodies of both Cuthbert and Bede; the inspiration of both were
powerful influences on the mentality of the monks who lived there.
Other new foundations included Battle (on the site of the battle of
Hastings), Lewes, Reading, Faversham and others. Some of these
were Cluniac houses and serve to remind us of the continuing influence of this greatest Benedictine abbey in Christendom, whose
example had permeated the regimes of both Dunstan and Lanfranc.
When William of Malmesbury compared the Canterbury community to that of Cluny, it was a very high compliment.

Meanwhile several reforming movements had begun on the
Continent, several of which founded houses in England. Among
these were the Savignacs, the Tironians, the Fontevraldines and the
Carthusians, whose single house at Witham and whose fine bishop
St Hugh of Lincoln fall outside the scope of this book, because
Carthusians were not properly Benedictines at all. The most
important of the reforming monastic movements which retained
the Rule of St Benedict as a principal element of their inspiration
was the Cistercian. To them are due not only the most beautiful
monastic ruins in the country—Fountains, Rievaulx and Tintern—
but also in their own time a much-needed element of self-questioning
and rethinking of monastic ideals which in the long run was a
benefit to the Black as well as to the White monks.

The rapid success of the Cistercians is one of the most phenomenal
in the whole of monastic history. From the humble beginnings of
the reform in the late eleventh century at Cîteaux until the death of
St Bernard in 1153 they grew to 300 abbeys from Spain to Poland

of which about 50 were in England and Wales. They were notably successful in the North and in Celtic areas. It has been customary to attribute their expansion to the charismatic and doctrinal influence of St Bernard, but it is quite clear that several other causes were also responsible. One was the quite new legal, constitutional organization of the houses among themselves. Initially these were always founded from some already existing Cistercian house and the aggregation of already existing houses was excluded. Even more important, their monastic ideal of self-sufficiency and rural settlement exactly co-incided with the needs of the time for continuous expansion of cultivated land owing to the greatly increasing population of the twelfth century. Then their development of lay brothers made the monastic life accessible to very many who had not been previously catered for by the Black monks, namely the illiterate, who were still the vast majority in contemporary society. The number of lay brothers is not known with accuracy, but they were almost certainly more numerous than the choir monks and were indeed an essential element of the well-planned Cistercian economy. Opinions will differ about whether this large addition to the community of 'second-class monks' was in the long-term best interests of the Cistercian Order: it was certainly highly beneficial in the short term. They provided free labour in both agriculture and building which were the foundation of Cistercian national economic impor-tance. Their special development of the wool-trade resulted in their producing the best quality wool in England, even though its total was less than a quarter of the whole national wool crop.

Cistercian criticism of the Black Benedictine regime was not fatal to the survival of the older monasteries. On the contrary, there was room for both. The diatribes of reformers did not always have wide circulation nor did they always carry conviction. Some modern historians, one may think, have summed up the differences between Black and White monks in a manner too one-sided, too favourable to the Cistercians. The great difference brought by such reforms was that it ended for ever the virtual, undesirable monopoly of the religious life by Black Benedictines.

Contemporary criticism of the White monks by sophisticated clergy and laity was no less telling. Well before the end of the twelfth century their wealth had become a byword. So had their alleged or real avarice. In the thirteenth century their recruitment of lay brothers dried up almost completely and so they could no longer maintain their earlier programme of work-organization. The extensive lands which they owned were exploited and rented out just like Black monk estates. As time went on, they became in practice very like the Black monks.

In the 1220s the religious world was vitally renewed by the coming of the Friars. The two most important of these Orders, the Dominicans and the Franciscans, arrived in England and soon expanded rapidly, particularly in the towns and in the southern half of the country. Inevitably there was some loss of recruitment for the Benedictines, first to the Cistercians and then to the Friars, but in general there was need for all three, as there was for the Orders of Canons, such as Augustinian or Premonstratensian. There was of course mutual influence between these various religious families. The Black monks, no longer enjoying the monopolistic position of earlier centuries, both maintained their traditional way of life and modified certain details of their outlook. From the Cistercians they gained a more effective organization between the various monasteries by having a Chapter and a regular system of visitation. From the Friars they obtained books of scholastic theology and reorganized their internal teaching to take account of these new insights into Christian doctrine: in the Canterbury and Durham libraries are some important and early manuscripts of the works of St Thomas Aquinas. Even if the Black Benedictines were not so 'fashionable' in the thirteenth and fourteenth centuries as earlier, they still maintained a dignified and spiritual way of life in the changing intellectual and economic conditions of their time. They sent their most promising monks to universities with active papal encouragement.

It happened less frequently in the thirteenth century than before that monks were called to the episcopate or attained positions of national importance. But in the fourteenth century there was a certain reflowering as in a late autumn. They initiated notable architectural improvements, of which the lantern tower at Ely and the East window and cloisters at Gloucester are the best known, but by no means the only examples. The surviving Cistercian buildings at Tintern and Rievaulx are predominantly products of the thirteenth rather than the twelfth centuries. The domestic buildings at Cleeve (Somerset) show clearly that Cistercians as well as Black monks lived in conditions of civilized elegance which are at first sight unexpected results of their initial urge towards simplicity, poverty and isolation, Other attractive examples include Beaulieu, Netley and Valle Crucis.

Also in the fourteenth century there were a number of eminent Benedictine bishops, abbots and scholars: Simon Langham of Westminster, archbishop of Canterbury and cardinal; Adam Easton of Norwich, scholar, theologian and later cardinal also; Thomas Brunton, bishop of Rochester; Thomas de la Mare, abbot of St Albans and Uthred of Boldon, monk of Durham and theologian. The last two of these receive separate treatment in this book.

It is notable that as institutions the relative importance of the old Black-monk abbeys and cathedral priories increased rather than diminished with the waning of the Middle Ages. While there was much levelling of standards as between themselves, the Cistercians and the Austin canons, in numbers the great old abbeys recovered better than most from the disaster of the Black Death. A first, superficial impression of continual decline from the twelfth century to the sixteenth, when they were dissolved, needs considerable modification. In every age there have been better and worse monasteries; in every age there has been fidelity and infidelity: the pattern is not always uniform as between one house and another, or even with regard to the same house in different generations. The historian must be humble enough to admit that there are plenty of questions which the surviving evidence does not allow him to answer. Among these questions should probably be included personal judgements about individuals' sanctity. It is easy to be subjective in such matters, and an unfavourable judgement about a notable individual's lack of mystical perfection or sanctity may in fact tell us more about the prejudices of the historian than the achievement of that particular person.

If this is true concerning individuals, it is equally so with regard to communities. Presuppositions about the degree of perfection actually achieved are often too prominent in judging the desirability or otherwise of the Dissolution of the Monasteries. It is also a mistake to assume that because this happened, it was inevitable.

Recent work on this fascinating topic has in many ways resulted in a greater convergence of view among historians of all religious persuasions or of none. The economic factors have been properly stressed, both as a motive by the Crown for the Dissolution and as a contributory cause to the decline, real or supposed, of the monasteries. These have sometimes been criticized both for being too remote from the mentality of contemporaries and for being too closely involved with the rest of society. There is some truth in both these apparently contradictory charges. But each factor does not date from the sixteenth century, but from the twelfth or even the tenth. Considerable involvement with local life went back to the days of Dunstan. The development of the obedientiary system in the twelfth century had undesirable consequences, both in a diminution of the sense of personal poverty and in the spending of considerable time away from choir on business. A medieval obedientiary could often become a law to himself, organizing, buying and selling, dealing with the business world for longer hours than he was spending in choir or at his *lectio divina*. Even more serious was the development of the life of the abbot, Benedictine or Cistercian, away from that of his community. This is clearly shown, among other evidence, by the survival of their country manors or separate abbots' houses in the most notable monastic ruins. It is difficult to see how, in these conditions of separation, comparative luxury and excessive involvement in local secular life, the proper duties of St Benedict's abbot, described on other pages, could be completely fulfilled.

The Visitation records of the later Middle Ages leave one with a disappointing impression of the quality of monastic life. They need to be read with reservations, insofar as they cannot and do not tell us the whole story. They were never intended to be mulled over by historians four or five centuries after their production; there could moreover be misunderstandings or even conspiracies of silence. In some cases what have survived are the visitor's rough notes of complaints rather than his final judgement on the state of the house. Allowing, however, for all these factors, there seems to have been a certain tiredness, even a lack of conviction, about the ideals of monastic life. Too much energy went into maintaining the *status quo*; life-giving initiative was largely lost. Further, one must consider carefully the effect on the communities of the presence within them of people unsuited to this particular form of life, but unable to move from it honourably because the contemporary Canon Law did not envisage (as it does nowadays) the possibility of legitimate dispensation from vows, often undertaken too young. Visitation records provide plenty of examples of human frailty, but they by no means justify the statements of the preamble to the Act for the dissolution of the smaller (i.e. the poorer) monasteries, with incomes of less than £200 per year. This preamble is rightly regarded by historians today as propaganda. There were misfits and oddities in the monasteries, there were a comparatively few notorious examples of houses apparently past redemption, when suppression by the ecclesiastical authority would probably have been best. But the great majority of the monasteries at the Dissolution were perfectly respectable, if not always very inspiring places. They had not changed very much over the past hundred years (some indeed were in a better state in 1535 than they were in 1515), but the attitude of society had altered towards them. Collectively they were still great landowners, although there were also plenty of houses, especially nunneries, which were very poor. By and large the smaller and poorer houses had a worse reputation, but the generalizations about vice within them were unjustified.

The dissolution of the monasteries, the smaller ones by suppression and the greater ones by surrender, was carried out ruthlessly on a national scale by King Henry VIII, helped by the efficient planning of Thomas Cromwell. He had learnt the technique of dissolving monasteries from Cardinal Wolsey's suppression of several small houses to benefit his foundations of Ipswich Grammar School and Cardinal College (now Christ Church) Oxford. The whole process took five years. The royal treasury was the principal beneficiary; there was widespread destruction and vandalism, books were burnt, statues destroyed, roofs stripped of lead and the walls left to fall down. Concrete suggestions to turn some of them into schools were rejected. In some towns the people bought the monastery church, or part of it, for use as the parish church: Tewkesbury, Romsey and Selby are obvious examples. St Albans, Peterborough and Gloucester became cathedrals of new sees, while the older monastic cathedrals suffered less than some, at least in terms of the survival of buildings. Durham is the most notable example of the survival of cathedral, monastic buildings and library with archives all together in the same original place. But, by and large, immense damage was done to the country's cultural heritage: even more to the religious life of the Church.

The dissolution took place *after* the break with Rome and was one of the consequences, originally unforeseen, of the king arrogating to himself supreme, papal power over the Church in England. It is easy to see in retrospect that once the abbots acknowledged on oath, as they were forced to do, that the king was 'Supreme Head' of the Church, no power on earth could save them if he should decree that monastic and religious life should cease. The most heroic resistance came from the London Carthusians, but it has often been claimed that three Benedictine abbots, of Glastonbury, Colchester and Reading, were likewise martyrs for the traditional teaching of the Catholic Church. This claim will be examined on another page. Although, as the later history of the Anglican Church was to show, there was no intrinsic incompatibility between it and monasticism, in the strongly Protestant current of opinion in sixteenth-century England there was no place for the life of the vows or for that veneration of saints which flourished at monastic shrines.

By 1540 all organized forms of monastic community life had been brought to an end in England. In a few cases there is record of small communities continuing to live together privately and unobtrusively, but they could receive no new subjects, so their extinction was inevitable. Twenty-five years later, under Mary, there was a short-lived revival of Benedictine life at Westminster Abbey (1556–9). It began with sixteen monks, but the numbers rose to forty when it was dissolved by Elizabeth. This time the Oath of Supremacy was refused and most of the monks went into exile; so did the members of the other revived religious houses, Carthusian, Dominican, Franciscan or Brigettine.

Once again was verified the old adage of monastic history: *succisa recrescit*. Cut down in one country, the old Benedictine tree-trunk showed its vitality once more by producing new shoots and new branches. These arose in Italy, Germany and Spain: for nearly three centuries corporate Benedictine life did not exist in this country. Until its reform young English men and women who wished to be Benedictines had to go abroad to do so. In the event, as will be shown elsewhere, some of them returned in spite of persecution and a few gained a martyr's crown.

Europe was never without Benedictine abbeys, but their number reached a dangerously low level in the late eighteenth and early nineteenth centuries. There was little to show that the next hundred years would witness a remarkable revival with the founding of several large, influential Benedictine Congregations which are still very important in the life of the Church. With remarkable sureness of touch Dom Guéranger revived the abbey of Solesmes in 1837 with the traditional Benedictine emphasis on the liturgy, on tried and approved methods of monastic formation and on scholarship. The Congregation which developed from it has been described by a Benedictine from a very different family as 'the central ray in the modern Benedictine spectrum, observant, regular and moderate'. Other Congregations which began in the nineteenth century include those of Beuron (1868), Austria (1889), Subiaco (1851–72) and St Ottilien (1884). The last two of these had a strong missionary impulse. This has resulted in many and sometimes large overseas foundations (reaching the number of 100 monks or more). The Subiaco Congregation, however, is almost like a small order within an Order, so diverse in origin, spirit and observance are its different houses. Some of these, such as Montserrat in Spain, a pilgrimage centre of national importance, existed long before the Congregation itself. Like the Solesmes Congregation it has English houses, while the others mentioned above do not. The two great American Congregations also date from the nineteenth century: the American-Cassinese (1855) and the Pan-American (1881). The first of these is the largest in the world and has the largest abbey, of 350 monks, at Collegeville. This community has outnumbered even the arch-abbey of St Vincent with its 270-odd professed monks.

These numbers alone reflect the changed balance in the twentieth century between the different families of Benedictines. Also they have both expanded, and suffered persecution, notably in the 'Iron Curtain' countries, while Australia, East Africa and Latin America all have growing Benedictine communities. The Cistercians, for their part, have made foundations in Brazil, the Cameroons and the Far East. This last is consequent in part on the rapid post-war expansion of the Order in the U.S.A. made known to many through the writings of Thomas Merton.

Monastic historians tend to be more interested in monks than in nuns; the abundance of materials for the one and their scarcity for the other makes this almost inevitable. No book on English medieval nunneries has been published since 1922; yet their history is full of interest.

In the late seventh century the two most notable nuns were Hilda and Etheldreda. Both were of royal birth, both ruled over 'double' monasteries, both were foundresses of justly famed institutions. When Boniface became a missionary in Germany, he was followed and helped by a distinguished group of nuns of whom the most famous are Lioba, Walburga and Thekla. The nunneries founded in ninth-century Wessex were still in existence when Dunstan and Ethelwold refounded their monasteries, but what little we know of them seems to suggest that they were in considerable need of reform. Ethelwold in particular was very interested in the Wessex nunneries, especially Wilton and Wherwell, while Amesbury was founded by King Edgar's widow. These three houses, together with those of Shaftesbury, Winchester and Romsey, formed a strong group in a small area and maintained close contact with royalty, whether Anglo-Saxon, Norman or Plantagenet. To judge from known statistics it seems that they reached their highest point, not in the twelfth century, but in the late thirteenth and early fourteenth. About the year 1300 most of these had communities of about 100 nuns. The same numbers were reached at about the same time by the houses of Fontevrault in the Midlands. Meanwhile the Cistercians had come to recognize nunneries who had asked for affiliation; eventually these numbered over 30 in England and Wales, many of them being small, poor and situated in Yorkshire and Lincolnshire, with a few in Wales.

Also in Lincolnshire arose and flourished the new Order of Gilbertines, who owed their existence to St Gilbert of Sempringham, the handicapped son of a Norman knight and himself both squire and parson before he became the founder, first of a convent of local girls, housed close to his parish church, and then, in response to pressure from local magnates, of a series of nunneries. He tried unsuccessfully to have these incorporated into the Cistercian Order; instead, the Cistercian pope Eugenius III appointed him Master of the Order. This eventually included canons, lay brothers and lay sisters as well as choir nuns. When the monasteries were 'double', they were built in such a way that there was complete separation between the sexes: the churches, for example, had two parallel choirs with a stone wall between them. The Rule of St Benedict was followed by the nuns, who always remained the principal element in this Order, the only purely English one ever in the Church. The convents seem to have been less aristocratic than those of Wessex: they enjoyed a high reputation and continued until the Reformation. They were never wealthy, although a few houses numbered 100 inmates, at least for a short time.

Like the monks, the nuns sometimes educated the young in their cloisters. These monastic schools were never on a large scale, but they were sometimes influential out of proportion to their size because of the wealth and standing of those who attended them. In the later Middle Ages especially, a convent education for girls seems to have been highly esteemed, but of course the school was never the *raison d'être* of the convent. Also in the later Middle Ages recluses or anchoresses flourished, whose history, like that of hermits, has yet to be written. At least some of the nunneries continued to flourish until the Dissolution: at Shaftesbury the abbess and fifty-six nuns surrendered in 1539, at some other Wessex nunneries the communities still numbered over thirty. This compares very favourably with the twenty at Rievaulx, the fourteen at Rochester and the twenty-one at Malmesbury.

After the Dissolution the nuns suffered more severely than the monks. They lost their homes, there were no careers for women, nor were they allowed to marry. Moreover their pensions were worth only about half those of the monks. When Benedictine nunneries were revived, English women such as Dame Gertrude More showed that sanctity was attainable in the new conditions of the seventeenth century.

In this volume much has been written about the history of the Benedictines. History was made, especially in the distant past, by comparatively few people. Saints and superiors who lived by the Rule usually have more historical, if not necessarily more spiritual, importance than multitudes of anonymous monks and nuns. The Life of Benedictines through the ages includes members of communities as well as their leaders, the uncanonized as well as the canonized, all those in fact who used to be liturgically commemorated in the feast of All Benedictine Saints. This feast, for better or worse, has been suppressed in recent calendar reforms and those whom it commemorated are included in the feast of All Saints.

Liturgical change has been by no means the only one to affect Benedictines since the second Vatican Council. The examination of the validity of past attitudes, the need for adaptation and restatement of ideals in a rapidly changing world, or questionings about the desirability of continuing the special work of a particular community, have all led to changes which some regard as transformation or metamorphosis rather than legitimate development. The debate, inside and outside the monasteries, is not yet over, but at least in some abbeys there seems to be a calmer attitude and more readiness to restate the validity of traditional views than was the case some years ago. Certain unwise experiments have produced unwelcome and bitter fruits. Others, better inspired, have resulted in desirable change. It would however need another volume to chronicle in detail such developments and to forecast possible future changes.

Looking back on the Benedictines' long history, this writer believes that they have contributed most at the deepest level to the Church's life when they have been most faithful to their initial calling to a life of prayer in separation from the world. Not every development has been good, nor every adaptation to society's needs necessarily bad. The impartial observer will find much to praise and much to blame. It is right that Benedictines should be judged principally by their most eminent representatives: opinions will differ on what should be their role today. Bede, Dunstan, Anselm can all be called pioneers, whether of scholarship, organized monasticism or of theology and devotional literature. But all three can also be called conservative (in the best sense) for the nature of their achievements, which however also revealed insights into the special needs of their own times.

In a world which often seems to have lost its sense of permanent values and its debt to those who have gone before, many people today look to the Benedictines to conserve all that is best in the doctrinal wisdom, in the living liturgy, in the educational standards and the monastic ideals of the saints and heroes of their own and of the Church's history. They are not expected to reject the accumulated treasure of the past, intellectual or artistic, for the latest or most superficial of experiments. Instead, just as Benedict saw the need for stability and obedience in the life of the individual monk, so is there need for the same qualities in communities today. When they are committed and convinced centres of stability, prayer, wisdom and good sense, then their influence for good radiates through the Church into society. Without them, both the Church and society would be immeasurably poorer. This traditional role seems particularly fitting in the pontificate of John Paul II, who has so effectively re-affirmed Catholic doctrine, morality and outlook in our own days.

by D. H. Farmer

BIBLIOGRAPHY

P. Schmitz, *Histoire de l'Ordre de S. Benoît* (7 vols., Maredsons 1942–56). English translation 1950.

D. Knowles, *The Monastic Order in England* (Cambridge 2nd ed. 1963).

D. Knowles, *The Religious Orders in England* (3 volumes, Cambridge 1948–59).

D. Knowles, *Christian Monasticism* (London 1969).

D. Knowles and R. N. Hadcock, *Medieval Religious Houses: England and Wales* (1971).

D. H. Farmer, *The Rule of St Benedict* (Copenhagen 1968).

D. H. Farmer, *Bede and Boniface* (forthcoming).

J. Leclercq, *The Love of learning and the desire for God* (London, 1978).

G. W. O. Woodward, *The Dissolution of the Monasteries* (1966).

J. Youings, *The Dissolution of the Monasteries* (1970).

See also particular bibliographies at the end of each chapter.

St Benedict (c. 480–c. 550)

It might be expected that the first chapter of a volume devoted to Benedictine figures and Benedictine history would be the Life of the founder. But, in the first place, St Benedict was not the founder of an Order in the ordinary sense of the term; he did not consciously legislate for an international organized body with a special task to perform, as did, for instance, St Ignatius when he founded the Society of Jesus. Benedict wrote a Rule for the monks of his own monastery, foreseeing no doubt that it might be adopted in other monasteries in other climates, but not intending any juridical link between them. The process by which autonomous monasteries living under the Rule of St Benedict have come to be grouped in loose federations has been long and complicated, but the autonomy of each monastery remains the norm. Even today the Benedictines are still not an Order in the common meaning of this word.

In the second place, it is not possible to write a Life of Benedict as one can write a Life of St Francis of Assisi or St Teresa of Avila. We do not have materials which would enable us to enjoy a vivid, intimate picture of his personality such as we find in the letters of St Teresa or St Francis of Sales, nor do we know more than the outline of his life. Leaving aside later legendary matter concerning his ancestry and his two disciples Maurus and Placid, which have left their traces in iconography and even in liturgy, we have only two sources: the second book of St Gregory's Dialogues, entirely devoted to Benedict, and then, Benedict's own Rule.

Gregory's Dialogues belong to a literary category difficult for the modern reader. They were written in 593–4, nearly fifty years after the probable date of Benedict's death, to show that sanctity and miracles did not belong only to the past, but that there were saints and miracle-workers in contemporary Italy. The narrative in Book II, as in the other three Books, is thus a sequence of miracle stories, interspersed with theological and spiritual reflections. It is not necessary to believe that miracles simply do not happen in order to be sceptical about many of those recorded by Gregory. Yet the narrative has great charm, while the theological reflections link its naivety to the deeper elements of Gregory's thought. These however tell us more of Gregory's mind than of Benedict's. Gregory is careful to cite his witnesses, while his topography has been confirmed in many ways by the excavations at Subiaco and Monte Cassino after the bombardments of the last war. But he does not

2

give us the material we would like for a Life of Benedict; he gives us no chronology and only slight glimpses of his way of living and thinking, as these emerge from the miracle stories. He does however give us a reliable outline of his life and an impression of his personality, austere and awe-inspiring, yet also tender and gentle. It is surely not fanciful to see a deep harmony between the character of Benedict as it appears in the Dialogues and Benedict's own ideal of the abbot, as he depicts it in chapters 2 and 64 of his Rule.

When all is said and done, we come to know Benedict mainly through study of the Rule. Quite apart from the monk's personal work on it, he hears it read aloud three times each year throughout his monastic life. Insofar as he listens with attention and sympathy, the mind and heart of its author come alive for him, not with the particular human intimacy with which we can know and love Francis or Teresa, but in a degree no less deep and personal.

When the Rule was written (c. 540), Christian monasticism already had over 200 years of history, so Benedict had an authoritative tradition on which to draw. From very early times men and women had pledged themselves to a life of prayer, austerity and celibacy while still living in the urban community; but if monasticism is defined by flight from the world, then its beginning dates from c. 270 when St Anthony of Egypt withdrew into complete solitude in an empty tomb. He soon became the guide of a group of hermits, and similar eremitical or semi-eremitical groups arose in the deserts of Scete and Nitria in Lower Egypt, whose spiritual teaching has come down to us in the collections known as the Sayings of the Fathers. A little later Pachomius, a convert soldier familiar with the organization of the Roman army, carried monastic development beyond the stage of the colony of semi-hermits to that of fully cenobitical monasticism. Large groups of monks, not merely under the guidance of a spiritual father but under the authority of a single superior, followed a uniform rule. This provided both an elaborate constitutional framework and an efficient organization of common prayer and common work. These early Egyptian monks, though there were some educated men among them, were for the most part simple peasants with characteristic shrewdness and wisdom. Cenobitical organization of a Pachomian type underlay the more cultivated monasticism of Basil in Cappadocia and Jerome in Bethlehem, known to us chiefly from the Rules of Basil and the Letters of Jerome.

In the West monastic life became known especially through Athanasius' Life of Anthony. In northern Gaul, the monasticism of Martin of Tours (d. 397) at Ligugé and Marmoutier seems to have been on the Egyptian model, while in the south, at Marseilles and in islands such as Lérins, there were flourishing groups of hermits and community monks. For these Cassian (d. 435), himself trained in Syria and Egypt, wrote his Institutions and Conferences which became and have remained a kind of *Summa* of monastic spirituality. In Italy there were clearly monastic settlements from the early fifth century, but we know few details about them.

It is against this background of monastic history and an already articulate monastic spirituality that we study the life and Rule of Benedict. Only approximate dates can be offered; but Benedict was born about 480, and this is why 1980 is being celebrated as the fifteenth centenary of his birth. The town of Nursia, now Norcia, in the Sabine country some seventy miles north-east of Rome, claims to have been his birthplace, though Gregory tells us that he was born 'in the province of Nursia', which suggests the neighbourhood rather than the town itself. We are told that the people of this hill-country had a reputation for physical and moral toughness and austerity. He was born *liberiori genere*, which suggests that his family belonged to what we would call provincial gentry rather than to the patrician background which later legend claims for him. His family was doubtless Christian and devout, for his sister Scholastica had been dedicated to God from her infancy, presumably by her parents. Benedict received his early education at home, but was then sent to Rome to study letters—'grammar school' rather than university studies. He was accompanied by his nurse, which does not mean that he was still a child, but rather that the servant, perhaps a slave, who had cared for him as a child, continued to look after his needs as a personal attendant to the young man.

We are not told how long Benedict continued his studies, but only that, fearing the temptations to which a career in the great city would expose him, he decided to abandon them. Gregory's *despectis litterarum studiis* suggests that he had not yet embarked upon the study of rhetoric or of Roman law. Instead he adopted the monastic life. So he set out for 'the desert', accompanied, somewhat unexpectedly, by his nurse; perhaps the devoted woman was difficult to elude. Had Benedict a definite destination in mind? In any case, the pair were at first detained by the insistent hospitality of the people of Enfide, now Affide, and lodged 'in' the church of St Peter there, presumably in one of its dependencies. Here Benedict's first miracle, a homely and attractive one, drew unwelcome attention to him, and he again took flight, eluding this time his unfortunate nurse, and found his way to Sublacus, now Subiaco, some fifty miles east of Rome. He was perhaps in his late teens, and if he was born about 480, then we can put his flight to Subiaco towards the end of the fifth century; his stay at Enfide seems to have been a short interlude.

At Subiaco, the gorge of the river Anio had been dammed by Claudius, and two lakes formed; by the side of one of the lakes, Nero had built himself a villa. The dam burst in 1305, and the lakes have consequently disappeared, so that it is difficult to imagine Subiaco as Benedict knew it. The youth passed the ruins of Nero's villa, and further up the gorge he fell in with a monk named Romanus from a monastery at the top of the cliff; to him he opened his heart, and from him he received the monastic habit, which in those days was equivalent to making monastic profession. In the face of the cliff was a deep cave, and here Benedict lived unknown and in complete solitude for three years. To one familiar with the structures which Benedict was himself to establish later in his Rule, the situation was anomalous. For one thing, if we infer from his desire for the monastic life at least some knowledge of its tradition, he might have learnt from Jerome and Cassian that the solitary life should only be embarked upon after a solid formation in the cenobitical life. But neither he nor Romanus appears to have envisaged his beginning his monastic life within the community little more than the cliff's height above his cave. Romanus cared for his bodily needs, but it is not suggested that he was Benedict's spiritual counsellor. Indeed, the very existence of Benedict in his cave was concealed from Romanus' abbot, a situation at least unconventional by more recent monastic or ascetical standards. It may be significant that Benedict, who must have had at least some contact with contemporary Italian monasticism, did not put himself at the school of any existing institution: in his cave, the Holy Spirit prepared him for a work which was to be at once deeply traditional and a new beginning. The cave is now embedded in a complex of delightful medieval buildings covered with fourteenth- and fifteenth-century frescoes; but it is itself untouched, and its identification as certain as such things can be: it is surely one of the more moving sanctuaries of Christendom.

Here Benedict lived for three years unknown to any but Romanus. We can only guess at the life he led, in his heroic novitiate for quite other things, from what we know of the lives led by the hermits of the Egyptian deserts. He no doubt observed the regular hours of prayer and psalmody already traditional among monks; he may have cultivated an exiguous vegetable garden by the mouth of his cave. He read and re-read the Scriptures, though not in these three years of near destitution did he lay the foundations of that wider reading which his Rule reveals. He grew towards a life lived in the awareness of God's presence; his seclusion was such that we learn, and are a little jarred to learn it, that the saint who was to tell us to long for Easter with the joy of spiritual desire, was once himself unaware that Easter had come.

Only after three years was complete solitude of life gradually lessened. We can only guess at the qualities of character required for, and enriched and deepened by, such an experience in one in his early twenties. Gregory underlines that the initiative for the contacts which now began did not come from Benedict himself, but rather from God: a priest was guided by a vision to seek out the solitary and to share with him his Easter meal. Later, Benedict was found by some shepherds, who brought him food and received in return spiritual instruction from him. Gradually his reputation grew, so the monks of a neighbouring monastery asked him to become their abbot. Benedict knew of their easy-going ways, and accepted only with misgiving. His attempts to reform them were perhaps over-hasty, and the monks decided to rid themselves of the saint by poison, which was evaded only through a miracle. Benedict returned quietly to his cave. But he would never find his old solitude again. Other and better disciples sought him out to be trained in monastic life. Over a period of some years Benedict built up at Subiaco, not a single large community, but twelve monasteries, each of twelve monks with its abbot. Benedict retained supervision overall and kept with him those whom he wished to form more closely. By this time his reputation had reached Rome, and some of the devout nobility sent their sons to him to be trained in monastic life. Gregory mentions by name Maurus and Placid, round whom later legends were to grow, but of whom in fact we know little.

These years at Subiaco must have been important for Benedict himself, both in the experience they brought and in the opportunity for that wider reading of the Fathers and monastic writers which is revealed by his Rule, and which would have been impossible during the years of solitude in his cave. But of this Gregory tells us nothing: he tells us only of some miracles wrought, and then of the circumstances which led Benedict to abandon Subiaco for Monte Cassino. Benedict's growing reputation and influence provoked the jealousy of a neighbouring priest, who, after another unsuccessful attempt at removing Benedict himself by poison, set out to destroy his monastic foundation by sending women to seduce the monks. Benedict realized that the underlying motive was merely jealousy of himself, and determined to end the persecution of his monasteries by moving elsewhere. He was accompanied by a few monks. His intention was thus not to resume the solitary life to which he had once returned after his unsuccessful attempt to reform the monks of Vicovaro.

Instead he settled at Monte Cassino, some eighty miles south of Rome, just off the Via Latina from Rome to Naples.

Cassinum itself was a town of diminished importance, with its small fortified *arx* on the summit of Monte Cassino, some 1,700 feet high. Massive prehistoric walls which survived the bombardments of 1944 show that this had been fortified in prehistoric times. There were Roman fortifications too, and a small temple of Apollo with sacred groves and, at the summit of the mountain, a separate altar of Apollo. The rustic population was still pagan or semi-pagan, and Benedict set himself to convert them: he transformed the temple of Apollo into an oratory of St Martin, cut down the groves, and on the summit, where the altar of Apollo had stood, he built an oratory of St John the Baptist which was to serve as a burial-place. The oratory of St Martin, together with the Roman fort no doubt transformed and enlarged, formed the monastery; only much later did the oratory of St John the Baptist, rebuilt on a magnificent scale, became the principal church above the tombs of Benedict and Scholastica. This drew the monastery to itself, so that the oratory of St Martin and the original fort-monastery became a secondary sanctuary, known today as the Torretta.

It seems unlikely that the mountain-top and its buildings could have been appropriated by Benedict as an abandoned property; he probably received them as a gift from some landowner, perhaps from one of the Roman patricians who had already befriended him at Subiaco. This would explain his authoritative way of disposing of buildings and of the pagan sanctuary to which the rustics had remained devoted. It seems likely too that the desire to deliver his monasteries at Subiaco from the persecutions of the jealous priest was not Benedict's only motive in embarking upon a fresh start at Monte Cassino. For it is clear both from the Dialogues and the Rule that in at least one important way the structures of Subiaco were not reproduced at Monte Cassino. At Subiaco, Benedict had grouped his monks in twelve small monasteries, each consisting of twelve monks under an abbot, while he himself retained oversight overall. The Rule, reflecting both Benedict's experience and the structure he established at Monte Cassino, shows us on the contrary a single, larger community, divided into groups of ten, each under its dean, appointed by and responsible to the single abbot. It is this structural change which indicates that the Rule itself was written not at Subiaco but at Monte Cassino. But it is impossible to do more than guess at the dates either of the move to Monte Cassino or of the composition of the Rule. It is generally suggested that the move to Monte Cassino took place about 530, so that Benedict would have spent some thirty years at Subiaco. If the Rule presupposes some years experience of the Monte Cassino observance, we may guess it to have been written about 540, though there are internal indications that it was not composed in a single operation.

As with the years at Subiaco, so with those at Monte Cassino, Gregory limits himself to a series of miracle stories from which we can glimpse Benedict's personality and the pattern of his life. Yet alike in the Church and in civil society, the background of his life was one of conflict. The schism in the Roman church on the election of Symmachus in 498 may have begun before Benedict's flight from Rome to Subiaco, and could even have played a part in his decision. This schism lasted until 514, and thus coincided with the first half of the years at Subiaco. In 537 the election of Pope Vigilius opened yet another troubled period, which ended only after Benedict's death, so that the ecclesiastical background of the Monte Cassino years was as full of conflict as had been that of his earlier years. Of all this there is no trace in the tranquil pages of the Dialogues and of the Rule. In the political sphere, during Benedict's boyhood and the years at Subiaco, Italy was well governed by Odoacer and then by Theodoric, until the latter's death in 526. In the Eastern Empire Justinian succeeded in 527, and in 535 there began the Gothic War to reconquer Italy for the Empire; the war, with its tragic consequences in suffering and famine, continued until the complete reconquest of Italy in 555. Of this there are only slightly more traces in the Dialogues: the hard-working Goth who enters the monastery at Subiaco, and the brutal Zalla who victimizes a defenceless peasant. But several miracles are evoked by famine conditions, and there is above all the visit of the Gothic king Totila to Benedict at Monte Cassino. This can probably be dated in 542, when Totila was marching through Campania on his way to Naples. Benedict was to be proclaimed one day Patron of Europe, but his influence lay, not in political nor even in ecclesiastical involvement, but in the creation of cells of intense Christian and cultural life.

Benedict's break with his family must have been complete when he slipped away from his nurse at Enfide and hid in his cave at Subiaco. But contact was evidently resumed, perhaps in the years at Subiaco when his reputation had reached Rome; for Gregory tells us, apropos of her last visit to him before her death, that his sister Scholastica used to visit him annually at Monte Cassino. His own death was near, and he had her buried in the grave intended for himself in the oratory of St John the Baptist at the summit of the mountain—an attractive glimpse of enduring human affection.

Before recounting Benedict's own death, Gregory tells us, in particularly solemn language, of a unique vision or spiritual experience granted to Benedict. There are many allusions in the

Dialogues to Benedict's absorption in prayer, as we also see him occupied in reading at the door of the monastery; and it would be wrong to regard these allusions as mere hagiographical commonplaces. But the experience described in chapter 35, the vision of 'the whole world gathered into one sunbeam and brought under his gaze', with Gregory's famous comment that 'all creation is small to the soul that sees the Creator', suggests a mystical grace of a very high order, and much has been written to try to determine the exact bearing of Gregory's language.

In the sequence of Gregory's narrative, Benedict's own death follows closely upon this experience. Six days before his death, he ordered his grave to be prepared in the oratory of St John the Baptist—presumably the grave in which his sister Scholastica had already been buried—and on the sixth day he was brought by his monks into the oratory of St Martin, where, after receiving the body and blood of Our Lord, he died standing upright, upheld in the arms of his monks, his hands raised to heaven, and words of prayer on his lips.

It has long been usual to suggest 547 as the year of his death, though recent scholars are inclined to put it later, even as late as 560. We learn from the Dialogues the names of his two successors as abbot of Monte Cassino, Valentinianus and Simplicius. But Benedict had been given prophetic foresight of the destruction of his monastery by the Lombards whose invasion of Italy began in 568. He received the prophecy of the destruction of his monastic home, not with cold detachment, but with bitter weeping and great sorrow: 'All this monastery that I have built, and all things that I have provided for the brethren, are . . . delivered to the barbarians. And I scarce was able to obtain the lives of my monks.' The prophecy was fulfilled in 581, when the monastery was sacked and the monks took refuge in Rome—a move no doubt of significance for the future propagation of the Rule. Monte Cassino was abandoned from 581 until its restoration by Petronax of Brescia in 717; but the new community—which included the Anglo-Saxon Willibald—represented a fresh start without continuity with the group which had left Monte Cassino for Rome in 581. According to a late seventh-century tradition, the abbot of Fleury on the Loire, having read the Dialogues and being distressed to think that the relics of Benedict and Scholastica lay abandoned in the ruins of Monte Cassino, sent a group to find the relics and bring them to Fleury. This took place in about 673. The relics of Scholastica were later taken to Juvigny in Lorraine. Those of Benedict made of Fleury a great pilgrimage centre, and gave it the name of St Benoît-sur-Loire; they are still venerated in the great romanesque church there. But Monte Cassino also possesses two sets of bones which are claimed to be those of Benedict and Scholastica, and rejects the Fleury tradition. This is not the place to discuss the relative claims of Monte Cassino and Fleury: one would naturally prefer to think that the saints lie, not in places they have never known, but in their own monastic home. But the case for Fleury is at least a serious one, and we may take comfort in Mabillon's phrase, 'the bones are with the Franks, the ashes with the Cassinesi'.

Gregory was aware of the limitations of the account he gives of Benedict in the Dialogues: and he himself refers us to the Rule: 'He wrote a Rule for monks which is remarkable both for its discretion and for the lucidity of its style. If anyone wishes to know his character and life more precisely, he may find in the ordinances of that Rule a complete account of the abbot's practice: for the holy man cannot have taught otherwise than as he lived.' From this Rule, studied and pondered upon and lived, the Benedictine reaches an insight into the mind and heart of Benedict as deep, if not so circumstantial, as that which others have of founders of whom detailed lives can be written.

By the time Benedict wrote his Rule, there existed already a corpus of monastic experience and teaching; to this Benedict refers us, not merely as a complement to it, but still more as the setting within which the Rule is to be read and lived. He sends us to the Scriptures, the Fathers of the Church, and the Fathers of monastic tradition, particularly the Rule of Basil, whom he calls 'our holy Father', to the writings of Cassian and the sayings of the Desert Fathers. The study of the sources of the Rule shows clearly that Benedict knew deeply these writings to which he sends us. But there is one source, in some ways the most important of all, to which he does not refer by name at all—the anonymous rule known as the 'Rule of the Master' because it is couched in the form of questions addressed to a 'Master' and answered fully by him. Dom de Vogué, the principal authority upon this Rule, believes it to have been composed in the neighbourhood of Rome, a little before 530. It is some three times longer than the Rule of Benedict, but the text of Benedict's Prologue and of the first seven chapters of Benedict's Rule is found embedded in the Rule of the Master; and the rest of Benedict's Rule follows broadly its sequence, though its text and prescriptions are totally independent and even largely divergent. The Rule of the Master survives only in three manuscripts, in contrast with some 300 manuscripts of Benedict's Rule; until 1940 it was always regarded as an interpolated and somewhat eccentric enlargement of Benedict's Rule, and thus dependent upon it. But in 1940 Dom Genestout of

Solesmes touched off something like an atomic explosion in the field of Benedictine studies by arguing that, far from the Rule of the Master being an interpolated and expanded version of Benedict's Rule, it is the Rule of Benedict which is, at least as regards its Prologue and first seven chapters, itself only an abbreviated edition of the Rule of the Master. Dom Genestout died before he had marshalled all his arguments, and some of his subsidiary theses have proved unacceptable; but after some thirty years of controversy, it may be said that the priority of the Rule of the Master is now generally accepted. It has taken some time to assess the implications of this. At first sight, it seemed to diminish considerably the prestige of Benedict as a spiritual and monastic teacher; for in many ways the Prologue and the first seven chapters of the Rule appear to contain the weightiest parts of its spiritual teaching, and it is precisely these parts which have been transcribed by Benedict from the Rule of the Master. But further reflection shows that the assessment of the relationship between the two Rules is not as simple as that. The judicious and sometimes severe pruning which has produced Benedict's Prologue and first seven chapters from the Master's Prologue and first ten chapters is in itself a very personal achievement which tells us much about the mind of the pruner; and the rest of Benedict's Rule, chapters 8 to 73, is entirely his own, and very different in character and spirit from the corresponding chapters of the Master's Rule.

The quality of the Master's Rule is not easy to assess. It contains in some areas a more explicit theology of the monastic life than does the Rule of Benedict, and much has been done to bring out its richer side; on the other hand it often has the character of a customary rather than of a Rule, and of a customary sometimes pedantic, small-minded, and even a little silly. The spirit of the two Rules is widely different; it is surely not possible to read the Rule of the Master, and then to read chapters 8 to 73 of Benedict's Rule, without coming to recognize that Benedict remains a spiritual master in his own right. These chapters contain, not only such masterpieces of human and spiritual wisdom as the chapters on the cellarer and on the election of the abbot, but also explicit and implicit monastic teaching as rich as that contained in the passages derived from the Master. On the other hand, once we recognize that Benedict wrote with the Master's Rule before him, the comparison of the two Rules, and reflection upon the points where Benedict decided either to endorse or to depart from the Master's prescriptions, furnish us with a new and invaluable instrument of exegesis. This has entirely renewed our study of Benedict's Rule: the two Rules can no longer be studied apart.

What is the purpose of the life legislated for in the Rule? Benedict took the answer to this question largely for granted, partly because it was fully dealt with in the monastic literature to which he refers us, and partly because the answer was in a manner taken for granted by those to whom the Rule was addressed. He defines the monastery as 'a school of the Lord's service', a way of life conceived as a way of serving God rather than as a school of self-perfection. But we serve God insofar as we attune our lives to his purposes through love of him, so that the monastery will be an effective school of the Lord's service in the measure in which its observances bring us to the love of him, expressed first of all in the life of prayer. Benedict does not ask himself the question which sometimes nags at us today: what is the usefulness of such a life to the Church at large, or to civil society? The existence of individuals, or of groups, living lives from which all non-religious elements have been as far as possible eliminated, and who exercise little or no direct influence upon their environment, has been an element in the Christian church—as indeed in most religions—from the beginning; it is less a religious paradox calling for an apologia, than a datum of Christian tradition and life whose significance it is important to penetrate.

In the first chapter of the Rule, Benedict, while leaving open to individuals the possibility of passing over to that eremitical life which he himself had experienced at Subiaco, states clearly that he is now legislating for cenobitical life—that is, for a form of monastic life in which the same rule is observed by all, with common prayer and work and meals, under the authority, spiritual and administrative, of a single abbot. But whereas in earlier monasticism the monk committed himself irrevocably to the monastic life, but did not commit himself irrevocably to leading it in any particular monastery, under the Rule of Benedict the monk, by the vow of stability, committed himself irrevocably to the monastic life in the monastery in which and for which he took his vows. This gave a peculiarly permanent quality to cenobitical life under the Rule of Benedict; the candidate embarked, not merely upon cenobitical monastic life, but upon this life in a particular monastery, where he would normally continue to lead it until his death, among the same brethren and in the same setting. The same framework of enduring relationships is strengthened by the position of the abbot. In the Rule, the abbot is normally chosen or 'presented' by the community, and this choice confirmed by the local bishop or by neighbouring abbots; but Benedict nowhere states that the appointment is only for a term of years, and this has from the beginning been taken to imply that the abbot holds office for life. This is still the more common Benedictine practice, though in some Congregations a retiring age has now been fixed, or election is made only for a term of years, indefinitely renewable. The Benedictine community has thus a unique quality of permanence, through the vow of stability which binds each monk to his own particular monastery, and through the prolonged tenure of abbatial office. It has become a commonplace to say that the Benedictine community is a family; and this should be true, not merely in the sense in which the expression may be used of any group of men living together, engaged in some common task in a climate of good-natured intimacy and comradeship, but in the deeper sense in which members of a family are bound together by the common inheritance and a common responsibility, by enduring relationships, by true and lasting affection. Not all of this can be found explicitly in the Rule, but it is implied on almost every page. Throughout Benedictine history it has been the spontaneous fruit of life according to the Rule, showing itself in the affection of the monk for his monastic home, for its beauty and its traditions, and giving its character to the spiritual and cultural influence of each monastery, exercised on those brought into contact with each local monastic family.

All authority in the monastery, spiritual, disciplinary and administrative, is vested in the abbot alone and all officials are appointed by him and responsible to him. If we are to understand his position in the Rule, we must not think in terms of later political categories, or ask if his authority is 'absolute' or 'democratic'. We shall find the clue neither in the Politics of Aristotle nor in the Roman paterfamilias, but in the New Testament, and in the position of the bishop in the local church as we find it for instance in the Epistles of Ignatius of Antioch: the abbot 'holds the place of Christ in the monastery'. He is to be first and foremost the spiritual father of his monks, guiding them in that search for God which has brought them to the monastery, by his teaching and example, by individual spiritual guidance, and also by maintaining in the monastery a level of observance which will help them in their quest. His disciplinary and administrative authority exists only to serve the purposes of his spiritual authority, which is one of service. In everything the ultimate decision rests with him alone. In serious matters he must take counsel of a few seniors, or in graver ones, of all the community, for even through the youngest the Holy Spirit may speak. For, just as the abbot is the father of the family, so the monks are its members; so that all work together responsibly, each in his own degree. The Rule supposes a real measure of co-responsibility for the common good, but the ultimate decisions rest, not with a majority vote, but with the abbot, who will have to give an account of all his decisions to God. The relationship between abbot and monks, and between the monks themselves, is to be one of affection, for the monastery is to be the school not only of the love of God but also of the love of the brethren which is inseparable from the love of God.

It is fairly easy to reconstruct the daily life lived by the religious family whose structure has been sketched above, for the Rule provides timetables for the three seasons—summer, winter and Lent —into which the year was divided. The day was divided between three occupations—community prayer, described as 'the Work of God', reading, and manual work. The time allotted to each varied with the three timetables, and each was somewhat lengthened or shortened as the days grew longer or shorter. It has been calculated that on an average over the year, some three and a half hours were spent in community prayer, four hours reading, and six and a half in manual work. This triple division is not the invention of Benedict, but had belonged to monastic life, in varying proportions, from the beginning.

Benedict legislates in great detail for community prayer, with the Vigils, for long now misleadingly called Matins, at about 2 a.m., and the other seven Hours at intervals throughout the day, concluding with Compline at nightfall. This community prayer is the principal spiritual exercise of the monk's day. It is primarily a work of praise and worship, centred on Christ through the liturgical year and the Christian interpretation of the psalms; it is linked also with the natural poetry of the seasons and of the sequence of day and night. Benedict's liturgy is fairly sophisticated and doubtless owed much to contemporary Roman usage. It consists primarily of psalmody, the entire psalter being recited each week; there were also responsories and hymns, while at Vigils there were readings from Scripture and the 'orthodox Catholic Fathers'. There was a conventual Mass on Sundays and feastdays and it is likely that, as in the Rule of the Master, the monks received communion daily. The community prayer was not the longest occupation of the day, but it took first place in the scale of values and gave to the daily timetable the framework within which, with a certain amount of elasticity, the other occupations were fitted.

The hours of reading, *lectio divina*, were not hours of study in the modern sense of the word, nor were they devoted simply to 'spiritual reading' in the sense of devotional or ascetical reading. They were spent, according to the capacity of each, in the prayerful reading of Scripture and the Fathers to whom Benedict refers us in several passages. This reading is more directly spiritual in its motivation than pure intellectual work, yet more doctrinal and, in the traditional sense, more theological than what we call 'spiritual reading'.

This reading enriches the monk's insight into the themes of community prayer and is in its turn enriched by them. This convergent influence of the liturgy and *lectio divina* proved very creative in early monastic culture, in the fields of both learning and art.

The Rule says nothing of set periods of relatively prolonged personal or mental prayer familiar to the rules of all religious groups since the later Middle Ages; these are a necessary corrective to the growing complexity of our lives. Personal prayer however was involved in sacred reading, which led spontaneously to it. Thus reading was the first rung of that ladder of which later writers spoke: reading, meditation, prayer, contemplation. On this personal, contemplative prayer Benedict is reticent, but what he says of it is firm and pregnant; he clearly regards it as an indispensable element in the prayer-life of his monks.

Manual work was partly that involved in the ordinary running of the monastery, partly craftwork—chiefly no doubt practical, but often artistic also—and partly what we would call kitchen-garden work. Benedict seems to regard farmwork or harvesting as something exceptional, required by the needs of a particular community. He assumes that the monastery will own and acquire property, and he speaks of the situation where the monks may be obliged to live by the work of their hands, as the early fathers of monasticism had done, a little wistfully: such a state of affairs monks should welcome, not resent.

The alternation and equilibrium of the three elements of the daily life, liturgical prayer, reading and manual work, was a source also of psychological balance. But, because the three elements were designed to converge upon the deepening of the life of prayer in the growing awareness of God's presence, they were to be lived in a setting of silence and seclusion. There is clearly no question in the Rule of absolute silence, nor of the sign-language which arose in the early Middle Ages; the Rule assumes that when there is need to communicate, the monks will do so by speech. But, necessary speaking apart, silence was continual, and there were no periods of purely recreative conversation. No doubt the balanced alternation of occupations provided the necessary release of nervous tension. This silent life was led in conditions of effective though not absolute seclusion. Gregory shows us Benedict preaching to the rustic pagans of the neighbourhood round Monte Cassino and his monks ministering to the spiritual needs of some neighbouring nuns. But in the Rule he requires that all things necessary should be provided within the enclosure, so that there might be no need for the monks to go outside; and exits were preceded, accompanied, and concluded by special conventual prayers for those who had to go outside the monastery.

Gregory has told us that if we wish to know Benedict, we will find him in his Rule: the spirit which inspires the letter of the Rule will reveal to us the mind and character of Benedict. It is hazardous to attempt to summarize the spirit of the Rule. Gregory describes it as 'remarkable for its discretion'. The modern connotation of the word does not evoke the most inspiring of virtues; but we shall not be far from Gregory's meaning if we see here in discretion the wise adjustment of means to their end, the end in this case being, as Benedict himself tells us, 'that love of God which being perfected casts out fear'. One of the most striking qualities of the Rule is the way in which it continuously sets before us the highest spiritual ideals, while showing a tender and even humorous patience with human weakness. It is clear from the text of the Rule that it was not composed simply for *âmes d'élite*, that there were wilful children and rough customers in Benedict's community, and that he was prepared to handle them appropriately if need arose. But this does not set the tone of the Rule, and it is wholly without the suspiciousness which is so present in the Rule of the Master. In a famous phrase, Benedict invites the abbot 'so to temper all things that the strong may still have something to long after, and the weak may not draw back in alarm'. This is sometimes interpreted as meaning that the abbot is to maintain a level of observance which the strong may find insufficiently demanding but which will not frighten away the weak. Surely what Benedict asks is something far more difficult; to maintain a level of observance which will not frighten away the weak, and which nevertheless holds a challenge for the strong.

The later chapters of this book will illustrate the almost bafflingly different ways in which the life of the Rule has been realized in the past and in the present. Benedictinism has never been a centralized organism with a single central authority to maintain uniformity of observance. Benedict wrote a Rule to be observed at Monte Cassino and which he foresaw would be adopted elsewhere. But he cannot have foreseen how widely it would be followed, and if he had, it would not have entered his mind to organize and centralize the monasteries which adopted it. Any monastery living under the Rule, just because it was a living thing, had at once to maintain its identity and to adapt itself to an ever-changing environment both in the Church and in civil society. Benedictine history since Benedict is the expression of this twofold law, as the monasteries strove to maintain the essentials of the life of the Rule, while responding to the pressures of their environment, sometimes wisely, sometimes too rigidly, sometimes too yieldingly. It may be useful to indicate some of the ways in which Benedictine life has evolved since Benedict.

Benedict himself was no doubt a layman, and his community was a community of laymen, including only a few priests who had either entered the monastery as priests, or had been presented to the bishop for ordination to serve the sacramental life of the community. It is this non-priestly character of the life of the Rule which led to its being adopted by nuns, from an early time; nuns under the Rule of Benedict have a long and distinguished history. The language of Benedict's community would have been Low Latin, but his monks would have had no difficulty in taking part in a Latin liturgy or in spending time in reading the Latin Fathers. But the process was already beginning whereby, in the 'latin' countries the Romance languages, Italian, French, Spanish, were beginning gradually to replace Latin as the spoken language; and elsewhere, the Germanic languages would be the vernacular used. These new languages were not yet able to express the thought of the Scriptures and especially that of the Fathers. There was no idea of a liturgy in the new vernaculars; thus a life focused on the Latin Liturgy and nourished by the Latin Fathers became accessible only to those who possessed or who could acquire a certain measure of culture. The monastic profession, from being accessible to all, became a learned profession. From a learned profession it rapidly became, in the West, a clerical profession, in which an increasingly large proportion of the monks were ordained to the priesthood. This was accompanied by a growing tendency to give to the liturgy a more elaborate and prolonged character. Hence was reduced the place given to manual work, either because it was thought unsuitable for priests, or because it was being crowded out by a more elaborate liturgical life and by a greater place given to study. Among these convergent tendencies, it is difficult to guess which is cause and which effect; but the predominant type of Benedictine life throughout the Middle Ages was one in which liturgical worship and study or reading had virtually eliminated the element of manual work. It was a type of monastic life which expressed a very real spiritual ideal and which produced saints and scholars; but something of the equilibrium of the life of Benedict's Rule had been lost. One of the most significant aspects of the Cistercian reform lay in its pruning away of the accretions to the liturgy of the Rule, and the recovery of its equilibrium of prayer, reading, and manual work. In this, as in the body of spiritual teaching which inspired it, the Black monks owe a great and not always acknowledged debt of gratitude to their White brethren.

In the meantime, other developments in the Church were having their impact on monastic life. During what Newman called 'the Benedictine centuries', the monasteries had been virtually the only centres of intellectual life. But with the eleventh and twelfth centuries came the rise, first of the cathedral schools and then of the universities; and with the arrival of the Latin translations of Aristotle came the beginnings of scholastic philosophy and theology. The monasteries were now only on the fringe of the intellectual life of their time, and their biblical and patristic culture seemed old-fashioned. Monasteries must not be backwaters, but need to be open to the intellectual life of their own day. They need also to be faithful to their own specific inheritance, both for their own sake and as something to be safeguarded for the life of the Church as a whole. The movement of the monasteries towards the universities in the later Middle Ages was no doubt justified, and was encouraged by the papacy; but it was not an unmixed blessing, as it brought with it a tendency to replace the traditional monastic culture, biblical and patristic, by a scholastic formation of inferior quality. Perhaps the new insights of the Renaissance would have been more easily integrated into the Catholic tradition, if they had been confronted not only with a decadent scholasticism, but with a living monastic culture based upon the Scriptures and the Fathers of the Church. But at a later phase, the influence of Renaissance scholarship came to revive in the monasteries the study of the Fathers, and the work of the Maurists in preparing critical editions of their writings is only the most striking realization of a widespread revival of interest.

Even among the Maurists, however, the study of the Fathers was an important form of work for a relatively small group of those apt for such a task; their spirituality, like that of many of their monastic contemporaries, was strongly marked by the spirituality of the Counter-Reformation. The hours of prayerful reading envisaged by the Rule had come to be concentrated into the relatively short periods of 'meditation' and 'spiritual reading': this left longer periods available for work of all kinds. Manual work had been considerably reduced, or even eliminated completely. For those with the necessary aptitudes, intellectual work came to take its place, and to win for Benedictines that reputation for learning which could in fact be merited only by a small minority.

Benedictine tradition had never excluded pastoral or educational work: in the nineteenth and twentieth centuries, in response to the ever-growing needs around them, pastoral and educational work have come to loom large in the overall picture of life under the Rule today. This has been a characteristic example of the working-out of the double principle of at once maintaining identity and adjusting to environment which has been a mark of Benedictinism from the beginning. But the monasteries which have inherited such commitments would be the first to insist that these must remain subordinate to the essential priorities of the Rule, and to recognize the healthy tensions they can involve alike for communities and for individuals.

We have seen that originally there was no juridical link between the monasteries living under the Rule, though from the beginning of the ninth century various attempts were made to achieve some uniformity of observance, either among pre-existing independent monasteries, as in the Carolingian Empire through Benedict of Aniane in 817, and in England under Dunstan in 970, or among monasteries springing from a single mother-house, as in the case of Cluny and its daughter-houses. But the Cistercians were the first to achieve a constitutional structure which safeguarded at once the autonomy of each house and a rigid uniformity of observance by a system of Visitations and General Chapters, thus realizing for the first time the modern conception of a religious 'order'. In contrast, the Black monks experienced the drawbacks as well as the advantages of the complete autonomy of each monastery, and the Lateran Council of 1216 laid down that in each ecclesiastical province a system of regular provincial chapters and a system of visitations should be established. England was the first country to implement the Lateran decree, so that the English Benedictine Congregation, which just survived the storm of the Reformation, still ranks as the oldest Benedictine Congregation. Today, almost all Benedictine monasteries, while retaining their autonomy, are grouped in loose federations called Congregations, some on a national basis, some on the basis of a common tradition and a common expression of Benedictine life; they vary considerably also in their degree of uniformity or centralization, and their constitutional history is complex and interesting. The observance of the monasteries within each Congregation is determined not by the Rule alone but also by Constitutions which adapt the Rule to present-day needs in function of the traditions and commitments of each Congregation. Since 1893, these Congregations have been grouped into a Confederation with an Abbot Primate as its chairman and *primus inter pares*, but the Confederation is not an Order, and the Abbot Primate is not a General.

To the outside observer, it is the variety of the manifestations of Benedictine life which is most striking. To the Benedictine, what is most striking is the unity of spirit and mentality which he recognizes beneath the variety of external observance. And this comes, beyond question, from the inspiration of the Rule itself, which is common to all, however differently they may live it out. It has been truly said that the Rule is 'elastic', and that, like good elastic, while responding to external pulls and pressures, it retains the tendency to return to its original shape. And here perhaps is the key both to Benedictine history and to the Benedictine present and future. All developments must ultimately be assessed by the standard of the Rule, which is not merely a spirit but also a letter. Like everyone else, Benedictines have been shaken by the aftermath of the Second Vatican Council, and by the self-questionings and misgivings which this has brought with it. There have been signs of what has been called a loss of monastic nerve, and there have been defections and unwise experiments as well as many wise ones. But the Rule is always there to provide a criterion and an inspiration. We must avoid a kind of monastic Protestantism, with a *sola Regula* to replace the *sola Scriptura*. It would be short-sighted to attempt to by-pass various specialized traditions, derived from saints and from great monks, through which different monastic families inherit the life of the Rule. There are inherited commitments of all kinds, some of which are enrichments which ought not to be shed, while others call for patient and sensitive development. On the other hand, with our deepening knowledge of the background of the Rule, both through the study of pre-Benedictine monasticism in all its forms and through the new insights brought by the study of the Rule of the Master, our understanding of the Rule itself is being immensely enriched. We also have at our disposal all the fresh vision which the Second Vatican Council has brought to the Church. If we can combine, as did our monastic forefathers at their best, faithfulness to tradition and openness to new insights, we will surely find ourselves on the threshold of a new and creative period of Benedictine history. Behind the Rule, expressed in it and revealed by it, stands the personality and holiness of Benedict, filled, as Gregory tells us, with the spirit of all the just. He still supports those whom his Rule guides in their search for God, not only by his teaching, but also by his intercession.

by Rt Rev Dom Aelred Sillem

BIBLIOGRAPHY

The Rule of St Benedict
La Régle de Saint Benoît, ed. A. de Vogué and others, seven volumes,
(*Sources Chrétiennes,* Paris 1972–7).
Sancti Benedicti Regula Monasteriorum: editio critico-practica, ed. C.
Butler (Freiburg 1912, 1927, 1936).
S. Benedicti Regula Monachorum, ed. Ph. Schmitz (Maredsous 1946).
Regula Benedicti, rec. R. Hanslik (*Corpus Scriptorum Ecclesiasticorum
Latinorum,* Vienna 1977).
The Rule of St Benedict, ed. Justin McCann (London 1951).
Household of God. An English translation of the Rule with a short
commentary, ed. David Parry (London 1980).
The Rule of the Master
La Régle du Maître, ed. A. de Vogüé, three volumes (*Sources Chrétiennes,*
Paris 1964–5).
The Rule of the Master. Translated by Luke Eberle (*Cistercian Studies,*
1977).

St Gregory's Dialogues
Critical edition by U. Moricca (Rome 1924).
A. de Vogüé is preparing a new edition of which the first volume
appeared in *Sources Chrétiennes* (Paris 1978).

Life of St Benedict
Justin McCann, *St Benedict* (London 1937; New York 1958).

Commentaries on the Rule
Paul Delatte (Paris 1913; English tr. London 1921).
Hubert van Zeller (London 1958).
Basilius Steidle (English tr. Colorado 1967).

General studies
Cuthbert Butler, *Benedictine Monachism* (London 1919 and 1924).
David Knowles, *The Benedictines* (London 1929).
C. Marmion, *Christ the Ideal of the Monk* (London 1925).
David Knowles, *Christian Monasticism* (London 1969).
Daniel Rees, ed., *Consider your Call*: a Theology of Monastic Life
today (London 1978).
Wilfrid Tunink, *Vision of Peace* (New York 1963).
Jean Leclercq, *The Love of Learning and the Desire for God* (London
1978).
Louis Bouyer, *The Meaning of Monastic Life* (English tr. London
1955).
Cardinal Hume, *Searching for God* (London 1977).

St Gregory and St Augustine of Canterbury

Few people would deny the immense importance of St Gregory the Great both as pope and as writer throughout the Middle Ages. He deserves indeed a book, not an article, to do him justice. For long both he and his disciple, St Augustine of Canterbury, were regarded as 'Benedictines' in the full and juridical sense. In the last twenty years or so, doubt has been cast on this assumption, which seems in some ways anachronistic and unhistorical. The purpose of this paper is to resume the main points at issue and to suggest that the role of Gregory in Benedictine history is just as important, if somewhat different from, traditional assessments. Opinions about the importance of Augustine in the evangelization of the Anglo-Saxons have also varied enormously, often in accordance with the presuppositions of the writers concerned.

Gregory was the son of a Roman senator and became a prominent civil servant. He was very wealthy, but at the age of about thirty-five, in 573, he sold his extensive lands to found six monasteries in Sicily and a seventh in Rome, on the Celian Hill, where he himself became a monk. This was like a 'basilican', and was obviously an urban monastery. Like others of its time and place, it was presumably one where the monks were the choir and the clergy, devoted both to the prayer of the liturgy and to the pursuit of the ascetical life. Gregory was noted for his austerity in his early years; his later ill-health may have been caused by some indiscretion in this way. But he always looked back afterwards with nostalgia for his early days in the monastery. From it he was called out by Pope Benedict I to become one of the seven deacons in Rome. This office was important, for the deacons played a prominent part in administering the finances of the Roman Church. Nor would the popes easily release one so gifted and experienced in government and finance. Pelagius II made Gregory an ambassador in Constantinople. Here he lived as far as possible the life of a monk and wrote some of his more important works. After six years he returned to Rome and became abbot of his monastery. Once again, after a few years, his repeated choice of monastic life was frustrated: in 590 he was elected pope. He took office at a critical time: floods, famine, a Lombard invasion and Byzantine dominance in Italy all claimed, and received Gregory's urgent attention. In the longer term the conversion of the barbarians who had overrun the old Roman Empire and caused it to disintegrate presented another immense problem to be solved. This one was not new; but in response to it he had chosen the isolated life of a monk rather than that of a diocesan priest or a politician. This may well indicate that he looked to monasticism as the deepest catalyst for the improvement of society, that the disordered world would in the long term be helped more by lives of prayer and self-sacrifice than by politics and welfare. However this may be, what gave urgency to the conversion of the barbarians was Gregory's deeply felt and often expressed conviction that the end of the world was near. Contemporary disasters were so numerous that they seemed to presage nothing else.

Before becoming pope, he had already taken some initiative with regard to the conversion of the Anglo-Saxons. There is no need to doubt the underlying truth recorded in the Northumbrian tradition about the angelic appearance of the slave boys in the Roman market nor about Gregory's own desire to evangelize them. This might reveal some unresolved conflict within him concerning the ideals of monk and missionary. The important fact to retain is that he initiated Augustine's famous mission in 596, after some previous correspondence. These letters reveal a plan for redeeming slaves and bringing them up in monasteries and a recognition that the neighbouring Christians were doing nothing about converting the Anglo-Saxons. Augustine was prior of Gregory's monastery of St Andrew on the Celian Hill in Rome. His band of about forty monks came presumably from this and other monasteries.

There is no clear evidence to determine the exact status of such monasteries. It is likely that Gregory had become a monk and an abbot in a monastery which did not know the Rule of St Benedict. He wrote the Dialogues only after he became pope, as late as 593–4. This, as had been shown elsewhere, was an account of many saints in sixth-century Italy, whose many miracles showed that sanctity was not dead. Benedict was one of these saints. In the last chapter but two of the book devoted to him occurs the famous passage about the Rule, praised for its discretion and recommended to the reader as a way of understanding Benedict more completely: for the saint, he said, 'was incapable of teaching a way of life that he did not practise'.

The question then arises: was the Rule of St Benedict known in Rome early in Gregory's life? The story that Benedict's monks fled to the Lateran basilica after its destruction by the Lombards is, according to Dom David Knowles, 'no more than a venerable tradition'. Nor even did Gregory join the Lateran community. Nor does he in the Dialogues describe the Rule in any detail or give any indication that he knew it already, still less followed it as an exclusive or dominant guide.

Evidence for the early use of the Rule outside Monte Cassino is weak; continuity is lacking. After a gap, it appears more clearly in France than Italy. Monte Cassino was sacked in 577 and was restored only in 717 by Petronax of Brescia and the Englishman Willibald. But the exterior form of the life under the Rule was basically similar to that of many other monasteries, especially rural monasteries, of the time. St Benedict was more a man of tradition than has often been asserted in the past: his clear dependence on the Rule of the Master makes this basic point even more evident. The division of the day between prayer, reading and work was traditional; so also, to a very large extent, was the spiritual teaching to which Benedict refers and which he makes his own. The self-conscious use of the word 'Benedictine' to describe a particular form of monastic life arose very much later: the first firm evidence for this particular development comes with the rise of Benedict of Aniane and Cluny.

In view of this, it seems anachronistic to ask Gregory and Augustine if they were 'Benedictines'. No doubt they would have answered that they were monks, living according to the received monastic tradition. At some point in his life Gregory learnt about the Rule, but there is no evidence that he was, like later monks, professed 'according to the Rule'. Augustine's 'Benedictinism' stands or falls with that of Gregory. There is no hard evidence that he ever brought the Rule to England. He may have done so, but it can be neither proved nor disproved. There seems to have been nothing 'un-Benedictine' in the Canterbury monasticism; it is interesting to note that Wilfrid's biographer Eddius does not say that Wilfrid introduced the Rule into England: he says that he introduced it into Northumbria. By the middle of the seventh century, then, the Rule was probably known in southern England: Wilfrid and Benedict Biscop are the important names for its use in the north. Their likely source was Gaul rather than Rome.

Two other questions remain. What was the effect of Augustine's mission in England, and how influential was Gregory in the development of Benedictine tradition?

Augustine's mission made history insofar as it was, so far as we know, the first time that monks were used by the papacy in this particular way. Augustine's initial band, about forty strong, hesitated on their way to Britain and needed to be reassured by Gregory who also strengthened Augustine's authority over them. They landed at Pegwell bay and met the Anglo-Saxon king Ethelbert of Kent in the open. It is extremely probable that the way was prepared for them not only by correspondence, but also by the presence of a Christian queen, Bertha, with her Frankish chaplain Liudhard; it is likely that there was some initial invitation from England for them to come. The notorious refusal of the British Christians to evangelize the Anglo-Saxons was one reason for the presence of missionaries from overseas at all.

The letters of Gregory (most of which were used in Bede's *History*) are the only contemporary source for the story of the mission. One fact that clearly emerges from Bede is that early on Augustine's monks were given a monastery, in which they followed their monastic life of the liturgy and the other usual occupations. This monastery was placed just outside the city walls, not far from the cathedral, but distinct from it. In the cathedral, there was a mixed group of priests and clerics, some of whom were married if they were in minor orders only. This is clear from Gregory's famous and authentic answers to Augustine which Bede attributes to the conditions of about 601 or the following years, presumably after the conversion of the king.

We know little about the details of evangelization. Augustine certainly baptized many men in Kent. Some of the monks were in his mixed episcopal household; once they joined it, it seems from Gregory's letters, they were no longer expected to live in a monastery or be bound by its observances. They were however expected to live the common life of the bishop's household. We hear nothing about monks travelling round Kent or elsewhere: instead, it seems, their principal influence on the Christianization of Kent was the equally valuable one of providing a stable and lively centre of Christian life, very close to the town, to which the faithful would come for further instruction.

Bede tells the story of the conversion very largely in terms of that of kings and their courts in different parts of England. Kings and magnates were the first providers of churches and of the necessary funds for the upkeep of bishops. But monasteries were very important in the consolidation of the Christian faith and practice; it was their task to bring to rural communities its spiritual power, its prayer and its teaching. In a predominantly illiterate society this was no small task. By later standards the population was extremely sparse; there was no parochial organization for some centuries to come. Italian monks ignorant of the Anglo Saxon vernacular had immense problems of communication. It is not altogether surprising that in some kingdoms the joyful acceptance of Christianity was followed by widespread rejection under pressure of changing fortunes. But these setbacks proved temporary, not permanent. It was partly the effect of the monasteries that this was so.

An interesting feature of early Canterbury was its close resemblance to Rome. This aspect was described by Eadmer, among others. So used have we become over the centuries to hear Rome and Canterbury speak with different, sometimes discordant voices, that it is difficult to realize that at the beginning they were in complete harmony. Augustine was, and gloried to be Gregory's representative. Gregory was regarded as the Apostle of England not only by Bede, but also by Aldhelm of Malmesbury and by the anonymous monk of Whitby, who wrote the very first (if inadequate) Life of Gregory. This writer indeed describes his role in the terms of Gregory himself:

> According to Gregory's opinion, when all the Apostles bring their own peoples with them and each individual teacher brings his own race to present them to the Lord on the Day of Judgment, he will bring us, the English people, instructed by him through God's grace. . . .
>
> When we seek to know what those marvels are which one and the same Spirit works, dividing to everyone as He wills, we find that they are to be recognized not only in the healing of the body, or the raising of the dead, but still more in the healing of souls, because it is in them that we are the image of God. . . . Therefore Christ avails us more when he speaks through Gregory than when he made Peter the Apostle walk on the waves.

The dependence on Rome was one of receiving not only the message of the Gospel, but also ecclesiastical organization and architecture. Canterbury was a miniature Rome in all these ways. Its cathedral of Christchurch had the same dedication as that of the cathedral of Rome, the basilica of St Saviour later called St John Lateran. Outside the walls of Rome were two monasteries dedicated separately to the Apostles Peter and Paul. At Canterbury there was but one monastery similarly placed, but it was dedicated to the same two apostles together. Rome had seven suburban sees; Canterbury had but one, Rochester. The churches of Kent strongly resembled in style those of contemporary Rome: sometimes they were also built in whole or in part of re-used Roman materials. Canterbury itself provides a rather rare example of Anglo-Saxons continuing to live in a town of Roman origin; usually they were country-dwellers who built up their own settlements apart from the remains of earlier towns.

The close Roman connexion with the Church in England was fostered by later popes, relished by English writers and consolidated by later archbishops like Theodore, Anselm and Stephen Langton. Papal sympathy and support for the monastic Order can also be seen at work in Canterbury and England for the first time. This element of papal interest in monasticism over the ages could indeed be the subject of another book. In early England it was shown in a stream of papal privileges of protection and later exemption, which although sometimes abused and falsified in the interests of current controversy, should still be remembered as the continuation by later popes of the close relationship initiated by Gregory.

The organization of the Church in England projected by Gregory also endured and served as a model for later missionaries on the Continent. Although Gregory seems to have been hazy about the reality of political power in Anglo-Saxon England of about 600, and to have been dependent on records of the government of Roman Britain for his geography, his division of England into two provinces endured through the Middle Ages and subsists in the Anglican Church today. Although he assumed that Augustine would have his see at London rather than Canterbury, while the metropolitan status which he foresaw for York did not emerge for over a century, his blueprint of two metropolitan sees, each with twelve suffragans, are an indication of his long-term provision for the future. Augustine's own rank as metropolitan of the south lacked its complete fulfilment because of the comparatively early deaths both of Augustine and of Gregory.

Augustine's achievement, which none can take from him, was the establishment of a strong local church in Canterbury, closely modelled on contemporary Rome. It was situated in the most important town of the most powerful and cultured Anglo-Saxon king of his time. Thanks to his predominance as *bretwalda* (or over-lord king), Christianity spread to London, where the first church of St Paul was built. With the small see of Rochester between them, there were three dioceses in all established before Augustine died in about 604. His efforts to obtain the co-operation of the British bishops in a more comprehensive missionary effort among Anglo-Saxons elsewhere in England failed. There is no reason to suppose that all the fault was on Augustine's side, although it may be that he was too self-conscious about being Gregory's metropolitan for the whole of southern England. Gregory's plan reproduced the organization of the former Roman empire, in which towns were the centres of both civil and ecclesiastical life; it may well be that he did not fully realize the extent to which Anglo-Saxons and British were tribal societies, living principally in the countryside.

Augustine seems to have had the quality of seriousness (*gravitas*) much esteemed by Gregory. It is entirely true to his character that he chose to consolidate Christianity on a narrow geographical front in south-east England rather than scatter his very limited resources on adventurous missionary enterprises further afield. This was all that could be expected of him in his seven or eight years at Canterbury. Others after his death and after dangerous pagan reactions would reap where he had sown. Eventually his plan for the unification of the Church in England would be realized by St Theodore of Canterbury (d. 690).

Monks were prominent among the early bishops in Canterbury, London and York. But they never had a monopoly of the apostolate in early England. Nor do we know for certain how many other early monasteries were founded in the south-east. Some survived; others did not. That in Canterbury itself was the most important and provided a model in its school and its teachers for the work of Felix in East Anglia. We know more of Kentish monasteries in the later seventh century; some of these were for nuns like Minster in Thanet, while a grange at Salmestone was early founded from Canterbury. This monastery, called St Peter and Paul at the beginning, was later called St Augustine's: it was the burial place of the early kings of Kent and archbishops of Canterbury.

Augustine, apart from his letters to Gregory, left no writings of his own. But there survives an Italian Gospel Book usually called 'The Gospels of St Augustine', which he very probably brought with him to England. It is a small book of the sixth century, written in uncial script. It is incomplete, but full of interest, not least for its illustrations of scenes from the life of Christ. These, it may be thought, were used as early 'visual aids' in the task of explaining the Gospel and could have served as models for larger paintings by local artists in the churches. In a largely illiterate society, the help of pictures and poetry in spreading knowledge of Christianity was very important and should never be underestimated.

Gregory was certainly deeply interested in iconography and stressed in a passage of one of his letters which became influential, that a picture represented the person or the mystery it portrayed, that it should not be adored, but only the reality of which it was the sign. His literary influence however, was far more extensive and important: it can even be called creative.

This was exercised principally but by no means exclusively in the monasteries of the Middle Ages. Here his teaching on ascetical and mystical theology was regarded as classical. It is often asserted, not entirely justly, that Gregory's thought was entirely derived from St Augustine and Origen. These were quite certainly deep influences on him, but his personal touch, his own skill in dealing with concrete situations by appealing to fundamental principles, are best revealed in his 854 letters. His other works, especially his Homilies on the Gospel, conspicuous for their good sense, and his *Moralia* on Job, remarkable for their development of the allegorical and moral senses of Scripture and for his teaching on the spiritual life, were even more widely read. Here are to be found his teaching on action and contemplation, on the virtues and vices and on other topics closely associated with the attainment of Christian perfection. He was certainly diffuse in his treatises, to such an extent that some famous medieval writers, William of Malmesbury and Stephen Langton among them, made a *defloratio* or a kind of digest, of extracts from Gregory on particular topics, in order to make his teaching more readily accessible. His influence was also important beyond the monastic order on writers such as St Thomas Aquinas and St John of the Cross.

Nor did he leave entirely unsolved the difficult task of training bishops and abbots. His book of the Pastoral Care describes the life and qualities of a bishop in terms of his task of shepherd of souls. This was particularly necessary in times when bishops were often chosen for their skill in administration, even for their military prowess. Written for Leander, bishop of Seville, this work rapidly attained a very wide diffusion, and was soon translated into Greek. King Alfred the Great (d. 899) asserted that it was brought into England by Augustine when he had it translated into Old English along with other Christian classics such as the Soliloquies of Augustine, the History of Bede and the Consolation of Philosophy by Boethius. By that time it had become a standard work. Its teaching is entirely consonant with that of the Rule of St Benedict and may well have been partly inspired by it. It is however difficult to detect much direct citation from Benedict. Nevertheless, Gregory's bishop, like Benedict's abbot, must not be ambitious for office, but must give a good example always. He should be

> discreet in keeping silence and helpful in his words: a near neighbour to everyone in sympathy but exalted above everything in contemplation; a familiar friend to good livers through humility, but unbending against the vices of evil-doers . . . not neglecting to provide for outward things in his solicitude for what is inward.

Elsewhere, in a passage which acknowledges its debt to St Gregory Nazianzen, he makes the point that one and the same kind of exhortation will not suit everyone because individual characters differ so greatly. In his homely way he reminds his readers that

> herbs which nourish some animals are fatal to others; the gentle hissing which quiets horses excites whelps; the medicine which cures one disease aggravates another; the bread which strengthens the strong sometimes kills tiny children. . . . Therefore teaching

should be fashioned to suit the qualities of the hearers . . . yet never deviate from the art of common edification. . . . Every teacher, in order to build up in all the virtue of charity, should touch the hearts of his hearers with one doctrine, but not with one and the same exhortation.

Gregory, like Benedict, practised what he taught. His ideal of authority was one of service, which explains his choosing for himself the title of 'the servant of the servants of God', retained by his successors to this day. There is no better sign of the permanence of Gregory's influence in the Church than the retention of this title and its re-presentation in the teaching of the Second Vatican Council.

Lastly must be mentioned Gregory's influence on the Liturgy. This was important, though its scope is still somewhat disputed. Some of the Collects in the Gregorian Sacramentary are his and many more are inspired by his thought. The chant called Gregorian, although it existed before him, owes much to his reorganization. It is sad to record that nowadays many of his collects are scarcely recognizable in the new so-called translations, while Gregorian Chant, although enjoying a slight revival, has been much neglected in recent years by the very communities who might have been expected to retain and cherish it. This neglect, one may think, was not intended by the Second Vatican Council; perhaps in the years to come, such elements of the Christian heritage will again be revalued as they deserve.

Gregory's influence on the medieval Church and on the monasteries in particular was deep and lasting. So ubiquitous are his works in medieval libraries that it is hard to name anyone more widely read. In the often undervalued role of writer he was perhaps as influential as in his more widely known office of pope. In this country we do well to recall with St Peter Damian his special role of *Anglorum apostolus*, apostle of the English. He deserved this title although he never set foot in our country. Both by his emissary Augustine and by his writings he did more perhaps to shape the Church in this country than any other pope. In his attitude to native, but harmless pagan customs he showed in his letter to Mellitus the kind of wisdom which made history in missionary technique.

Augustine was a lesser man than Gregory. His rôle was to plant the seed which would bear much fruit later. The Canterbury monastery which he founded was of immense long-term benefit to the spread of Christianity: from its earliest days the sight of a community devoted to prayer and Christian living was a powerful factor in conversion. Some of the monks he brought took an active part in evangelization.

For this evangelization he depended greatly on the direction of Gregory; some of his queries reveal much unfamiliarity with pastoral needs. From the base which he established and with the help of missionaries from both Ireland and Gaul the Church in England developed into a coherent structure on Gregorian lines.

For some centuries monasteries in the West lived under mixed rules. Their founders often made their own collection of extracts from many sources. For this reason it seems inaccurate to describe Gregory and Augustine as 'Benedictine' in the self-conscious and narrow sense. Such apparent uncertainty is a consequence of Benedict not aiming at 'founding an Order'. The Rule slowly won its way. In this process Gregory was important, both for his Life of Benedict and his appreciation of the Rule. Its diffusion little by little led to its adoption, certainly in the ninth century and quite possibly before, as the basic monastic code of many monasteries. Seldom, if ever, has it been observed without any additions. Such additions in the early centuries were the whole or the parts of other rules: later there were traditions which were also regarded as fundamental; with the Cistercian reform came constitutional innovations of great wisdom and the development of a new class of monk, the lay brother; in modern Congregations there are also Constitutions which form part of the monks' juridical and spiritual inheritance.

Such being the case, one might hazard the opinion that to seek a 'pure' Benedictinism in the Rule alone without any additions whatever is to seek a mirage. Benedictines, whether Black or White, belong and have always belonged to living institutions for whom a refusal to grow or develop can be fatal. Fidelity, it may be thought, to St Benedict implies something deeper and more subtle than a material adherence to the letter of the Rule. The flexibility shown in the lives of many early monastic saints, who passed at different times of their lives from conventual to eremitic regimes or from either to a spell of missionary work, reveals in the early Middle Ages an element of variety which many might envy in today's more circumscribed juridical monastic regimes. Within this wider tradition Gregory, Augustine, Wilfrid, Cuthbert and Bede all have a place as witnesses to the persistent influence of the Rule of St Benedict. Paradoxically all these were in some measure 'Benedictine', yet none was so in an exclusive, modern, juridical way.

by D. H. Farmer

BIBLIOGRAPHY

B. Colgrave (ed.), *The Earliest Life of Gregory the Great* (Kansas City 1968).

B. Colgrave and R. A. B. Mynors (ed.), *Bede's Ecclesiastical History* (Oxford 1969).

F. H. Dudden, *Gregory the Great* (2 vols. London 1905).

P. Battifol, *Grégoire le Grand* (Paris 1928; Eng. tr. 1929).

C. Butler, *Western Mysticism* (London 1922 and 1926).

D. Knowles, *The Monastic Order in England* (2nd ed. 1966), pp. 1–23, 750–2 and references.

G. Ferrari, *Early Roman Monasteries* (Rome 1957).

H. Mayr-Harting, *The Coming of Christianity to the Anglo-Saxons* (London 1972).

J. Leclercq, *The Love of Learning and the Desire for God* (London 1978).

R. A. Markus, 'The chronology of the Gregorian Mission to England' *Journal of Ecclesiastical History*, xiv (1963), 16–30.

P. Meyvaert, *Gregory the Great and Bede* (Jarrow Lecture 1964) 'Bede's text of the Libellus Resposionum' in *England before the Conquest* (ed. P. Clemoes and K. Hughes, Cambridge 1971).

Gregory's works in P.L. lxxv–lxxviii; critical editions in *Corpus Christianorum, Series Latina* (1963 and 1971); his letters are in P. Ewald and L. M. Hartmann, *Registrum Epistolarum* (*M.G.H. Epistolae*, vols. i and ii, 1891–9). Translations in the *Ante and Post Nicene Fathers*.

St Cuthbert and St Wilfrid

In about the year 634 two boys were born into the ranks of the Northumbrian nobility. Their radically different personalities were to give the lie to the belief that monasticism can be defined in terms of the personalities who embrace it. A study of the lives of Cuthbert and Wilfrid forces one to the conclusion that there is no particular pattern of traits that characterizes the monk.

Nevertheless there were similarities in their background. Before the age of twenty both had gone to Celtic monasteries, Cuthbert to Melrose and Wilfrid to Lindisfarne. Both received early training in the rigorous asceticism and spirituality of the Irish. Both in varying degrees were to become familiar with kings and princes. Both became bishops in the ancient kingdom of Northumbria. Yet the peaceful, retiring Cuthbert, happiest in the solitude of Farne Island was very different from the dynamic, forceful and even bullying Wilfrid.

Through the partisan words of Eddius, his biographer and disciple, and through the cooler account of Bede, Wilfrid appears as a vibrant individual, the kind of man who inspires only extremes of feeling. A period of nearly 1,300 years does not diminish his compelling personality, Even for modern readers of Eddius Wilfrid evokes love or hate, but always mingled with admiration.

On the other hand Cuthbert emerges with difficulty from the mists of legend and hagiography. The 'Anonymous Life' written by a monk of Lindisfarne shortly after Cuthbert's death and Bede's prose Life present a dazzling array of miracles. Cuthbert is a holy man but not a fully concrete human being, a shadowy paper-saint, rather like the Galahad of the 'Quest of the Holy Grail'.

The posthumous fame of either saint takes a quite unpredictable course. Devotion to Wilfrid, despite his missionary activities in several parts of Britain and on the Continent, is not especially noticeable. He becomes one of many great monastic saints. But Cuthbert's fame increases in leaps and bounds. Over the centuries a quantity of literature grows up dedicated to him. The historical Cuthbert fades and the Cuthbert of legend takes over. He is the patron of Durham, a place he probably never saw in his lifetime. He is the best-loved saint of the north of England. As late as the Second World War a dense fog which shielded Durham from the threat of the enemy bombers is attributed to the patron's defence of his city. Much of Cuthbert's early fame can be traced to the advocacy of Bede and to the incorruptibility of his body. But this does not explain fully why this mysterious monk caught the imagination of the north.

The world into which Cuthbert and Wilfrid were born was not one of tranquillity. Christianity itself was new. Pope Gregory I had sent the mission of St Augustine to Kent in 597. In 601 he had sent Paulinus to England. When Ethelburga, the daughter of King Aethelberht of Kent went north in 625 to marry Edwin, king of Northumbria, she took Paulinus with her. Already consecrated bishop at Canterbury, Paulinus had great success in the north. On Easter Eve 627, Edwin and many of his people were baptized in the wooden church of St Peter at York. For the following five or six years Edwin and Paulinus strove successfully for the spread of Christianity. But in 633 Cadwallon, the British king of Gwynedd in North Wales, in alliance with Penda, the pagan king of Mercia, invaded the northern kingdom and slew Edwin at Hatfield Chase. Paulinus fled south with the queen and her baby daughter, Eanflaed, later to become Wilfrid's patron. Christianity in Northumbria weakened.

The kingdom, divided into the two great regions of Bernicia, roughly from the Forth to the Tees, and Deira, modern Yorkshire, was now ruled by Eanfrith and Osric. The worship of Woden and Tiw prevailed. But Oswald arose in 634 and defeated a huge army under King Cadwallon. Oswald and his brother, Oswiu, fighting to restore Christianity, called upon the assistance of Aidan, an Irish monk of Iona. They established him at Lindisfarne, a few miles from the royal city of Bamburgh, and there he founded a monastery.

But a further clash with the pagan Penda at Oswestry resulted in the slaying of Oswald on 5 August, 642. Bernicia came under the sway of Oswiu and Deira under that of Oswini. Although both were Christians and both encouraged Aidan in his work, Oswini was murdered at the instigation of Oswiu. Aidan died in 651 but his work continued and expanded under his disciples Chad, Cedd and Eata. The great affection aroused by this humble Irish monk who spoke the Northumbrian language but poorly is amply reflected in Bede's *Ecclesiastical History*.

From this brief summary of the national events of the early years of Cuthbert and Wilfrid, three central factors emerge. Firstly, the politics were essentially concerned with dynastic struggles; the success or failure of missionaries was inexorably linked to the king or family branch that they supported. This fact is arrestingly displayed in the life of Wilfrid.

Secondly, the tension between Christianity and paganism was still considerable. Hence there was still missionary work to be done

3

at the most basic level. As late as the 680s Wilfrid was working in
the last pagan stronghold in England, west Sussex. Furthermore,
the seed of Christianity, once planted, needed much care before it
took root and flowered. This is proved by the attempt to restore
paganism after the death of Edwin.

Thirdly, quite apart from paganism, there was the tension within
Christianity between the Celtic and Roman forms of practice. Just
as paganism itself in the face of the increasing Christianization of
Europe, and indeed of the British Isles, must have appeared as an
obsolescent backwater, so too did Celtic Christian practice begin
to seem small and provincial in the face of Roman universalism.
The question of the date of Easter about which so much controversy
reigned appears quaint and strange to us today. Bede reports the
unsatisfactory situation in 662. King Oswiu followed the Celtic
forms while his queen, Eanflaed, the daughter of Edwin, followed
the Roman. 'When the king, having ended the time of fasting kept
his Easter, the queen and her followers were still fasting and
celebrating Palm Sunday.' Much greater divergences than this
were possible.

But the Easter question was one issue among several. There was
the problem of the status of bishops vis-à-vis the monasteries.
Although St Patrick himself had not been a monk, the Irish church
had become essentially monastic. The monasteries were the centres
of Christianity and the bishops exercised the powers of their order
under obedience to an abbot. On the other hand the Roman system,
as characterized in Merovingian Gaul, saw the bishop as a great
official, powerful in both Church and state. A certain external dignity
was the necessary concomitant of spiritual authority. The case
of the bishop of Naples whose love of ships drove him to the sea-
front each day in dirty old clothes was far from pleasing to Pope
Gregory. Wilfrid's concept of his episcopal office was Continental
through and through. He would have fitted comfortably and uncon-
troversially into the Merovingian church. Cuthbert's view on the
other hand was more along the Celtic line. It was only in the
peculiar, hybrid system of the English church that two bishops,
Cuthbert and Wilfrid, could occupy such different positions with
regard to their concepts of their office.

Needless to say, the anomalies could not remain. In 663 the
synod of Whitby opted for the Roman system. Some, such as Colman,
could not accept the decision. Abandoning his see of Lindisfarne he
fled back to Ireland. But the Celtic position would not survive for
long. The south of Ireland had conformed already; the north
capitulated in 696, Iona in 720, North Wales towards the end of
the eighth century and South Wales and Cornwall later still.

Others, realizing that the Celtic past could not prevail over the Roman future, accepted the synod's decision. Cuthbert was in this camp. Nevertheless, intellectual acceptance or even conviction does not always sever emotional ties. Cuthbert gives the impression that while faithful to Rome and its ways, he remained most at ease in the context of his Celtic background. Perhaps the exhaustion which terminated his short period of episcopacy was emotional as much as physical.

Wilfrid, the spokesman for the Roman position, had no difficulty. For him, Roman was right and, despite his early training on Lindisfarne, Celtic was to be viewed with suspicion. Provincialism repelled him and he followed his convictions with a ruthless consistency that did not enhance his popularity. Men in his position frequently lack the sensitivity to understand the emotional ties of others. For them everything is black and white and a nuanced view is not possible. Yet a nuanced view is essential for the successful politician. The Northumbrian kings were shrewder than their bishop. A pro-Roman decision at Whitby did not entail, contrary to Wilfrid's hopes, a total obedience to Rome and a wide-scale eradication of Celtic ways. The forces of nationalism and of popular, frequently conservative, feeling were strong. While backing the winning side Wilfrid was insufficiently aware that a lasting victory for Rome would require a greater level of balance and compromise than he was capable of achieving.

Before we begin our exploration of the actual lives of Cuthbert and Wilfrid it might be asked from where we obtain our information on people and events of thirteen hundred years ago. Much has been written on Cuthbert over the centuries. But the earliest work is the *Anonymous Life* written by a monk of Lindisfarne between 699 and 705, that is within twenty years of Cuthbert's death. Bede's *Life of St Cuthbert*, written about 721, is based on the *Anonymous Life*, which it amplifies and develops. The earliest life of Wilfrid is that by Eddius Stephanus. It was written shortly after its subject's death and probably before 720. It is likely that the *Anonymous Life* of Cuthbert inspired the community of Ripon to urge Eddius to produce an account of their patron. It seems that these works were considerably influenced by earlier examples of hagiography such as Evagrius' Latin translation of Athanasius' *Life of Antony* and Sulpicius Severus' *Life of Martin*. Despite such influence they are still of historical importance. They can be supplemented by one of the earliest and most famous examples of English historical writing, Bede's *Ecclesiastical History of the English Nation*. By comparing the various works and by attempting to read between the lines we can build up a picture of our subject.

History is not merely a chronology of facts. Rather, it is concerned with interpretation. The Lindisfarne monk who wrote Cuthbert's life sees a very specific purpose to his work: 'This record of St Cuthbert is of great gain and value to myself. Indeed it is in itself a ready path to virtue to know what he was.' If Cuthbert is to survive as a figure relevant to the lives of the men of today, he must emerge as a man in possession of qualities which are always alive, always compelling and always inspiring.

Cuthbert was born into a well-to-do if not noble family. We can reach this conclusion for several reasons. We find him as a youth riding on horseback, at that time a privilege of the noble classes. This was why St Aidan would not ride unless compelled to do so by necessity. At a young age he was sent to foster parents, another custom of the nobility. He had a servant.

He must have been born somewhere in the region of Lammermuir in the border country, then in the northern part of the ancient kingdom of Northumbria. As a child of eight his youthful agility and high spirits were called to sobriety by a prophecy of his future high office. While still in his youth Cuthbert came up against local nostalgia for paganism. Bede tells how he stood on the north bank of the Tyne watching the monks from the monastery at South Shields bringing timber on rafts. A gale sprang up and swept the rafts out to sea amidst the jeers and hoots of the spectators who despised the monks because they had 'taken away our old religion and given us one that none of us can understand'. Needless to say, Cuthbert's prayers and reproofs saved the monks and won over the crowd. Later he apparently did military service, presumably defending Northumbria against one of the incursions of Penda.

His major conversion experience came one night as he was feeding his flock of sheep in the hills above the river Leader. Suddenly he saw a vision of a holy soul being born to heaven as if in a globe of fire. Later he heard how at that very hour of the night St Aidan had died. Shortly afterwards Cuthbert set off for the nearby monastery of Melrose to test his vocation. The abbot of this Celtic monastery was Eata, a pupil of Aidan, and the prior was Boisil whose name is preserved at St Boswells in the Borders. Although the anonymous biographer states that Cuthbert received the Roman or Petrine tonsure, it is more likely that he received the Celtic. The former left a ring of hair around the head in commemoration of our Lord's crown of thorns. The latter shaved the head completely up to an imaginary line joining ear to ear over the top of the head. Hair was grown behind this line. Cuthbert soon adapted to the strict pattern of Celtic monastic life with its long fasts and vigils. But his biographers do not hide the fact that his physical make-up was not sufficiently robust for the full rigours of Irish asceticism.

Meanwhile the strength of King Oswiu was waxing and in 655 at a river called Winwaed in the region of Leeds a decisive battle was fought between the forces of Northumbria and those of Penda of Mercia and his allies. Although outnumbered, Oswiu prevailed and Penda was slain. Northumbrian suzerainty extended over Mercia and the south until the rise to power of Penda's son Wulfhere who was proclaimed king of Mercia in 657.

Oswiu made his son, Alhfrith sub-king of Deira and the latter founded a monastery at Ripon. Eata of Melrose was invited to become the first abbot, and thither he went taking the young Cuthbert as his guestmaster. It is a great tribute to Cuthbert's qualities of tact and kindness to have been appointed to a responsible job at so young an age. (We hear that one of his guests turned out to be an angel in disguise.)

Bede suggests that Cuthbert had considerable experience of angelic ministrations. Such claims, however sceptically we may view them, reveal an important fact. Cuthbert is seen as an exemplar of the traditions of the monks of the Egyptian desert and of the Irish monasteries. He would fit into Egyptian Scetis without any difficulty. He was the timeless holy man, brought close to God by extraordinary asceticism and detachment. The consequence of this extreme spirituality was a great power with the Almighty and with his creation. Like the desert fathers, Cuthbert was able to control natural phenomena and animals. Nevertheless his was not a negative spirituality of hatred of matter. He would come to love the rough beauty of the Northumbrian coast. This is one of the timeless aspects of monasticism. It is the mood which underlies St Benedict's virtue of stability which is one of the vows that Benedictines make. It entails a sense of love for and harmony with the actual geographical environment. It flowers into a respect and reverence for creation. Monasticism can thus avoid an unhealthy dualism between matter and spirit and take full account of the fact that Christianity, at its core, is sacramental, based on incarnation, the union of matter and spirit.

Life at Ripon continued until Wilfrid's return from Rome. He fired King Alhfrith with his enthusiasm for Roman ways. In 660 Eata who had resisted the Roman intrusions of Wilfrid was expelled from Ripon and returned to Melrose with Cuthbert. Wilfrid took control of Ripon.

Shortly after the return to Melrose there was a terrible attack of plague, the effects of which apparently remained with Cuthbert for the rest of his life. His old friend Boisil was smitten with this disease and died, but only after prophesying that his young protégé would one day become a bishop. The prediction did not please Cuthbert.

Boisil died about 662 and Cuthbert, still in his twenties, found himself prior of Melrose. During the next few years he made many missionary journeys around the northern part of the kingdom and into the territory of the Picts. It is possible that one such visit is the explanation of the name of the town of Kirkcudbright, 'the church of Cuthbert'. On the other hand it is more likely to have been founded by disciples of Cuthbert or to be associated with the later flight of his relics. On another occasion he visited the monastery of Aebbe, the sister of Oswald and Oswiu, near Coldingham. Aebbe has given her name to St Abb's Head on the east coast of Scotland and also to Ebchester in county Durham. While he was there Cuthbert went out one night and walked along the seashore in prayer. Then he entered the water up to his neck. A cleric from the monastery had furtively followed the saint to see what he would do. When Cuthbert emerged from the water, two otters appeared, warmed him with their breath and dried him with their fur. The monkish spy was so amazed and remorseful that he fell ill, but on confessing his fault, the saint cured him.

Meanwhile King Oswiu was concerning himself with the establishment of Christianity throughout his kingdom. The tension between Celtic and Roman forms was becoming more pronounced. It would soon come to a head and the situation had to be resolved. Colman, the Irish bishop of Lindisfarne, found growing opposition to his views. The supporters of the Roman system included Queen Eanflaed, Alhfrith, the sub-king of Deira and Wilfrid, now abbot of Ripon. For them, as perhaps for the younger generation of clergy, to claim that 'Rome is wrong, Jerusalem is wrong, Antioch is wrong; only the Irish and Britons know what is right' seemed fatuous. In 663 the synod of Whitby convened and Wilfrid's eloquence on behalf of the Roman cause won the day.

But before Colman left the kingdom he persuaded Oswiu to make Eata abbot of Lindisfarne. Now holding the abbacies of both Melrose and Lindisfarne, Eata sent Cuthbert to the latter as prior. Although only thirty, Cuthbert's experience and tact served him in very good stead. Bede tells us that 'by his life and his doctrine [he] taught the monastic rule to the brethren'. The reference to 'monastic rule' inevitably raises questions for the historian of Benedictinism. What rule is referred to? Did Cuthbert live under the Rule of St Benedict? Was he in fact a Benedictine? We can be fairly certain that Wilfrid was the first to introduce the Rule into Northumbria, but that does not preclude Cuthbert's using it very shortly afterwards. The *Anonymous Life*, possibly written as little as twelve years after Cuthbert's death, refers to the Rule only once: Cuthbert 'arranged our rule of life which we composed then for the first time and which we observe even to this day along with the Rule of St Benedict'. Apparently he found the discipline at Lindisfarne somewhat lax. The 'rule' which he introduced was probably the traditional, not codified observance of Melrose. Bede frequently compares Cuthbert to the St Benedict of Pope Gregory's Dialogues. Nevertheless, he makes no reference at all to Cuthbert's introducing the Rule to Lindisfarne. Thus while it must have been introduced before 699, it is only probable, not certain, that Cuthbert should be linked to it. The later pre-eminence of the Rule can make us forget that in the sixth and seventh centuries there were many rules. Several could be observed in any one monastery. Cuthbert probably knew the Rule and was influenced by it, but we must conclude that he did not live under it as a sole guide, and was therefore not a Benedictine.

With regard to his tightening up at Lindisfarne, many of the brethren were unwilling to abandon their older usage. There were stormy scenes in the daily chapter meeting. Nevertheless, by courtesy, patience, self-control and gentle persistence he gradually won the whole community to his point of view.

St Benedict sees the hermit life as a higher way to which some are called 'after long probation in a monastery . . . well taught by the companionship of many brethren'. It seems that Cuthbert's interest in the communal life began to wane. According to Bede his heart was drawn more and more to things of the spirit. It is difficult to describe one's own inner state, let alone that of another man. There is no simple answer to why a man thirsts for solitude. Cuthbert was no social misfit. He moved familiarly and comfortably among all manner of men and women. His supposed misogyny, dating from a Norman legend, has no basis in fact. He was deeply devoted to his foster-mother, Kenswith; he was on warm, friendly terms with ordinary wives no less than with queens and royal abbesses. Several of the incidents of his life are concerned with women and reflect the generally high position held by women in Anglo-Saxon society.

Cuthbert's was the reserved, humble personality that attracts by its peace and gentleness. Judging by his relations with such men as Boisil and Herbert of Derwentwater, he had a great gift for friendship. Despite his ascetical training he was a man of strong, not always controlled feelings. Bede tells us that 'when celebrating mass he could never finish the service without shedding tears'. Presumably, like St Dunstan and several of the desert fathers, he had the gift of tears.

While still ruling Lindisfarne Cuthbert began to spend increasing periods of time on a rocky islet off the Lindisfarne shore. But here he found too many distractions and finally, in about 675, with the blessing of Eata and the community he moved to the Inner Farne where, years before, Aidan had spent his Lents. This island is about one and a half miles from the coast and some six miles south-east of Lindisfarne. It is about sixteen acres in area. On the west, the landward side, it is rocky and precipitous. The land falls away to the east where there is a small beach, the only possible landing place. Peaceful and pleasant in summer, the island is lashed by the north-east storms of winter. Sometimes it is entirely covered with flying foam and spindrift. Here Cuthbert lived for nine years, surviving by a mixture of resourcefulness and supernatural help. He was not without visitors, all of whom were graciously received. Although he was drawn more and more to prayer, his fame in the outside world spread.

In 681 the kingdom of Bernicia was divided into two dioceses, Lindisfarne and Hexham. The former was held by Eata and the latter by Tunberht. The expulsion of Tunberht for an unknown reason resulted in Hexham's falling vacant. Now the day Cuthbert had long feared arrived. He was chosen as bishop, but he did not accept the appointment until King Ecgfrith himself came to Farne to plead with him. Eata kindly offered to exchange sees, and on Easter Sunday, 26 March 685, Cuthbert was consecrated bishop of Lindisfarne at York.

Cuthbert laboured in his diocese until the end of 686. These cannot have been happy months for the hermit. Finally, worn out by his efforts, he returned to his beloved Farne to spend the last few months of his life in solitude. Bede describes in detail the last few weeks of his life. He suffered from great pain and sickness and yet until the end he displayed solicitude and consideration for those who attended him. Much against his wishes he agreed that after his death his body should be taken to Lindisfarne. He exhorted the brethren to unity and charity: 'Always keep peace and charity among yourselves. . . . See to it most earnestly that you are unanimous in your counsels.' He gave the strange and momentous instruction that 'if necessity compels you to choose one of two evils, I would much rather you should take my bones from the tomb, carry them with you, and departing from this place dwell wherever God may ordain'.

On 20 March, a Wednesday in that year, 687, in the early hours of the morning, Cuthbert died. At once a brother rushed out on to higher ground with a blazing torch in each hand. The flickering sign was seen over the miles of waves from the watch-tower of Lindisfarne. At that very moment the brethren, chanting their night-office, had reached the line of the psalm: 'O God, thou hast cast us off and broken us down . . . '

'Simply to know what kind of man he was', writes Eddius, rather fondly, of his master Wilfrid, 'is in itself a sure way to virtue.' Wilfrid's life begins miraculously in a way similar to that of the Cuthbert of the *Anonymous Life*. The house in which his mother was in labour looked as though it were on fire. Then she gave birth to her son. Eddius tells us that 'from his boyhood he was obedient to his parents, beloved of all, handsome, well-proportioned, gentle, modest and controlled, with none of the silly fads common to boys'. It is quite possible that Wilfrid did have some of these qualities. He was able to inspire very strong affection. But on the other hand he had difficulty in maintaining the affection he inspired. Instances are his friendships with Kings Ecgfrith and Aldfrith, both of which turned sour.

He lost his mother while still young but must have been a precocious boy because at the age of fourteen, disturbed by a harsh stepmother, he left his father's house. He was able to move with easy familiarity and confidence among the nobility, and he soon arranged to be presented to Oswiu's queen, Eanflaed. His good looks and sharp mind made considerable impact upon her. Under her protection he entered Lindisfarne and made a favourable impression on the entire community. There he remained for a few years, and there he must have met Aidan who was to live until 651.

But it seems that he was not entirely happy there. His gifts were not such as to give him contentment in the quiet but rigorous asceticism of a Celtic monastery. He had a quick and retentive mind and before long he wished to escape the insularity of Lindisfarne. His eyes turned towards the Continent and Rome. With the assistance of Queen Eanflaed he left Northumbria and journeyed to her cousin Erconberht, king of Kent, upon whom he made a good impression. Finally, after a long wait he set out for Rome accompanied by Benedict Biscop, a Northumbrian nobleman like himself, who would later found Bede's monasteries of Jarrow and Wearmouth.

Wilfrid delayed for a year in Lyons. He won the favour of the archbishop, Annemundus, who offered him a governorship and the hand of his niece in marriage. But Wilfrid refused and pressed on to Rome. In the Papal City he met the archdeacon Boniface who taught him the four Gospels, the calculation of the date of Easter and aspects of canon law. Finally, with the pope's blessing, he retraced his steps northwards and reached Lyons. Here he tarried for three years and made sound progress in his studies. He received the Petrine tonsure at the hand of the archbishop. An internal revolution resulted in the archbishop's murder. Wilfrid's foreign blood narrowly saved him from the same fate. At last he set his steps towards Northumbria.

These formative years on the Continent had a far-reaching effect on Wilfrid. In contrast with his early Celtic training he now came into close touch with the broader ways of the Roman system. In Gaul he found a wealthy, land-owning and consequently powerful episcopate. This and the splendours of the papal court were more congenial to his proud nature than the simplicity of Celtic Northumbria. A broadened vision, a sharp intellect and considerable powers of inspiration and leadership must have bred in him a certain scorn for narrow and eccentric Celtic ways. This would explain his firm opposition to them. Nevertheless, if there was personal self-seeking in Wilfrid then it was always subservient to his missionary zeal. His passionate integrity and devotion to spreading the Gospel cannot fairly be doubted. But while pomp and circumstance might be natural characteristics of the Gaulish episcopate they would not endear Wilfrid to the simple Celtic mood of many of the Northumbrians.

Returning home, Wilfrid met Alhfrith, the sub-king of Deira and son of Oswiu. Alhfrith had strong Roman sympathies and a great bond of friendship grew up between him and Wilfrid. He gave Wilfrid ten hides of land at an unknown place called Aet-Stanforda and then the monastery of Ripon with thirty hides. It was at this point that Eata and Cuthbert fled back to Melrose. A young man in his mid-twenties, Wilfrid found himself abbot of Ripon and a landowner. Eddius is at pains to point out that the land was used for purposes of almsgiving. In 663, at the request of the king, Bishop Agilberht of Dorchester ordained the new abbot of Ripon a priest.

The first major opportunity for Wilfrid to display his considerable learning and knowledge of the Continental church was the synod of Whitby. He spoke on behalf of the Roman cause with eloquence and success. Colman had argued from a principle of conservatism and tradition, but Wilfrid scorned the idea that two remote islands should oppose all the rest of the universe. Oswiu closed the proceedings with the humorous question: 'Tell me, which is greater in the kingdom of heaven, Columba or the apostle Peter?' Rome had won the day.

On Colman's departure, Oswiu appointed Tuda to the see of Lindisfarne. But the new bishop lived only a few months. Meanwhile Alhfrith had sent Wilfrid to Gaul to be consecrated by Agilberht, now bishop of Paris. It seems that the plan was to have Tuda as bishop of Bernicia and Wilfrid of Deira. The latter's consecration was a splendid occasion; he was carried into the oratory on a golden chair borne by nine bishops. But when he returned to Northumbria the situation had again changed. Alhfrith had apparently rebelled against Oswiu and been either killed or exiled. Oswiu had appointed Chad as bishop with his see at York. From the Roman point of view Chad's consecration had been of questionable regularity.

With his patron gone Wilfrid returned to his monastery at Ripon, taking with him singers, masons and artisans. A most receptive disciple of Continental influences he greatly patronized the arts so that his churches at Ripon and Hexham were to become a wonder to all who would see them. One of the gifts he gave to the church of Ripon was 'a marvel of art hitherto undreamt of . . . a book of the gospels done in letters of purest gold on parchment all empurpled and illuminated'. Of the church at Hexham Eddius says 'we have never heard of its like this side of the Alps'. Although Bede claims that Biscop was the first to bring glassmakers to England, it seems that Wilfrid had employed them even earlier on the church at York. The love of art, so strongly evidenced in the life of Wilfrid, would become an important feature of later Benedictine monasticism. It is another aspect of the sacramental love of creation. Stark, untouched nature appealed to Cuthbert, but it was man's moulding of matter into art that caught Wilfrid's imagination.

It was perhaps during this time at Ripon that Wilfrid introduced the Rule of St Benedict. When attacked at the council of Austerfield in 703 he would plead in his defence: 'Did I not bring monastic life into line with the Rule of St Benedict, never before introduced into these parts?' Although the Rule may have come to England with Augustine in 597, it was Wilfrid who first brought it to Northumbria. He would use it as the basis of uniformity throughout his confederation of monasteries. It would be anachronistic to say that Wilfrid was a Benedictine. Nevertheless he was more Benedictine in spirit than most of his contemporaries. His propagation of the Rule would have a far-reaching influence on the development of English monasticism.

The Greek Theodore of Tarsus arrived in England to take up the vacant see of Canterbury. In 669, observing the irregularity of Chad's appointment, he restored Wilfrid to full episcopal jurisdiction. Even the partisan Eddius acknowledges Chad's saintliness. The latter must have impressed the archbishop because Theodore completed his ordination after the Catholic manner and afterwards made him bishop of the Mercians with his see at Lichfield.

The following nine years saw Wilfrid at the height of his power.

With his see at York he ruled a diocese coterminous with the kingdom of Oswiu. During this period his land-holdings increased and his building schemes at Ripon, Hexham and York progressed.

Oswiu died in 670 or 671 and was succeeded by his second son, Ecgfrith. It was Wilfrid's interference in the affairs of Aethilthryth or Etheldreda, the wife of Ecgfrith that largely contributed to his fall from royal favour. Several years older than her husband she had refused to consummate the marriage, wishing to remain a virgin. At Wilfrid's instigation she left her husband and entered the monastery at Coldingham under Abbess Aebbe, the friend of Cuthbert. Ecgfrith's second wife, Iurminburg heartily disliked Wilfrid and suggested to her husband that the bishop with his huge estates, his retinue and his pomp and ceremony was a threat to the royal dignity. It is not easy to see why this magnificent, generous, powerful and gifted man should have aroused hatred in some women. Probably he lacked the sensitivity and charm that made Cuthbert so popular.

It was not until 678 however that the controversial division of the Northumbrian diocese was carried out by Ecgfrith and Theodore, apparently without even consulting Wilfrid. Eddius' suggestion that the venerable archbishop was bribed by the Northumbrian royal pair is surely scurrilous. The purity of Ecgfrith's motivation is indeed questionable, but Theodore was merely following the policies on his council of Hertford, which had taken place in 672. His views on diocesan organization derive ultimately from Gregory the Great. This pope had held that 'a pastor should be a neighbour in compassion to everyone'. Men should have recourse to a pastor's understanding 'as to a mother's bosom'. Northumbria was certainly too large an area to enable one man to exercise neighbourly compassion and motherly understanding. Nevertheless, Theodore's method was highly irregular.

With his energetic, pertinacious character and his familiarity with canon law, Wilfrid was not one to take virtual deposition sitting down. He set off for Rome to plead his case at the papal court. Even under his own adversity, missionary fervour seized him as he passed through pagan Frisia. This mission would later be pursued by his disciple Willibrord. In 679 he entered the territory of Dagobert II, a Frankish king whom he had helped while the Frank had been in exile in Ireland. Dagobert received Wilfrid with enthusiasm and even offered him the see of Strasbourg. But Rome drew him on. The outcome of his appeal to the pope was that while his rights were vindicated, the principle of dividing the diocese was also affirmed. Wilfrid returned to Northumbria bearing letters for Ecgfrith and Theodore.

But it seems that Ecgfrith was more concerned with the removal of Wilfrid than with the diocesan divisions. The bishop was seized and flung into solitary confinement for nine months. He bore this with patience and fortitude. At the entreaty of Abbess Aebbe Ecgfrith finally freed Wilfrid and sent him into exile. But the Northumbrian queen stirred up hatred in Mercia and Wessex, and the bishop found peace only among the pagans of Selsey whom he set about converting with energy and eloquence. In his missionary endeavours in Frisia and Selsey Wilfrid avoided the methods of confrontation and violence used elsewhere by Columba and Columbanus. In accordance with Pope Gregory's policy towards the Anglo-Saxons of leading them step by step to the gospel, Wilfrid was gentle and reasonable. In 686 he helped the exiled Wessex prince Ceadwalla to regain his throne, and the latter helped Wilfrid in his missionary endeavours on the Isle of Wight.

It was shortly after this that the ageing Theodore of Canterbury, stricken with remorse if Eddius is to be believed, sought reconciliation with Wilfrid and even wished to make him coadjutor to the see of Canterbury. Through Theodore Wilfrid was received back to Northumbria by Aldfrith, the new Irish-trained king. In 686 he was restored to the see of York and given back his monasteries of Ripon and Hexham. But by 688 there were new bishops at both Hexham and Lindisfarne. Wilfrid's power was but a fraction of what it had been.

Around 691 fresh disputes arose between Wilfrid and the king, largely over land-holdings. The outcome was that the bishop fled to Mercia. We know little of what Wilfrid did in the years 692–703. He apparently acted as a bishop in Mercia and founded several monasteries. With varying degrees of probability Peterborough, Brixworth, Evesham and Wing have been claimed as his. In 703 Archbishop Berhtwald called a council at Austerfield, South Yorkshire, to decide on Wilfrid's position. Berhtwald suggested that Wilfrid abandon all episcopal function and retire into what was virtually a house arrest at Ripon. It seems that the main bone of contention was the question of his monastic holdings rather than of his episcopal position. But the fiery old man refused to concede and once more set off for Rome to plead his case. He was strongly supported by Aethelred, king of Mercia. He must have done sterling work during his eleven Mercian years. It is difficult to believe that the council was inspired by anything other than envy. Bede makes no mention of it.

After a long, careful consideration, Rome once again vindicated Wilfrid. During his return journey he became gravely ill but was cured by a vision of St Michael. Incidentally, this is the only miracle of Wilfrid's reported by Bede, although Eddius records many. Aethelred greeted Wilfrid joyfully but not so Aldfrith. Wilfrid was old and had been away a long time. The Northumbrian sees were satisfactorily occupied. It was only on Aldfrith's death that peace was finally achieved. His young son Osred succeeded him after a few months. Then in 705 the synod on the river Nidd took place. The decrees of the Holy See were explained, but still the bishops resisted. They did not relent until Abbess Aelfflaed convinced them that on his deathbed Aldfrith had accepted Wilfrid's point of view. An unconditional peace was made and Wilfrid received back his monasteries of Ripon and Hexham, together with the see of Hexham.

The old man's life was drawing to an end. He fell ill again. In 708 he divided his treasure at Ripon into four parts. One was to be sent to the Roman basilicas; one was for the poor; one was for the abbots of Ripon and Hexham so that 'they may be able to buy the friendship of kings and bishops'; the last was for his followers who had shared his exile. In 709 or 710, in the seventy-sixth year of his life, Wilfrid died.

Wilfrid's is a dauntingly complex personality. His story is so closely linked with the power politics of his time that it is difficult to confront the inner man. Despite the clarity of incident, the magnificence of achievement and the strongly delineated traits one is left with the impression that the real man has eluded us. Cuthbert fits well into the common understanding of a monk as a quiet, humble man fleeing worldly concerns in favour of the single-minded search for God. But Wilfrid has characteristics which seem to be the very antithesis of the monk. He is proud and forceful, gregarious, dominant and rigid, a great leader and fighter rather than a retiring contemplative. He is reminiscent of Jerome and Thomas Becket and several of the fierier desert fathers. Yet in the long run it is Wilfrid who is the more important and the more encouraging figure. Amidst the turbulent welter of persecutions, hatred and danger, he had also to contend with his own passionate and contradictory nature. How easy Cuthbert's search for God appears in comparison!

Wilfrid turned down too many opportunities for worldly and ecclesiastical advancement for us to doubt that his single purpose was 'that our nation might grow in the service of God'. His loyalty to the gospel, to the Christian mission and to the Roman Church was total and untiring. Moulded by his Gaulish experiences he saw pomp and wealth as the best way in which he could play his part in society and in the Church.

Yet in terms of their posthumous fame it was Cuthbert who

prevailed. In 698 while Wilfrid was working in Mercia, Cuthbert's body was taken up and placed in a shrine above the floor level of the church at Lindisfarne. This was the ancient equivalent of canonization. Now the body could receive fitting veneration. The monks were amazed to find that the corpse showed no signs of corruption. Devotion to Cuthbert increased and Bede took up his cause.

Then in 793 the Danes appeared off the Northumbrian coast and the country entered a dark period. Lindisfarne was pillaged, but the bishop and some of the monks were able to escape. On their return they discovered that the body was still safe. In 875 the Danes attacked again. This time, remembering the Saint's dying injunction, the monks fled taking the body with them. For several years they journeyed back and forth over the ancient kingdom before settling at Chester-le-Street where they remained from 883 until 995. Finally at the very end of the tenth century the body came to rest at Durham. During much of this later period the body was guarded by a community of married canons. This did not suit the austere tastes of the Normans and in 1082 Bishop William of St Carileph brought in Benedictine monks. In 1093 the foundations of the present Durham Cathedral were laid. Cuthbert's tomb was opened in 1104 before its transfer to the new cathedral. To the surprise of the various attendant dignitaries the body was incorrupt. Ralph, abbot of Séez and later archbishop of Canterbury, commented: 'Behold, my brethren, this body lies here, lifeless indeed, but as sound and entire as on that day on which the soul left it to wing its flight to heaven.' Throughout the Middle Ages St Cuthbert's shrine was the greatest in the North.

At the destruction of the shrines in around 1537 the king's commissioners were embarrassed to find Cuthbert 'lying whole, uncorrupt'. The incorrupt body was left in the sacristy until 1541 when instruction came for it to be buried underneath where the shrine had been. The official position is that the body buried under the blueish slab carrying the word 'Cuthbertus' is that of the Saint. The tomb was opened in 1827 and again in 1899. Remains were found as were the relics now on display at Durham.

But there are insistent Catholic traditions that these human remains are not those of the Saint. As early as the 1620s references are found to a supposed removal of the body and to its being hidden elsewhere in the cathedral. Three members of the English Benedictine Congregation were custodians of the secret of the resting place, and as one died the secret was passed on to another. The secret is still extant and is held by the Abbot President and by certain other members of the English Benedictine Congregation. But perhaps the time is ripe for the tradition to be tested by excavation.

Devotion to Cuthbert is strong in the North. At least eighty-three churches were dedicated to him, seventeen in Scotland and sixty-six in England of which forty-nine are in the northern six counties. Wilfrid's cult was less popular. Centred understandably at Ripon and Hexham, it spread farther afield later, especially through the translations of his relics claimed by Canterbury and Worcester. Forty-eight ancient churches were dedicated to him.

What are the defining characteristics of monasticism such that we can situate Cuthbert and Wilfrid in that way of life? The search for God is a necessary though not a sufficient feature. Cuthbert's search was simple and straightforward. Blessed with the contemplative personality, he was drawn to solitude, even though this desire for solitude was not always satisfied. Wilfrid's search was more tortuous. Always fired with a single missionary aim and a rigid integrity, he was led through a web of politics, travels and wrangles.

Community is not essential for monasticism; Wilfrid lived amidst a retinue while Cuthbert spent years in solitude. Perhaps a particular asceticism is an element. This would include celibacy, detachment from property, ambition and personal comfort, all for a higher ideal. Although both were trained in the spirituality of the Celtic church, it is Cuthbert who impresses us more on this front.

Monasticism is not easily defined. But in retrospect as well as in the eyes of a contemporary such as Bede, Cuthbert was the better monk. His life witnesses the principles of monasticism with greater success. Nevertheless, in the long run it was Wilfrid's achievement that would be more influential and far-reaching for the growth of monasticism. Wilfrid disseminated the Rule of St Benedict, the moderation of which was bound to prevail over Celtic extremism; he studded the country with monastic foundations; he initiated missions which would carry Christianity and the Benedictine way of life far afield; he stimulated the development of art, music and architecture.

Cuthbert and Wilfrid between them anticipated the rich diversity of Benedictine life, the solitary and the contemplative, the communal and the missionary, the artistic and the pastoral. The single area they failed to exemplify was the literary and scholarly. That would be left to their younger contemporary, Bede.

by Dom Edmund Power

BIBLIOGRAPHY
B. Colgrave (ed.), *Two Lives of St Cuthbert* (Cambridge 1940).

J. F. Webb, (ed.), *Lives of the Saints* (Harmondsworth 1965).

F. M. Stenton, *Anglo-Saxon England* (3rd ed., Oxford 1970).

H. Mayr-Harting, *The Coming of Christianity to Anglo -SaxonEngland* (London 1972).

C. F. Battiscombe (ed.), *The Relics of St Cuthbert* (Oxford 1956).

D. P. Kirby (ed.), *St Wilfrid at Hexham* (Newcastle 1974).

St Hilda and St Etheldreda

Consecrated virgins have been known throughout the Church's history. From the time of Philip the evangelist's four daughters in the Acts of the Apostles, women have responded to Christ's call to belong to him alone. Setting aside the human love of husband and children, they lived in their own homes, small groups or large communities, and often became the spiritual daughters, friends and counsellors of saintly monks and bishops. Such were Olympias (363–405), deaconess of Constantinople and friend of St John Chrysostom, and Marcellina, the sister of St Ambrose, 'dearer to him than his life and eyes' to whom he wrote many letters and treatises. In sixth-century Gaul Queen Radegund (d. 587), virgin deaconess, founded the monastery of Poitiers on land given her in reparation by her contrite husband Clothair. It was for her that Venantius Fortunatus wrote the famous processionals *Vexilla Regis* and *Pange lingua gloriosi* which became the marching songs of the Crusaders. Partly, no doubt, because of its geographical position, this great Frankish monastery did not have as much influence on Anglo-Saxon England as two others, near Paris: Faremoutiers-en-Brie following the rule of St Columban, and Chelles, refounded by Queen Bathild, an Anglo-Saxon formerly a slave.

This study is concerned with two Anglo-Saxon monastic pioneers, both of royal families. Hilda, the older by about twenty years, belonged to Northumbria; Etheldreda, though some eventful years of her life were spent in Northumbria, was from East Anglia. They died within a year of each other—Hilda in 680 at the age of sixty-six, Etheldreda in 679 at the age of about forty-five. Two intensely contrasted threads run through their lives: years in the magnificence and violence of an Anglo-Saxon court followed by years of religious seclusion, though certainly not obscurity. They are striking examples of great saints emerging among people many of whom were still idol-worshippers at heart.

A cursory reading of Bede's *Ecclesiastical History* suggests an England in the flower of Christianity, an island of saints ruled over by holy kings—an all too simple picture. Skullduggery and blood feuds abounded; murder, exile and death in battle were the lot of king and common man alike, while Christianity's official position depended on the sway of the political pendulum. Hilda and Etheldreda lived in this world, renounced it, and survived through tenacity and strength of will. Each became a notable example of the influence which could be exercised by women in early Anglo-Saxon society, counterparts of their first-century Germanic forebears of whom Tacitus wrote: 'They believe that women possess an element of holiness and a gift of prophecy; and so they do not scorn to ask their advice, or lightly disregard their replies.'

The two saints knew each other, and their families were related by marriage. This was sufficient to make a strong bond, for Anglo-Saxon family life was close-knit and affectionate, embracing even distant relations. Welfare of tribe or family always took precedence of the individual. Loyalty was a prime virtue. Everyone, from the king's hearth-companion to the common man, received food, gifts and protection from his liege lord, to whom he gave unswerving fealty even to death. The most wretched of fates was to be exiled, cut off from kin, from the warmth and companionship of the mead hall.

'Sundered from my native land, far from noble kinsmen, often sad at heart, I went in wretchedness with wintry care upon me, sought the hall of a treasure-giver who might comfort me.' Hilda's father could well have shared this lament of the Anglo-Saxon poem, called *The Wanderer*, for his exile is one of the few known facts about her early life. A probable course of events is suggested here. The exiled Hereric and his wife Bregosyth took refuge at the court of King Cerdic of Elmet in Yorkshire, one of the few British kingdoms left in the wake of the advancing Anglo-Saxons, where their two daughters, Hereswith and Hilda, were born. When Hereric was poisoned, Hilda and her mother fled to the protection of King Edwin of Northumbria, Hereric's uncle. Uniting politics with the solemn duty to avenge a kinsman, Edwin conquered Elmet and drove out Cerdic.

Since Hilda probably remained at her great-uncle's court until she was twenty, something must be said about King Edwin. Like other Anglo-Saxon kings, he claimed descent from the gods. Son of that Aella whose name prompted Pope Gregory's pun 'Alleluia should be sung in that land', Edwin had himself spent many years in exile, and at length gained his throne with the aid of King Redwald of East Anglia, Etheldreda's great-uncle. Fickle in his loyalties both political and religious, Redwald sacrificed to Christ and pagan gods on adjacent altars, and was probably the king commemorated with such magnificence by the Sutton Hoo ship burial. In 625 Edwin married Ethelburga, daughter of that king of Kent whom Augustine first converted. The chaplain who accompanied her to a Northumbria which still worshipped Woden and Thor was Paulinus the Roman, of whom Bede has given us a pen-portrait rare in the literature of the time: 'tall, with a slight stoop, black of hair, lean in face, and having a slender aquiline nose, his features both venerable and majestic'. Hilda must have known that appearance well. There can be no doubt that her great-aunt and Paulinus initiated the Christian training which was to become the guiding force of Hilda's life.

Edwin was the unquestioned overlord not only of Northumbria, but also of the kingdoms south of the Humber. Hilda would have accompanied the court from one royal estate to another, seeing the glitter and pageantry of a royal progress. Banners were borne before Edwin as he rode through his dominions accompanied by a guard of hardened warriors, their swords and shields adorned with precious metals. His was a strong hand that crushed lawbreakers, and it was said that a woman with her new-born babe could walk through the island, from sea to sea, unmolested.

Paulinus had been granted freedom to preach the gospel, and the eyes of the Church turned towards Northumbria, the conversion of which largely depended on one man's will. Pope Boniface IV wrote persuasive letters and sent Ethelburga most unpapal, but truly feminine, gifts of a silver looking-glass and a gilded ivory comb. When Edwin and Ethelburga had been married a year, the turning point came. An attempt was made on Edwin's life. One of his thanes thrust himself between king and assassin's knife, dying for his lord in the finest Germanic tradition. That same night the queen gave birth to her first child. As the king thanked his gods, Paulinus praised Christ and ascribed the safe delivery to him. Edwin's adherence to paganism began to waver. He allowed his infant daughter Eanfleda and eleven others from his family to be baptized, the first-fruits of the Church in Northumbria. After the famous Witan had declared in favour of Christianity, the high priest mounted the king's stallion and rode forth, spear in hand, to overthrow the pagan idols. The thirteen-year-old Hilda was an onlooker at these events, but in what followed she eagerly participated. On Easter day, 627, she was among those baptized with Edwin in a wooden church at York. We can imagine her watching her greatuncle and his thanes at the font, then stepping forward in her turn, serious of face, fully aware of the significance of this step. With her characteristic generosity 'she embraced the faith and mysteries of Christ and preserved them undefiled until she attained to the sight of him in heaven'. The seed of her religious vocation may have been planted during the years which followed. Her great-aunt, later a nun herself, would have learned from her mother, a Parisian princess, about the austere life led at the monasteries of Chelles and Faremoutiers, and passed the stories on.

With Edwin's conversion the Church's future in Northumbria

seemed assured. Mass baptisms, at the king's command, took place in the Trent and Swale, and Paulinus gave himself unsparingly to preaching and catechizing. But in 633 all was shattered, and for the second time Hilda's home was destroyed.

Cadwallon, a British king of Gwynedd, North Wales, took bitter vengeance on Edwin, his former fosterbrother, for the annexation of Anglesey and Man. He invaded Northumbria in alliance with Penda, the future king of Mercia, who dominates the history of the next twenty years. Under this warrior who exemplified the swaggering, gift-bestowing heroes of Germanic saga, Mercia grew from a tribe to a power rivalling Northumbria and Wessex. Undefeated until his last battle, Penda waged a relentless war against Christianity, exploiting for political ends the rivalry between the many gods and the One, at the same time tolerating missionaries within his kingdom. It was as Cadwallon's ally that Penda took the first step in his ascent to power. In a great battle at Hatfield, Edwin was killed. Paulinus took Queen Ethelburga and her young daughter to safety in Kent. As Northumbria lapsed into heathenism, Cadwallon, nominally a Christian but described by Bede as 'a barbarian more savage than any pagan' ravaged the country for a whole year, putting women and children to death with merciless cruelty. It is likely that Hilda was in Northumbria during this terrible year. The slaughter and rapine were only ended by the 'most Christian king' Oswald, who emerged from exile among the Celtic monks of Iona to slay Cadwallon and establish peace, and Christianity, once more.

One of his first acts was to send to Iona for a bishop. The story of how Aidan, Northumbria's second apostle and Hilda's friend, was selected, tells us much about this 'man of outstanding gentleness, holiness and moderation'. The first missionary chosen returned home, declaring to the monastic council that he had been able to do nothing because of the 'barbarous and stubborn disposition' of the Northumbrians. Aidan gently taxed him with having failed to feed his hearers first with milk and not with meat, according to the apostle's precept. Predictably, Aidan was forthwith consecrated bishop and sent on the mission. He was given the island of Lindisfarne as his see, and from there he travelled round his diocese on foot, making friends with rich and poor, and drawing everyone to Christ by his gentleness. Like his disciple, Bishop Chad of Lichfield, he was given a fine horse for his episcopal rounds. Chad was commanded by his archbishop to keep his mount, but Aidan promptly gave his away, countering his royal benefactor's protest with a mild rebuke: 'Is that brood of the mare dearer in your sight than that son of God', the poor man to whom the gift was given.

With Aidan's coming, Hilda, baptized and nurtured in her faith by the Roman Paulinus, learned the customs of the northern Celtic church, which had developed in isolation for centuries and retained its own way of life. But Celtic custom never held the monopoly of religious practice in Northumbria. Paulinus' deacon James, a saintly and steadfast man who lived until Bede's time, stayed at his post, continuing to preach, baptize, and teach the Roman manner of chant.

The fact that Hilda and Aidan became friends must mean that she remained in Northumbria after Edwin's death. From this time we know nothing about her until her thirty-third year, except that she remained single and 'spent her life nobly in secular occupations'. In a world where women normally married, this demonstrates a high degree of resolution. With no male relative to protect her, she yet remained in a Northumbria seldom free from the ravages of war and Penda's persistent raiding, though there was a ready refuge with her sister, who had married into the royal house of East Anglia.

Since the reign of the great Redwald, East Anglia had suffered a decline in temporal power, nor had Christianity prospered there until the accession of a king who was baptized while an exile in Gaul. During his reign, East Anglia received from Archbishop Honorius of Canterbury a Burgundian bishop, Felix, and with him teachers trained in the Canterbury methods. Felix seems to have had a special call to evangelize England in the seventh century, as Dominic Barberi was to have in the nineteenth. Unlike Barberi, however, Felix saw thousands of souls won for Christ during his seventeen-year ministry. He baptized Anna, Etheldreda's father and, when Anna became king, continued to strengthen his faith. Thus, Etheldreda and her three sisters received a Christian upbringing from an early age. All four became religious, all four saints.

The sisters grew up during the unknown period of Hilda's life in Northumbria. Their aunt by marriage Hereswith, Hilda's sister, was deeply religious; possibly it was from her that they imbibed the ideal of a life lived for Christ. After some years of marriage Hereswith's husband, Ethelhere, agreed to his wife leaving him and their two sons to enter the monastery of Chelles. The church authorities granted a permission which today would scarcely be given, and Hereswith crossed to Gaul 'to seek an everlasting crown'. There were at the time no monasteries for women in England. Hilda resolved to follow her sister. Bede's words vividly evoke her whole-heartedness: 'She desired to forsake her country and all that ever she had, and go into France, there to lead a pilgrim's and exile's life for our Lord's sake.' The plan was never carried out. On her way to Gaul Hilda delayed for a whole year in East Anglia. What prevented her crossing to Chelles we do not know, but it is probable that her prolonged stay had a profound influence on her four young relatives. At the very least, her enthusiasm for the religious life would have further inspired hearts set on fire by Hereswith.

Bishop Aidan recalled Hilda to Northumbria, where he gave her a small plot of land on the north bank of the river Wear on which to live the monastic life with a few companions. After a year, he installed her as abbess at Hartlepool where, not long before, he blessed Heiu, said to be the first Northumbrian woman to become a nun. Hilda ruled Hartlepool for eight years, 647–55. She 'began immediately to establish order and regular life under the guidance of learned men. For Bishop Aidan, with other religious men that knew and loved her, frequently visited and instructed her.' Her wisdom became renowned, and she began at Hartlepool to train those in her charge with the remarkable teaching that was to bear even greater fruit at Whitby.

Meanwhile, Etheldreda approached marriageable age in the surroundings of a royal court. As the Sutton Hoo treasure indicates, the East Anglian royal house was immensely rich, a wealth probably equalled, or even exceeded, by that of Northumbria. Shields and swords decorated with garnets set in gold filigree, silver spoons and bowls, jewellery of inestimable value, testify to a court which glittered with splendour. The gathering in the tapestry-hung great hall at night, seen through fumes of smoke and ale, must have been brilliant. As the bards declaimed the heroic deeds of great ancestors or, in Christian times, those of great ascetics, the assembly quaffed ale or mead from silver goblets and took their turn with the harp. The women served the men, neither queen nor princess being exempt. Perhaps Etheldreda, wearing gold armlets and rings and a heavy gold necklace of intertwining circles set with garnets and pearls, took part in scenes similar to that depicted in *Beowulf*: 'Queen Hygd, who loved her people, went round the hall with vessels of mead, and placed goblets in the hands of the fighting men . . . urging the young men to eat and drink, sometimes presenting a gold ring to one of the warriors before she retired to her seat. Sometimes Hrothgar's daughter, young and adorned with gold, carried goblets of ale to the senior chieftains.'

Before the age when women normally married, Etheldreda had, according to Ely tradition, decided to dedicate her virginity to Christ. Her elder sister Sexburga was already married to King Earconbert of Kent, and suitors for Etheldreda's hand came from far and wide, attracted by her beauty and gentle character. The young princess succeeded in refusing all offers until Tonbert, prince of the South Girvii, pressed his suit. King Anna exerted his authority in the face of his daughter's protests, and she was forced by her sense of family and tribal duty to agree to the proposed marriage.

It is at first difficult to imagine why her father, praised by Bede as 'marvellous godly and notable for virtue both of word and deed', should have insisted on her marriage. But Anna was also an Anglo-Saxon king, with his fair share of the ruthlessness needed to maintain that rank, and a duty to protect his people. The South Girvii territory around the Wash made a buffer state between East Anglia and north-east Mercia. Since two of Anna's predecessors had been killed by Penda of Mercia, whose power was still in the ascendant, Anna would be anxious to strengthen friendly ties with these valuable allies. His daughter's resolution weighed little against political expediency. However, there is no need to assume that her marriage was all penance. Probably a Christian, Tonbert respected his young wife's desire, and they lived in continence. This may seem strange to us, but it is by no means unfamiliar to Christian asceticism, ancient or modern.

In 654, two years after Etheldreda's departure to live in the fens, Penda again attacked the East Angles. Henry of Huntingdon, a Christian chronicler of the twelfth century, has preserved a vivid account of the battle: 'He marched furiously against the doomed army of King Anna, like a raging wolf he rushed on the sheepfold. On all sides ran streams of blood, nor did he stay till all the kin were destroyed. So King Anna and his army were swallowed up by the sword in one moment.' We may doubt whether Anna and his army were as helpless as sheep, but slaughtered they were, and Anna was succeeded by his brother Ethelhere, Hilda's brother-in-law. Anna's death possibly gave his two younger daughters the chance to enter religion unopposed. Ethelburga entered the double monastery of Faremoutiers and became abbess. Withburga became a recluse first at Holkham, Norfolk, then at Dereham, where she founded a monastery.

Tonbert died after three years of marriage. One would have expected the widow to hasten across the Channel to Chelles or Faremoutiers. She did not. Perhaps organized religious life did not yet appeal to her, or perhaps she was still uncertain what form her consecration to God should take. Whatever the reason, she retired to the Isle of Ely, a marriage gift from Tonbert. In those days Ely was truly an island, surrounded by miles of reeds and swamps. Unlike the trackless fens, its fertile fields and woods abounded in all kinds of wild life, and its surrounding waters teemed with fish. The families living on the island had been in Etheldreda's care for the previous three years. Now, leaving the estate in her steward's hands, 'She began to live with herself. Fixing her whole mind on heavenly things, she gave herself up to fasting, vigils and unceasing prayer.' as the Book of Ely says.

When, in 642, King Oswald was slain in battle by Penda, his brother Oswy succeeded him. Eager for more power, in 651 Oswy instigated the betrayal and murder of King Oswin, a friend and disciple of Aidan. The murder broke Aidan's heart and he died soon after, in a tent pitched for him outside Bamborough church. Hilda was at Hartlepool when she was deprived of her friend and counsellor. For a time things must have seemed black. Penda was raiding far into Northumbria, destroying all he met with fire and sword. Though Oswy tried to buy him off with great treasure, Penda refused all bribes.

By 655, Oswy was forced to fight for his kingdom against heavy odds, in spite of the fact that his younger son Egfrith was held hostage at the court of Mercia. He 'vowed that if he should be victorious, he would dedicate his daughter to God in holy virginity' and found twelve monasteries. His gamble succeeded, and in the ensuing battle at Winwaed near Leeds Penda was killed.

One of Penda's allies at Winwaed was King Ethelhere of East Anglia, who is said to have caused the war, though we are not told how. His death, only a year after that of King Anna, dealt a blow to East Anglia from which, perhaps, that kingdom never fully recovered.

In a complete reversal of fortune, Oswy became overlord of kingdoms both north and south of the Humber. His ten-year-old son Egfrith returned to him from Mercia. True to his promise, he entrusted his daughter Elfleda, scarcely a year old, to Hilda to be trained for the religious life.

Two years after Winwaed, Hilda was given a tract of land, perhaps one of the twelve Oswy gave in fulfilment of his vow, at Streaneshalch, known since Viking times as Whitby. Perched high on ancient cliffs, with the sea dashing against the rocks below, the site is impressive. Streaneshalch, or 'bay of the lighthouse', is indeed a city set on a hill. Even the low buildings of Hilda's time must have been visible to fishermen far out to sea, for the ruin of the later, much larger, monastery church still acts as a beacon through the dangerous rocks. It is unusual for monastic buildings to be situated in such a commanding position. The choice of this site in preference to a fold of the moors by a running stream would seem to indicate that Hilda was a woman of freedom and breadth of spirit who looked for no shelter from the storms of life, but opened herself to the mighty power of God.

Whitby was a double monastery, that is a community of monks and nuns who shared conventual life to an extent that varied from place to place. This type of foundation flourished especially in the seventh century. It came to England by way of Gaul, where the nunneries of Poitiers, Chelles and Faremoutiers-en-Brie all had associated houses of monks, who gave the sacraments and preached in the surrounding villages. During the period when Christianity was spreading and before parishes were established, these monasteries provided a centre from which to evangelize a district. In England the superior was invariably the abbess, usually a woman of royal blood, born to rule. No accusation of immorality has ever been made against these monasteries; they owe their disappearance to factors other than moral laxity. Apart from Gilbert of Sempringham's twelfth-century revival, and the Bridgettine house of Syon, they have been few and far between since Anglo-Saxon times. In our own day there are one or two, including a foundation made by the Eastern Orthodox Church in Essex.

At Whitby, Hilda found full scope for her talents of teaching and organization. She taught 'the strict observance of justice, piety, chastity and other virtues, and particularly of peace and charity; so that, after the example of the primitive church, no one was rich and none poor, all property being held in common . . . she obliged those who were under her direction to make a thorough study of the scriptures and occupy themselves in good works, so that many were found fitted for Holy Orders and the service of God's altar'. A remarkable statement on the position of women in the church in those days! This prudence, care for having property in common, and love of scripture, reminds one of the Rule of St Benedict. However, Hilda probably never used this rule. Aidan would have introduced her to the rule and customs of Iona, which followed the teachings of St Columba, and these were probably followed at Whitby. Hilda's training of her monks was so thorough that no fewer than five of them became bishops, a startling achievement when one considers that there were then only about twelve bishoprics in all England.

Modern excavations at Whitby hint at its rich and varied life. Within a two-feet thick stone wall were two churches, one for monks and one for nuns, and a number of other buildings. The discovery of bookcovers and styli indicate a scriptorium and library, and two-roomed cells each with a hearth were grouped in Celtic fashion. Spindles and loom weights tell of weaving wool from the hardy moorland sheep, while a touch which brings these seventh-century monks and nuns close to us is the number of personal items uncovered: buckles, pins, tweezers, needles, all of bronze or bone. 'Guests are never lacking in a monastery,' as St Benedict observed, and Whitby was no exception. Scholars, kings and nobles with their retinues, to say nothing of the poor, called for extensive accommodation. The kitchen with its open fire equipped with spits and large iron cooking pots, must have been kept busy. Folk came from far and near to seek spiritual and temporal relief, finding in Hilda, so Bede tells us, a counsellor of wisdom and prudence with, we may guess, a warm loving heart. 'Mother', as everyone called her, was penetrating in her discernment and fostering of talent. This has already been touched on in the case of her monk-bishops, and Caedmon is another example. Middle aged and shy, he was one of the laymen who tended the animals on the monastery estates. He avoided taking his turn with the harp at feasts because he could not sing, but in a dream he was bidden to sing about the creation of the world, verse to which he added when he awoke. Only nine lines of this have been preserved by Bede, who is careful to tell us that these are not Caedmon's exact words, but the gist of them:

> Praise now the maker of the heavenly kingdom
> the power and purpose of our Creator,
> the deeds of the Father of glory.
> Let us sing how the eternal God,
>   author of all miracles,
> first created the heavens for the sons of men
>   as a roof to shelter them.
> And how their almighty Preserver gave them
>   the earth to live in.

This has been criticized as clumsy and repetitive, hardly justifying Caedmon's title of the Father of English poetry. However, it should be remembered that his originality lies in using the technique and language of barbaric saga to clothe Biblical stories in a form the common man could appreciate. Then, as now, folk listened more eagerly to song than to preaching. Presented with the unexpected gift of a brother taught by God to turn scripture into song, Hilda quickly realized its value for conveying the fundamental beliefs of Christianity to people who could not read. She instructed that Caedmon should be received as a monk and taught the whole series of sacred history, which he reproduced in verse. For ordinary people, the songs reinforced and elaborated such stories as the Exodus and the Acts of the Apostles, depicted on the church walls.

While Hilda busied herself with her community at Whitby, king Oswy was seeking a wife for his second son Egfrith, a boy of fifteen. His choice fell on Etheldreda who, by the year 660, had spent five years as a recluse. On grounds of personal character his choice was excellent, but why choose an anchoress senior by some eight years to the bridegroom? Oswy cannot have been ignorant of Etheldreda's religious life and asceticism, but possibly the union of two dynasties outweighed the disadvantages of such a match. Perhaps his devout wife Eanfleda was behind the choice. She was that daughter of Edwin whose birth thirty-four years before had tipped the scales in favour of Christianity. Inheriting some of her father's strong character, she had forced her husband to found a monastery in memory of the murdered King Oswin; she was quite capable of insistence in the matter of her son's wife also. Etheldreda's uncle, King Ethelwold, had little choice but to consent. It was unthinkable to refuse an overlord, on whose favour the ruined fortunes of his kingdom depended. Once again Etheldreda gave up her own will and, after a splendid marriage ceremony, went to live at York in 660.

Unaccountable as it may seem to us, the couple loved each other, and their early married life was happy, resembling the sketch given by an Anglo-Saxon poet: 'Battle and warfare shall be strong in the man, and the woman shall thrive, beloved by her people, be cheerful of mind, keep counsel, be liberal with horses and treasures. In the hall before the band of comrades she shall present straightway the first goblet to the prince's hand, and be ready with wise counsel when they plan together how to run their household.'

The years from 660 to 670 coincide with the rise of Wilfrid, the fiery bishop who bestrides the second half of the seventh century and played a major part in Etheldreda's life. Probably already known to her by reputation, for her sister Sexburga, queen of Kent, had helped the young Wilfrid on his way to Rome, the abbot of Ripon became Etheldreda's spiritual adviser. Infuriating in his stubbornness, he was extravagant in the corresponding virtue of loyalty to friends and ideals, as Etheldreda was to discover.

There may have been a difference of liturgical custom between Egfrith and Etheldreda, as between the king and queen. Eanfleda, brought up in Kent, adhered to the Roman dating for Easter, to which the church in Southern Ireland had also conformed; Oswy kept the ancient Celtic date still retained by the Irish of Iona and its dependencies. 'As the king broke his fast and celebrated the feast of Easter, the queen and her attendants, still fasting, kept Palm Sunday.'

This diversity was tolerated during Aidan's lifetime, but when his gentle restraining influence was withdrawn, the controversy blazed up with a vehemence which finds its parallel in the differing liturgical opinions of our own day. Even the gentle Bede was roused to indignation. After a list of Aidan's many virtues, he sternly remarks:

'But that he observed not Easter at its proper time, this I neither commend nor allow.'

In 663 a synod was summoned, with protagonists from both sides, under the presidency of King Oswy. That Whitby was chosen for the meeting is a measure of Hilda's achievement. In seven years she had transformed a desolate cliff top into a thriving monastery which could house two kings, several bishops, an abbot and their retinues. Hilda, a supporter of the Iona observance, attended the sessions with some of her nuns; whether Etheldreda was present is uncertain, indeed there is no hint that Hilda and Etheldreda ever met in Northumbria. The chief speaker on the Roman side was abbot Wilfrid, recently ordained priest. Bishop Colman of Lindisfarne vigorously defended the Scottish usage as being derived from John the Apostle, but Wilfrid's eloquence could not be gainsaid. His triumphant conclusion quoting the promises to Peter in Matthew 16 prompted Oswy to declare that he would stand with St Peter; otherwise, the doorkeeper of heaven might shut him out. There the matter ended. Colman and some others, taking some of Aidan's bones with them, retired to Iona. Most of the Irish-trained clergy remained, conforming to the Roman observance, but handing on the spirit of simplicity, poverty and missionary zeal which characterized the Celts. We are not told of Hilda's reaction. Forsaking the custom of her friend Aidan must have been painful, but in her later years Whitby became ever more Roman. A small dependent monastery founded the year before her death was built more on the Roman pattern, while in her successor's time there was at Whitby a cult of that eminent Roman, Gregory the Great, of whom a Whitby monk wrote the earliest life extant.

In the year 670 King Oswy died, a death almost unique among the kings in Bede's history in that it was of sickness, not violence. His widow Eanfleda joined her young daughter at Whitby, which they later ruled jointly. Egfrith's accession to the throne may have brought to a head the growing rift between him and his wife. He began urging the consummation of their marriage. Etheldreda held courageously to her religious vow and pressed in her turn for leave to enter a monastery, a step which must have seemed the best solution to the difficulty. Egfrith persisted, and Wilfrid, now bishop of York, was called in to arbitrate. 'Egfrith promised much land and money if he could persuade the queen to pay the marriage duty, for he knew she loved no man more than himself.' Wilfrid, heedless of the consequences of crossing the king, encouraged Etheldreda. At last, after many arguments, Egfrith was prevailed upon to give his consent, the queen took off her royal regalia, and entered Coldingham, a double monastery on the Celtic pattern.

These events do not present Etheldreda in an attractive light. We consider her unfeeling, and compare her unfavourably with her sister Sexburga, who bore children and waited for widowhood before entering religion. Yet the woman who built a marriage from such unlikely materials and was so reluctantly allowed to leave it, must have been warm and loving as well as resolute. Her hold over Egfrith is suggested by the legend which tells how he attempted to take her from Coldingham, then pursued her to the borders of her own fens, where he was thwarted by a sudden flood. However, it seems unlikely that the king would make any such attempt after refraining from coercion for several years past. He married again, but had no children, and was killed during a raid against the Picts when he was forty. He was succeeded by his illegitimate half-brother Aldfrith, a learned and virtuous man whose encouragement of scholarship during a long and peaceful reign made possible the great achievements of Bede.

Coldingham was probably chosen for Etheldreda's entry into religion because the abbess, the king's aunt Ebba, was well able to keep her nephew in order. Her memory is kept alive by the place-name of St Abb's Head of Berwick, and to her also belongs the doubtful honour of ruling the only monastery in Bede's history which earned criticism. Although formidable on occasion, Ebba in later life was easy-going and less than eagle-eyed in the running of her house, where the religious spent much time in feasting and drinking, and slept instead of attending the night office. When an Irish monk brought this to Ebba's attention she remedied matters, though after her death discipline again lapsed. Etheldreda remained at Coldingham for only a year, a period which suggests the probationary period enjoined in the Rule of St Benedict, which Wilfrid had recently introduced. Having made her profession and received the veil at Wilfrid's hands, she handed over to him the property at Hexham which had been her marriage gift from Egfrith. There, of blocks from nearby Roman ruins, he built a house of God 'of wonderfully polished stones, supported by many pillars and porticoes, with walls of unbelievable length and height', which was thought by his biographer Eddius to have no equal north of the Alps.

In 673 the ex-queen returned to Ely and set up a monastery for both monks and nuns, where a community soon gathered round her. She may have used the Rule of St Benedict exclusively, or at least as one among several. The site for monastery and church was that of a chapel reputedly built by Augustine of Canterbury and afterwards destroyed by Penda. If Etheldreda emulated Wilfrid by building in stone, the brothers may have brought material by boat from the Roman ruins at Grantchester, sixteen miles upriver.

Bishop Wilfrid installed and blessed the new abbess. Perhaps on this occasion the responsories and antiphons were sung entiphonally 'according to the custom of the early church', on the introduction of which Wilfrid prided himself. The task of the new superior was to establish regular life and to instruct the religious by precept and above all by example. Like Queen Radegunde, she practised austerities without enjoining them on others, and felt so powerful an attraction for prayer that, after the lengthy recitation of the night office, she remained in church until dawn.

Five years after Ely's foundation, Wilfrid was expelled from Northumbria and his diocese divided. Before taking ship in order to appeal to Rome, he visited Ely and promised Etheldreda to obtain from the Pope a recognition of the rights and liberties of the abbey. Upon his return after a two-year absence in the course of which he had converted many Frisians, he found she had died. Etheldreda is said to have prophesied not only the pestilence from which she died, but also the number of her flock who would succumb to it. She accepted with joy the suffering caused by a great swelling under her jaw, seeing in it a means of atonement for her youthful pleasure in wearing fine jewels: 'For I remember, when I was a little girl, bearing round my neck the useless weight of gold and precious stones.' She died on 23 June 679, and at her own request was buried in a plain wooden coffin in the common cemetery.

Sixteen years later her sister Sexburga, the ruling abbess, decided that the bones should be exhumed and more fittingly interred. In the presence of Wilfrid, exiled once more from his see, and surrounded by the monks and nuns singing appropriate chants, the grave was opened. Sexburga cried, 'Glory to the name of the Lord!', for the body was seen to be 'as free from corruption as if she had died and been buried that very day'. The body was placed behind the high altar in a beautifully decorated Roman sarcophagus from Grantchester. It is noteworthy that the bodies of Etheldreda's two sisters, Withburga the recluse and Ethelburga of Faremoutiers, were also said to have been found incorrupt.

Etheldreda's prominent place in monastic calendars is evidence of deep interest in her during the Middle Ages. In an eleventh-century Sarum missal she has a proper Mass Preface and is named in the Canon. Incidents from her life are sculpted round Ely's great Lantern Tower, while late medieval paintings of her survive in East Anglian rood screens. Under her Norman name she is remembered to this day in St Audrey's Fair, still held at Ely, where the cheap trinkets sold in her honour gave the English language a new word, 'tawdry'. Her tomb, surrounded by those of her sisters Sexburga and Withburga and her niece Ermenilda, the third abbess, survived until the Reformation, but today, the only relic of Anglo-Saxon times in Ely Cathedral is a memorial cross to Owine, Etheldreda's steward.

During most of Etheldreda's short rule, Hilda at Whitby was afflicted with a fever, in spite of which she continued to give instruction to the whole community as well as private counsel in her small two-roomed cell. For six years she suffered, giving thanks to God herself, and instructing others to praise him in all adversity. About cockcrow on her last day, 17 November 780, after receiving Holy Viaticum, she summoned all her nuns. Begging them to keep peace among themselves and with others, she reiterated the peace and charity which was the essence of her rule. As she was still speaking, she passed, with a smile, from death to eternal life.

That same night, a nun at Hackness thought she heard the passing-bell and, looking up, saw a great light in which Hilda's soul, accompanied by angels, was borne up to heaven. A Whitby nun who loved Hilda dearly received a similar vision in the novitiate quarters, which were remote from those of the community. So both the Hackness nuns and the Whitby novitiate were roused in the night to pray for their mother, the news of whose death was received by them at daybreak.

Hilda's influence on the Church of her day was immense, equalled by no other abbess. She not only inspired respect on the human level from men and women alike, but evoked deep love and devotion. It was above all because she was a woman of great spiritual stature who sought God, that she drew men to him. When Hilda was a child, her mother dreamed about a jewelled necklace which illuminated all Britain with its splendour. This dream came to pass in the life of her daughter.

Hilda's cult must have begun almost at once after her death, for her name appears in an early eighth century calendar of St Willibrord, Northumbrian monk and apostle of Holland and Luxembourg. Though Whitby was completely destroyed by the Vikings about 860, Hilda's supposed relics were translated to Glastonbury about 150 years later. Her cult was always strong in the North, especially after the revival of Whitby as a monastery for monks only in the late eleventh century. Had it not been for Bede, we should know nothing of her; but Bede has kept her memory green, and in the nineteenth and twentieth centuries she has been aptly chosen as patron of churches and colleges.

Hilda and Etheldreda well deserve a place in this book. Although neither of these great saints can strictly be called Benedictine, they paved the way for many centuries of Benedictine monasticism in this country. How perfectly they would have responded to St

Benedict's call to take up strong, shining weapons and follow their Lord to glory. Channelling their ancestors' warlike spirit into an energetic love of God, they gave their lives fighting in the service of Christ, their true King.

by Dame Etheldreda Hession

BIBLIOGRAPHY

Bede, *Historia Ecclesiastica Gentis Anglorum*, ed. C. Plummer (Oxford 1956).

Eddius Stephanus, *Life of St Wilfrid*, ed. B. Colgrave (Cambridge 1927).

The Earliest Life of Gregory the Great, ed. B. Colgrave (Lawrence, Kansas 1968).

Liber Eliensis, ed. E. O. Blake (*Camden Series* 1962).

D. Whitelock, *The Beginnings of English Society*, (Harmondsworth 1952).

F. M. Stenton, *Anglo-Saxon England*, 3rd edition (Oxford 1970).

H. Mayr-Harting, *The Coming of Christianity to Anglo-Saxon England* (1972).

D. P. Kirby (ed.), *St Wilfrid at Hexham* (Newcastle 1973).

P. Hunter Blair, *Northumbria in the Days of Bede*, (London 1976).

M. S. Carey, *Ely Cathedral* (*Pitkin Pictorials*, 1975).

J. Godfrey, 'The Double Monastery in Early English History', *Ampleforth Journal*, lxxix (1974), 19–32.

St Bede the Venerable, Monk of Jarrow

'*The candle of the Church lit by the Holy Spirit*'.   St Boniface.

'*One of the saintliest characters ever produced by the Church of Christ in this island. . . . We have not, it seems to me, amid all our discoveries, invented as yet anything better than the Christian life which Bede lived, and the Christian death which he died.*'   Charles Plummer, 1896.

'*Bede was a pioneer: the first Englishman of his type, the first scientific intellect produced by the Germanic people of Europe. . . . He was the most unexpected of all products of a primitive age, a really great scholar.*'
Sir Richard Southern, 1964.

In 796 Viking marauders erased the great twin monasteries of Monkwearmouth-Jarrow from the map of the civilized world for a millennium; by some strange whim of modern man's admiration a monument to a pair of these destroyers has lately been placed in today's Jarrow. In spite of this, the two monks who more than any others in their period succeeded in preserving the glory of an old civilization and building a new one, Abbot Benedict Biscop and the Venerable Bede, are still remembered there with veneration. Their work was achieved and disseminated: a single span of monastic tradition had bridged for our European civilization the old, fast disappearing and the new, a first renaissance.

Bede was not alone in his work, just as St Thomas Aquinas centuries later was not alone in his. Both blossomed as a quintessential flowering to a process that seemed to require them to give it final value. For the friar, it was the long-germinating scholastic movement, which had begun with St Anselm of Bec; for the earlier monk, it was the steady build-up of the monastic church of Canterbury and Northumbria, with its recovery of the learning of secular Rome and the faith of papal Rome. For all that, when Bede emerged in his time, he has been rightly judged by W. H. Hutton as 'a perfect example of the concentration of interests, religious and educational, afforded by the monastic life'. He was uniquely the ideal monk-scholar as conceived by St Benedict, his mind being prompted ever by the material of *lectio divina* as that was understood in the Rule. Though Bede knew the Rule, he did not live exclusively under it, but he proved its perfect model.

We might ask why Bede, brilliant as he was, remained a monk-priest all the days of his life, unelected even to office in his own house. The moment came in 716, when Ceolfrith, the founder-abbot of Jarrow, resigned and made his way to Rome to visit the see of Peter, but died on the way. On Whit Sunday the many brethren of St Peter's Monkwearmouth and St Paul's Jarrow met to elect Hwaetberht. Bede gives us a vivid eyewitness account of it in his *Historia Abbatum*, his account of the abbacies of his own house. None had considered him for abbot, it seems, though he was then forty-five and at the height of his powers. Had he been elected, his best writings would probably never have reached the world. He was anyway too modest and retiring (as his lack of intrusion into his own pages suggests to us), and too given to speculation ever to make a good father and administrator. The temperamentally natural scholar is a poor leader, and vice versa. Bede was a man of thought and peace, of geographical and spiritual stability who, like Newman in his day, needed the steady structure of his community about him as a back-cloth for unremitting study or letter writing. Both of them had a call beyond their confreres to their age and ages beyond.

Edward Gibbon, explaining his life, suggested that the scholar at his desk who travelled little and scarcely participated in the activities of his generation could yet travel more in the mind than any man of action. Man as reflective spirit, capable of broad synthesis, aware of the play of the past and the possibilities of the future, able with a powerful imagination, a disciplined intellect and a clear judgement to bring order and meaning to large masses of unordered human record, can travel vast regions of human experience without ever leaving his cell or desk or oratory. So it was with Bede.

Bede travelled more in the mind and less in the body than perhaps any other major scholar of Christendom. Monk, priest, theologian, scriptural exegete, Church historian, he scarcely ever left the rather undistinguished spit of land a few feet above the waters of the Tyne opposite what is now dockland and shipyards at Jarrow, symbol of modern economic recession. Concerning the area above the Jarrow mud-flats, Bede wrote in all simplicity thus:

> I was born on the lands of the monastery of the blessed Apostles Peter & Paul at Wearmouth and Jarrow, and on reaching the age of seven years, my family entrusted me first to the most reverend abbot Benedict [d. 689] and later to abbot Ceolfrith [d. 716] for my education. I have spent the remainder of my life in this monastery, and devoted myself entirely to the study of the scriptures.

There is an astonishing constancy and stability about such an existence. Born in 672 just before Benedict Biscop founded Monk-wearmouth, called to the cloister in 680 just before his abbot went on to found St Paul's at Jarrow (the dedication stone of whose church bears a date which can be referred to the year 685, and arguably marks a new beginning for civilization in Britain), Bede thereafter 'observed the regular discipline and sang the choir offices daily in church', finding his chief delight in study, teaching and writing at no other place than Jarrow, till he died in 735 after over fifty-five cloistered years of prayer and work.

Ordained a deacon at the unusually young age of nineteen, Bede neither searched out other places than Jarrow for the exercise or stimulation of his gifts, nor sought any promotion at St Paul's. He was ordained a priest at the direction of abbot Ceolfrith when he was thirty (St Benedict having been no more in his life than a deacon), probably because the monks were increasingly being called upon for pastoral duties requiring the priesthood and it became the custom for the more able monks to be ordained. From then on he continued to learn and to teach and write (at first for the needs of his house) excellent Latin, some scrappy Greek and Hebrew, much involved scripture commentary, and a little history—enough to earn him the title 'father of English history'.

It was a strangely concentrated existence, *ora et labora*, with scant time either for friends or for travel; it was a total ordering to the values most expressly monastic. Bede, so it seems, never left North-umbria nor journeyed farther south than York, and that late in life to see a former pupil. His homily upon his first abbot recorded his gratitude to him that his journeying abroad to Gaul and Rome had allowed successive monks at Wearmouth-Jarrow to remain peacefully in their cloisters 'to serve Christ in secure freedom'. In collecting and collating his sources for the great *Ecclesiastical History of the English People*, Bede did travel over to Lindisfarne, but scarcely further, rely-ing on those of his friends who did travel to sift the libraries and record collections of Rome, Gaul, Ireland and southern England. As he tells us in his preface, he particularly commissioned Nothelm, a priest of the Church of London destined to be archbishop of Canterbury: he 'visited Rome, and obtained permission from the present Pope Gregory [II, 715–31] to examine the archives of the holy Roman Church. He found there letters of Pope Gregory [I, 590–604] and other popes.'

To emphasize how utterly Bede's mind and body was topo-graphically bounded by the place where he passed his human existence, it might be worth recalling what Bede's commentator, Charles Plummer, described as a 'beautiful and touching' incident about a little boy, who might well have been Bede himself. It concerns the pestilence of 686 which swept away all at Jarrow who could read or preach or sing the antiphons and responses—all except abbot Ceolfrith himself and a young boy, who, if it were Bede, would have been aged fourteen by then. After conducting the Divine Office without antiphons for a week, the abbot could no longer tolerate so truncated an Office; so with the help of that young boy he restored the full service, the two of them carrying on together until the abbot could train more choir monks. Who was this boy? Bede just tells us: 'one who had been brought up and taught by [abbot Ceolfrith]; and who now, at this day, being in priest's orders in the same monastery, duly commends the abbot's praiseworthy acts both by his writings and his discourse'.

Who taught Bede? Part of the answer lies in the tradition of learning brought to the house by its abbots, especially its founder Benedict Biscop. The libraries of Monkwearmouth and Jarrow, while they had some startling gaps (as is to be expected), were marvellously replete by the standards of the time. Alcuin's list of books at York would nearly all have been familiar to Bede from his monastic copies. He knew his Virgil, quoting him frequently. He made lengthy quotations from Pliny's *Natural History*. He was introduced to the Latin authors by those at Jarrow who knew Latin well, as he soon did himself.

One of his scripture teachers was the monk Trumberht, who had been educated at Bishop Chad's Lastingham house, and who probably gave Bede so many details for his account of Chad and the Northumbrian Church at the time of the Synod of Whitby. Bede seems to have learned a little from John of Hexham, the bishop who ordained him deacon in 691 and priest in 702; and from Acca, a later bishop of Hexham, to whom Bede was to send a number of his scriptural works out of respect. It may have been from John, founder of Beverley minster, who had been a monk of Whitby, that he learned so much of the great Yorkshire double monastery, and about Theodore of Canterbury under whom John had studied before being consecrated to Hexham in 686.

Bede's first writings were school-books, probably initially intended for his own monk-pupils. He addressed his *De Arte Metrica*, which he wrote as a deacon, to his 'dearest son and fellow deacon Cuthbert', a curious greeting for one so nearly his own age. He wrote later to Plegwine, a monk of Hexham, as 'most loving' and 'dearest brother'. To a priest in 705 he sent his verse *Life of Cuthbert*, greeting him as John, 'my most beloved Lord in Christ', saying 'how much I am moved by your love and delighted by your presence, if it can be so.' His commentary on the Apocalypse he sent in 708 to his 'most beloved brother' Hwaetberht, who had been in Rome transcribing materials for his scholarship. Later, after 716, Bede addressed Hwaetberht as his 'most beloved abbot', dedicating another work to him. Such greetings reveal a warmth and intimacy between the early Anglo-Saxon monks of a kind the monks of the twelfth century Renaissance thought they were pioneering—Anselm in his letters, Aelred in his dealings with recalcitrants. If the Normans and Cistercians were conscious of their friendships, it seems that the monks of Bede's day took them for granted.

Bishop Acca of Hexham, who succeeded the turbulent Wilfrid in 709, seems to have been particularly close to Bede. The bishop persuaded Bede to write his two commentaries on Luke's Gospel and Acts, and he in turn sent copies of his commentaries to the bishop. Acca seems to have been Bede's major source for his *Ecclesiastical History* chapters on Willibrord and the Frisian mission, after a visit there in 703 en route to Rome; and he must have provided him with details of Wilfrid's life. Acca was a man after Bede's own heart, enriching Hexham with works of art and learning, with relics of martyrs and altars raised to them, with music and musicians. So Bede wrote warmly to him in several of his Prefaces: 'the most dear and beloved of all bishops who dwell in the land', 'ever revered with the deepest love', and so forth. The two monks kept in touch till the end, even in face of Acca's trials—the year the *History* appeared (731), the bishop was driven from his See and never reinstated.

Such were Bede's friends beyond his cloister. Another is clearly Albinus, who in 710 succeeded Hadrian as abbot of St Peter and St Paul, Canterbury, whose name appeared a lot in Bede's Preface to the *History*, notably as the *auctor* and *adjutor* of the great work, the 'promoter' and 'begetter', 'authority' and 'adviser', and 'eminent scholar of the Church of Canterbury . . . due to whose persuasions I was encouraged to begin this work'. If we take to be Bede's friends beyond Jarrow those with whom he had literary correspondence, or to whom he dedicated a piece of writing, they include a certain 'dearest sister in Christ' perhaps from Whitby; Bishop Eadfrith of Lindisfarne and several of the brethren of that monastery; Bishop Daniel of the West Saxons; Bishop Cyneberht of Lindsey; and 'the most reverend abbot Esi', with the brethren of Lastingham. It is a fair sprinkling; a list of them suggests to us that, as might be surmised, men of letters in those half-lettered days all knew and respected one another, exchanging their writings and their friendship. And, as today monks from many Communities know one another in a wide network, all the more would they have so known one another in those sparser and spartan days, when friendship was more a necessity than a luxury.

Of the monks of his own house that Bede numbered among friends or pupils or both, three should be mentioned here. One is Wilberht, who was present at Bede's death-bed, and took dictation of his final words upon the Fourth Gospel that Bede so desired to finish translating. Another was Egberht, a king's brother who became bishop of York in 732 and was the recipient of Bede's famous last letter-treatise of 734 instructing him on the needs of the Northumbrian Church, when Bede grew too infirm to make visits to his old pupil at York minster. And another was the young Cuthbert, one day to become abbot of Bede's own monastery, who as a lector wrote the moving account of Bede's last hour so much in the style of the master, that were he not the subject of the death it might have been Bede writing.

The picture given us, if we piece it together, is of a monk surrounded by the support and friendship of his own large community, from above in encouragement when he was young, from below in gratitude as he grew older; friendship in reverence from his fellow monks throughout England dazzled by the persistence of his scholarship and the way it enhanced the religious life of a Church so far from Rome; and friendship in learned companionship from those who shared the responsibilities of Church governance. Though Bede never travelled, his name did and his various works did, bringing affectionate admiration. Cuthbert his pupil was not alone in feeling that 'the whole race of the English in all provinces wherever they are found' should give thanks to God for granting them Bede.

Before we look to Bede's monastic life or his phenomenal scholarship (which is not beyond modern reproach) we should look to the conditions under which he lived and some of the assumptions of his society. He lived in the remotest north at a time of very deep significance for western Christendom. He mentions in his works the Saracens, who in the century before he died had sliced the Christian world in half, depriving the Church of many of its most ancient and cultured centres. What was left was a Gaul sunk in violence and immorality, an Italy locked in civil strife, and a sea of paganism as yet unchecked. Hope lay only in conversion of faith and heart, and not from abroad. Yet Bede found the English 'intellectually slothful', poor tools for such a considerable conversion.

Bede lived when books were a labour to make, both their production from pelts and their scribing one by one by skilled hand. There were no indices nor cross-references, nor library cataloguing systems. The Bible had not yet been divided into chapters (till Archbishop Stephen Langton did so after 1200), never mind verses (provided for controversy at the Reformation). Rooms were scarcely

lit at night and scarcely heated by day, visibility through what glass
there was available being pathetic by our standards—nor were there
opticians to salve tired eyes. Yet Bede's monastic fastness seemed
to become by degrees the clearing house of the North, open to influences from Africa and Asia Minor, from Gaul and Italy, from
Celtic Ireland. The doctrines of the Church, hammered out at
General Councils or in the writings of the Fathers, reached Bede's
monastery intact, with sound texts of the scriptures to support them.
The primary need for Anglo-Saxon England was to sift them and
serve them up with brevity and limpidity for the instruction of the
clergy, simple men of hardy ways who were to go out and convert
all England. What was wanted then was not illumination upon
monastic matters, but the Word of God, undistilled in good biblical
texts and distilled in good commentaries. Bede's life and works met
these needs admirably: *aperta magis brevitas quam disputatio prolixa.*

Bede's teaching was wholly orthodox, which says much for the
intellectual communication of his time, even if it lacked exploratory
interest. He fought to preserve the unity and universality of the
Church against Celtic particularism. He stressed the primacy of
Peter and the hierarchical authority of the bishops in apostolic
succession. He clearly saw the proper work of the Church as teaching
(which he did himself), governing (which he left to others) and
sanctifying (which was the cause for monks to be ordained priests),
insisting that essential to the spiritual life of any soul was the life of
the Church. Grace, eucharist, sacraments, all are found in Bede's
pages, so that his works appear modern beyond their time. And the
virtue he valued most was humility, coupled with the will to make
gradual progress before God—what the monks call *conversio morum.*
He was well tuned to become the teacher of his time.

What of the problem of miracles in Bede's writing: are they period
pieces that detract from his critical authenticity, or are they an
element of religious truth which escapes the modern historian? It
has long been noticed that Bede introduces no miracles into his
History of the Abbots of his own monasteries, where he had a first-hand
knowledge of all the circumstances; and that in the *Ecclesiastical
History* and his hagiographical writings, where he had authenticated
occurrences related to him, he included only those miracles which
were sufficiently substantiated, providing his evidential authorities
for all to see. It has long been suggested that, where miracles are
retailed, Bede wanted to edify rather than to record hard fact, to
underline some value: his purpose was didactic and moralizing.
In a word, Bede's world was at the same time practically historical
and religiously fanciful; as with Scripture, his belief and intention
lay at two levels.

Bede's world happily accepted the miracles of both Old and New Testament, and God's righteous intervention into the law of creation, miracles being linked essentially with man's salvation. It accepted fundamentalist interpretations of the Fathers at face value, albeit with a practical restraint which made it attribute to the miraculous only what was necessary. Moreover, with Augustine and Gregory, Bede and his world saw spiritual miracles of conversion as more significant than physical miracles of nature. And yet all three viewed their world as a place for wonder, medical phenomena being part of that wonder. Bede indeed narrates a single miracle done to himself (as does Gregory similarly in the *Dialogues*): in the Preface to his verse *Life of Cuthbert*, he tells us that he was healed 'in his tongue' at the time when he was recording Cuthbert's miracles, which are so numerous, Bede wrote, that new ones are daily effected by his relics and old ones come to light from those who are in a position to know. The meaning is not determinative, and it may be that J. A. Giles' interpretation of Bede's words is right: 'I myself experienced such a miracle in the guidance of my tongue while singing Cuthbert's miracles', i.e. Bede became inspired by his study.

Bede's world was not only full of physical trial and spiritual wonder, but it was a world not of market adjustments, supply and demand or meritocratic promotion; it was a world beholden to aristocratic and royal favour within the context of beholdenness in faith to God. Indeed Mr James Campbell devoted the 1979 Jarrow Lecture (the twenty-first since 1958) to 'Bede's Kings & Princes'. From his attention to them in the pages of the *Ecclesiastical History* we learn a great deal in passing about the contracts of early Anglo-Saxon life, even though Bede's intention is to edify by writing religious and not social history. Thus we are told more of Edwin and Oswald and Oswy than of Penda of Mercia. Nevertheless, the feuding and sudden exiles appear in his pages, and equally sudden returns to power and favour. It is so also with the bishops, notably Wilfrid, who cannot escape being drawn as a secular nobleman in a cowl and cope. The element of weapons as coinage of power, of treasure as political patronage, of fighting bands able to exert their corporate will, all this cannot be entirely overlooked by the peaceable Bede. The conversion of England had to be effected by the conversion of kings: Bede's fullest account of a conversion is that of Edwin of Northumbria, and Edwin made certain that his fellow monarch in East Anglia joined himself and Ethelbert of Kent in baptism to Christendom. Kings persuaded other kings, for reasons political as well as religious. So it was that the kings of Wessex and Essex and Middle Anglia were baptized in Northumbria, with Oswald and Oswy as godfathers. Such events had importance in linking overlords with lesser kings, thereby uniting dignified sub-ordination with mutual obligation.

In Bede's *History* there is ample evidence that a new power establishes a new faith, and a new faith a new power. Christianity brought Mediterranean civilization, good government and a docile society—provided that royal conversion had then succeeded in effecting subsequent popular conversion. Bede, desiring to encourage, in fact disguises the slowness of the conversion of England. His eye on the princes, he does not admit that, as in later ages, much had to be done by a full century of pastorally orientated monasteries and missionary priests doggedly working at Christianizing the countryside. Rome is not built in a day.

Between the east-flowing rivers of the Tyne and Wear were founded in 674 St Peter's Monkwearmouth and in 682 St Paul's Jarrow. Their founder was a Northumbrian nobleman who had spent his early years at the court of King Oswy and had then come under the influence of the Lindisfarne monk, Wilfrid. Wilfrid, discontented with the Celtic mode of religious life, had studied the Roman tradition at Canterbury and had decided to make the arduous journey to Rome itself; so in 653 the two Northumbrian noblemen, Benedict Biscop (628–90) and Wilfrid (634–709) set out for the capital of Christendom. Wilfrid returned after three years at Lyons, with England's first copy of the *Regula Benedicti* to become abbot of Ripon and Hexham; Benedict returned earlier to wait his time before making a novitiate at Lerins in southern Gaul in 666. Both of them became inveterate travellers on behalf of the Church of Northumbria, especially travelling to Rome to consult the pope and his chapel or chancery. Benedict Biscop made that exacting and perilous journey six times in all, bringing back not only many manuscripts for what was to become the richest library in northern Europe, and with them paintings and relics; but he even brought back abbot John (formerly of St Martin, Tours), the arch-cantor of the Apostolic See in 680 'to teach his monks the chant for the liturgical year as it was sung at St Peter's, Rome'.

What Benedict Biscop did for his abbey was most significant; it became a model of conduct for Charlemagne under Alcuin's direction. Over a century later, Charlemagne sent to the papal chapel to have all its liturgical books copied exactly for the royal chapel at Aachen; he sent also to Monte Cassino to have the authentic *Regula Benedicti* copied for the standardizing reforms of St Benedict of Aniane. Then he required all churches and monasteries in the Carolingian empire to model their ritual and procedures on these, the definitive texts of liturgical and monastic order. Thus

Roman rite and Benedictine Rule were to drive out current customs and expressions of religious life. Benedict of Wearmouth/Jarrow was not as ruthless as the later Benedict, with his *Capitulare Monasticum*; but here were the ingredients of ultramontane standardization that Bede was so much to approve in his *Ecclesiastical History*, as he narrated the demise of Celtic custom with little trace of compassion.

Abbot and arch-cantor John, following papal instruction, taught the cantors of Monkwearmouth in the far north

> the theory and practice of singing and reading aloud, and he put into writing all that was necessary for the proper observance of festivals throughout the year. His teachings [Bede tells us] are still followed in this monastery, and many copies have been made for other places. . . . Proficient singers came from nearly all the monasteries of the province to hear abbot John, and he received many invitations to teach elsewhere.

So from its inception in 674 Monkwearmouth became a touchstone of Roman orthodoxy, to which all Northumbria looked for guidance. As Rome had emerged among the Mediterranean Churches as a centre of consultation, so in its lesser way Abbot Benedict's monastery became the repository of Roman Church usage in the northern limits of civilization.

> This indeed had been the purpose of Abbot John's embassy, for in addition to his task of teaching singing and reading, he had also been instructed by the pope to make careful enquiries about the faith of the English Church, and to report upon it when he returned to Rome. And he had brought with him the decisions of the Council recently held in Rome by the blessed Pope Martin and 105 bishops. These he handed over for a transcript to be made in the monastery.

Bede is referring to the deliberations of the 679 Roman Synod, confirmed the following year at the sixth Ecumenical Council, Constantinople III, concerning Monthelitism (the heresy that Christ had only one will). John the arch-cantor duly summoned his own synod to establish that no such heresy had any credence in England, and his delegation reported this to Pope Agatho on its return. 'John's testimony to the Catholic Faith of the English was taken on to Rome, where it was received with great satisfaction by the pope and all who read it.' Bede showed in this passage not only that orthodoxy reigned in the north, but that Abbot Benedict Biscop's monasteries there were in direct, authoritative and educative touch both with Rome and with dependent houses throughout the North. This provided that vital climate of internationalism and exactitude which was to be the making of Bede, and then of his reputation.

What may we say more directly of Bede's monastery? We know that Bede's first abbot, Benedict, reputedly introduced the use of glass for windows and stone-built churches into English life. One of the prize exhibits in the Jarrow museum opened on 26 May 1979 is coloured glass from this period, discovered in the excavations of the last few years. When in 682 Ceolfrith (who was to succeed Biscop as abbot of the conjoined houses in 689) was entrusted with the foundation of the Jarrow extension, he inherited the vision of his abbot. Indeed when Benedict made two further journeys to Rome to bring back books, relics, works of art and expertise (which included glaziers) for his two houses, he brought Ceolfrith with him on the first of the journeys.

The books brought back from the Continent to enhance the monastic library and to give further inspiration to northern monastic scribes by the influences of the stately uncial scripts of the Mediterranean, included fine sixth-century manuscripts among which was a copy of the Bible written in Cassiodorus's own house at Vivarium, the *Codex Grandior*. This splendid work inspired Ceolfrith's scribes to produce three enormous 'pandects'—copies of the whole Bible in a single volume—one of which, the famous *Codex Amiatinus* in Florence's Laurentian Library, survives to this day. Designed as a present for the pope, it is ten inches thick and weighs over seventy-five pounds. Unlike its contemporary and peer, the *Lindisfarne Gospels*, which owed their style largely to the Celtic art tradition, it is a magnificent reflection of Italian style, and was thought indeed at one time to be of Italian provenance. Alas, the other two copies, which were placed on the lecterns of the two monasteries of Monkwearmouth and Jarrow, did not survive the Reformation—except for a few leaves, now in the British Library—although they had survived the Viking depredations.

Bede's own writings, particularly the scriptural and theological ones and of course the great *History* at the end of his life, came to be in such demand that many copies were made by scribes in the Jarrow scriptorium. These reserved their Italian stately uncial for ceremonial books, and developed a fluent practical minuscule hand in the Anglo-Saxon tradition. An example of this can be seen today in the oldest extant copy of Bede's *History*, the 'Moore Bede' at Cambridge, written between 734 and 737 and so probably begun in Bede's lifetime soon after the work was completed. There is another of the same in the so-called 'Leningrad Bede', dating to about 746, which has a good claim to contain the earliest historiated initial in European illumination.

The sites of Monkwearmouth and Jarrow where Bede spent his entire adulthood have been subject to extensive excavation under the direction of Professor Rosemary Cramp of Durham University during the last fifteen years, and the work continues. The sites compare favourably with those of all other houses in the North-east, notably Lindisfarne and Whitby. Both St Peter's and St Paul's were within close reach of a great natural harbour, with the possibility of Continental trade. The excavations reveal buildings made by Continental techniques of construction, but with a layout adapted to existing insular custom. 'White-plastered stone buildings with their magnificent colour-glass windows would indeed have appeared as something new in the northern English landscape.' When Jarrow was chosen for the community's expansion, the monks quarried stone from surviving Roman buildings. St Paul's church appears to have had close parallels with Wilfrid's church of St Andrew at Hexham—successfully pillaged, as we know, from Roman ashlar. The other main buildings are interpretable partly as a monastic layout (with chapter-house, abbot's cell, etc); and partly as a great secular hall layout. Small wattle huts nearer the river seem to have been used for workshops; and evidence of glass-making and other crafts has been found there. The whole campus must at its zenith have been enormous by the standards of the day. In an age when villages seldom numbered more than 300 souls, Bede tells us that in 716 the brethren of Wearmouth and Jarrow together numbered 600 (more than the vaunted Rievaulx maximum in St Aelred's time). The scale of their agricultural activities can be judged by the fact that the three great Bible pandects referred to above would have required the skins of 1,550 calves. Such a monastic complex would in those days be the nearest approximation to a town that the English could know.

What is clear from literary texts and excavations is, in Professor Cramp's judgement, that

> the man-made environment at Wearmouth-Jarrow was in many ways the visible expression of an ideal, just as were Aidan's buildings at Lindisfarne. The houses in which Bede lived were founded in a period of peace and political stability, in which the first missionary enterprises were successfully completed. Their founder succeeded in freeing their inmates in some measure from the old bondage of status, family inheritance, and dependence on royal favour.

If the links with Roman splendour had been snapped, at least Roman buildings had been plundered or re-employed, by the use of advanced construction techniques to evolve new local models.

Where Northumbria's villages were made up of simple timber houses, Bede's monastic sites were covered with fine stone edifices. It must have been a main source of pride to the Jarrow monks, who— excavations indicate—had none of the imported pottery, nor knick-knacks, nor coinage of such as Whitby to divert the possessiveness. Bede's monks, it seems, kept close to the Rule concerning freedom from personal property. Their pride lay in public prayer, public functions, and public buildings to house their liturgy and work.

The monk-scholar of Jarrow abbey is known first as 'father of English history', principally for the work he undertook in the last five years of his long life when he was in his late fifties (old by the standards of his time). He has inevitably been compared, to his advantage, with Eusebius of Caesarea, called the 'father of Church history'. Bede's *Ecclesiastical History* brought him into the field of learning on the Continent in the days of Boniface, Willibrord and Alcuin; and into English learning through all the centuries down to the present day, with a gap that king Alfred deplored and attempted to repair. In our time, for instance, a commemorative conference was held, gathering up the best Bede scholars of the realm, at Durham in September 1973 to mark the thirteenth centenary of the birth of Bede; and a commemorative volume was produced. To remind ourselves of the span of reflection upon Bede's writings, let us recall that the last two of those essays were concerned with the seventeenth-century 'Smith & Son, Editors of Bede', and the nineteenth-century Charles Plummer, editor of and commentator on Bede's historical works.

But the venerable old scholar of 731, who had so recently filled his mind with the history that has brought him his most permanent respect, still evidently held himself to be primarily a student of Scripture, who delighted in 'study, teaching and writing' from the *sacra pagina*. From his thirtieth birthday he had spent thirty years of his priesthood working 'both for my own benefit and that of my brethren', as he says, 'to compile short extracts from the works of the venerable Fathers on Holy Scripture, and to comment on their meaning and interpretation.' In 731 he listed nearly all his writings as we know them, and most are commentaries upon the Old and New Testament books. Suitably he started with *The Beginning of Genesis*, up to the birth of Isaac and Ishmael's rejection: four books. Suitably Mr Gerald Bonner gave his 1966 Jarrow Lecture on 'Saint Bede in the Tradition of Western Apocalyptic Commentary', Bede having written three books on *The Apocalypse of St John*, the last work in scripture. As though to confirm the point, Bede's next enterprise after listing his works at the end of the *Ecclesiastical*

History was his *Retractatio in Actus Apostolorum*, a return to what he conceived as his proper last. Therefore not to view the scholar of Jarrow primarily as a biblical exegete and theologian would be—at least in his own estimation—a loss of perspective. And further, it would lead to a loss of understanding about his intention as a historian.

It might be well to survey Bede's other interests in order to see how much they help to build a bridge between Bede as exegete and Bede as historian. It is worth saying at once that much of Scripture is sacred history, salvation history requiring some of the arts and skills of the historian (albeit theological); and much Church history in its turn needs the insights of a biblical exegete, for it can be regarded in some manner as the continuation of the *sacra pagina*, under the inspiration of the Holy Spirit, into our own time.

Bede was endlessly curious about chronology, a strand of the historian's craft; and that brought him to persistent ruminations about the dating of Easter, so much so that it came partially to mar his *Ecclesiastical History* by its obsessive intrusion into the narrative. The problem is with us still today; any who have a love both of the Church in the west and of the Eastern Church will know how perplexing it can be when—as happened in 1978—their separate Easter Days (a datum for all days back to post-Epiphany and forward to Trinity Sunday) are caused to fall at a five-week interval, admittedly that being the extreme. One mourns in purple while the other rejoices in white; one fasts, the other feasts; one is vigilant in teaching, the other goes on to baptize or marry with pomp. Bede saw not only the chaos of such disunity in the Celtic and Roman traditions, but saw the danger of such date computations becoming the banners of separate loyalties, leading to the collapse of centralized unity focused on the Apostolic See at Rome. So he fought to the end of his days to establish the decision of the Synod of Whitby. It is however worth observing that, in Bede's account of the 664 Synod, it was St Peter the keeper of the gate of heaven rather than St Peter as bishop of Rome, for whom King Oswy settled in his sagacious decision.

Besides chronology, Bede interested himself in what would become the duties of the Precentor in later abbeys. Precentors had to provide the local element of the liturgical office, particularly accounts of saints' lives. Bede's interest in that quarter prompted not only his scriptural commentary (much of which would be needed at the lectern) but also his *Martyrology* of the feast-days of the holy martyrs, 'in which I have carefully tried to record everything I could learn not only of the date, but also by what kind of combat and under what judge they overcame the world'.

Lives of saints naturally came to interest Bede, with the needs both of his brethren and his society in mind. He wrote, besides *The Histories of the Saints*, a prose translation of Paulinus' metrical *Life and Sufferings of St Felix*; revised the translation of the Greek *Life and Sufferings of St Anastasius*; and composed his own *Life* of 'our father, the holy monk and Bishop Cuthbert', both in heroic verse and in prose. He then wrote a *History* of the abbots of his own two houses, abbots Benedict Biscop, Ceolfrith and Huaetberht—'rulers of this monastery in which I delight to serve the Divine Goodness'. All of this must have made Bede's society conscious that, under the Holy Spirit, the process of sanctification continues down the centuries into their own lives and their own homes. A community of monks able to perceive in detail the blessings of their immediate forbears, particularly of those who 'hold the place of Christ in the monastery', should be doubly conscious of their need to pursue the one thing necessary. It was Bede who by his pen reinforced those values in their lives.

Observing, as he did, the regular discipline and singing the choir Office daily in church, Bede naturally turned his pen to '*A Book of Hymns in various metres and rhythms*', which has not come down to us. St Hilary of Poitiers (d. 367) had written the first *Liber Hymnorum* and St Ambrose (d. 397) soon followed him. St Columba of the Irish Church and St Gregory of the Roman both wrote collections of hymns, so the tradition was in existence before Bede: it was to be expected of him that he should continue it, and indeed his *corpus hymnorum* influenced the next generation.

Finally we should record Bede's little works that do not fall into the categories of biblical exegesis or commentary, history or chronology, martyrology or hagiography, or liturgical pieces. He prepared one of the first Latin dictionaries in England, '*Orthographia*, arranged in alphabetical order'; and that puts him in the same category as Dr Johnson, the great lexicographer. He prepared *A Book of Epigrams in heroic or eligiac verse*, and that perhaps makes him a forerunner of the compilers of *The Oxford Dictionary of Quotations*. He wrote on *The Art of Poetry*, appending a small work on the figures and manners of speech found in the scriptures. And he wrote a number of long epistles of an ecclesial-political nature, of which the most significant is his last in 734 to Bishop Egbert of York, an old man's warning to his erstwhile pupil about the degeneracy of the Church in the North: it was a sort of supplement to his *History*, rather in the style of the Joannine Epistles. Old men grow fearful of the survival of what they most cherish, not always entirely without cause.

It is important to be brief when discussing Bede as a historian. To his *Ecclesiastical History of the English People* (which has run to many editions and had many editors and commentators over the years), Bede owes the major part of his fame. And yet, putting his writings in the context he wishes us to accept, at the end of the *History*, he shows that he remembers himself as monk, priest, biblical scholar and then as historian. His *History*, however long it may have been in gestation (and that may have been quite a dozen years, with the constant amassing of evidence), was finally written when he was almost sixty. It was indeed the work of a master who by then had acquired an enormous control over much disparate and often doubtful source material, which he admirably orchestrated to his purpose. What was his aim? He tells us this in his Preface:

> If history records good things of good men, the thoughtful hearer is encouraged to imitate what is good: or if it records evil of wicked men, the good religious listener or reader is encouraged to avoid all that is sinful and perverse, and to follow what he knows to be good and pleasing to God.

This passage and the whole tale was read out meal by meal in monastic refectories all over the realm, all down the ages.

Isolated as he was in the North, but possessed of so remarkable a library and traffic in ideas, Bede—as we have seen—had a mass of contacts in script from the Roman past and in person from the monasteries of England and the civilized world. He could draw on many models for the draft of his *History*—from Eusebius, Jerome, Orosius (whom he used much) and Gregory of Tours. His opening twenty-two chapters up to the coming of St Augustine and his band of monks to Kent in 597 derive from just such sources. Thereafter, Bede's source-flow becomes more patchy and he is required to be more inventive to make up the mosaic. How well he has done, in his own estimation, may be gauged by the words of his own Preface, which ends with an inversion of what we have come to expect from the research student and might have expected from so humble a monk as Bede. He says:

> Should the reader discover any inaccuracies in what I have written, I humbly beg that he will not impute them to me, because, as the laws of history require, I have laboured honestly to trans-mit whatever I could ascertain from common report for the instruction of posterity.

It is a very disarming comment. It gives no inkling into the selectivity that every historian must exercise (except Bede's predecessor Nennius, who confessedly made a heap of all he could find and transmitted it for the reader to make some sense of it). It gives no inkling into the fact that every historian comes to his task with a theory, a philosphy or even a theology of history in his mind, which strongly colours his weighting of evidence and his selective processes. And equally, it gives no inkling into the difficulties historians encounter where they have not been able to ascertain enough of, or the inner truth of, circumstances that remain still opaque to their understanding: they cannot presume to write until they know with sufficient detail how to procure an approximation to the whole truth as it was. That must have been exceedingly difficult for Bede in an age that did not use or keep documents much, nor consider the retention of the ingredients of history as a normal part of social habit. Indeed, in a society where the concept of historical record is dim, to set out to write history was a very courageous venture.

Towards the end of his life, Bede was well fitted to deal with doubtful sources, being by then a master in the correlation of chronological data from diverse provenance. And yet, curiously, many of the faults in his *History* are chronological. Admittedly he had to struggle with disparate dating systems—regnal, consular, and the rest—and conflicting evidence, some made up to suit the needs of a credulous society; and he had to compile his five books as material came to hand, with insertions continually being made after the main draft was done. But we should not hasten to judge the old monk, as he pioneered the road of English Church history, as though he were a young student with all modern techniques to hand. It is marvellous how well he did. What comes forth beyond all technique is his capacity to absorb and retransmit the atmosphere and implications of all he gathered up. He was the first Englishman to understand the past; the first to put his mind across the chasm which the collapse of the Roman empire had caused, linking it with the subsistent social and religious cultures in the provinces that had arisen in its place. Bede brought intelligibility to it all.

Sympathetic but discerning critics of today such as James Campbell show how Bede has intelligently doctored, even suppressed, and more generally fashioned his huge stock of evidence to tell a moral truth rather than a literal one. His is a tract for his times; but is not all history that at root? He interweaves ecclesiastical and secular life to show how God's work prospers and evil brings certain nemesis, etching out the successful interaction of Christianity with the needs of a dynasty in a particular climate of Custom and expectation. He outlines the duties of kings, thegns and prelates, calling on a gallery of good examples and bad. When, as with Wilfrid, the examples are ambiguous, he tailors them to his plan, leaving men like Eddius to tell the rest. Even if he has used history to teach religion, he has nevertheless managed to produce the record of most of what we shall ever know of English history in his time, and that with unusual skill and power. The *Ecclesiastical History* is one of England's great books.

In his last days, after his great work had gone out to the world, and with only four years to live, Bede grew fearful, uncertain, despondent and unhopeful of English Church life. His writings, now diminished to a trickle, included a *Retractatio* (as St Augustine had retracted some of his younger opinions in his twilight years) of some of his earlier Commentary on the Acts of the Apostles. A letter-treatise ascribed to him, on thunder and magical arts, prompted a bio-grapher to write, 'Those who love Bede cannot bring themselves to believe that he wrote it.' He visited St Peter's monastery less often, content, as old age stole upon him, to look out from his St Paul's cell upon a darkening world. The sense of invincible progress that had pervaded the pages of the *History* in 731, had already lurched to a halt that same year when King Ceolwulf had been forcibly ton-sured and imprisoned in a monastery. Among the clergy ignorance and corruption were in the ascendant; among the nobility too many religious houses had been founded too richly endowed, as invest-ments; among the episcopate, too little visiting was done and too few bishops laboured under too much fruitless work. Bede, in a spirit of humility, put all this before his old pupil, now bishop of York, in his long letter of 5 November 734, asking for more exalted standards of pastoral duty, of learning among priests, of sacramental activity, of episcopal devotion. He was painting a new and different picture from that of a decade earlier, one of gloom surely half warranted but equally surely half induced by his own fatigue of spirit.

A little before Easter 735 Bede had great trouble in breathing, and grew weaker. He continued to teach and pray, but slept little at night, preparing his mind for the great journey. He grew more sentimental, as old men do, breaking down for instance at the words *ne derelinquas nos orphanos*. His own brethren often enough caught his mood and wept with him. To his pupils, he said: 'Learn quickly, for I know not how long I shall be with you.' He was engaged on his last scriptural task, an English translation of the Fourth Gospel for his own house. On the eve of Ascension Day he worked his scribes harder, as if in desperation, till they had to leave him for their liturgy. The boy Wilbert remained, but hesitated to press the dying scholar: 'No, no,' said Bede, 'take your pen and write quickly.' In mid-afternoon he called his brethren to a farewell, distributing small parting gifts. By evening, Wilbert roused the old man to this dialogue—

'Dear master, there is still a sentence which is not written down.'

'Well, then write it.'
'Master, it is written.'
'You have said the truth; it is finished.'
At Bede's request, his brethren propped him up against the wall facing towards the sanctuary. He quietly sang a *Gloria Patri* and breathed his last. By then it was Ascension Day.

Alcuin in his *Carmen* sang of miracles wrought by Bede's relics, as did others in later centuries. The venerable monk was accorded a feast day in the Church of York, with that title accruing. His bones were stolen from Jarrow in 1020 and finally given a resting place beside those of St Cuthbert in the great church of Durham, together those bones being the proudest possession of the cathedral priory. Later still they were enshrined in a silver feretory, gold enriched. At the Reformation the remains were not lost, but buried in the Galilee, where they now rest in honour. Called by his near contemporaries *doctor eximius*, Bede was raised by Pope Leo XIII to that greatest distinction, being proclaimed a Doctor of the Universal Church in 1899.

by Dom Alberic Stacpoole

BIBLIOGRAPHY

Bede's *Ecclesiastical History* is most easily accessible in the editions by B. Colgrave and R. A. B. Mynors (Oxford 1969) or C. Plummer (Oxford, 1896 and 1946): English translation only by L. Sherley-Price, revised by R. E. Latham (*Penguin Classics*, 1968). Critical editions of his other works in *Corpus Christianorum* (Turnhout 1955–). Studies on Bede include:

A. H. Thompson, (ed.), *Bede: his Life, Times and Writings* (Oxford 1935).

J. Campbell, 'Bede' in *Latin Historians* (ed. T. A. Dorey 1966).

P. H. Blair, *The World of Bede* (London 1970).

H. Mayr-Harting, *The Coming of Christianity to Anglo-Saxon England* (London 1972).

G. Bonner (ed.), *Famulus Christi* (London 1976).

P. H. Blair, *Northumbria in the Days of Bede* (London 1976).

P. Riche, *Education and Culture in the Barbarian West* (1976).

W. H. Marnell, *Light from the West: the Irish Mission and the Emergence of Modern Europe* (1978).

See also the series of Jarrow Lectures (1958–80), especially H. Mayr-Harting, *The Venerable Bede, the Rule of St Benedict and Social Class* (1976).

St Boniface in his Correspondence

To the German peoples St Boniface is always known as their Apostle, just as St Amand is the Apostle of Belgium, St Willibrord the Apostle of Friesland and St Anscar the Apostle of Sweden. It was the title the Germanic peoples gave to their great missionary founders and it is significant that all those just named were Benedictine monks. From the end of the sixth century missionaries had been setting out for Germany; Columbanus and his Irish monks travelled widely, wandering priests with no fixed centre for their activity, also with no close connexion with Rome. After the conversion of England, the Germanic lands were destined to be a far wider field of Benedictine missionary activity, securing for the black monks some of the most glorious achievements of their long history.

St Gregory the Great had sent monks from the Celian monastery in Rome to convert the English. In this he was making the monastic family broader in its outlook, for he saw that the monks could be used like an army in reserve, capable of demonstrating Christian living, as well as of teaching Christian doctrine. Gregory had continued to guide the monks in England by sending them directions for the conduct of their work, the creation of dioceses and the establishment of monasteries. Their task was completed in a century; it was to be on similar lines that the mission to Germany was to be carried out. The monks were to adapt the pagan temples for Christian worship; the heathen festivals were to be transformed into Christian festivals; the service of the God of the Christians was to be maintained in the face of the pagan peoples.

Frisia, the part of northern Holland beyond the Zuider Zee, was destined to be the first field of Benedictine missionary work among the Germanic peoples. In 679, on his way to Rome, St Wilfrid had spent a winter there; others had followed him, notably St Willibrord, who came to Antwerp in 690, moving thence to Utrecht, where he prepared the way for the coming of Boniface. Willibrord had proved himself to be a great missionary; Boniface was to become the great organizer of Germanic Christianity. He first saw Frisia by journeying up the Rhine in 716, spending a year there without much result. Then he returned there by another route to work with Willibrord for three years, so beginning the thirty-six years he was destined to spend in the German lands. The two men parted for good in 722, perhaps differing on questions of missionary method, but Boniface was to keep warm the memory of his early work in Frisia, returning there in 753, to meet his death after only one year of living among its people. Frisia was a difficult mission field; the lands to the east of the Zuider Zee were long to remain a pagan stronghold.

The monk Wynfryd, later to be named Boniface, was said by John de Grandisson, bishop of Exeter from 1327 to 1369, to have been a native of Crediton in Devon. The bishop may well be noting down a local tradition, dating from long before Crediton became an episcopal see. Wynfryd must have been born about 672 or 673; he became a monk at Exeter and then at Nursling, now within South-ampton. Instead of becoming abbot of Nursling in 717, he went off to Rome in 718, armed with a letter from the bishop of Winchester. Pope Gregory II is said to have given him the name of a Roman martyr, Boniface, though it seems that he already used this name earlier. His training was thoroughly Benedictine and this perhaps derived from Canterbury; just as the English church remained very conscious of its Roman origins, so Boniface would always maintain close contacts with the popes. He was to make the journey to Rome three times, spending about a year there on his last visit. While all the correspondence of Willibrord is lost, there survives a large collection of letters from and to Boniface, with a similar dossier for his successor, Lull. Some of the letters are official, others are intimate, even trivial; they inform us abundantly about his missionary activity, his anxieties and his problems. He is eager to receive advice and suggestions from his correspondents, who form a wide social circle, including Anglo-Saxon kings, abbots, bishops, and former pupils now his friends. His attractive exchange of letters with nuns and abbesses has already been much studied; they were keenly interested in his movements, for he was to give a special place to women in forming native communities.

Many nuns came to help him in his mission field; others who stayed on in England continued to keep in touch with him by correspondence. It must be remembered that the Anglo-Saxon nunnery, aristocratic in its recruitment, served its age as an orphan-age and as a boarding-school, for many of the nuns entered as children, without regard for vocation or age. Even the boy Wynfryd, we are told by his biographer, Willibald, had wanted to enter the cloister at four or five and was only prevented by the opposition of his father. For young women the monastery was almost the only institution affording education in a society only then beginning to be literate. The monastery of this period was not rigidly cut off from the secular world: itinerant royalty frequently stayed there, and others, too, of lesser degree in the days before inns became respectable. Nor were the nuns entirely cut off from the society of men. Indeed, in such an age of violence and perpetual warfare, it was not even wise for a community of women to live isolated and without the protection of men, even if these were only employees for maintenance or for the stables. Here lies the deeper explanation of the existence of the double monastery, ruled by the abbess, as at Whitby or at Wimborne, and of the double monasteries which Boniface was to establish in Germany. For a lady of high birth, the choice lay often between the cloister and a marriage to a partner as planned by the families. The occasional references to nuns in the works of Bede only serve to corroborate all that we find in the correspondence of Boniface. Therefore we need not be surprised that in the days before monastic enclosure, nuns had a longing to go on pilgrimages, or to undertake missionary work, any more than that they were in a position to send out gifts or money to Boniface.

Among these Anglo-Saxon nuns there breathes still an atmosphere of naïvety, cheerfulness and uninhibitedness. Egburg (unknown to us, unless she is to be identified with Bugga, of whom much is known) at some time between 716 and 720 wrote thus to her true abbot and friend Boniface : 'Since I am deprived of seeing you in your bodily form, yet I will always cling to your neck with the embrace of a sister.'

Whether these nuns had in fact known and seen Boniface must remain uncertain; what is remarkable is that they were deeply conscious of being of one and the same family, needing spiritual conversation and development from mutual contact. They obviously enjoyed writing long letters and more still receiving them from Germany, therein learning all the details of the missionary expansion. We may guess how eagerly such letters were passed around, how each nun was anxious to have a spiritual guide among such courageous bearers of the Gospel good news. These nuns wrote in fluent Latin and at length ; they composed verses and were anxious to receive emendations in return. For the missionaries they would copy books and illuminate texts, or make garments and coverlets against the winter cold. They were in no sense absorbed in high intellectual matters.

However, it would be a mistake to consider life in the Anglo-Saxon nunnery as completely idyllic. Around the year 720, Eangyth, abbess of an unidentified double monastery, confided lengthily her troubles to Boniface, for she was weighed down by her responsibilities. The king and the notables had turned against her. There were disputes and divisions among the nuns, with opposition from the monks, so that life for her had become burdensome. If only Boniface were nearer, or she could be transported, like Habakkuk, to receive counsel and consolation. She would like to betake herself to Rome, as so many others were doing these days. She felt she stood alone with her friends dead, for only her beloved daughter, Bugga, remained with her.

Yet from this company of nuns, mostly cloistered since childhood, was to come a group ready to break through and penetrate into the wilds of Germany. Such were Leoba, or Leofgyth, who had been educated at Minster, in Thanet, and had become a nun at Wimborne; also Kunihilt, Kunitrud and Thekla, future abbess of Kitzingen, who all went to Germany at the call of Boniface. Leoba was to become abbess of Tauberbischofsheim, near Mainz, the earliest nunnery to be founded in Germany by Boniface; she seems to have made the journey in about 737. Boniface had asked that she should come, leading a group of about thirty. For all his foundations Leoba stood as the venerable mother, comparable to St Hilda of Whitby. But from Leoba we have only her letter to Boniface after he had been elevated to the archbishopric, and before she left England. She reminded him that he had been a friend of her father now deceased; her mother also was dead—she was in fact related to the saint. She sent him a little poetic exercise, bidding him improve these four lines. However, we have collective letters for Leoba, Thekla and Kunihilt when they were working in Germany, wherein Boniface begs their prayers that he may not flee from the wolf prowling around the fold. In another letter he approves of the abbess undertaking the education of a girl. Leoba was evidently a person of great charm and is better known to us from a *Life* and from her place in the history of the German nunneries. She spent twenty-eight years as abbess of Tauberbischofsheim, and when she died in *c*. 780 she was laid to rest near St Boniface at Fulda. The nunneries founded by St Boniface were not, of course, the earliest foundations in Germany, but through his influence at the Council of 742, the Rule of St Benedict was imposed on all the convents of nuns. Leoba with Kunihilt, Kunitrud and Thekla implanted into their nunneries the standards and usages of Anglo-Saxon England. After the death of St Boniface in 754, Leoba kept alive his spirit for another quarter of a century. Boniface had been able to treat with Charles Martel and Carloman; Leoba was to appear at the court of Charlemagne.

Of the letters to nuns or abbesses who remained in England, far more have, of course, survived. Among the recipients of these the most outstanding is the abbess of Minster, Eadburga or Bugga. Writing to Boniface after he had returned from Rome in about 721, she congratulated him on what he himself had told her of the successful course of events. He had already recounted his dream that he would be busy harvesting the sheaves for the heavenly Kingdom, to ensure that she would the more fervently pray for him. Though as yet she could not send him the passions of the martyrs, she, poor *vilis vernacula*, would be consoled to receive from him a little selection of scriptural texts. She sent him fifty shillings and an altar cloth, regretting she could not send him something larger. Perhaps some four years later, Boniface wrote to Bugga, describing her as 'his sister to be preferred to all others of the feminine sex in the love of Christ'. She had, it seems, written to him of her desire to go on a pilgrimage to Rome. Boniface was not prepared either to persuade or dissuade her. He clearly would prefer her to remain in quiet contemplation within her cloister rather than to try to avoid the pressure from secular folk by attempting to secure freedom for contemplation near the tomb of St Peter. At any rate it would be unwise to consider such a journey just when revolts and Saracen invasions had begun to assail the eternal city. Boniface had not found the time to compose for Bugga the spiritual bouquet she had wished for.

From very much later there is a last letter to Bugga, after she had made her pilgrimage and had since been beset by the many trials of old age. News had reached Boniface of all her many tribulations, after years of silence due to her journeys; she knew now that she had sought relief from her responsibilities as abbess, only to meet greater trials. With many citations from Scripture Boniface consoled her:

'He who is the father and lover of your chaste virginity, who in the days of your earliest youth called you to be his daughter, inviting you to Himself with the voice of his fatherly love. . . . He it is who now in your old age desires to beautify and adorn the form and comeliness of your soul with toils and tribulations. . . . Do you, dearest sister, as you rejoice in hope of the inheritance of your heavenly home, hold out the shield of faith and patience against every adversity of heart or body.'

It was Bregowine, archbishop of Canterbury, who was to inform Lull of the death of abbess Bugga:

'The day of her burial was 27 December. She earnestly begged me while yet alive that I should transmit this to your beatitude. Do you take care to do for her as she hoped and trusted you would, for her father and patron in Christ was bishop Boniface.'

Other nuns less closely linked with Boniface in spiritual friendship were eager to have if only a few words from him. Many of these remain unknown to us, as are most of his priest correspondents. But it would be incorrect to think that the saint only sought the prayers of the nuns among his acquaintance. His letters bear on many topics. Of about the year 717, shortly after Boniface, as Wynfryd still, had returned to England from Frisia, is the account he wrote for Eadburga, abbess of Minster, of the strange vision to a monk of Much Wenlock. The reliable version she had desired was supplied by Hildelith, abbess of Barking. He would write to Optatus, abbot of Monte Cassino, requesting a union of charity and prayer with him and his community:

'That, as you live out the spiritual life according to the Rule, your fraternity may deign to pray for us in our frailty in the peaceful tranquillity of brotherly concord.'

He was in correspondence with Torhthelm, bishop of Leicester from 737 to 764, though only one letter survives, written to Boniface and encouraging him in his mission to the Saxons. To Pecthelun, the first bishop of Whithorn in Galloway, he appealed for advice on a problem of marriage between partners spiritually related. Not only are his correspondents from various social groups, but they are widely scattered geographically.

The early letters contain many requests for books, although St Boniface brought with him for his use the Roman liturgical and service books, derived from Italian sources. Just as it is now difficult to picture the Benedictine monk without books, so Boniface would write to the nun, Bugga, the abbess of Minster, asking for copies of books, suggesting the passions of the martyrs, the *Responsiones* which Gregory the Great sent to St Augustine of Canterbury, any treatises on the epistles of St Paul (other than those he already had on Romans and Corinthians). She also sent him money, altar linen, incense, clothing. From the same abbess he requested a copy of the epistle of St Peter, written out in gold script so as to impress his people. From all these holy nuns he was asking prayers for his work, knowing how closely he was still united to his Benedictine family in England in a deeply spiritual friendship.

The earlier intellectual life of the monks in England had been centred in Northumbria. With the nuns and Boniface, after Aldhelm of Malmesbury, we see the beginning of the contribution of Wessex and the south of England to Benedictine learning. In the centre may be placed the influential bishop of Winchester, Daniel, a former monk of Malmesbury. In 718, as Boniface was setting out on his missionary journeys, Daniel wrote a letter of commendation of Boniface to all the notables—kings, dukes, bishops, religious and spiritual sons of Christ. One is inclined to wonder whether it was not through Daniel that Boniface came to the special notice of Gregory II. From the bishop of Winchester we have a long letter of advice on missionary method, even supplying arguments to convince the unbeliever:

'If the gods are omnipotent and beneficent and just, then they should not only reward those who worship them, but also punish those who reject them. . . . Why do they spare the Christians, who are turning almost the whole world away from their worship and overturning their images?'

It is curious that Bede nowhere mentions Boniface, for it was Daniel who supplied Bede with the historical data for Christianity in Wessex, Sussex and the Isle of Wight, which he needed for his *Ecclesiastical History*. Boniface repeatedly requested copies of Bede's commentaries and treatises. In his old age Boniface wrote to Daniel for a copy of the book of the prophets, which abbot Wimbert of Nursling had copied for his monastery, pleading, on account of his failing sight, that it would need to be written in large characters and without the customary abbreviations. In exchange for some letters of Gregory the Great, Boniface requested from Egbert, archbishop of York, some treatises of Bede, 'whom divine grace has vouchsafed to shine forth in your province, that we too may enjoy that candle which the Lord has bestowed on you. . . . To have a particle, a spark from the candle for the Church, which the Holy Spirit has made to shine in your province.'

He particularly wished to have the homilies on the liturgical lectionary and Bede's commentary on the Proverbs of Solomon. From Hwaetberht, abbot of Wearmouth, Boniface asked again for more of the writings of Bede, 'that wisest of investigators into the Scriptures . . . shining like a candle of the Church by his knowledge of the Scriptures.'

The missionary in his isolation, beset by anxieties and the hostility of opponents within the Church, suffering also from the cold so that he was obliged to ask for gifts of clothing and cloaks for travelling: 'If it is not too troublesome for you, send us a cloak which would be a great consolation', yet maintained his reading as he would have done inside a monastery.

If the correspondence with four popes is official and less intimate, it remains profoundly significant for the history of the Church in Europe. We need to keep clearly in mind certain signposts into the life and movements of St Boniface. The proper field of his activity was central Germany and he was there first as a priest, then as bishop, and finally as archbishop. More simply we may divide his life into his years as a missionary, followed by the years in which he undertook the organization of the German and Frankish churches. We need also to look back at the map of the Germanic lands and rediscover where exactly lay the provinces in which St Boniface laboured and to realize the distances to be covered, often through dense forests or over mountainous country—Frisia, Hesse, Thuringia, Bavaria, Saxony.

Boniface was to work under popes Gregory II, Gregory III, Zacharias and Stephen III. If Boniface remained steadfastly loyal to Rome, from Rome he was followed with great interest in all that he did. His relations with these four popes were good, yet, as we shall observe, with certain differences. The missionary naturally looked back for a pattern to Augustine of Canterbury, who had also sought papal guidance and approval. Boniface was a man of tradition rather than a man of new ideas; he was strengthened to be enterprising by his firm faith, yet he always felt the need to be fully authorized in what he undertook.

Boniface had written to Gregory II for advice on certain problems of marriage, such as were persistently to trouble him. He had already consulted Nothelm, who in 735 would be archbishop of Canterbury, as to the authenticity of pope Gregory the Great's permission for marriage between second and third cousins. Replying to Boniface in 719, Gregory II encouraged him in the work that was being undertaken of instilling the truths of the Christian faith into pagan minds. The pope was here thinking particularly of the heathen tribes of the east bank of the Rhine. There has been some dispute about the date when Boniface became a bishop, but it must have been in 722 or 723, when he took an oath of fidelity to the Holy See. The pope proceeded to send out letters commending Boniface and his missionary work, one to all Christian people, another to the clergy, and one to the Thuringians, requesting them to build a suitable residence for Boniface and to assist him in setting up churches. To the Old Saxons the pope wrote, calling upon them to leave their idols. More important for the future was his recommendation of Boniface to Charles Martel (d. 741), who gladly agreed to protect the missionaries and their work. Later, in 741, Boniface would write to Charles Martel's son, Gripo, just after his father's death, asking him to continue to protect the Christians of Thuringia. During these years he was writing to England, asking prayers for the conversion of the Saxons, a work he was undertaking at the request of two popes.

In 732 Pope Gregory III sent to Boniface the *pallium*, the symbol of the plenitude of the episcopal office and of jurisdiction. Boniface was now an archbishop, with instructions to set up other bishops among the Saxons, as numbers should require. In his letter the pope adds his reply to various questions of detail in the conversion of pagans—for example, they should be discouraged from eating the flesh of the wild horse. Boniface was to make the journey to Rome in 737–8, where he stayed for a council; the pope would later recommend his archbishop to hold synods and councils for the German peoples. After this meeting the pope followed the pattern of his predecessor in sending out to bishops and nobility letters recommending the work which was already assuming a definite shape. Boniface seemed happy about the mission; the pope was able to congratulate him on the hundred thousand Saxons converted with the help of Charles Martel. Boniface himself would have liked to remain among the Saxons, but the pope had wider visions, desiring him to turn to Bavaria; Boniface was once again recommended to set up four dioceses with their bishops. It is interesting to note here that Boniface the monk would have preferred to work from a fixed centre, meaning, no doubt, a monastery. Gregory III thought differently, writing in 739: 'You are not permitted to stay in one place, when once a task is completed; you are to go where the Lord opens out the way and not to be slow to undertake arduous journeys.'

From the next pope, Zacharias, there is a very long letter of encouragement and advice. Boniface had set up bishoprics at Würzburg, Erfurt and Büraburg, near Fritzlar in Hesse, and he wished the pope to confirm these by charters. As usual, he had also sought the advice of the pope on problems of marriage and had not shrunk from pointing out that the scandals of the carnivals held in Rome were handicapping his own preaching. Carloman, the eldest son of Charles Martel, was begging him to attend a synod of the Franks, among whom he declared that no synod had been held for eighty years and ecclesiastical discipline was consequently in a sorry state. Carloman was closely linked to the Benedictines; he had been brought up by the monks of Saint Denis, and he gave St Boniface great support, until he abdicated to take up the monastic life in 754. The pope confirmed the three bishoprics, trusting they were located in reputable towns; he then wrote letters to the three new bishops. As to the holding of a council, Zacharias gave advice, particularly insisting that unworthy bishops and priests should be prevented from taking part. Councils were held in 742 and in the following year, and the pope confirmed their acts, congratulating Boniface on being aided by Pepin and Carloman. He sent the *pallium* to each of the bishops now set up as metropolitans at Rouen, Rheims and Sens.

Boniface very frequently complained of the difficulties and dangers of his work; his boat was perpetually tossed about by the Germanic waves and storms. He was also naturally anxious about the choice of his successor, so that the ground gained for Christendom might be securely held. But his request to the pope that he might nominate a successor did not receive the approval of Zacharias. The most Boniface could secure, and that as a special favour, was the permission, when he was at the point of death, to send the man of his choice to Rome. Later the pope would even correct Boniface on a question of rebaptism. Yet Boniface continued to receive consolation and encouragement from the pope, now that he was to

care for the Franks as well as Bavaria. Zacharias approved of
Cologne becoming a metropolitan see. By 748 Boniface was already
advanced in years, was weak in body and had difficulty in reading.
The pope at last permitted him to nominate a successor, whereupon
Boniface sent Lull, a monk of Malmesbury, to Rome in 751, bearing
a letter, in which he tells how he had tried to avoid being in communion with bad priests—thereby only underlining the difficulty.

By 751 Boniface was happy to tell Pope Zacharias of the foundation of the abbey of Fulda, in Hesse, where he himself wished to be
buried. He described it to the pope.

'There is a wooded place in an expanse of the deepest solitude, in
the midst of the peoples to whom we preach; there, building a
monastery, we have established monks living under the Rule of
St Benedict, men observing strict abstinence from flesh and wine or
cider, and without servants, being content with the work of their
own hands.'

The whole construction was the result of the labour of the monks
and the foundation afforded both satisfaction and promise. One of
the monks was Carloman, the former ruler of the Franks, who in
744 had given Boniface the land where Fulda stood. In 754 he had
abdicated in order to live a monastic life—he was to end his days at
Monte Cassino, after having built a monastery on Mount Soracte.
Pope Zacharias was to declare Fulda independent of its local
bishop and dependent on the Holy See. Later, when Lull was
archbishop of Mainz, he was at odds with Sturmi, the abbot, on
the question of this exemption. The pope was still attentive to all
the demands for advice which Boniface continued to make regularly,
even to those points which to us seem most curious or trivial. Though
he was established as an archbishop, it is clear that there were still
pagan attacks on the missionaries around him and he himself was
still just as much in need of consolation as he faced hostile clergy
and persecuting local chiefs. Zacharias was to declare Mainz a
metropolitan see for Boniface, with five bishoprics for Tongres,
Cologne, Worms, Spire and Troyes.

Writing to the new pope, Stephen III, in 753 Boniface declared
that he intended to remain as filial towards him as he had been
towards his three predecessors; they had always strengthened and
aided him by their counsel and the authority of their letters. He
reminded the pope that he had now been acting in his legation for
thirty-six years; should the pope find anything which ought to be
amended, Boniface would readily respond. If he had been slow in
writing to the pope, this was due to his preoccupation with recon-
structing those churches which had been burnt down by the pagans
—more than thirty of them had been destroyed. He then proceeded

to put before the pope the question of the difficult relations between the bishoprics of Utrecht and Cologne. Years before, in 690, Willibrord, the Northumbrian monk, had set out to evangelize West Frisia and in 693 he was consecrated archbishop of the Frisians. The Frankish king, Pepin the Short, son of Charles Martel, had given him a site for his cathedral at Utrecht. Willibrord was to spend fifty years preaching to the Frisians. When, in 739, he died, Carloman entrusted Boniface with the choice of a bishop for Utrecht. Thereupon the bishop of Cologne claimed rights over the see of Utrecht, on the basis that king Dagobert (d. 638) had originally given the castle of Utrecht with its chapel to the diocese of Cologne, as a base for the mission. The chapel had been restored from its ruinous state by Willibrord, but it had since been destroyed. However, the condition of King Dagobert's grant had been that the diocese of Cologne should undertake the conversion of the Frisians. But the conversion was not begun until Pope Sergius (d. 701) sent Willibrord. None the less Cologne now wished to take back Utrecht, on the basis of the grant of Dagobert, though the condition had not been upheld. Boniface desired that Utrecht should be made subject to the Holy See, arguing that the intentions of Pope Sergius should be followed, for the majority of the Frisians were still pagan; but to this Cologne would not agree. Hence Boniface appealed to Pope Stephen to intervene in the dispute, suggesting that he should send a copy of whatever directions Pope Sergius had sent to Willibrord. Pope Stephen must have approved of these proposals for Utrecht, since Boniface appointed to the see Eoba, an Anglo-Saxon.

And this is the last of the long series of letters of Boniface, written in 753. It is in every way typical of the man and his preoccupations. He shows his devotion to the work of converting the Frisians and his firm loyalty to the papacy, to which he always looked for a final decision. Late in 754, Cuthbert, archbishop of Canterbury, wrote to Lull about the martyrdom, adding that he had decided to celebrate the anniversary of the event, for in Boniface they now had 'a patron before Christ the Lord, whom in life he always loved and in death magnificently glorified'. Mildred, bishop of Worcester from 743 to 775, also wrote to Lull, begging that the loss of their common father might more closely unite them in charity. However, neither of these letters tells us of the circumstances of the death of Boniface and these have to be sought elsewhere. When, in the vigour of manhood, he had faced the heathen at Geismar and felled the oak of Thor, he had been supported by the presence of the military strength of the Frankish rulers; as, in old age, he faced the pagan Frisians, he no longer had any such support. Even if no poet put into verse the story of the martyrdom of Boniface, it has every element of a saga from the northern parts.

By ship down the Rhine from Mainz, Boniface had reached the scene of his earliest missionary labours in a country that had never known any Roman culture. Among his effects, along with his books, he had taken a shroud for his burial. There, in Frisia, near the modern town of Dokkum, their camp was attacked by a pagan horde, while the saint encouraged them all: 'Take cheer in the Lord and fix the anchor of your hope in God.' After the martyrdom a funeral procession of boats carried the body of Boniface first to Utrecht, then to Mainz and thence to lie in his abbey of Fulda. Some fifteen years later, Willibald, an Anglo-Saxon monk of Fulda, wrote for posterity a *Life of Boniface*. And at Fulda Boniface still lies and the bishops of Germany demonstrate their devotion to him as their Apostle by holding their official gatherings around his tomb.

But the letters far outstrip the various Lives in importance. They form, according to Sir Frank Stenton, 'the most remarkable body of correspondence which has survived from the Dark Ages'. There we encounter a man of courage and vision, yet a man who longed for the consolation which the contacts with his wide circle of friends could afford him. It was indeed a wide circle, though of set purpose we have given most attention to the letters to and from the popes, for from this continuous link Boniface received the guidelines for his missionary work and still more for his restoration of the Frankish church. Through the collaboration with Pepin, he had secured a workable co-operation between the court and the papacy, and, in the great councils held between 742 and 747, Boniface had proved himself a great statesman and organizer, giving shape to Europe. Christopher Dawson declared him to be 'the man who had a deeper influence on the history of Europe than any Englishman who has ever lived'.

If, when organizing ecclesiastical life for the mission countries, Boniface did not allow matters of detail to disturb the great lines of his projects, everything shows that, when dealing with individuals, he could descend to practical details or to a tender regard for those in distress. The saint did not act differently towards kings than towards the nuns. He knew what was most suited to each. Several letters are from or to kings then reigning in England. Elfwald, king of the East Saxons, requested his prayers. In a long letter to Ethelbald, king of Mercia, Boniface begged him to amend his life, yet sent him gifts of a hawk and a pair of falcons, two shields and two lances. It was the nun, Bugga, who recommended Ethelbert II, king of Kent, to seek the prayers of Boniface; the king begged the saint's intercession, sending him gifts, only asking Boniface to send him in return a pair of falcons for hunting cranes, since in Kent falcons were scarce. Boniface fully realized how helpful to a mission was the support of a king. One of his last letters is addressed to Fuldred, abbot of St Denis, where Charles Martel had been buried. Boniface begged the abbot to thank Pepin the Short for all the good which he had been able to do through the king, their father's staunch support. He trusts that, as his end is near, Pepin will continue to help his monks and all who have worked with him, when Lull succeeds him.

It is a great good fortune to possess the correspondence of St Boniface and of Lull. The letters can be used to give a picture of life in the eighth century, as well as the portrait of a busy missionary and his friends. Yet the spirit which pervades all this endeavour is always seen to derive from a family in which everything bears the mark of the Rule of St Benedict. The missionary monks are conscious of the support of their brethren, as they serve God in the face of a pagan people. They go out to their work from their monasteries which have become centres of faith and of civilization, yet remain always united in spiritual friendship with their absent brethren. All this missionary zeal added a new dimension to the Benedictine ideal, unforeseen by St Benedict, testing its flexibility and its adaptability to the full.

by Dom Frederick Hockey

BIBLIOGRAPHY

M. Tangl, *S. Bonifatii et Lulli Epistolae* (MGH 1916) : translated by E. Kylie (London 1924) and by E. Emerton (New York 1940).

C. Albertson, *Anglo-Saxon saints and heroes* (New York 1967).

E. S. Duckett, *Anglo-Saxon saints and scholars* (New York 1947).

C. H. Talbot, *The Anglo-Saxon missionaries in Germany* (London 1954).

W. Levison, *England and the Continent in the eighth century* (Oxford 1946).

F. M. Stenton, *Anglo-Saxon England* (3rd ed., Oxford 1970).

C. Dawson, *The Making of Europe* (London 1935).

Cluny: Silentia Claustri

Cluny is a daunting subject; no contribution of this size will do it justice. Cluny existed for nearly nine hundred years in all. For its first two centuries it was closely bound up with the development of the Church in Europe, in particular with the Gregorian Reform. It also became a force to be reckoned with in European politics, in the Crusades, in the elaboration of the feudal system and in economic development. But essentially it was a monastic community, providing a way of life which was specifically Benedictine in character and spreading it generously wherever it was asked. To this it owed its appeal, its growth and its long life: this factor has determined the scope of this article.

When the Roman Empire fell, sound government to a large extent fell with it. Insofar as its hold was lost on its extensive territories, disintegration set in. Under the pressure of successive waves of barbarian invasions France, Germany and England broke up into units governed by independent or semi-independent lords. As the seventh and eighth centuries wore on, many traces of Roman civilization disappeared, society returned to a state of lawlessness when might, not right, was the title of possession. Eventually feudalism was born. Under Charlemagne (768–814) disintegration was arrested, but the conflicts between his sons after his death led to its renewal.

The monastic Order during this period reflected the contemporary state of society. Thanks to Christian missionaries, many of whom were monks, the invading Goths, Franks and Saxons had become Christian, and the Church was firmly established in their lands. Many of them wanted to assure their eternal salvation by building monasteries. This they did with generosity, but often the canker was in the fruit. Their legal ownership of the monasteries led to their interference in its internal life, to lay appointments of abbots, to the partial sequestration of the monastic revenues, to the residence in the abbeys of the lords and their families. If they were kings, they gave their monasteries to relatives or faithful servants who were their vassals. The evil effects of this state of affairs is obvious; Bede, among others, protested in 734 against secular interference in monastic affairs. Despite the respite of the Carolingian renaissance (c. 780–850) secularization continued, the second half of the ninth century being one of the darkest periods in medieval history. But a new day was at hand and it dawned in the early tenth century; Cluny, then small and unknown, was founded on 11 September 909.

Before we consider this in detail, it must be stressed that the Carolingian renaissance, in spite of apparent failure, sowed good seed which bore fruit later. Charlemagne wanted an orderly empire. Every institution felt the effect of his keen organizing and centralizing power. The Church was no exception, nor were the monasteries. In the Church as a whole he promoted liturgical, ultramontane reforms; for the numerous monasteries he legislated about abbots' duties in numerous capitularies and extolled, like his predecessors, the excellence of the Rule of St Benedict.

Meanwhile a notable monk was deeply concerned about restoring high standards in monasteries. This was Benedict of Aniane, a truly remarkable figure, whose influence on Benedictine life can still be felt today. Aniane, near Montpellier, the monastery he founded on his own estate, was the first object of his reforming zeal. The results of this spread from the south of France right up to the north, resulting in the foundation of Inde (Cornelimünster) close to the imperial city of Aachen.

Two features characterized his work: he kept all the houses under his own rule and he instituted in each of them full Benedictine observance. He was thus able to ensure the permanence of his work. In maintaining his personal authority over all the houses he dealt a fatal blow to the cause of widespread monastic decadence, secular appropriation; by giving each community sound internal discipline, he guaranteed their monastic future.

It was not Charlemagne but his successor, Louis the Pious, who recognized in Benedict a great monastic teacher; he determined to give his official backing to his work of restoring monastic life in the Empire. This he did by calling together all the abbots at Aachen in 817. With their help was drawn up a *capitulare institutum*, a body of prescriptions added to the Benedictine Rule, to be observed in all the monasteries. A system of visitation was also elaborated to maintain good observance once it was introduced.

Benedict was a teacher as well as an organizer. He produced two works of considerable importance: the *Codex Regularum*, a collection of monastic rules, and the *Concordia Regularum* in which he shows how St Benedict of Nursia had assimilated all that was best in the rules that were written before him and handed it down in his own rule. This second work was much in vogue for some time after its author had disappeared, and it went far to consolidate the position of the Rule of Saint Benedict in contemporary monasticism. Benedict of Aniane died in 821; Louis the Pious followed him in 840. The political turmoil that ensued reduced society to chaos, with the inevitable result that monasteries once again fell victims to lay interference and to the Scandinavian invasions that punctuated the remaining decades of the ninth century.

But the scheme failed for another reason too: the model monasticism so much desired by the Emperor was foreign to Benedictine thought and polity. From the days of St Benedict his disciples had always cherished the autonomy of each monastery and its individual family spirit as a characteristic of its life. Each house developed its own life and had its observances, coloured by national traits and by circumstances social and cultural. Though at times monasteries were closely related, either through foundations, where daughter was obviously linked with the mother house, or when—as in the case of Benedict of Aniane—an abbot governed several monasteries, the individual character of each house was always safeguarded. In attempting to restore good observance by imposing a body of regulations and a common observance on all the monasteries of his Empire, Louis ran counter to this tradition. In centralizing this at Aachen in the hands of Benedict and planning regular visitations or inspections of all the monasteries he was courting certain failure. The attempt was well intentioned and was meant to rehabilitate monasticism; although it was short-lived, it sowed seeds that were to bear an abundant harvest later. It did not attack the root of the trouble, secular intervention in monasteries, but it codified or standardized what had become common Benedictine observance, and introduced the idea of confederation, as distinct from centralization, into Benedictine circles.

If the work of Benedict of Aniane failed as part of the politics of the Emperor, it succeeded as a spiritual formation in the monasteries he had influenced through Aniane. This house had in fact helped many another to put its affairs in order, amongst them Saint-Savin-sur-Gartempe near Poitiers, and monks from here had rendered a like service to the Abbey of Saint-Martin at Autun (870). Some sixteen years later St Martin was called upon to restore monastic life once more in the monastery at Baume in Burgundy, and to carry this into effect it designated one of its members, Berno. Member of a very fervent community, Berno introduced the Aniane observance both at Baume and at Gigny, a monastery he founded soon after and which he kept under his authority. Both these houses attracted attention at the time, and it is not surprising that when William, duke of Aquitaine, decided, like many another nobleman of that age, to found a monastery, he appealed to Abbot Berno. The place designated for the foundation was Cluny, the date 11 September 909.

In that very same year Baume had attracted a promising young priest of thirty, Odo, in search of monastic life, destined sixteen years later to become abbot of Cluny. He had been brought up in the court of William of Aquitaine, but had entered the clerical state as a boy of eighteen at Tours, and, after initial studies in that city, had gone to Paris, to sit at the feet of the learned Remigius, a teacher of considerable reputation in the cathedral school. It was from here that, in his late twenties, he began to look for a monastery and was told by his friend Adhegrinus about Baume, recently restored by Berno. Odo made his profession there and became master of the claustral school, a post for which he was highly qualified. He also taught music to the young monks.

In founding a monastery at Cluny, William of Aquitaine had nothing more in mind than setting up a house in which monastic life would flourish and which would be properly safeguarded from lay interference. To secure both these aims, he could not have chosen a better man than Berno. In the first place, Berno had been trained as a monk in the spirit and observance of Benedict of Aniane, and he knew what was best in monastic tradition. This was to prove an invaluable foundation for the life of the new community at Cluny, and gave it the characteristics that marked it for centuries. Secondly, Berno realized how undesirable were the results of lay interference in monasteries. To avoid its recurrence, he subjected the houses for which he was responsible, not to the weak local duke, but directly to the Holy See. So with a good basic tradition for its community life, and with security against all secular intervention, Cluny was set on a safe course. William, its founder, was also meticulous in safeguarding the right of the community to elect its own abbot, and in making over the abbey and all its temporalities to the Holy See. He abandoned his possessions to the Apostles, and gained their protection and defence in return. Just before Berno died, the monks elected Odo to succeed him. He decided to leave Baume definitively and devote all his care to Cluny.

What did Odo find at Cluny? A monastery where monastic ideals were held in esteem and where the observance was good; a solitude where he could seek God and find God in prayer, penance and study. Such a house was rare indeed in the decadent years of the early tenth century, when monastic discipline had all but disappeared. Almost in despair of finding such a place, he had adopted a hermit's life near Tours. Meanwhile, his friend, on a similar quest, stumbled on the peaceful foundation of Baume, in the mountains of Jura, and shared his good news with him. Together they took the habit, and under Abbot Berno learnt the *ordo monasticus*, the way of life in the monastery. This they discovered was not just the Rule of St Benedict, though that was its foundation and its chief inspiration, but a way of life that had become more complex over the centuries, yet was still basically the same. John of Salerno, Odo's contemporary biographer, tells us that the customs observed at Baume were those of St Benedict of Aniane, so when Cluny was founded, they were automatically introduced there.

At this period Rule and custom were inextricably bound up together and thought of as one: together they formed the *ordo monasticus*. Just as for a long while the Rule of St Benedict was only one of the monastic rules frequently observed alongside several others in a single monastery, so later on that Rule was not considered separately from the body of further prescriptions added to it by tradition. Benedict of Aniane should not be considered an innovator in this respect, but rather a codifier of existing customs or contemporary adaptations. It should be remembered—and the fact is important in the light of subsequent developments at Cluny—that more than one factor had contributed to upset the simple balanced life of St Benedict's Rule. One was the migration of monasteries from their country setting to towns and cities. This was the case in Italy where monks served Roman basilicas, and where, perforce, they adopted a more developed liturgy and exchanged manual work for study. Another fact was the increase in the number of priests in a community and the consequent importance attached to study and to the copying of books, over and above those hours of *lectio divina* provided so generously by the Rule. These and other factors modified Benedictine life considerably and, in a sense, permanently.

Prayer has always been the essential element in monastic life right from its birth in the Egyptian desert; the importance attached by St Benedict to both liturgical and private prayer shows that he continued this tradition. At the date we are discussing, however, a transformation had appeared, namely that an ever-growing importance was being attached to liturgical prayer, and the monks of St Benedict of Aniane were devoting far longer hours to the Divine Office than their predecessors. Odo found this at Baume and at Cluny, but far from being peculiar to those monasteries, it was characteristic of this reform movement wherever it appeared.

In any attempt to assess this transformation of the daily life of the monasteries we must bear in mind two important factors. First of all, for the monks themselves the liturgy and the long psalmody it implied was prayer. Every monk knew his psalter, and much else of the liturgy, by heart; it was his form of prayer, and he would spontaneously express himself in the beautiful and varied text of the psalms. In Odo's day a Benedictine community added many psalms over and above the number prescribed for the day and night

Offices of the liturgy; to us the burden may appear intolerable, but it was not so to the monk of that day, it was his prayer. Today in most monasteries you will find monks praying privately, for example, before Matins in the early morning; Odo's monks did so too, but recited psalms, sometimes as many as fifteen, in preparation for the important and lengthy office of Matins.

Their devotion to Our Lady, to the Saints and to the Dead gave rise to additional Offices added to the main Divine Office. Their eucharistic devotion was expressed in more elaborate ceremonial at the daily Community Mass, and even by their celebration of another Mass earlier in the morning. The Divine Office itself was gradually enhanced by more beautiful music and ceremonial: nothing was spared in their zeal 'to put nothing before the Work of God' (*Rule of St Benedict*, ch. 43). To sum up: monasteries were houses of prayer, but mainly of liturgical prayer, of the prayer of the Church, in which generation after generation of monks found what they sought: a school of the Lord's service in prayerful solitude.

The second factor to be considered is the place that monasteries held in the society of the age. They were centres of intercessory prayer, first of all for the founders of the particular house who nearly always instituted them for the salvation of their souls and those of their families, and secondly, for the Christian body at large, who grew to depend on their prayers for their well-being and prosperity. Many of the additional psalms alluded to above were prescribed for the founders and benefactors living and dead of the community. As time went on, anniversaries accumulated in monasteries and added considerably to the quantity of prayers and Masses. Christendom valued its centres of prayer.

This is what Odo found when he became abbot of Cluny; a monastery pure and simple, with no other ambition but to live the life of the Benedictine Rule and offer it to all who knocked on its door. It soon attracted many. The state of society was chaotic; petty rulers and feudal lords were in constant war with one another; moral standards were low; the Church was caught up in the net of feudalism. The ordered life of a monastery like Cluny could not fail to stand out in bold relief. Added to this, its abbot, Odo, was a man of culture and letters, as well as an ardent follower of Christ and the Gospel, and a clear exponent of the monastic way of life.

It is not surprising that within a few years of his becoming abbot Odo's prestige stood high. Monastic houses in need of reform turned to him with his experience and deep appreciation of a sound tradition: in the course of his rule he introduced good observance into a number of houses, including Aurillac in Aquitaine, Romain-moutier in Burgundy, Jumièges in Normandy, St Paul's outside the

Walls in Rome, Subiaco and St Elia at Nepi in Italy, and at the celebrated abbey of Fleury. Through Fleury, Odo's influence was felt in England, as there were already Englishmen in that community when St Ethelwold sent Osgar, one of his monks, there to learn monastic life before introducing it at his monastery at Abingdon. Germanus, another member of his community, had been trained at Cluny itself. St Oswald, bishop of Worcester and later archbishop of York, who restored monastic life in seven monasteries, was professed at Fleury and introduced its observance elsewhere. It was precisely in this way that the influence of Cluny made itself felt during Odo's abbacy. It was not a concerted campaign of reforming zeal, but the gentle force of a fervent community spreading to other communities and kindling their ardour. We shall see later on that it was a different procedure when Cluny made a direct foundation in England.

In the age of unrest and lawlessness in which he lived, Odo set great store by peace and purity of life; he saw monastic life as a powerful means of restoring both to the world. He would do anything in the cause of peace. At the request of the pope, he undertook four difficult journeys to Rome between 933 and 940 to negotiate peace between Alberic, ruler of Rome, and Hugh, king of North Italy. This leads us to say that although he was primarily the restorer of peace and order in houses of monks, his concern extended to the Church at large. His monastic doctrine was in fact theologically based on that of the Church as the Mystical Body of Christ, in whose peace and unity he saw the salvation of the troubled world in which he lived. Monasticism, as he saw it, was to be a powerful means to the reform of the Church by its purity and other-worldliness. Most of all, however, he saw the Eucharist as the symbol of the union of Christ and his Mystical Body; and in the Real Presence, which he propounded in the most literal way, he recognized the source of its transforming power. The Church as the Mystical Body was central to his teaching and held priority among the spiritual values from which Cluny was born. Other-worldliness, purity (*munditia* is his favourite word) and a total commitment to Christ were the elements that contributed most to the spiritual climate that obtained in Odo's monastery. Silence and recollection were stressed in accordance with the Benedictine Rule; prolonged prayer, mainly psalmody, was intended to colour a monk's daily life and all his activities. It was this way of life that commended itself so strongly to Odo's contemporaries. His main work during his twenty-odd years as abbot was consolidating this spirit and deepening it. All things considered, it was this spirit, and the observance it inspired, that lay at the heart of Cluny's growth and influence, both in the monastic order and in the Church at large.

An important factor in the growth of Cluny was that it was ruled during its first two centuries by a succession of great abbots. These men were both saints and administrators; they shaped the destiny of their house with wisdom and prudence. Five of them stand out in bold relief: Odo, Mayeul, Odilo, Hugh and Peter the Venerable. Odo, as we have seen, gave the house its spiritual character; his dynamic personality established the course it was to take. Before he died (944) he appointed an abbot-coadjutor to help him in his duties; this was Aymard, who was duly elected abbot after Odo's death. There was precedent for this, for we may remember that Odo himself had been appointed by Berno a little before he died. Aymard in his turn appointed Mayeul to be coadjutor and his successor (948) with the approval and consent of the community. Mayeul nominated Odilo to succeed him (994). Odilo died without appointing a successor, and Hugh, his prior for some years, was elected by the community (1049), thus bringing to an end a practice which, although directly counter to the Rule of St Benedict, gave Cluny a succession of outstanding spiritual leaders. Hugh was to rule for sixty years (1049–1109). After a lapse of thirteen years, during which Pons was abbot (1109–22) followed by Hugh II, the community elected Peter the Venerable, who was a worthy successor of Hugh I. He united both the spiritual leadership and the outstanding human qualities of his predecessors. He ruled as abbot from 1122 to 1156.

We know little of Aymard, Odo's coadjutor and successor, apart from the fact that he proved equal to the task of maintaining the traditions of his master and consolidating his teaching. Unfortunately he went blind, and after only ten years handed over the government of the community to Mayeul.

Mayeul came from a distinguished family of Provence. Invading Saracens pillaged the family domain, so Mayeul left for Mâcon where he became archdeacon. He studied at Lyons, and, like Odo before him, came to Cluny with a well-equipped mind and a wide experience of men. Appointed abbot at an early age, Mayeul governed his monastery for forty years. These were years of expansion on every level. In the first place, gifts of land came in rapid succession—sixteen different acquisitions are mentioned in one year—so that the monastery became securely endowed. Secondly, more and more monasteries turned to it for help either temporary or permanent. Monks left Cluny to introduce its ways of life elsewhere, and a number came to the monastery itself to be trained. Mayeul began the construction of a new monastery, and first of all the church, which was consecrated on 14 February 981. His influence was far-reaching both in Church and State; the prestige of Cluny rose high. Though nothing of his writing has come down to us, his contemporary biographers depict him as an ardent student, particularly of Saint Gregory the Great and the pseudo-Denis the Areopagite, whose mystical writings he delighted to ponder.

Odilo ruled for fifty-five years. He was born in Auvergne into a family of considerable importance. His father was both an outstanding soldier and a wise counsellor. During his long rule Odilo combined gentleness and energy in a remarkable degree, and brought his gift for administration to the rapidly increasing network of Cluniac houses, which now included the greater part of France, Northern and Central Italy, and Spain. Sancho the Great, King of Navarre, took in hand the restoration of monasteries destroyed by Islam; he sent Paternus and some companions to Cluny about 1000 to learn monastic life. On their return to Spain they were installed at San Juan de la Peña, and from there the Cluniac way of life spread rapidly throughout the peninsula, first to Oña, Leyre and San Pedro de Cardena, then to many other monasteries.

But Odilo did not attempt to create a centralized congregation based on Cluny. Some monasteries never lost their autonomy, and others regained it after a period of restoration; no link beyond the personal influence of the abbot bound them to Cluny. Many houses maintained that link permanently. Odilo's preoccupation was the furtherance of good monastic life, and he made every effort to create houses of prayer wherever he was called upon to help. Two of his initiatives always interest historians. The first was the institution in his monastery of an annual commemoration of the dead on 2 November. This he was prompted to do by his great charity. From Cluny this observance spread, it was eventually adopted by the whole Latin Church. His second initiative was in the political field, where through family connexions his influence was decisive. In a vigorous attempt to promote peace in Europe, he persuaded the rulers to agree upon the *pactum Dei*, which protected certain persons and properties from violation, and the *truga Dei* or truce of God, whereby certain times of the year and specified days were consecrated to peace: on these days fighting was forbidden.

More to our point is the fact that the oldest customaries of Cluny were compiled during Odilo's abbacy. The first was put together between 996 and 1030 from older fragments, one dating from Odo's day, the other going back even further to Berno's and to pre-Cluniac observance. This customary is basically liturgical. It is short and does not throw much light on the day-to-day life of the monks. Fortunately we possess another, generally known as the Customary of Farfa, which is more detailed and allows us to catch a glimpse of life at Cluny under Odilo. It was written for this Italian monastery, whose abbot Hugh was trying to restore good observance and had invited the disciples of St Romuald to help him. Unfortunately this attempt failed, so he appealed to Odilo who was then on a journey in Italy, and agreed with him to introduce Cluniac observance into his monastery. About the year 1000 John, one of his monks, was sent to Cluny to make a copy of the customary and bring it back to Farfa. The copy we possess represents a customary drawn up between 1023 and 1030 together with additional material judged useful by John, the date of the whole compilation being roughly 1042. This additional material constitutes a second part of the customary, the first being strictly liturgical covering the whole year from Advent to November. In part two we are given information about the novitiate, the installation of a new abbot, the monastic habit, the claustral prior, what monks should do on a journey, manual work and the monastic penal code. Then follow a list of miscellaneous 'dos and don'ts', the cellarer's duties, procedure at meals and washing up, the tonsure and shaving. Next come arrangements for Mass, processions of all kinds, blood-letting, guests, the stables, the poor, the care of the rooms and furniture, the larder, the sacristy, the sick brethren and, finally, the ritual prescribed for the dying and for funerals. From this abundant material we can reconstitute life at Cluny in its main lines. One characteristic stands out above all others—its orderliness. Nothing is left to chance; everything is foreseen and provided for; people know what they have to do and do it; every department of the life is catered for. This reflects in a practical way the untiring efforts of the abbots of Cluny for peace, and the supreme importance they attached to the *tranquillitas ordinis* in building up a house of prayer. Experience in every age has shown the wisdom of this; its inspiration is in the Rule of Saint Benedict itself, where it is prescribed that 'everything may be fulfilled at its proper time' (ch. 47).

Before making further deductions from this customary, let us analyse two items contained in its second part which cast considerable light on the life it describes. The first is a detailed description of the church and the monastery with measurements. The church, we remember, was rebuilt by Mayeul and consecrated on 14 February 981. The monastery was rebuilt by Odilo and was obviously an extensive and noble building, capable of housing a community of about seventy-five monks. Refectory, dormitory, scriptorium, kitchen and other buildings were on a generous scale, and so were the novitiate, the guest-house and the servants' quarters. In Odilo's day Cluny probably had a population of about two hundred and fifty. The whole was harmonious and of beautiful proportions, and there was plenty of light. There was sobriety about it as well as dignity, and this was intentional. The material beauty of their home was meant by Mayeul and Odilo to be an important element in the spiritual growth and well-being of the community. Like the beauty of the liturgy and its perfection in ceremonial and chant, the beauty of the monastic buildings themselves led the monk to prayer and to that other-worldliness so characteristic of his life. Odilo became a great builder of churches and monasteries: twelve at least owed their buildings to him, twenty welcomed his work of restoration, and hundreds of beautiful romanesque churches in different parts of France were inspired by Cluny at different times. In the words of his biographer Jotsaud, Odilo left a cloister of marble wherever he found a cloister of wood.

The second item of interest contained in the Farfa Customary enables us to reconstruct still further the life led at Cluny. Saint Benedict prescribes that at the beginning of Lent the abbot shall give each of his monks a book to be read '*ex integro et per ordinem*', that is right through consecutively, during the hours of *lectio divina*. It became the custom (which still obtains in some monasteries) to compile the list of these books with the names of the monks who received them, and hang it up at the door of the chapter house. John of Farfa found such a list and included it in his customary, thus giving us not only the list of the monks resident at Cluny, but also some idea of its library. The community consisted of sixty-four monks at this date (1042–43) in the last years of Odilo's abbacy, and the titles of the volumes distributed include, besides various books of the Bible, commentaries on Scripture by Origen, Ambrose, Jerome, Augustine, Chrysostom, Cassiodorus, Gregory, Bede, Ambrose Autpertus, Rhabanus Maurus and Haymo, theological treatises by Cyprian, Augustine, Eugippius, Gregory, Isidore, Julian of Toledo and Alcuin, books of ascetical theology by Benedict of Aniane, Ephrem the Deacon, Basil and Cassian, different collections of saints' lives, and finally historical works one would hardly expect to find in such a list: the *Antiquities* of Josephus, Eusebius's *Church History*, works of Paul Orosius and Ethnicus (whose *Cosmography* circulated under the name of Jerome), Bede's *Ecclesiastical History* and Livy's *History*. This list shows us that reading and study were in high repute, and that the copying of manuscripts had gone on perseveringly in the scriptorium of the monastery ever since Odo had arrived a hundred years earlier with his hundred volumes. Beside their heavy liturgical observance, the monks of Cluny cultivated letters both divine and secular; later catalogues reveal an ever-increasing supply of books.

It is obvious from the customaries that for the monks of Cluny the choral Office, the daily round of prayer and praise, was the core of their life. It was the most important though by no means the only occupation of their busy days. It was carried out with great care seven times a day and once at night. It was not only the basis of their spiritual life and the source of their strength, but the *raison d'être* and the inspiration (with their *lectio divina*) of their wide artistic achievement in many media. They rose between 1.30 and 2.30 a.m. for a long service called Vigils or Matins, which was preceded and followed by additional psalmody, the whole amounting to about two hours. Lauds followed, after an interval devoted to reading, at daybreak, and Prime after sunrise. The work of the day then started; it was carried out either in the scriptorium or in the different offices and workshops of the monastery, or in the garden or on the farm. Studies were always in high esteem, especially under Odilo, when, for example, Ralph Glaber wrote his histories (1047), and under Peter the Venerable, when Alger of Liège, Peter of Poitiers and Richard of Poitiers produced theological and historical works. Peter the Venerable was himself a poet. Cluny also had a school of illumination, music and stone-carving which maintained a high standard. At the end of the morning, broken by the Office of Terce and the short Morrow or Chapter Mass, came the solemn Community Mass about midday, preceded by Sext and followed by dinner. After that there was a period of rest or optional reading until None. By this time the afternoon was well advanced and Vespers was sung at about four o'clock, followed by supper on certain days or a drink, and a period of reading in common called *Collatio*. Compline brought the long day to an end about six o'clock.

Odilo died in 1048 and was succeeded by Hugh, who was to rule for sixty years. He was only twenty-five years old when elected abbot, but as grand prior of Cluny he had already shown promise. He was to maintain the spirit and observance of his predecessors. He went further in strengthening the links which bound other houses to Cluny, but even in his day there was nothing comparable to the organization and centralization that appeared in monastic circles and in the orders of friars at a later date. Although the abbot of Cluny had control of all the houses dependent on him, and even appointed the superiors in some of them, and despite the fact that novices made their profession into his hands, the independence of each house was respected, and there was never any question of tampering with the local stability of each monk. In fact, the dependence on Cluny was viewed as a protection from secular interference, always to be feared in a feudal society, and a safeguard of good observance, always in danger of deteriorating in any community. Like his predecessor, Hugh was a great builder. The rapid increase in numbers of his community from about 100 when he became abbot to 200 thirty years later, and indeed to 300 at the time of his death, compelled him to enlarge his monastic buildings, particularly the dormitory and the infirmary, and to project the rebuilding of the church. Work on the latter began about 1085 and it was ready for consecration by Pope Urban in October 1095. It was at the time the largest church in Christendom, only to be surpassed five centuries later by the rebuilt basilica of St Peter's in Rome. Dr K. J. Conant, who began excavations at Cluny as far back as 1927, has made a close study of the successive churches built by Odo (Cluny I), Mayeul (Cluny II) and Hugh (Cluny III).

Under abbot Hugh the first Cluniac foundations were made in England. This is not to say that the influence of the great Burgundian monastery had not been felt long before. First of all, through Fleury, it had assisted the monastic reform of the tenth century for which Dunstan, Ethelwold and Oswald were responsible. Secondly, through William of Dijon and Bec, it had profoundly influenced the Norman monasticism that came to England with the Conquest. Lanfranc's Constitutions reflect the practice of Cluny rather than Bec.

In his attempt to obtain worthy bishops and abbots for England, William the Conqueror asked Hugh to send him a dozen good monks, but Hugh refused. It was not in the spirit of Cluny either to get involved in ecclesiastical and feudal matters or to impose their way of life on an unwilling community. Not long after this, however, William de Warenne, one of the Conqueror's trusted followers, planned like many another knight of that time to found a monastery on his estate in Sussex. He discussed the matter with Lanfranc, the archbishop of Canterbury, and started off with his wife on a pilgrimage to Rome. On their way they stopped at Cluny and were so deeply impressed that they asked Hugh for a group of monks to make the foundation. Reluctantly he consented, but rather dragged his feet and sent only three monks—a number quite inadequate for the purpose. He subsequently sent a group of monks under Lanzo, a very remarkable man, as their prior (1072). One of the stipulations made by William was that the abbot of Cluny was to choose the holiest and wisest monk of his community to be prior of Lewes, who was to be in some degree independent. Lanzo indeed measured up to this, and during his rule of thirty years won a reputation for sanctity. William of Malmesbury has left us a touching account of his death, when he was carried by his monks to the presbytery of the church and died before the high altar of St Pancras. His community too was widely esteemed. When Henry I founded the abbey of Reading in 1121, it was to Lewes that he turned for the abbot and monks to people it.

During the century that followed, further Cluniac foundations were made up and down the country, either from Cluny itself like Montacute and Lenton, or from important dependencies of Cluny such as La Charité, whence Bermondsey, Wenlock and Pontefract, or from S. Martin-des-Champs in Paris, whose very small foundations were in Devonshire (Barnstaple and Exeter) and Wales (St Clears, Dyfed), or from Ste Foy de Longueville, which possessed two small houses, Great Witchington and Newington. These small foundations never developed; in the long run they proved to be a weakness in the monastic body. Wenlock, Thetford, Pontefract and Lenton developed into normal-sized communities, though their numbers were never big. Lewes and Bermondsey alone became really large. The latter was founded in London about 1085 from La Charité-sur-Loire; being close to the city it attracted rich benefactors, including William Rufus who gave them the land on which it was built. Several of its priors were men of distinction who were promoted to be abbots of Glastonbury, Abingdon, Evesham, Faversham and St Ouen at Rouen. One of its community, Thomas of Elmham, is best known to us as the chronicler of St Augustine's abbey, Canterbury.

Abbot Hugh's reluctance to make foundations as far away as England proved well founded. Cluniac strength lay in its particular observance and on the close ties with Cluny itself. Both of these were difficult to maintain at a distance. The houses, except for Lewes and Bermondsey, never had the full quota of monks needed for the full character of the life to endure, so discipline suffered. The distance from England to Burgundy was too great for practical purposes; gradually the influence of the mother house all but disappeared.

Cluniac influence in England, however, was far wider than the foundation of these immediately dependent houses. Two royal foundations were manned by Cluniac monks: Reading was founded by Henry I in 1121 with monks from Cluny and Lewes, and Faversham by Stephen in 1148 with monks from Bermondsey. Both grew to be large and influential. Neither of them was Cluniac in the full juridical sense, but Reading kept up cordial relations with Cluny and Lewes for some years and in 1199 provided Cluny itself with an abbot in the person of Hugh V.

Henry I showed his great esteem for Cluny by contributing substantially to the building of its huge church. He and his successor Stephen appointed two outstanding Cluniacs as bishops in England. One was Henry of Blois, whom Henry sent to be abbot of Glastonbury in 1126. A man of outstanding ability with a taste for classical archaeology as well as art patronage on a lavish scale, he reformed the finances of England's richest abbey before being promoted to

England's richest see, Winchester, three years later. He retained the abbacy in plurality, much to the disgust of St Bernard, but sent Robert of Lewes to represent him and consolidate his work. For a whole year he supported the whole abbey of Cluny and set its finances on a sound basis. Although he never again resided at Glastonbury, he did not lose interest in its development, but retained the affection and esteem of the community. He died in 1171.

King Stephen called on Gilbert Foliot, prior of Abbeville, to be abbot of Gloucester in 1139. Here he found excellent standards left by his predecessor, the saintly Serlo, and maintained them. When he became bishop of Hereford in 1148, he resigned the abbacy of Gloucester. In 1163 he became bishop of London. He is perhaps best known as a bitter opponent of St Thomas of Canterbury, but he deserves to be remembered also as a theologian and canonist of some distinction and an able diocesan bishop. Both Henry and Gilbert had brilliant careers in ecclesiastical and political life; they made a powerful contribution to the life of twelfth-century England.

In 1161 Adam, prior of Bermondsey, became abbot of Evesham, while in the same year William, prior of S. Martin-des-Champs, became abbot of Ramsey. Moreover Abingdon had a Cluniac abbot in 1175 in Roger, prior of Bermondsey. The fact that William became abbot of Cluny later is a further sign that there were no hard and fast distinctions between Cluniacs and other Benedictines; certainly no hostility. We must conclude that monastic life in twelfth-century England owed much to Cluny; when William of Malmesbury compared the Canterbury community to Cluny, he paid them a very high compliment.

Let us return to Abbot Hugh and the community he ruled with such success in the second half of the eleventh century. Two other features of his rule must be noted. The first affects our knowledge of life at Cluny itself—the codification of its customs. This code was first drawn up by Bernard, a monk of Cluny, at the request of St Hugh, and is generally dated *c.* 1075; and there followed a second redaction ten years later. Unfortunately, this valuable customary is only available in a rare volume, Hergott's *Vetus Disciplina Monastica* (Paris, 1726), but it will appear, it is hoped, in the *Corpus Consuetudinum Monasticarum* edited by Dom K. Hallinger, now in course of publication. Some twenty-five years had elapsed since the appearance of the Farfa Customary referred to above, and obviously customs had changed with the fast-growing community and the increase of external commitments that called for more frequent coming and going to help other communities. Hugh was calling for an assessment and Bernard compiled his customary. The second redaction was drawn up by another monk of Cluny named Ulric, and was asked for by William, abbot of the German monastery of Hirsau. He certainly drew on Bernard's work, but he handles his material in another way. However different in method, both cover the same ground; they describe the whole liturgical year from Advent to Advent, and they detail for us the different duties of the officials of the monastery, including the novices. In this way the whole life is considered, and we can get a clear picture of the day-to-day existence of the monk. The customaries of Bernard and Ulric circulated widely in the monasteries of France and Germany, and in particular Bernard's was used by Lanfranc when he drew up his *Consuetudines* or *Statuta* for his cathedral monastery of Christchurch at Canterbury.

The second feature of Hugh's rule was the foundation by him of the double monastery of Marcigny in the diocese of Autun. He was dissatisfied with the existing convents of nuns, and as both his mother and sister wanted to embrace the monastic life he was anxious to provide a suitable monastery for them. So he founded one himself. He gave them substantially the life of Cluny, but what was particularly appreciated in his day was the fact that he gave them proper enclosure. He also saw to their spiritual care and formation; for this and for their temporal needs he founded a priory of monks under a spiritual and capable prior alongside the convent. Hugh wanted this house of nuns to consist of experienced and mature women, so he insisted strongly on careful selection and sent them back to St Benedict's Rule (ch. 58) in this connexion. The superior was not an abbess but a prioress. Marcigny was treated like any other dependency and was an integral part of the congregation. During his first exile St Anselm of Canterbury visited Marcigny, so Eadmer tells us, and met Hugh. This foundation is important as illustrating Hugh's creative genius and reflecting his deep spiritual and monastic ideals.

Before we leave Hugh and pass on to the last of the great abbots, Peter the Venerable, we must stop to consider the misfortune that befell his immediate successor Pons. Briefly what happened was this. Pons was duly elected at Hugh's death, and carried the heavy responsibility well. He was both a capable administrator and a well-loved father of his monks. During his rule and probably before, a growing opposition was felt both from the local bishop of Mâcon and from the archbishop of Lyons to whose province Cluny belonged. Callixtus II, the first non-monk pope for many years, adopted a conciliatory attitude to all parties and did not uphold the ancient exemption of Cluny as firmly as his predecessors. In the end abbot Pons lost patience, went to Rome and resigned his office into the pope's hands. His resignation was accepted and his community proceeded to an election. Their choice fell upon an elderly monk, Hugh, who died a few months later. They then chose Peter the Venerable, a young prior of great promise, who was duly confirmed and installed. Pons, however, had second thoughts, and after a pilgrimage to the Holy Land, returned to France and, when Peter was away, forced his way into the monastery and declared himself still abbot. There were scenes of violence. The whole episode is beyond belief and difficult to explain. The pope intervened, called both abbots to Rome, and after a hearing confirmed Peter in his office. Pons died the same year (1126). Capable administrator and astute diplomat as he was, Pons was at times high-handed and impulsive. In recent years both his great qualities and his serious flaws of character have been recognized.

When Peter the Venerable came on the scene, there were serious problems to be faced and solved. The resident community had reached the number of something like four hundred monks. The network of dependent priories ran into hundreds, as did the many independent or quasi-independent abbeys and priories. It must be remembered that there existed no organization to hold this widely scattered and numerous family together. It was the personal influence of the abbot of Cluny and the *ordo Cluniacensis* (the way of life of Cluny handed down either by oral tradition or the written description of the customaries) that kept the unity. This *ordo* was still very strictly adhered to, and it was unhealthily and almost exclusively liturgical. In a word everything had grown too big, and in all departments there were indications that things were not well. Not that Cluniac influence abated; it even increased during Peter's rule, but it became clear that personal contact and influence could not be satisfactorily maintained.

Peter made efforts to obviate this difficulty not only by assiduous visitations of monasteries—he visited England in 1130—but also by summoning all the abbots to a meeting at Cluny in 1132, the first of its kind. A few years later he promulgated a series of statutes, seventy-two in number, modifying customs that had become obsolete, and generally reforming the daily life by eliminating many of the extra psalms and prayers that had been attached to the Divine Office over the years. This was long overdue. It would, however, not be correct to talk of relaxed discipline on a big scale. At the very beginning of his rule he had invited Matthew, Prior of the Paris house of S. Martin-des-Champs, to come and help him restore the observance of his monastery, and as Matthew returned home after a brief two years this does not appear to have been a very difficult task.

Peter's statutes and the reasons he adduces for the modifications they introduced reflect the change of climate in the monastic world in the early twelfth century when the influence of other movements, Cîteaux particularly, was being felt. Peter was sensitive to this. He had to cross swords early on with Bernard of Clairvaux; the interchange of letters is well known. But the two men were big enough to understand one another, and the friendship that ensued was beneficial to Cluny in many ways. We must remember that Hugh his predecessor had ruled for sixty years, and that inevitably his hold on his vast community had grown slack and many abuses had crept in. Throughout his thirty-four years of rule, Peter consolidated both the prestige and the influence of his house.

His personality is better known to us than any of his predecessors' thanks to the collection of his letters which has come down to us, and which has recently been superbly edited by Giles Constable. Peter's kindness to Abelard will never be forgotten. After Abelard's condemnation at the Council of Sens in 1140, Peter wrote to Pope Innocent II asking him to approve of the suggestion that Abelard should spend his last years at Cluny '*dimissis scolarum et studiorum tumultibus*' where he would be a help to the monks, and where 'like the sparrow he would find a home and like the turtle dove a nest' from which nobody would expel him. The suggestion was carried into effect, and when two years later, on 21 April 1142, Abelard died, Peter wrote to Héloise breaking the news and describing the old man living in the community, humble and effaced, poorly dressed, sparing in food and drink, silent, prayerful, still bent over his books, offering the sacrifice of the Mass as often as he could, a wonderful example to all. '*Mens eius, lingua eius, opus eius, semper divina, semper philosophica, semper eruditoria meditabatur, docebat, fatebatur.*' He wishes Héloise could have come to live at Cluny too, or at least with the Cluniac nuns at Marcigny. And he concludes by reminding her that their saintly love for each other had been strengthened and enhanced by their love of God, and that at the final coming of the Lord, Abelard would be given back to her. The whole letter is a masterpiece of humanity and deep spirituality. It also reflects the atmosphere of Cluny itself, where somebody of Abelard's stature could be made welcome and happy. Some time later, Peter went to the abbey of the Paraclete where Héloise was living, taking Abelard's body with him for burial there.

Also under Peter eremitical life developed and flourished. The number of monks living, temporarily or permanently, as hermits was considerable. This fact, together with the need to staff its small foundations, meant that the conditions of life for the individual were more varied than is often supposed.

Regretfully we must leave Peter the Venerable. He died on Christmas Day 1156. With him went the 'golden age' of Cluny. In many ways he epitomized its spirit; he was essentially a man of prayer and a man of the cloister. His closest friends and admirers were monks: Bernard of Clairvaux, Basil, Prior of the Grande Chartreuse, and many others. He wrote a work recounting the inspiring lives of monks he had known entitled *De Miraculis*; in it we can see what he himself loved and admired in the monastic life. One passage may be cited among many; it is a pen portrait of Matthew of Albano, Prior of St Martin-des-Champs:

> After a varied career in the world, he dwelt uninterruptedly with the brethren in the monastery. Fully intent upon his sacred reading, which he perseveringly pursued, he was like that very column of the cloister, firm and unmoved, against which he had his desk. Though he was prior, it was with difficulty that he could be persuaded to leave his brethren for an hour to transact business, and once his mind was fixed on God no worldly cares could move him. Though he could not escape completely from the claims of Martha, all the desire of his heart was to sit with Mary. He loved community life—the common cloister, the common oratory, the common dormitory—wherein he might dwell the more safely, away from the tumult of the world. . . . He was a most fervent lover of the cloister and the monastic life.

The strength of Cluny became its weakness. For two centuries it had relied on the mighty men that ruled it—five outstanding abbots succeeded one another. In the fifty years that followed the death of Peter the Venerable there were no less than eight abbots, not one of them of the calibre of their predecessors. One of them, Hugh V (1199–1207), who had been prior of Lewes and abbot of Reading, was responsible for the first system of organization amongst the Cluniac foundations. Provinces were formed and provincial chapters set up, which appointed visitors to make visitations in all the houses. A general chapter was also introduced to meet periodically at Cluny, but the personal responsibility of the abbot of Cluny over all the monasteries was carefully maintained.

With the rise of Cîteaux during the twelfth century and the coming of the friars in the thirteenth, Cluny became less fashionable, less central. Her work for the reform of the Church was accomplished. But her continued existence demonstrates the continued demand for her way of life. As time went on, particularly in the fourteenth century, she lost hold of her dependent priories, which one after the other left her and gained their normal status of independence. All the English houses, after a succession of less able superiors, were denizened from 1351 onwards; the German and the Spanish houses followed suit. Cluny became and remained French. She did not however fall into decadence. Her monastic spirit remained good; whenever it appeared to decline, attempts were made to maintain it throughout the thirteenth and fourteenth centuries. Like all other Benedictine houses Cluny sent monks to the universities, and Abbot Yves I de Vergy (1257–75) founded the famous Collège de Cluny in Paris. She could always rely on the favour and protection of the French kings and the nobility.

In the fifteenth century there were serious attempts at reform. It was the age when the spirit of reform was in the air; in the Benedictine family such important movements as that initiated by Ludovico Barbo in Italy and John Dederoth in Germany inspired two abbots of Cluny, Odon de la Perrière (1423–56) and his successor Jean III de Bourbon (1456–85), to put their house in order. The latter was the last abbot to be elected by the community. After his death and up to the French Revolution the disastrous system of commendatory abbots obtained here as elsewhere, with its inevitable consequences for the life of the monastery and for its financial situation. Two of these commendatory abbots, however, must be mentioned: Richelieu (1635–42) and Mazarin (1654–61), both of whom took to heart the reform of Cluny. The ambitious scheme of the former to unite all the Benedictines in France under his authority failed completely, while Mazarin's attempt to get Cluny and the Congregation of St Maur to unite also broke down. The only outcome of all these efforts was the division of Cluny into two separate groups: the common observance and the strict observance. This solution was due to the wisdom of Dom Jacques de Veny d'Arbouze who, as prior, encouraged a number of his monks to follow a stricter observance (1621); after Richelieu's failure and death in 1642 they were established as a separate body with their own constitutions and superiors. Both observances henceforth lived side by side. The common observance dwindled considerably and was suppressed by Louis XVI and Pope Pius VI in 1788; the strict observance lasted until the Revolution. Its last superior general, Dom Courtin de Neubourg, and two of his monks died at the guillotine on 29 March 1794 for their faith.

The history of the abbey came to an end in 1790. Its commendatory abbot Dominique de la Rochefoucauld, Cardinal Archbishop of Rouen, did nothing to protect it. The inhabitants of the town failed in their attempts to keep the noble church for their spiritual needs or to preserve the monastic buildings. The last Mass was celebrated in the empty monastery on 25 October 1793, after which the place was pillaged and its furniture sold by auction. Passing that way years later, Napoleon refused to visit the town that perpetrated such vandalism. Fortunately, the noble and beautiful tower and transept still remind us of Cluny's one time grandeur and send our thoughts back to its days of prosperity and sanctity.

It would certainly be unjust and ungracious of us to take leave of Cluny in the day of its misfortune. Let us return to it when it was still a flourishing community after the time of Peter the Venerable in the second half of the twelfth century. To the abiding value of its monastic ideal and its way of life at that time we could scarcely find a more impartial or more appreciative witness than the Carthusian monk-bishop St Hugh of Lincoln. His biographer Adam tells us that, after the Carthusians, the monks of Cluny were the dearest to him because they cultivated the silent life of the cloister—*silentia claustri*—and turned their busy leisure—*otium negotiosum*—to spiritual profit. When in old age he visited Cluny in 1200, he was struck by the good order that reigned there in the choir, in the cloister and in the refectory. He was admitted to share their life in community for three days and to celebrate Mass, and before he left he said to the abbot: 'Truly, if I had seen this place before I fell in love with the Carthusians, I should have become a monk of Cluny.'

by Dom Joseph Warrilow

BIBLIOGRAPHY

K. J. Conant, *Cluny: Les Églises et la Maison du Chef d'Ordre* (Mâcon 1968).

G. Constable, *The Letters of Peter the Venerable*, 2 vols. (Cambridge, Massachusetts 1967).

H. E. J. Cowdrey, *The Cluniacs and the Gregorian Reform* (Oxford 1970).

J. Evans, *Monastic Life at Cluny 910–1157* (Oxford 1931).
The Romanesque Architecture of the Order of Cluny (Cambridge 1938).
Cluniac Art of the Romanesque Period (Cambridge 1950).

R. Graham, *English Ecclesiastical Studies* (London 1929).

N. Hunt, *Cluny under Saint Hugh 1049–1109* (London 1967).
Cluniac Monasticism in the Central Middle Ages (London 1971).

G. Sitwell O.S.B., *St Odo of Cluny* (London and New York 1958).

D. L. Douie and D. H. Farmer, *The Life of St Hugh of Lincoln* (London 1961–2).

Dom J. Leclercq, *Pierre le Vénérable* (Fontenelle 1946)
'Pour une histoire de la vie à Cluny,' *Revue d'Histoire Ecclésiastique* lvii (1962), 385–408 and 783–812.

Dom J. Hourlier, *Saint Odilon, abbé de Cluny* (Louvain 1964).

St Dunstan and the Monastic Reform

Dunstan was born in about the year 909 at Baltonsborough near Glastonbury, in the heart of a Wessex still recovering from a long and bloody war against the Danes. Only thirty years before, King Alfred had emerged from his fenland retreat at Athelney and inflicted a severe defeat on the Danes at Edington, the decisive turning point in the struggle. By the time Dunstan was born, Wessex had been made secure, and in 910 Alfred's son, Edward the Elder, beat the Danes again at Tettenhall in Staffordshire and began the rapid reconquest of the Midlands kingdom of Mercia. Dunstan was a boy when the English and the Danes settled to peaceful coexistence, with Wessex incorporating the kingdom of Mercia, and the Vikings independent in the North in their Danelaw. His childhood was thus set against the background of the re-assertion of the power of the royal house of Wessex, and with it the prosperity of the Christian Church. He was born into a noble family, related to many of the leaders of the political and religious restoration, and a kinsman of the king, and marked out himself at an early age for the ecclesiastical life when he was sent to Glastonbury for his education.

Earldormen and bishops, priests and thanes worked together to repair the damage brought by the wars. The Church had declined badly during those years, partly through plunder and killing but largely through neglect amid the turmoil and uncertainty of the Viking invasion. Alfred described the state of the Church as he found it on his accession in his introduction to the Anglo-Saxon translation of St Gregory the Great's *Pastoral Care* written more than twenty years afterwards:

> there were very few on this side of the Humber who could understand their [Latin] service books in English, or even translate a message from Latin into English, and not many, I think, beyond the Humber. So few there were that I cannot call to mind even one person south of the Thames when I came to the throne. . . . When I thought on this, I thought also of what I once had seen, the churches throughout all England standing full of treasures and books, before all was ravaged and burnt down.

Perhaps Alfred exaggerated this sorry condition of learning to heighten his own work in encouraging scholarship, English writing and monastic life. He certainly had to call on men from beyond the borders of Wessex to lead the revival, and the monastery he founded at Athelney to commemorate his own darkest hour had a monk from Germany, John of Saxony, as its abbot. Yet it never flourished, perhaps because it was so inaccessible in the fens. His son, Edward, was more successful, founding two new monasteries at Winchester, the New Minster for men and the Nunnaminster for women, and subdividing the two Wessex dioceses of Winchester and Sherborne by creating three more, Ramsbury, Wells and Crediton. Dunstan's uncle, Athelm, was the first bishop of Wells, appointed in the year of Dunstan's birth, and later archbishop of Canterbury.

At Glastonbury, Dunstan showed himself a devout and quick-witted boy. One strange episode is recorded of those years, when delirious with fever he climbed up onto the church roof, and having got down again safely, fell asleep between two sleeping keepers in the church. It seemed that he had been divinely protected from danger, and his parents decided to dedicate him to God in the monastery. In about 923, at the age of about fourteen, he was ton-sured and embarked upon his ecclesiastical studies. He read widely among the books that were available to him, and studied with Irish pilgrims who came to Glastonbury because of its associations with St Patrick. He became skilled also in writing, painting and music. His harp was said to play itself, as he was so dexterous on the instru-ment. But his life there was different from the monastic life develop-ing on the Continent at the same time. In 910, the monastery at Cluny was founded which was to have a profound effect on monastic-ism throughout Europe. It set a pattern of liturgical life and common observance, more demanding even than that prescribed in the Rule of St Benedict. Society was seen as threefold: the military men, who fought for the rest; the peasants, who worked for the rest; and the monks, who prayed for the rest. The monks at Cluny gave a great part of the day to singing the Divine Office for the living and the dead, and soon became the centre of a network of lay involvement, with men in the world associating themselves, by giving alms and visiting the monastery, with the prayers of the monks. The Cluniac style of monasticism, with its magnificent churches and its elabora-tion of the liturgy, was mirrored in other reform movements: in Germany at Gorze; in Flanders at the monasteries reformed by Gerard of Brogne; in France at Fleury; and in England in the houses founded and reformed by Dunstan and his companions.

Monasticism was not an important influence in the Saxon Church at the beginning of the tenth century. It was rivalled by the shared life of canons set out in the Rule of Chrodegang of Metz, priests who worked and lived together but kept their own property and even at times dwelt apart in their own houses. Chrodegang had lived in the eighth century, and his Rule had been prescribed by Charlemagne as compulsory on all clerics living together unless they were monks under the Rule of St Benedict. It had been translated into Anglo-Saxon, and it seems that many houses where Benedict's Rule had once been followed had accepted instead a life similar to that described by Chrodegang. Asser, a Welshman made bishop of Sherborne by Alfred the Great, wrote in his life of the king:

> Now for many years past the desire for monastic life has been utterly lost to all this people, and also to many other peoples. Many monasteries, it is true, still remain standing. Yet no one keeps in due order the Rule of monastic life, and I know not why. Perhaps the cause lies in these raidings by men of foreign race, who very often make assault by land and by sea, perhaps in the super-abundance of wealth of every kind in England.

Dunstan entered Glastonbury, perhaps one of the very few centres of monastic life still preserving the old tradition in England, and known as 'the royal island', at about the same time as his uncle Athelm was translated from Wells to Canterbury. Dunstan soon joined Athelm's household, and from there became a member of the king's court. In 924, Edward died and was succeeded by his son Athelstan, whose fifteen-year reign marked the apogee of the work of restoration. The court was international; Athelstan married off sisters to the duke of the Franks, to the king of Burgundy, to Otto the future Emperor of Germany, and to the Viking king of York. He was attended by several exiles, among them Louis d'Outremer, later king of France, Alan of Brittany and Haakon of Norway. He received kings from Scotland and Wales paying him homage. He destroyed the Viking kingdom of York and absorbed Cornwall into Wessex. He styled himself 'Basileus', the Byzantine title for king, of England. Among the prominent ecclesiastics at the court, Dunstan knew Aelfheah the Bald, a monk, perhaps of Glastonbury, to whom he was related and who became bishop of Winchester in 934, the same year that another of his relatives, Cynesige, was made bishop of Lichfield.

With his intelligence and his learning, and his skills in music and art, and with his influential connections, he seemed ideally suited to a career at court. But he was far from popular with his contemporaries. Perhaps they envied his easy accomplishments, and he was accused of 'studying the vain poems and futile stories of the pagans and of being a magician'. He was expelled from the court, but their ill-feeling was so strong that a group of them waylaid him, tied him up and threw him into a bog. Beaten and bruised, dirty and humiliated, he made his way to a friend's house where he was set upon by the dogs until they recognized his voice.

This failure led him to despair of any future in the clerical life and he began to think of marriage, but a severe illness provoked a crisis. He asked his kinsman, Bishop Aelfheah of Winchester, to visit him, and took monastic vows. He was then ordained by the bishop in company with another young courtier who was to become a life-long friend, Ethelwold, and another man called Athelstan who later abandoned the monastic habit and remained an apostate to the end. Dunstan now retired to Glastonbury, where he devoted himself to music and art and a life of seclusion, but did not entirely lose contact with the royal family, as he certainly visited and ministered to the king's niece, Ethelfleda, to whom he was related.

In 939, King Athelstan died and was succeeded by Edmund, who brought Dunstan back to court and made him a councillor. Once more he became a figure of controversy, and though he tried to live a life of prayer in private as well as that of an adviser to the king in public, his time at court was brief. His enemies once more secured his fall, and he retired into obscurity. But shortly after, the king was hunting near Cheddar Gorge, in hot pursuit of a stag that threw itself over the cliff followed by the hounds. The king's horse was galloping wildly towards the edge, and Edmund momentarily repented of his act of injustice to Dunstan. The horse brought its rider at that point to an abrupt stop, on the brink of the precipice. The king rode back to the court at Cheddar, and summoning Dunstan took him at once to Glastonbury, where he set him upon the throne as abbot.

Perhaps this fulfilled the private hopes of Dunstan. It certainly salved the king's conscience while avoiding any further rows at court. It was this event, in the year 940, that marked the beginning in a new phase in English monastic history. Dunstan affirmed the Rule of St Benedict at Glastonbury and set a standard of observance that had not been seen in England for generations. He made his own brother, Wulfric, the procurator to administer the business affairs of the house to ensure that no one else would have to travel about. He was joined at Glastonbury by Ethelwold, who threw himself into monastic studies, the scriptures, and also metrics and grammar, and devoted himself to prayer, fasting and vigils. He was a man of severe temperament, only a little younger than Dunstan himself, but he accepted the new abbot as his mentor and guide.

Glastonbury benefited from royal patronage. After Edmund's assassination in 946 and his burial at Glastonbury, his brother Edred who succeeded him kept the royal treasure there. When Ethelwold asked to go abroad to study at a Continental house and imbibe something of the spirit of the reform movement, Edred chose instead to give him a derelict monastery at Abingdon, on the advice of his mother, Queen Eadgifu. Ethelwold thus established the second monastery in England following the Rule of St Benedict strictly in about 954, taking with him three monks from Glastonbury, Osgar, Foldbricht and Frithegar, a clerk from Winchester called Ordbricht and one from London called Eadric. He sent Osgar to Fleury in France to complete the studies he could not embark upon directly, and received at Abingdon monks from Corbie skilled in chant. The king endowed the original forty hides of land with 100 more, and was clearly impressed by Ethelwold's energy and dedication. New buildings were planned and the king came over every day to observe the progress. The monks built the new monastery themselves, and typically Ethelwold threw himself into the work until he fell off the scaffolding and broke his ribs.

Dunstan was equally highly regarded. When Edred died in 955, he left £200 in his will to Dunstan to care for the people of Somerset and Devon. He too was buried at Glastonbury. The abbot of Glastonbury was invited to the coronation of the new king, Edmund's son Edwy, who was still only a youth, and he must have seemed in the eyes of many one of the most imposing figures present. Young Edwy disgraced himself by abandoning the banquet to enjoy the company of a girl whom he was shortly to marry and her mother in a neighbouring room. The archbishop of Canterbury, Oda, a man of Danish family who had been one of the leading advisers of King Athelstan and had become a monk at Fleury at about the same time that he was appointed archbishop, about 942, asked Dunstan and his kinsman, Bishop Cynesige of Lichfield, to bring Edwy back. They followed him to the room where he was sitting between the two ladies, his crown thrown on the floor. Dunstan picked up the crown and pushed it back on his head, and taking him by the arm led him back to the banquet. Of course, neither the king nor the ladies could forgive Dunstan this insult, and he soon found himself for the third time in disgrace, and now forced into exile abroad.

Dunstan went to Ghent, and stayed at the monastery recently reformed there by Gerard de Brogne dedicated to St Peter. For about a year, he lived the Rule of St Benedict in the atmosphere of austerity and full liturgical worship created there in imitation of the German reform at Gorze. In 957, a revolt in Mercia against young Edwy made his brother Edgar king of all England north of the Thames, and Dunstan was recalled. Edgar was still a youth, and had been trained by Ethelwold, and must have seemed a more attractive prospect to the thanes of Mercia than Edwy. Dunstan was at once made bishop of Worcester, and then of London, and in 960 when

Edwy had died and England was once again united, Dunstan was made archbishop of Canterbury.

Thus, twenty years after becoming abbot of Glastonbury and beginning the long process of reviving English monasticism, Dunstan was made archbishop and given the chance to forward the cause of Church reform. On his recommendation, Edgar chose Oswald, a young man of Danish family and related to Archbishop Oda of Canterbury and Oskytel of York, who had become a monk at Fleury after being a canon at Winchester, to succeed him at Worcester. In 963, Ethelwold was made bishop of Winchester. The next twelve years in Edgar's reign were a time of rapid monastic expansion.

Ethelwold was the most vigorous in his determination to make the English church more monastic. The secular clerks of his cathedral did not share his enthusiasm, and the *Chronicle* of Abingdon condemned their lives in colourful terms:

> At that time, there were in the Old Minster, the seat of the bishop, clerks of bad habits, so given over to pride, arrogance and self-indulgence, that some of them even refused to take their share in the celebration of Masses. They broke the law by marrying and then cast off their wives for other women. They were given over to a constant round of gluttony and drunkenness.

These three areas for criticism, their liturgical indifference, their comfortable life and their taking wives, reflect three of the central issues underlying the reform: the re-assertion of celibacy and austerity of life; of communal living rather than living in separate families; and of the supreme importance of liturgical worship. The clerks were dismissed, and replaced by monks in the year after Ethelwold's consecration as bishop, but accounts vary as to whether it was Edgar directly or Ethelwold who expelled them. The most dramatic, that of Aelfric, describes Ethelwold leading a small group of monks brought from Abingdon by Osgar with a royal official called Wulfstan into the cathedral at the end of Mass on the eve of the first Sunday in Lent, confronting the assembled clerks and offering them the alternative of either vacating their stalls or becoming monks. Three eventually chose to join the new community, the others were dispossessed.

Encouraged by this success, Ethelwold proceeded to reform the other two houses in Winchester, the New Minster and the Nunnaminster, pulling down the houses of people who lived nearby to make them more secluded, and imposing a stricter observance of the Rule. He probably reformed the monasteries at Chertsey and Milton also, sending one of the first five monks at Abingdon, Ordbricht of Winchester, as abbot of Chertsey. He purchased property at Medehampstead later known as Peterborough, at Ely and at Thorney, where he established new communities, building a church at Thorney with an apse at each end.

Ethelwold was also a tireless builder, rebuilding the cathedral at Winchester and introducing an enormous organ with 400 pipes and thirty-six bellows. The monks often worked alongside the builders. It all reflected his energy and temperament. He travelled around the religious houses he had founded, as Aelfric described him,

> establishing good usages by admonishing the obedient and correcting the foolish with rods. He was terrible as a lion to the disobedient or undisciplined, but gentler than a dove to the gentle and humble. He was a father of the monks and nuns, a comforter of widows and a restorer of the poor, a defender of churches, and a corrector of those going astray.

Of less ferocious character, but equally successful, Oswald also laboured to introduce monasticism into his diocese. On becoming bishop of Worcester, he chose a monk whom he had known at Fleury, an Englishman called Germanus of Winchester, to be first abbot of a new foundation at Westbury on Trym. He introduced monks to the cathedral at Worcester according to a later tradition in 969, but did so with far less distress than Ethelwold had provoked at Winchester. In 971, he founded a monastery at Ramsey and in 985 asked one of the foremost scholars of Fleury, Abbo, to become its abbot. Abbo ruled there for two years before returning to become abbot of Fleury. Later he was killed tragically in a brawl between the monks and servants at a monastery he was visiting in 1004. Between 972 and 975, Oswald founded monasteries at Evesham and Pershore, appointing Frithegar and Foldbricht as their abbots, two of the original five monks that Ethelwold had taken to Abingdon twenty years before.

In all this, Dunstan seems to have been overshadowed. Later tradition attributed to him the foundation of five monasteries, including Malmesbury and Westminster. In the earliest anonymous life of Dunstan, there are references to his having had monks with him at Canterbury in company with the secular clerks, but they seem to have been only a few attendants. He did not emulate the precedent of Ethelwold, and perhaps that of Oswald, in introducing monks to the cathedral and making its worship and government monastic. That was left to a later generation. Yet the anonymous life does describe him 'going about the country visiting the monasteries in his care', and he clearly retained some influence, if not direct authority at Glastonbury, for when he visited Bath the provost of the abbey came out to see him and ask his advice. It seems that Dunstan assumed the role of a rock of stability, rather than an active force in introducing monasteries all over southern England. Authors always alluded to his monumental qualities. To Adelard, he was the magnificent man, the pillar of God, an unshakeable mountain. To Aelfric, in his life of Ethelwold, Dunstan

> was made archbishop and remained in Kent for thirty-seven years like an immovable pillar, pre-eminent in doctrine, almsgiving and prophecy.

In the anonymous life of Oswald, he is described as the glory of all his country, and to Abbo of Fleury, he was a man exceedingly well loved, supreme in holiness. In the earliest life of Dunstan, he is four times called constant, resolute. Clearly, he struck those who lived in the shadow of his memory very differently from those who had known him as a young man, unpopular, uncertain of his future, experimenting with a new form of life little known and perhaps little appreciated.

Dunstan was not only a great churchman, but also young Edgar's principal adviser. He watched the king rise to maturity and follow a vigorous policy, ensuring peace in the Danelaw, purging the country of brigands, ravaging Thanet in 969 to flush them out, introducing a new system of coinage based on a series of mints producing pennies each stamped with its own device, building up the kingdom's security against naval attack with a stronger fleet. In an Anglo-Saxon vernacular account of the establishment of the monasteries often attributed to the pen of Ethelwold, Edgar was described as

> availing himself continually of the counsel of his archbishop, Dunstan; through his admonition he constantly inquired about the state of his soul, and not that only, but likewise about all the welfare and religion of his dominion.

He seems to have played a large part in the legislation of the reign, notably the code promulgated at Wihtbordestan in about 963, which asserted the rights of the Church along with those of the king, and a system of open witnessing and neighbourliness to ensure that no one could steal something and claim that it was his property.

Perhaps nothing testifies to Dunstan's strength and towering personality more than that he was taken by Ethelwold as his spiritual mentor. Long after Ethelwold had become a bishop, a zealous reformer feared for his severities towards himself as much as towards others; Dunstan was the only man whose advice he would take to relax his fasting for the sake of his health. Once more, Dunstan assumes a tone of calm assurance that contrasts with the extremism of Ethelwold's character. Dunstan had learned a great deal through his bitter experience of rejection. Three times he had been disgraced and fallen from positions of security and influence, and each time he had returned with greater knowledge and greater integrity. But he suffered from uninspired biographers, unlike Ethelwold, and perhaps also from his monumental character. We cannot see now why men either loved him or hated him. He aroused the most violent antagonism, and also the deepest affection. But his biographers can give us no insight, no real feeling of his personality. He left no writings, nothing by which he might be judged, save perhaps a small picture of himself prostrate at the feet of Christ believed to be a self-portrait. In a simple monk's habit, with a tonsure, in a gesture of supplication, the figure is tiny beside Christ enthroned significantly not in majesty, but as the beardless philosopher, holding a rod, the incarnation of holy wisdom.

By 970, the progress of the reform was sufficiently marked for its leaders to gather and lay down some principles by which the English monasteries were to live. It sprang from such varied sources: the traditions of Glastonbury, the enthusiasm and example of many churchmen and the practice and inspiration of several different reformed monasteries on the Continent. A council was summoned to meet at Winchester, and drew up the basic customary, the guide to monastic daily life expanding and explaining the Rule, known as *Regularis Concordia*. It is a short Latin document, one of a family of customaries produced in the tenth century reflecting the new reformist spirit. There, if anywhere, the philosophy underlying the reform will be found.

The preface stresses the role of the king as the patron of the new monasteries. Having chased out the negligent clerks, like the Good Shepherd he cares for his sheep, and the synod has been called because the monasteries are not united in their observance. Monks from Fleury and Ghent have been invited to attend, along with the abbots and abbesses of England. They are all enjoined to pray for the king 'by whose bounty, under Christ, we are maintained,' and it recognizes his advisory and consultative role in abbatial and episcopal elections. It is stressed that his protection saves monasteries from the inroads of secular lords. The epilogue is also concerned with property, stressing that abbots and abbesses should not amass private fortunes and alienate monastic property.

The first chapter sets a general outline of the monk's life from the moment he wakes until he goes to bed at night. As in the Rule of St Benedict and many other early rules, it selects appropriate texts from the scriptures to accompany the actions of the day. As soon as he wakes, the monk makes the sign of the cross and says 'Lord open my lips', and then the whole of Psalm 69, which begins with 'O God come to my assistance'. This is before attending to the necessities of nature. He then goes down to choir, saying Psalm 24 on the way, which begins 'To Thee, O Lord, I lift up my soul', and when he has arrived he says the seven penitential psalms while everyone is assembling, together with the Our Father and three collects. The community then all say the fifteen gradual psalms together, and then at last they begin Matins. This is all in the middle of the night, and far from the experience of most modern monks, but it reflected the spirituality that they shared in common with St Benedict, the sanctification of the ordinary actions of the day by small acts of devotion. Thus from the moment the monk wakes until he goes to bed at night, when they are sprinkled with holy water in the dormitories, the day is full of specified acts of devotion intended to bring the mind always to a state of recollection.

The next few chapters take the reader on a breathless sweep through the day's and then through the year's cycle of liturgy. Having recited Matins and Lauds for the day in the middle of the night, they then sing the Matins Office for the feast of All Saints, and then Lauds of the Office for the dead, before they reach Prime. They have two Masses, a morrow Mass when all are enjoined to communicate, a unique English prescription at this time, and then the Conventual Mass sung with great splendour. The rest of the day is punctuated by the little Offices of Terce, Sext and None. Then in the evening, they sing Vespers of the day, followed by Vespers of All Saints, followed by Vespers from the Office for the dead. This great weight of liturgical prayer, filling the larger part of the waking hours of the day and rivalling the liturgical observance of Cluny, was supplemented by even more psalms and prayers for the king and the royal family.

The description of the seasonal liturgy contains much colour and drama. For example, on Good Friday, the deacons are instructed to strip the altar like thieves. After the veneration of the Cross it was placed in a sepulchre constructed in the church. Here, at the third lesson of Easter Sunday Matins, one monk shall sit wearing an alb and holding a palm, and three others, vested in copes and holding thuribles approach the tomb, as though searching for something, in imitation of the women coming to anoint the body of Jesus. A series of versicles and responses are then sung, by way of conversation, which leads into the Easter proclamation and the *Te Deum*.

Thus the *Regularis Concordia* is for the most part a ritual, a ceremonial, laying out the way that the office will be performed at different times and seasons. But it also includes other detailed regulations. For example, money is to be given at the gate of the monastery daily to the poor, 'in whom Christ shall be adored who is received in them' and the abbot is enjoined in particular to be attentive to

Plate I: Marian chapel in Norman crypt of Minster Abbey (Thanet):
founded 670, destroyed 840, revived 1027, dissolved 1538, refounded 1937.

Plate II: Blessed Sacrament chapel, Worth Abbey (Sussex).

this duty. The sick are to be taken Holy Communion each day, but not merely by an individual priest, but by the whole community in procession. 'If the sickness improves, the visiting shall be discontinued, but if not, it shall be kept up until the death of that brother': an order that perhaps encouraged many to recover quickly simply to escape the daily liturgical sollicitations of the entire community.

The emphasis throughout is upon adherence to custom, to established rituals. Holiness in such a life is the holiness of patience, of perseverance, of acceptance and self-effacement. But the text is also conscious of the difficulties of enduring such a demanding routine. In common with many monasteries, notably Cluny, an official is designated, the circa, who tours the cloister to ensure that the brethren are properly employed, and is equipped at night with a lantern to ensure that no one falls asleep in choir during Matins. The Rule of St Benedict is endowed with a significance almost equal to that of divine revelation. The monks are told to keep it strictly,

> lest by careless neglect of the smallest precept of the Rule a monk becomes guilty as the apostle says of all the commandments, which God forbid.

Regularis Concordia stresses the role of the king as the patron and protector of English monasticism. Perhaps it was written by Ethelwold and Dunstan. It certainly took its inspiration from the Continental reform, rather than some royal passion for order and discipline. In its detailed regulations, it went far beyond anything known to secular Saxon society. But the fortunes of the reform had entirely reflected the interest and enthusiasm of different kings. Dunstan and Ethelwold had been brought up at court, and both owed their first abbacies to royal favour. It was the enduring support of Edgar that gave them their chance to develop monasticism in England as it was found abroad. The monks were enjoined regularly to pray for the king. The monasteries were centres of support for royal authority, nowhere more obviously so than in Winchester where the royal palace was adjacent to the two minsters.

The distribution of monasteries forms a pattern, especially along the Severn valley and the edge of the Danelaw, areas where the royal writ needed to be strengthened by powerful local landowning interests. Both Edred and Edwy had given land to bishops on long leases to protect them from intrusion or influence by laymen, the bane of monasticism, and it had become the custom on the Continent to ensure the independence of monasteries by granting them financial security and either royal or papal protection. In England, this was taken to exceptional lengths. The monasteries were not merely protected and their autonomy guaranteed by the king. They became

6

part of the system of government. They were given authority over local government as well as extensive lands. For example, Ethelwold received the lordship over the hundreds of Chilcomb in Hampshire, Downton in Wiltshire and Taunton in Somerset, and he took the market tolls and burgage rents of Taunton, the earliest example of a borough not in the direct hands of the king. Oswald received the three hundreds of Oswaldslow, excluding the power of the Earl-dorman of Mercia and his deputies. The only monastery that was not near the border of the kingdom, apart from Glastonbury and Winchester, was Abingdon, and this was most richly endowed by Edgar with 600 hides of land.

This was the culmination of a long process of the re-assertion of royal power begun by Alfred the Great. The Church had played a major role in the restoration of English society, and now Edgar had accepted the monasteries as a valuable asset in his attempt to unite and pacify the realm under his government. Monasteries were also an excellent way of taming the Church. Where secular clerks might alienate the property of churches and cathedrals and assert some kind of family claim to them, especially as marriage and concubinage were rife among them, monks by contrast were a corporation of men vowed to personal poverty. Thus the monastic cathedrals flourished, Winchester and possibly Worcester in Edgar's reign, Canterbury and Sherborne later in the tenth century.

But Edgar did not pursue this policy of lavish endowment simply for hard political reasons. He believed firmly that God's worship and devotion demanded respect. His laws, framed jointly with Dunstan, echo repeatedly the view that men must pay their tithe and other church taxes out of respect for God, as His due. Pestilence was regarded as the penalty for withholding God's tribute, but just as a secular landlord will forgive if the tenant who has not paid his rent is penitent, so the Almighty also will forgive, or else men risk 'either sudden death in the present life or indeed the future death in everlasting hell for any withholding God's dues'. It was exactly the same attitude that inspired the monks to give so much of their day to prayer in church, and especially intercessory prayer for the living and the dead. They were the part of society who prayed for the rest, and the others had an obligation to God to support them. When the monks came under attack after Edgar's death, many distinguished laymen supported the monks, and the anonymous life of Oswald quotes the arguments used by one of them, Aelfwold, to maintain his position:

If my life is preserved unharmed by Christ, I wish to preserve the things that are mine, and give them willingly to whoever pleases me and is obedient to my authority. If indeed Christ is prince of all things, shall he not have the portion which religious men gave to Him for the redemption of their souls, but be driven far from us? How can we guard our own without His great help? By Him who caused me to be re-born, I may not tolerate that such men be ejected from our territories, by whose prayers we can be snatched from our enemies.

In zeal for endowing the Church, there could be nothing more appropriate than giving lavishly to monasteries whose express purpose was intercession. Edgar was not the only layman to have profound respect for the monks. He had the Rule of St Benedict translated into Anglo-Saxon to imbibe its wisdom.

Yet Edgar, as a young man, was far from saintly in his private life. In Goscelin's life of Wulfhilda, abbess of Barking, he is depicted trying without great subtlety to seduce a nun at Wilton. It was perhaps his immoral living that caused his anointing as king to be delayed until 973, the year after Oswald's visit to Rome to receive the pallium as archbishop of York, a see he held in plurality with Worcester. But with the anointing, Edgar was taken up beyond the ranks of ordinary men, and the unity of priest and king was closer than ever.

Edgar's death in 975 of course provoked a reaction. The Earldorman of Mercia, Aelfhere, had been the man most affected by Edgar's scheme for enriching monasteries and putting local government in their hands, creating a ring of royalist centres around his own strongholds. At once he evicted the monks from Evesham and distributed their land; he also closed houses at Winchcombe and Deerhurst. The nobility was divided, but it is an indication of the strength of the monasteries that they weathered not only the storm in Mercia, but also the collapse of Dunstan's hopes when Edgar's heir and his young protégé, Edward, was killed at Corfe three years after succeeding to the throne in 978. The accession of Ethelred, known to later writers as the unready, a false translation of the ill-advised, or the king without advisers, marked the decline in Dunstan's power at court.

Though Edgar had personally done so much for the reform, it had shown that it could survive without him, even against considerable hostility from one of the most powerful men in the realm. The revival of monasticism was not merely a political tactic, but responded to genuine spiritual needs and entirely suited the outlook of early medieval society. It also inspired a great revival in art and music, notably at Winchester. The illumination of manuscripts there soon surpassed the best Continental scriptoria, and the Benedictional of St Ethelwold, produced for him probably some time after 971, is one of the most lavish illuminated books from the tenth century. This art of painting and drawing, closely connected with the interests and skills of Dunstan himself, was matched by an extremely high standard in metalwork and sculpture, especially carving in ivory.

Winchester too was the home of vernacular writing. Aelfric had been a pupil there of Ethelwold's, and later became abbot of Eynsham. He wrote sermons for parish clergy, lives of saints and translations from scripture. Oswald showed some interest in scholarship, encouraging Abbo of Fleury to settle at Ramsey, where his immense learning contributed to the later work of Byrhtferth in studies of calendars and chronology both in Latin and English. He also granted a three-life lease of Bredicot near Worcester to the priest Godingc on condition that he produced the manuscripts needed by the cathedral. But the standard of learning in most of the cloisters was not high. The libraries were old fashioned and ill equipped. The Latinity of many of the monks was poor, as can be seen from the mistakes they made in manuscript copying, betraying an inadequate familiarity with the language. The monasteries were more important for their pastoral and artistic influence than as homes of scholarship. As they were not founded upon a scholarly tradition of learning, but derived from the needs and hopes of many people, laymen as well as monks, this was not surprising.

As they were great centres of liturgy, it is also not surprising that they did much to develop early polyphonic music. The Winchester Troper is the first book of English polyphony. Plainchant was already giving way to more elaborate forms of music, and the huge organ that Ethelwold installed at Winchester was a sign of the mood of the age.

Nothing presents so convincing an indication of the importance of the monastic revival in the Church and society of the late tenth century than that the monasteries should have provided nearly nine-tenths of the bishops in all English sees until the accession of Edward the Confessor in 1042, and though they supplied fewer men during his reign, three-quarters of the bishops until the Conquest overall had been monks. The monastic revival was the foundation of the influence of the Black monks following the Rule of St Benedict in the English Church even after the Norman Conquest. The four cathedrals that the Normans found in the hands of monks, a unique English institution whereby the monks sang their Office in the cathedral and acted as its chapter, electing the bishop, with their prior as the dean, were supplemented by five more, Norwich, Durham, Coventry, Rochester and later Ely. It was the beginning of six hundred years of uninterrupted monastic life in those houses that grew to be some of the largest and richest monasteries in Europe, and beyond that of a tradition of monastic life even after the Reformation. The first printed edition of *Regularis Concordia* was that of Dom Clement Reyner, an English Benedictine, in his massive *Apostolatus Benedictinorum in Anglia* (Douay 1626), an historical vindication of the post-Reformation Benedictines' claim to inherit the rights and position of their medieval forbears.

At the heart of the reform were three great men, Dunstan, Ethelwold and Oswald. Ethelwold, the severest of the three, lived the Rule he had established at Winchester in its full austerity to the last, suffering greatly from illness but not abating his steady work and regular life. Aelfric depicts him in his last years never returning to bed after Matins, his old eyes squinting to catch the light from a candle, and once falling asleep over his book, and the page catching alight, but being caught in time before damage was done by another monk. He died worn out with his exertions in 984.

Four years later, still at the height of his powers and with his energy not lessened by age, Dunstan died. He preached three times on Ascension Day, 988, and two days later died in his eightieth year. Oswald was the last to die, also active until the end, administering his two dioceses. By 991, it had become clear that he might not survive the coming winter, and his farewells at Ramsey after his visitation there were more heartfelt than before. He spent the winter at Worcester, and began Lent in earnest as usual, washing the feet of twelve poor men each day. It was as he completed this task on the last day of February 922, reciting the Gradual psalms, that he died. But their passing did not mark the end of an era—it was a beginning.

by Dom Bernard Green

BIBLIOGRAPHY

W. Stubbs (ed.), *Memorials of Saint Dunstan* (Rolls Series 1874).

D. Whitelock (ed.), *English Historical Documents*, vol. I (London 1968), pp. 394–401, 826–43, 846–9.

T. Symons (ed.), *Regularis Concordia* (London 1953).

J. A. Robinson, *The Times of St Dunstan* (Oxford 1923).

E. S. Duckett, *St Dunstan of Canterbury* (London 1955).

E. John, *Orbis Britanniae and other Studies* (Leicester 1966).

D. Parsons (ed.), *Tenth-Century Studies* (London 1975).

D. H. Farmer, *The Oxford Dictionary of Saints* (Oxford 1978).

Lanfranc and St Anselm

Lanfranc and Anselm were both Benedictine monks, both Italians, both archbishops of Canterbury. Each of them was closely associated with Norman kings—Lanfranc amicably with William the Conqueror, Anselm controversially with both William Rufus and Henry I. Both of them for this reason have their place in the history books. Each of them not only built up the Church in this country between 1070 and 1109, but also was significant in the development of Church-State relations. Each represented different generations and different facets of the Gregorian Reform. These important aspects of their careers have been studied many times; here we are concerned rather with the interior, monastic life of each of these great monks.

In 1034 or thereabouts, a small group of men settled to lead a simple monastic life on land just north of Brionne in Normandy, mid-way between Lisieux and Rouen. Their leader, Herluin, was a former knight, a man of great strength and skill as a soldier, who had abandoned his career after twenty years in the service of the count of Brionne and resolved to dedicate himself to God. Attracted by the monastic way of life, he had visited several monasteries to learn more about it, but was so depressed by the low standards he encountered, self-centredness, affectation and even violence, that he would have turned away in despair were it not for one incident which his biographer, Gilbert Crispin, regarded as a miracle. He had stayed behind after the night Office, intending to pass the night in prayer in a secluded corner of the church. The other monks had left, apart from one who remained and stood nearby, and, unaware of Herluin's presence, continued in prayer until dawn, sometimes on his knees, sometimes prostrate, often with tears. That monk's prayer, as one scholar has observed, might be said to have changed the course of history. Inspired by this example Herluin returned north and with a few companions founded his community.

Others joined them but the community remained small, obscure and poor. Gilbert Crispin describes their life in these early days. 'When the Office was ended,' he wrote, 'you would see the abbot leading his monks out to work in the fields, with a bag of seed round his neck and a rake in his hand, or wielding a hoe, and remain busy in agricultural activities until the end of the day. Some would clear the land of briars and thornbushes, others would scatter manure, some would weed, others would sow the seed. None lingered over their food, and whenever it was time to say the Office all would meet in the Church again.' After a few years however, the inadequacy of the land, waterless and unproductive, compelled them to move to the meadows where a small tributary joined the river Risle, and from this rivulet, known only as the beck, the community took their name, *Le Bec*. Soon they were joined by one, who, like Herluin, had turned his back on a successful career when nearing middle age, and whose presence was to give a new significance to the name of Bec.

Lanfranc was an Italian. Born in Pavia, he had spent some years as a teacher of law, grammar and logic in his native town before moving north across the Alps. He had then settled in Normandy and taught for a while in Avranches where the fame he enjoyed attracted many students. But he had become dissatisfied with this life, and, challenged by Christ's words, 'If anyone wants to come after me, he should deny himself, take up his cross and follow me', he had decided to seek a life of solitude. Thus he made his way to Bec, believing there could be no other community so poor and insignificant. It happened that when he arrived, Abbot Herluin was at work on building an oven, and Lanfranc was so impressed, both by the humility of Herluin's behaviour and the dignity of his speech, that he chose without hesitation to stay.

At first, it seems, even the life at Bec was not austere enough for him and he considered leaving to become a hermit, but Herluin, perhaps understanding him better than he understood himself, dissuaded him from such an extreme measure. Soon, to help the impoverished community, he began to take pupils. News of his whereabouts spread and many of the most able young men came to study under him. In a short time Bec had become one of the intellectual centres of Europe.

Among Lanfranc's students were many, who, like the future pope Alexander II, were to play an influential part in the years to come, but none was so outstanding as the young Italian, Anselm, who came to Bec in 1059. Anselm had been born in the Alpine town of Aosta in 1033, only a year before Herluin founded his community. His mother, Ermenberga, a native of Aosta, whom he loved and admired, had died while he was still a youth and he was left with his father, Gundulf, an undisciplined man with whom he had little in common. Relations were strained and Anselm soon left home, making the difficult journey north across the Alps by way of Mont Cénis. It was Lanfranc's reputation as a scholar which drew him to Bec, and there he became an enthusiastic student, 'wearying his body with late nights, with cold and with hunger', as his biographer later wrote.

But Lanfranc's devotion as a monk was also to have a profound effect on him. He began to wonder whether he too should become a monk, or perhaps a hermit, or whether he should return to the estates he had inherited on his father's death and give what help he could to the poor. He asked Lanfranc's advice, but Lanfranc, understandably reluctant to take sole responsibility for this decision, took him to Archbishop Maurilius at Rouen. So great was Lanfranc's influence on him at this time, he later said, that had Lanfranc told him to stay in a wood through which they were journeying and never come out, he would have done so. The archbishop recommended the monastic life, a decision which must have pleased Lanfranc. But where should he make his profession? The scholar in Anselm was still strong. He feared that if he joined the famous monastery at Cluny, where an elaborate liturgy was well established, he would have little time for study. If, on the other hand, he joined the community at Bec, he would be overshadowed by the greatness of Lanfranc. He soon realized how wrong these thoughts were. 'Is this being a monk,' he said to himself, 'to desire to be set over others, to receive more honour and glory than others? Far from it. So put aside your rebelliousness and become a monk in that place where, rightly and for God's sake, you will be lowest of all.' And so he took the habit at Bec. This was probably in 1060.

Three years later Lanfranc left Bec, albeit reluctantly, to become abbot of the monastery of St Stephen's at Caen, newly founded by the powerful Duke William of Normandy, whose trusted adviser Lanfranc had already become. During the twenty years he had spent at Bec the community had grown, become established and ordered itself according to the Rule of St Benedict. Lanfranc himself had had an influential role in moulding the community and for many of those years he had been Abbot Herluin's right-hand man as prior. These same years had also seen a remarkable expansion of monasticism in Normandy. To the six monasteries already existing another twenty had been added and with the increase in numbers there had been a growth in the intellectual and the spiritual life alike. In this Bec had had its own distinctive part to play.

Lanfranc was to remain at Caen for only seven years. Events of great significance for the history of England were soon to take place and Lanfranc was to move even farther north. In 1066 Duke William became King of England and in 1070 he summoned Lanfranc to take an influential post in the English Church as archbishop of Canterbury.

If Lanfranc had left Bec for Caen with a certain reluctance, it was with even greater reluctance that he left Normandy for England. Nor did his first experiences change his attitude. A year or two after his arrival he wrote to his former pupil, Pope Alexander II, who had been instrumental in effecting the Conqueror's wish, begging to be released from his obligation. 'In vain did I plead my own incapacity, my ignorance of the language and of the barbarous people. . . . I gave my consent, I came, I took the burden upon me, and such are the unmitigated cares and troubles to which I am daily subjected . . . the meanness, the evil conduct I see around me, such the danger to which I see the Holy Church exposed, that I am weary of my life. . . . I entreat you, for God's sake and for the Lord's sake, since it was by your authority that I was involved in these difficulties, by the same authority to extricate me from them and permit me once more to return to the monastic life, which above all things I delight in.' Fortunately his wish was not granted.

When Lanfranc arrived in England, there already existed at Winchester, Worcester and Sherborne, an institution peculiar to England at this time, the cathedral-monastery. In these the monastic community acted as the cathedral chapter and the bishop as abbot. The early history of the community of Christchurch at Canterbury is obscure. A monastic community existed there from around 1000 though it had perhaps suffered more than others from the decline in monastic fervour during the reign of Edward the Confessor. Thus Lanfranc found himself in a position where he could combine his monastic commitment with his role as archbishop. The situation, however, must have seemed far from promising. Three years earlier the buildings had been badly burnt and now stood almost in ruins. Lanfranc's response to this was characteristic. 'Though the extent of the calamity drove him to despair,' wrote Eadmer, one of the Christchurch monks, in his *History of Recent Events in England,* 'he soon recovered himself and with firm determination, postponing all thought of providing for his own convenience, he set urgently to work and completed the building of dwellings needed for the use of the monks.' These first buildings soon proved too small and after a few years Lanfranc had them pulled down and replaced by ones which were larger and more impressive. Nothing now survives of these buildings save a few stones, but there can be no doubt that they would have been constructed in that style which had already become a characteristic of the monastic architecture of Normandy and which can still be seen in the church Lanfranc knew at Caen. Lanfranc also introduced a feature, which had become standard in Normandy, but which Eadmer notes as being the first of its kind in England, that of enclosing the various monastic buildings within a surrounding wall.

Such buildings, with their sense of spaciousness and orderliness, must have given the monks a new confidence and sense of purpose.

Buildings, however, though they may provide the scope for a richer monastic life, cannot of themselves create that life. With this in mind Lanfranc drew up a new set of constitutions for his monks. In writing these he showed again his determination to introduce at Christchurch all that he thought best in the monasticism on the Continent. He seems to have made no use of the constitutions already existing in England, the *Regularis Concordia*; nor was he content merely to introduce the customs he had known at Bec, which he had doubtless had some hand in creating and which he had introduced to the new monastery at Caen. Instead he selected what he felt to be best from a number of Continental customs, including those of Bec, but especially those written by a monk named Bernard for the monastery of Cluny, where the richest and most elaborate liturgy was practised. Yet he always kept the particular needs of Christchurch in mind and whenever necessary made the appropriate modifications and adaptations. 'We send you the customs of our monastic life,' he wrote to the prior and monks of Christchurch, 'which we have compiled from the customs of those monasteries which in our day have the greatest prestige in the monastic order. We have added a few details, and have made certain changes, particularly in the ceremonies of certain feasts, considering that they should be kept with greater solemnity in our church.'

A monastic customary was by tradition intended to be a liturgical directory and Lanfranc's is no exception. At least half of his work, following through the liturgical year in logical sequence, is devoted to detailed instructions for the correct procedures for the various feasts, such as the Maundy Thursday ritual of the washing of the feet of the poor, or the Palm Sunday procession through the streets of Canterbury, with the singing of the hymn, *All glory, laud and honour* . . . at one of the city gates (a custom which was not known at Cluny and seems to have been a tradition introduced from Poitiers). Other matters, such as discipline or the last rites, come in the second part of the work, apart from those, like the bath taken before Christmas and Easter, which are dealt with at the appropriate moment in the liturgical year.

One of the most interesting and best known of these passages is the one in which Lanfranc gives instructions for the annual distribution of books at the beginning of Lent, the time prescribed in the Rule of St Benedict. 'Before the brethren go in to chapter,' he wrote, 'the librarian should have all the books save those that were given out for reading the previous year collected on a carpet in the chapter-house; last year's books should be carried in by those who have had them, and they are to be warned by the librarian in the chapter the previous day of this. The passage from the Rule of St Benedict concerning the observance of Lent shall be read, and when a sermon has been made on this the librarian shall read out a list of books which the brethren had the previous year. When each hears his name read out he shall return the book which was given to him to read, and anyone who is conscious that he has not read in full the book he received shall confess his fault prostrate and ask for pardon. Then the aforesaid librarian shall give to each of the brethren another book to read. . . .'

Little is known about the library at Christchurch before Lanfranc's time. A few service-books and others survive, beautifully executed, which are known to have belonged there, also some collections of private devotional prayers. It is possible that the library was affected by the fire which caused so much damage in 1067. As a scholar Lanfranc was naturally anxious to see the library well stocked with reliable and useful texts, so that each monk could have at least the one book, the minimum prescribed for meditative reading during the year. In building up this library he turned for assistance to the Norman monasteries, particularly Bec, arranging to have copies made from the books in the libraries there. One of the works he purchased from Bec, a collection of canon-law, is now in the library of Trinity College, Cambridge, and contains the note, *Hunc librum dato precio emptum ego LANFRANCUS archiepiscopus de beccensi cenobio in anglicam terram deferri feci et ecclesie Christi dedi.* (I Lanfranc, the archbishop, have paid for this book, arranged for it to be brought from the monastery of Bec into England, and have given it to Christchurch.) It was not always easy to obtain the copies he wanted. On one occasion, at Lanfranc's request, his former pupil Anselm, who was by now abbot of Bec, engaged a scribe to copy the *Moralia* of St Gregory the Great. Anselm wrote to say that he was confident that the matter was now in hand, and that, as far as he knew, the scribe had started work, and added that he was also endeavouring to have copies made of the works by St Ambrose and St Jerome which Lanfranc wanted, but as yet had had no success. Later he wrote to say that things were not turning out as he had hoped in regard to the *Moralia*. There had been a disagreement with the scribe, and since none of the monks at Bec was in a position to produce the required copy, the abbot of St Stephen's had taken the Bec book to Caen and was going to look for a scribe there. Despite these difficulties Lanfranc built up a good collection of patristic texts at Christchurch, works of Augustine, Ambrose, Jerome and Gregory the Great, some of which still survive, books of fine quality written in a clear and regular script. Lanfranc also developed the scriptorium at Christchurch itself; by the end of his life copies were being produced there in a characteristic script which owed much to the influence of the manuscripts from Normandy.

One of the dangers of copying by hand is that any slip made by the scribe, either through carelessness or tiredness or misunderstanding what he is reading, will be copied by the next scribe and thus creep into the text. Lanfranc was anxious to eliminate as many errors of this kind as possible and by careful comparison of manuscripts to produce as accurate a text as he could. Two manuscripts which he worked on still survive in France with the words *Lanfrancus ego correxi* (I, Lanfranc, have corrected this); and though no such manuscript survives from Christchurch there is good reason to believe the words of the obituary notice which states that when Lanfranc came to Canterbury 'he bestowed upon that Church the special ornament of a valuable library, and many of the books which it contained were corrected with his own hand'. Lanfranc took measures to see that the library at Christchurch was well stocked, not so much with the secular works which would develop the monks' grasp of logic and grammar, as with the patristic texts which would deepen their understanding of their monastic commitment, and he was concerned to ensure that the texts made available for them were as reliable and accurate as possible.

In the wealth at his disposal as archbishop, in the elaborate liturgy he prescribed, in the books, buildings and vestments with which he endowed Christchurch, Lanfranc may seem to have strayed far from his early ideals, when even the harsh and simple life at Bec was not austere enough for him. Yet the daily life of the monk as envisaged in his Constitutions, in keeping with the spirit of the Rule, was a hard one, and there is no reason to believe that Lanfranc did not share in the life of his monks whenever possible. He was not a man for solitude but one who found his greatest fulfilment in contact with other men, as a teacher and a statesman, and above all in the life of the monastic community which he loved so much. He had high standards, a stern disposition and at times a sharp tongue; but he could be kind. Eadmer records one charming story which reveals the way the monks themselves best pictured him. It had been Lanfranc's practice to give one of the monks, perhaps Eadmer himself, thirty shillings each year to help support his mother, paid in instalments when she visited him. On one occasion, engrossed in conversation, she failed to notice the five shillings her son was slipping into her hand in a cloth and it fell to the ground, but this did not transpire until her next visit, when she asked why she had not received the money. The son was worried when he realized what had happened and afraid that Lanfranc would be angry with

him for his carelessness, but Lanfranc, who had in the meantime
come into the cloisters and sat there, as he often did, noticed how
upset the monk was when he came away from speaking with his
mother. He took him aside privately and asked what was wrong.
'On being told,' wrote Eadmer, 'with a look of the utmost kindness,
as was always his way in dealing with those in trouble, he said, "Is
that the cause of your distress, my dearest son? Why, God must
purposely have given that money to someone else whose need of it
was perhaps greater than your mother's. Keep quiet and take care
not to say a word about it to anyone. That what has happened may
not trouble you in the least, in place of those five shillings I will
have seven shillings given to you today for your mother." ' In this
Lanfranc was true to his own conception of the role of the abbot,
which he saw as symbolized in the Maundy Thursday ritual of the
washing of the feet. 'In this day's Office,' he said, in words which
are to be found in no monastic customary but his, 'if the abbot alone
can wash the feet of all the brethren, he should do so, for St Benedict
declares that he holds the place of Christ in the monastery, and this
is especially true of this service.'

Lanfranc's work of monastic reform extended beyond Christchurch through his policy of introducing Norman monks into
England. Though too critical an assessment of English monasticism
at the time of the Conquest would be unjustified, for some of the
monasteries, like Evesham under the saintly Abbot Aethelwig, still
had a high standard of monastic life, even the best of these had
grown out of touch with developments on the Continent. Lanfranc
was anxious to enlist men who could infuse the new monastic
vigour of Normandy into the monasteries of England. In this he
had the support of the king who, for his part, was anxious to secure
the loyalty of the monasteries, having been opposed by most of the
English abbots, and was able to make use of a royal prerogative
which already existed in England and entitled him to appoint an
abbot. Thus Normans were appointed to almost all the bishoprics
and abbacies in England, whenever a vacancy arose.

Lanfranc himself appointed Henry, a monk of Bec, to assist him
as prior of Christchurch and brought other monks from Bec as well.
His nephew, Paul, a monk of Caen, was appointed abbot of St
Albans. Serlo, a monk from Mont S. Michel, became abbot of
Gloucester. The appointment of men such as these sometimes
caused friction. Abbot Thurstan of Glastonbury, for instance, a
monk from Caen, is said to have been so enraged at his monks'
refusal to accept the customs he was imposing that he brought in
soldiers to enforce it, with the result that in the ensuing battle in
the church, in which the monks defended themselves with benches

and candlesticks against spears and arrows, several of the monks were killed or wounded. Thurstan's behaviour, however, was exceptional.

The majority of the Norman abbots, when appointed, followed the policy of Lanfranc at Christchurch, rebuilding in the Norman style, introducing the Norman customs they were familiar with, and raising the standard of the intellectual and spiritual life; and though they sometimes showed a tactless disregard for the cult of the English saints, they seem like Lanfranc to have won the love and respect of the monks in their charge. Typical of these was Ralph, a monk from Bec who was first prior of Rochester and later abbot of the monastery founded by William the Conqueror on the site of his victory, Battle Abbey. Of him the Battle Chronicler wrote:

> Vigilant as he was in his care for external matters, let it not be thought burdensome if we also relate how zealously he promoted the good of souls. . . . He always adapted himself to the characters of his monks and never gave them orders like a master. He bore with the weaker brethren, but encouraged them to more arduous efforts. He practised what he preached and lived as he taught. He told his monks to hasten to the Divine Office and would be in choir before others younger than himself, even when in old age he needed a stick for support.

When Lanfranc first came to England, he had felt he could achieve nothing, yet during his nineteen years as archbishop the numbers in his own community at Christchurch had risen to a hundred, partly through the introduction of monks from Normandy but chiefly through the new recruits it attracted. These developments at Christchurch were echoed in the monasteries throughout England. Though Lanfranc was less concerned to establish new monasteries than to encourage a revival in existing ones, he had also given his support to the foundation of two new cathedral-monasteries, Rochester and Durham. His Constitutions, though written primarily for Christchurch, in the hope that that community at the head of the see of Canterbury, would set the right example, were adopted by some of the other monasteries, such as St Albans and Rochester. The copy produced at Christchurch for the new community at Durham still survives. Lanfranc himself wrote nothing on the monastic life except his Constitutions, which may seem to concentrate on external matters, but his view of that life, expressed succinctly in the preface to the Constitutions, inspired both the *Octo Puncta* of Ralph, probably that same Ralph who became the beloved abbot of Battle, which takes the form of a commentary on eight aspects of the monastic life, and the writings of the Christchurch monk, Eadmer, which these same values underlie.

> What we have to consider with the greatest care [Lanfranc wrote] is that what is necessary for the soul's salvation should be safe-guarded in every way; faith, that is, and contempt of the world, together with charity, chastity, humility, patience, obedience, penance for faults committed and a humble confession of them; frequent prayers; silence in fitting measure; and many other things of this kind. Where these are preserved it may truly be said that the Rule of St Benedict and the monastic life are kept.

When he died on 24 May 1089, an old man, but one whose sharpness of mind had remained unimpaired to the last, he had indeed become, in the words of one of the monks of the rival community at St Augustine's, Canterbury, written fittingly not in Latin but English, *muneca fader & frouer* (the father and protector of monks).

Four years after Lanfranc's death his former pupil, Anselm, the most outstanding monk Bec had known, became the new archbishop of Canterbury. He was already sixty years old when he came to England. He had had a distinguished career at Bec, having become prior when Lanfranc vacated the post in 1063 and abbot when Herluin died in 1078. Unlike Lanfranc, to whom the customs and language of the English were unfamiliar when he first came, Anselm had long had contact with England, both through his continuing friendship with Lanfranc and the correspondence that passed between them, and through his links with the other monks who had come from Bec. He had visited England on at least one occasion when he came in 1079 to inspect the English lands belonging to Bec and spent some time at Christchurch.

The circumstances of his appointment also differed from Lanfranc's. Whereas Lanfranc had come at the wish of the king, Anselm received his invitation from certain leading nobles who were anxious for the welfare of the Church in England, and the king, William the Conqueror's son, William Rufus, who was enjoying the revenues of the vacant see, would not agree to the appointment until a serious illness brought him to the point of death. Similarly, whereas Lanfranc, for the greater part of his time as archbishop, had been able to work in co-operation with the king, Anselm's unpromising start heralded a stormy career which was to see him twice in exile. An old sheep had been yoked to an untamed bull, Anselm shrewdly observed, and tension soon broke out between the king and his archbishop.

Under the influence of the reforming work of Pope Gregory VII, Anselm refused to receive the pallium, the symbol of his office, from the king, since he believed that his first allegiance was to God and to the pope as head of the Church, not to a secular ruler. William Rufus refused to let Anselm go to Rome to fetch the pallium and himself had it brought to England. Anselm compromised and took the pallium from the altar at Canterbury; but conflict soon arose again when William Rufus refused to agree to Anselm's demands for reform in the English Church. Since he would not let Anselm go to Rome to discuss the matter with the pope, Anselm set off, threatening to walk to Rome naked and barefoot if need be, and was not allowed to return to England for the remainder of the king's lifetime. In 1100, however, William Rufus was killed in a hunting accident, and his brother, Henry I, summoned Anselm back immediately. Again conflict arose because Anselm refused to do homage to the king for the symbol of his office as archbishop. Again he went into exile, but in 1107 a compromise was reached in which Henry conceded Anselm's demands in regard to investiture and reform in the Church.

Despite these vicissitudes Anselm was able to gain further recognition for the primacy of Canterbury, wishing, like Lanfranc, to see the Church in England united under one head. Lanfranc had obtained recognition from the archbishop of York, though not without difficulty and only for his lifetime. Anselm, though he succeeded in procuring a papal letter confirming the primacy of Canterbury as it had been enjoyed by his predecessors, whatever that might mean, was unable to obtain the same recognition from York. He succeeded, however, in establishing a certain amount of authority over both Wales and Ireland, Scotland being cut off from him by the see of York which lay between, and thus made some move towards establishing a united Church in Britain.

Anselm was happiest however when he could be with his monks at Christchurch. 'Just as an owl is glad when she is in her hole with her chicks,' he said to them on one occasion, 'so it is with me. For when I am with you, all is well with me, and this is the joy and consolation of my life.' In the tranquillity of the cloisters he often used to talk with them, recounting incidents and conversations from his past life, which the monk Eadmer later recorded in his biography. The formative and creative work of monastic reform in England had already been done by Lanfranc; Anselm's task was merely to consolidate. It was in his writings, most of which had been completed before he came to England, that his distinctive contribution to monasticism lay. In these Anselm showed himself a thinker of far greater originality than Lanfranc. Though Lanfranc had had an outstanding reputation as a teacher and had made a name for himself in his refutation of the heretical teaching of Berengar on the Eucharist, and though his commentary on the Pauline Epistles met with immediate success, his writings had little lasting value, and his work on the subject of the famous controversy, *De corpore et sanguine Domini* (On the Body and Blood of the Lord) was already outdated ten years after it was written. Anselm's works, on the other hand, though little read in the thirteenth century, have not yet lost their power to fascinate.

Anselm never taught in a secular school attached to the monastery as Lanfranc had done, but among the monks to whom he gave instruction were some of the finest intellects in northern Europe. At Bec, the historian Orderic Vitalis observed, almost all the monks were philosophers. These young men, like Anselm himself, shared the current interest in questions of logic and grammar, but as monks they were also well read in the Fathers of the Church, particularly Augustine, and committed to gaining a deeper understanding of the faith they professed.

Anselm's earliest writings reflect the lively discussions which took place at Bec, which he himself would have done much to provoke. He wrote, for instance, a treatise entitled *De Grammatico*, which was an advanced introduction to logic, and his first major work, the *Monologion*, so named because it took the form of a monologue, was written at the request of the monks. 'Certain brothers,' he said, 'have insisted in urging me to write out for them, in the form of a meditation, a number of things which I had discussed in non-technical terms with them regarding meditating on the Divine Being and related topics.' They requested that the arguments in this work should be clear and simple and that they should not be supported by quotations from the Bible or the Fathers. Anselm sent the finished work to Lanfranc for approval, but though Lanfranc had himself been responsible for introducing the interest in logic and grammar at Bec, he failed to appreciate Anselm's purpose and criticized it for lacking the very thing Anselm intended it should lack, quotations from the Bible and the Fathers. But Anselm became dissatisfied with the *Monologion*, not because of Lanfranc's response, but because it consisted of a number of arguments, such as the one that the degrees of goodness which we observe in the universe point to the existence of an absolute goodness, so he began to wonder whether there might not be one single argument which would in itself suffice to prove that God exists. Thinking about this, he later told Eadmer, took away his desire for food, drink and sleep, and even disturbed the attention which he ought to have paid to Matins and to Divine Service until one night during Matins the idea came to

him in a sudden moment of inspiration and a great joy and exulta-
tion filled his inmost being.

Thinking that others might feel the same pleasure and satisfaction
at his discovery, he decided to write it down in his next treatise, the
Proslogion, so named because it took the form of an address to God,
but which he first called *Fides quaerens intellectum* (Faith in search of
understanding). The argument is tantalizing in its simplicity.
Anselm begins with the words of the psalm, 'The fool has said in his
heart, "There is no God"' (Psalm 14,1). With his interest in
grammar and definition of terms, he asks what 'the fool' understood
by the term 'God' when he made the statement 'There is no God'.
By definition, Anselm said, God is 'that than which nothing greater
can be thought'. 'The fool' understands these words, and therefore
the concept of 'that than which nothing greater can be thought'
exists in his mind if not in external reality. But a being who existed
in reality would be greater than a being who existed merely as a
concept in the mind. Therefore God, who is 'that than which nothing
greater can be thought' must exist in reality because if he merely
existed as a concept in the mind, he would not be 'that than which
nothing greater can be thought.'

Whether or not the argument has given others the same sense of
delight it gave Anselm, it has certainly provoked a lively interest,
and throughout the centuries leading thinkers have debated both
the meaning and the validity of his argument. One of the criticisms
to be brought against it was made almost immediately by a fellow-
Benedictine Gaunilo, a monk from Marmoutier on the Loire.
'People tell of an island existing somewhere in the ocean,' he said in
his short treatise *On Behalf of the Fool*. 'Some call it Lost Island. . . .
They say it abounds with inestimable plenitude of riches and delights
of all sorts.' What would he think, he asked, of someone who said
that this perfect island must exist, because if it did not, any really
existing country would be more excellent than it. He asks in effect
whether an island has to exist to be perfect, and in this anticipated
the argument of the eighteenth-century philosopher, Kant. Is not
one's picture of the perfect island the same, whether it exists in the
mind or in reality? Does existence add anything to that picture?
Anselm countered Gaunilo's argument by saying that his argument
was not applicable to any perfect thing but only to that one unique
being who was by definition that than which nothing greater can be
thought. 'With confidence I reply,' he said, 'if beside that than
which nothing greater can be thought anyone finds anything else
. . . to which he can apply the logic of my argument, then I will
make him a present of that lost island.'

Anselm opens his *Proslogion* with a moving prayer:

Teach me to seek you
and as I seek you, show yourself to me,
for I cannot seek you unless you show me how. . . .
    I do not seek to understand so that I may believe,
but I believe so that I may understand. . . .

For this reason it has sometimes been suggested, notably by the Swiss theologian, Karl Barth, that Anselm's argument is not intended as a philosophical one, intelligible to human reason working unaided by divine grace, but as an exposition of faith. Anselm himself however, though he starts from a position of belief, 'we believe you are that than which nothing greater can be thought', assumes that the unbelieving 'fool' accepts the same definition of God and is capable of recognizing the contradiction inherent in the statement, 'God does not exist', given that definition. He therefore seems to regard his argument as a piece of logic acceptable to the working of a rational mind. 'Why does the Fool say in his heart, "there is no God", when it is perfectly clear to the reasoning mind that you exist most fully of all? Why, except that he is indeed stupid and a fool?' Whether Anselm is doing any more than draw out what is already implicit in his definition, and whether he is justified in starting from that definition, is of course another question, but if he does not start from that definition, what definition should he start from?

There has been a tendency to focus attention on those three chapters of the *Proslogion* which contain Anselm's 'ontological' proof for the existence of God, but in the Preface Anselm announces a fuller programme. 'I began to ask myself,' he said, 'if it would be possible to find one single argument to prove that God really exists, that he is the highest good . . . and to prove whatever else we believe about the nature of God.' Having argued to his own satisfaction that God exists, Anselm turns to the question of what God is. He continues to build on his formula. 'What are you then, Lord God, you than whom nothing greater can be thought? You are just, true, blessed and whatever it is better to be than not to be.' It is, however, one thing to say that God is these things; it is another to understand the full significance of what these terms mean when applied to God, and here Anselm recognizes that his powers of reasoning have limitations. His understanding is imperfect and incomplete. 'I strive to see more . . . but I see that I cannot see further because of my own darkness.' This, too, has a direct connexion with his initial formula. 'Lord, you are then not only that than which nothing greater can be thought; you are something greater than it is possible to think about.' Since it would be possible to conceive of a being who was greater than we could think about, Anselm continues, God must be that being, for if he were not he would not be 'that than which nothing greater can be thought'. What Anselm feels to be true in his experience, his reason affirms to be a logical deduction from his initial formula. For Anselm, influenced as he was by St Augustine, moral and intellectual limitations prevent a full understanding of God which will only be possible in Heaven, but however imperfect our understanding there is need for development towards a fuller one.

> Truly in this life,
> 'neither has eye seen, nor ear heard,
> nor has it entered into the heart of man',
> how much they will know and love you in that life.
> My God,
> I pray that I may so know you and love you
> that I may rejoice in you.
> And if I may not do so fully in this life,
> let me go steadily on to the day when I come to
> that fullness.

The language of prayer which he uses with such effect in his *Proslogion* is expressive of an idiom he had already developed in his *Prayers and Meditations*. These works were of a different kind from his philosophical treatises but like them, were produced at the instigation of others and like them break new ground. Though following the traditional pattern which had been established for several centuries, Anselm's prayers are written with a sensitivity to the changing mood of the times. There was, for instance, a growing interest in the humanity of Christ, seen in art in the contrast between the depictions of the infant Christ as it were as a small adult, and those depictions of the nativity which show the baby Jesus in the manger with the animals standing around and the midwife testing the temperature of the water with her elbow. Anselm's prayer to Christ expresses this new feeling.

> Why, O my soul, were you not there
> to be pierced by a sword of bitter sorrow
> when you could not bear
> the piercing of the side of your saviour with a lance? . . .
> Why did you not see with horror
> the blood that poured out of the side of your Redeemer?
> Why were you not drunk with bitter tears
> when they gave him bitter gall to drink?

With the growing sensitivity to the humanity of Christ, there was also a growing sensitivity to his mother. This, too, is expressed in the same prayer,

> My most merciful Lady,
> What can I say about the fountains
> that flowed from your most pure eyes
> when you saw your only Son before you,
>   bound, beaten and hurt?
> what do I know of the flood
> that drenched your matchless face,
> when you beheld your Son, and your God,
>   stretched on the cross without guilt,
> when the flesh of your flesh
> was cruelly butchered by wicked men?

Another feature in keeping with the prevailing mood, seen particularly in the prayers to the saints, is a fuller expression of self-abasement, which may at times seem excessive, and a more heightened contrast between the saint who has reached glory and the sinner who still has far to go. Thus, for instance, in his prayer to St Benedict, he writes:

> Holy and blessed Benedict,
>   the grace of heaven has made you rich
>   with such full blessing of goodness
> not only in order to raise you to the glory you desire,
> to the rest of the blessed, to a seat in heaven,
> but that many others be drawn to that same blessedness. . . .
>   I have vowed to live according to your Rule,
>   however carnal a monk . . .
>   It would be too long a story to tell
> of all the gluttony, sloth, inconstancy, impatience,
> vainglory, detraction, disobedience,
> and all the other sins which my wretched soul commits,
>   deriding me each day.
> Sometimes my sins drag me here and there,
> mocking at this wretched and tattered little man. . . .

If this expression of inadequacy seems exaggerated, it should be remembered that one of the purposes of the prayers was to stir the reader out of complacency. They were intended, as Anselm himself said, to be read quietly, slowly and carefully, concentrating on a section at a time, in order to 'stir up the mind of the reader to the love or fear of God, or to self-examination'.

The first known recipient of the prayers was the young daughter of William the Conqueror, Adelaide, to whom a copy of the collection in its early form was sent in 1071. The following year three additional prayers to the Virgin Mary, were sent to Gundulf, the monk of Bec who had joined Lanfranc at Christchurch. By these prayers, which gained immediate popularity and attracted imitators in the next century, Anselm did much to influence the developing interest in the humanity of Christ and devotion to his mother, and inspired much devotional literature of the later Middle Ages.

For Anselm human love, like human understanding, was an imperfect anticipation of that which would be enjoyed in Heaven, as he said in the closing passages of his *Proslogion*, and in his beautiful Prayer for Friends. In this he sees his love for his friends as an expression of his gratitude to God for his love to him.

> What return can I make to my God,
> except to obey his commandment from my heart?
> For this is your commandment, that we love one another.

It is not easy to form an assessment of Anselm's relationships from the language of his letters, most of which were written to aspirants to the monastic life or to monks who had left Bec to join Lanfranc in England. Sometimes he uses language of intimacy to those he hardly knew. At other times he writes with surprising coldness to his closest friends. But it is easy to see from Eadmer's biography why, in Eadmer's own words, 'there grew up a wonderful and unbelievable love for him among all the people'.

If the monks of Bec shared something of Anselm's questioning, philosophic mind, the Christchurch monk, Eadmer, shared something of his sensitive and intuitive outlook. As Eadmer travelled with him, or listened to him talking in the refectory, he took careful note of what he said and did. He noticed how upset he was when he allowed himself to be persuaded against his will to refuse the request of a young girl who wanted him to confirm her. He remembered how he had reined in his horse when a hare chased by dogs ran under it for protection, and had spoken sharply to those who were laughing around, 'You laugh, do you? There is no laughter for this unhappy beast'. He listened when Anselm spoke of the advice he gave to an abbot who complained about his inability to discipline the young boys in his community. 'You never give over beating them?' Anselm had asked.

> Now tell me, my lord abbot [he continued], if you plant a tree-shoot in your garden, and straightaway shut it in on every side so that it has no space to put out its branches, what kind of a tree will you have in after years? . . . Without doubt this is what you

do with your boys. . . . You so terrify them and hem them in on all sides with threats and blows that they are utterly deprived of their liberty. And being thus injudiciously oppressed, they harbour and welcome and nurse within themselves evil and crooked thoughts like thorns. . . . But the weak soul which is still inexperienced in the service of God, needs milk—gentleness from others, kindness, compassion, cheerful encouragement, loving forbearance, and much else of the same kind.

This biography, which Eadmer wrote with such sensitivity to Anselm's personality and awareness of his sense of values, might never have been completed, for when Eadmer had begun to transcribe the first draft which he had written on wax tablets on to parchment, Anselm asked him what he was writing. He seemed willing to help Eadmer at first, suggesting alterations and corrections, but after a few days ordered Eadmer to destroy the whole thing. As a monk, trained in the school of obedience, Eadmer did not find it easy to disobey but as an author he was understandably reluctant, as he said, 'to lose altogether a work which I had put together with much labour.' He destroyed the quires, but not until he had transcribed the writing on them to other quires.

Though most of Anselm's works were written at Bec, one of his greatest, his study of the redemption entitled *Cur Deus Homo* (why God became Man) was not started until he became archbishop of Canterbury. It was completed while he was in exile during the reign of William Rufus. Like his earlier works it is an attempt to argue the rational nature of Christian belief. Anselm's friend, Gilbert Crispin, the Bec monk who had written the Life of Herluin and who was now abbot of St Peter's, Westminster, had written a work entitled *A Dialogue between Jews and Christians*, and Anselm's own work may have been provoked in part by the argument of Jews. 'The unbelievers deride our simplicity, objecting that we do God an injury, . . . when we assert that . . . he suffered . . . death on the cross among thieves.' His *Monologion* had been a monologue and his *Proslogion* an address; his *Cur Deus Homo* takes the form of a dialogue with one of the Bec monks, Boso, who was spending some time in Canterbury.

In this work too, Anselm takes a new line. He rejects the view, which had become predominant, that the achievement of Christ's death was to destroy the Devil's rights over mankind, since the Devil had overstepped his limits in taking the life of the sinless Christ. 'I cannot see what force this argument has,' he says. 'If the Devil or man belonged to himself or to anyone but God . . . perhaps it would be a sound argument. But the Devil and man belong to

God alone, and neither one stands outside God's power.' For Anselm the central issue is not the Devil's rights, but God's. Man was made for blessedness, Anselm argues, but he has failed to give God the obedience he owes him. Anselm uses the imagery of contemporary feudal society. God's honour has been offended by man's disobedience, and satisfaction must be made. The satisfaction must be made by a man, however, because it is man who caused the offence. An angel is not in a position to do this. But man himself is incapable of making that satisfaction because in his sinful state he is incapable of offering God anything perfect. Therefore the satisfaction can only be made by the God-man, who fulfils both the requirement of perfection and of manhood.

Stated as such, the argument has a strongly legal tone and may seem to represent God in an undesirable light. Underlying the feudal imagery, however, Anselm's thought is essentially that of the New Testament, particularly that of the Epistle to the Hebrews. He sees sin as an act of the will. Though sinful actions may result, sin itself is wilful disobedience against God. He recognizes the serious nature of sin. 'You have not yet considered what a great weight sin is,' he says to Boso. He sees, too, that God cannot lightly overlook sin. Reconciliation between man and God could not be effected by mercy alone. It could only be effected by the God-man who acted in perfect obedience to God through his own free and loving choice, since his will was one with the will of the Father. 'Christ came not to do his own will, but the Father's, because the righteous will which he had was not from his human but from his divine nature.' Whatever the limitations of Anselm's argument he puts the emphasis back on God, God whose goodness has been offended by man's sin and whose love takes the initiative in reconciling man to himself.

As a monk obedience was important to Anselm. Soon after he became archbishop of Canterbury he wrote to the monks of Bec: 'When I made my profession as a monk, I denied myself . . . that is, I did not live according to my own will but according to obedience. Now true obedience is given either to God or to the Church of God, and after God primarily to religious superiors. . . .' It is obedience which lies at the heart of Anselm's theory of the atonement, man's disobedience on the one hand and Christ's perfect obedience on the other.

Characteristically, though in his seventy-sixth year and much weakened by a stomach complaint, he was still pondering a problem in the days before his death, as Eadmer records. 'Palm Sunday dawned and we were sitting beside him as usual. One of us therefore said to him: "My Lord and father, we cannot help knowing that you are going to leave the world to be at the Easter court of your Lord". He replied: "And indeed if his will is set on this, I shall gladly obey his will. However, if he would prefer me to remain among you, at least until I can settle a question about the origin of the soul, which I am turning over in my mind, I should welcome this with gratitude." '

He passed away as dawn was breaking three days later, on 21 April 1109, when the monk reading to him the Gospel for the day had reached the words, 'You are the men who have stood by me faithfully in my trials; and now I confer a kingdom on you, just as my father conferred one on me: you will eat and drink at my table in my kingdom.'

His long and varied life had been one of fidelity to the obligations of his monastic profession. He had also, more than most of his contemporaries, contributed to the development of a monastic theology and a monastic devotion which were to endure for centuries to come. These indeed may perhaps be best seen as the most characteristic activity of, and the most fitting memorial to one who, in St Benedict's words, truly sought God and preferred nothing to the Work of God. The element of genius in Anselm's mind helped to make his search for God memorable and of permanent interest.

by Margaret A. Harris

BIBLIOGRAPHY

D. Knowles, *The Monastic Order in England, 940–1216* (2nd. ed., Cambridge 1966), pp. 83–144.

A. J. Macdonald, *Lanfranc: A Study of His Life, Work and Writing* (2nd. ed., Oxford 1944).

M. T. Gibson, *Lanfranc of Bec* (Oxford 1978).

R. W. Southern, *Saint Anselm and his biographer* (Cambridge 1963).

G. R. Evans, *Anselm and talking about God* (Oxford 1978).

K. Barth, *Anselm: Fides Quaerens Intellectum* (trans. I. W. Robertson, London 1960).

J. McIntyre, *St Anselm and his Critics: a reinterpretation of the Cur Deus Homo* (Edinburgh 1954).

J. Hopkins, *A Companion to the Study of St Anselm* (Oxford 1972).

R. W. Southern, 'St Anselm' in *Medieval Humanism and other studies* (Oxford 1970).

A. Fiske, 'Saint Anselm' in *Studia Monastica* 3 (1961), 259–90, reprinted in *Friends and Friendship in the Monastic Tradition* (Cuernavaca 1970).

The following texts also contain useful introductions.

i. Texts in translation:

Eadmer's History of Recent Events in England (tr. G. Bosanquet, London 1964).

The Prayers and Meditations of Saint Anselm (tr. B. Ward, Harmondsworth 1973).

Anselm of Canterbury (ed. J. Hopkins and H. Richardson), vol. 1 (London 1974); vols. 2–3 (New York 1976).

ii. Texts in Latin and English:

The Monastic Constitutions of Lanfranc (ed. D. Knowles, *Nelson's Medieval Texts* 1951).

The Life of St Anselm by Eadmer (ed. R. W. Southern, *Nelson's Medieval Texts* 1962).

St Anselm's Proslogion (ed. M. J. Charlesworth, Oxford 1965).

iii. Texts in Latin:

Gilbert Crispin's Life of Herluin in J. Armitage Robinson, *Gilbert Crispin, Abbot of Westminster* (Cambridge 1911), pp. 87–110.

Lanfranci Opera (ed. J. A. Giles, 2 vols., Oxford 1844).

D. H. Farmer, 'Ralph's Octo Puncta of the Monastic Life', *Studia Monastica* 11 (1968), 19–29.

A new edition of Lanfranc's letters, edited by H. Clover and M. T. Gibson, has just been published (Oxford 1980).

St Ailred of Rievaulx (d. 1167)

'How clearly the Gospel has come to life in them . . . a happy race of men whose habit, whose diet, whose entire life savours of the Gospel! God alone is their portion, so that they abide in God and God in them. . . . The Gospel seems as it were to live again in them.' This was how the group of Cistercian monks, who had founded the monastery of Rievaulx, appeared to some of the Benedictine community of St Mary's at York.

The Cistercians, known as White monks because of their habit made from undyed wool, were members of the Benedictine family; they belonged to a 'protest' group which just over thirty years earlier had founded the new monastery of Cîteaux in a solitude in Burgundy. They were protesting, not against the Rule of St Benedict, but against customs and interpretations which had grown up round the Rule since its composition in the sixth century, and had obscured its original directness and simplicity. Some of these customs were cultural; others, liturgical ones, had been introduced to suit contemporary devotion, while others were perhaps 'mitigations' of the austerities of the Rule, austerities that were there not for their own sake, but as means or tools to be used by men who belonged to a race which had, in some deeply mysterious way, once turned away from God, but were now trying to journey back to God in response to his call.

The Cistercian movement was not simply a negative criticism of the Black monk's way of life. It developed at a time when renewal was in the air, and the first Cistercians came from the Benedictine monastery of Molesme which had itself been founded not many years earlier by a group of hermits who were seeking a more fervent way of life. But Molesme in its maturity had lost something of its first inspiration.

The group who founded Cîteaux, under the leadership of Sts Robert, Alberic and Stephen Harding, also wanted solitude. Not precisely so that individuals could lead a hermit life, but solitude for the community as a whole, to provide an atmosphere of quietness and peace for prayer, away from the busyness of the ordinary life of the world. They also wanted a real poverty which united them to the poor Christ, and also to the poor of Christ whom they saw living around them. This desire for poverty was also inspired by the early Christian community as described by St Luke, where all things were held in common and there was a sharing among them according to the needs of each—a sharing which united them into a community having one heart and one mind.

In a spirit of unity they discussed their new way of life at Cîteaux. They simplified: modified their clothing, bedding and diet, and rejected customs that had grown up around the Rule of St Benedict. They made their structures minimal, as we would say today. They paid special attention to Chapter 73 of the Rule which looks beyond St Benedict to the Desert Fathers and the early monks of the Thebaid.

After ten years, an Englishman from Dorset, Stephen Harding, became their third abbot. He was a man of deep prayer and a lover of solitude, pleasant and homely in speech, cheerful, and liked by everyone. He had a great love of scripture and of beautiful books and manuscripts. In spite of their ascetic life and the hard work involved in clearing the ground, Cîteaux became under Stephen a unique centre of monastic culture. This small community out in the wilds initiated a liturgical reform, made a collection of what they believed to be the authentic hymns and gregorian melodies, brought out an edition of the Bible and composed a document for monastic government (later known as the Charter of Charity) which was full of wisdom and foresight. The four volumes of Stephen's Bible completed in 1109 (just eleven years after the foundation of Cîteaux) constitute one of the richest treasuries of contemporary French miniatures. Two years later they finished a copy of Gregory's *Moralia* illustrated with little pictures of monks harvesting, weaving, gathering grapes, felling a tree and so on, a witness to the outstanding artistic gifts and culture of this small community.

Stephen was a man of inexhaustible charity and saw to it that the monastic purse was an open treasury to all in need. There was a famine and his own brethren were in need; there was no food and no money, and there were deaths in the community. We are told God visited them in two ways; first through Elizabeth de Vergy, described as one of the most attractive personalities of twelfth-century Burgundy. She gave, and inspired friends to give them farms, vineyards and meadows. Cîteaux was at the spiritual cross-roads; would it be the story of Molesme all over again? But the monks re-affirmed their decision for renewal and took steps to safeguard their apartness from the world, their poverty and simplicity, even in regard to their church and their form of worship. So renewal became something that was built into Cistercianism.

Secondly, God visited them through vocations, with the coming of St Bernard and his companions. Two or three years later Bernard was sent with a small group to found Clairvaux, and it was from Clairvaux in 1132 that he sent the men who were to establish

Rievaulx. It was no haphazard venture; the matter was discussed with the English king, Henry I, and with the local Baron who donated the land, Walter Espec. As leader, Bernard chose William, his own secretary (later venerated as St William), who was himself an Englishman. These men brought to Ryedale the Cistercian life, with its two great characteristics of love of the Rule in all its simplicity, and love of solitude. It was just thirty-four years after the foundation of Cîteaux.

Ailred entered the novitiate of Rievaulx two years later in 1134, being about twenty-four years old. His father Eilaf had been the priest at Hexham and at one time treasurer of Durham. Eilaf, like his father and grandfather before him, was a married priest and belonged to an Anglo-Saxon family of old Northumbrian stock. They had lived through the devastation of the North by William the Conqueror, and survived the tensions caused by having Norman bishops intent on reform introduced at Durham. Eilaf himself was a learned, respectable and conscientious man, well known to the neighbouring king of Scotland; and King David's son Henry and his own boy Ailred grew up together at Hexham and at the royal court. Later the king made Ailred his seneschal or steward. It was a position of trust and responsibility and gives evidence not only of David's affection for the young man but also of Ailred's capabilities as a practical administrator. He had a clear head for the understanding of affairs and a gift for dealing with men; because of these qualities the king sent him on a matter of business to Thurstan, archbishop of York. While he was in Yorkshire, he heard of the monks at Rievaulx and, having finished his business in York, he rode out to Walter Espec's castle at Helmsley where he spent the night. Walter, the founder of the abbey and one of King Henry I's leading barons, has been described as a huge man with a great black beard and a voice like a trumpet. He gave Ailred a great welcome and the next day took him to Rievaulx to meet the monks. This visit undoubtedly made a great impression on Ailred, but he returned at the end of the day with Walter to Helmsley. Early next morning he said goodbye to his host and set out on his journey home to Scotland. Their way took them along the top of the ridge overlooking the valley of the Rye (now beautifully laid out with lawns and known as Rievaulx terrace). The view across the valley is one of the most exquisite in England. But Ailred, looking down through the trees would have seen, not the lovely Gothic choir that is there today, nor even the severe Norman nave, but a cluster of temporary buildings set between the slopes of the hill and the fast-flowing stream. The peace of the setting, the simplicity of the monastery and above all the meaning of why it was there—a school of Christ, a school of the Lord's service—all this stirred Ailred to the depths. When they reached the narrow road that wound down the hill to the gatehouse he asked his companion if he would like to go down to the abbey again. Ailred later admitted that all had depended on the man's reply. It was yes. Ailred was stirred but he was not yet committed. The monks for their part questioned him, investigated his motives, and may even have used persuasion. But once he had made his decision he could hardly wait for the four days to pass before he would be admitted as a novice. After a year he made his profession according to the Rule of St Benedict.

His biographer, Walter Daniel, a monk of the house and later Ailred's infirmarian, tells us that he was a cheerful hard-working member of the community. Though not strong, he was deft and practical, cool in a crisis, and did what he had to do without fuss. Above all he developed a taste for prayer. All this did not go unnoticed, and Abbot William made him a member of his council, discovering in him unsuspected depths of wisdom and prudence together with a gift for disentangling difficult cases. He was also a good speaker, knew what he wished to say and said it well. As a result he was sent by his abbot on a diplomatic mission to Rome in connexion with the appointment of the new archbishop of York. On his return he was made novice-master of the fast-growing community which already numbered 300. Also, at the request of Bernard, whom he had met at Clairvaux, he began to write his best-known work *The Mirror of Charity* which was a treatise on the place of love in the growth of man's personal relationship with God, and with his fellow-men.

After only a few months as novice-master he was appointed first abbot of Revesby in Lincolnshire—the third foundation of Rievaulx. Five years later in 1147 he was elected abbot of the house of his profession and returned to Rievaulx as its third abbot, a position he occupied until his death in 1167.

Ailred seems to have had a special charism for his ministry as abbot. But we must not forget that first and foremost he was a Cistercian monk who had vowed to seek God along the way traced out by the Rule of St Benedict. He had grasped the basic Christian teaching, which the Cistercians made especially their own, that we would not be seeking God unless we had already been found by Him; that God loved us first while we were still sinners, and actually gives the power to men to return love for love. Life was a journey and the end of the journey, whose whole meaning was love, was already there in germ at its beginning. Ailred, steeped as he was in the Scriptures, saw this journey, this monastic/Christian life in biblical terms. St Benedict was a second Moses, a leader taking his monks, the special people of God, out of the bondage of sin—out of the Egypt of this world—through the desert of life to the promised land of heaven and the city of Jerusalem, which was no longer simply the vision of peace, but the vision of God himself. Christ had gone on before; St Benedict followed with his monks on this journey back to the Father. Christ himself was also the way. The monk followed this way by committing himself to Christ in faith, a faith that was not simply an act of the mind, but a surrender in absolute dependence to the care of God; a surrender which was truly radical because it reached to the roots of a man's being where he is most alone and most in need of security. This faith was expressed by a commitment of love to the person of Christ and by a merciful, compassionate bearing love towards one's brothers. It was a love that would find its full flowering in the face-to-face vision of Christ who would be fully recognized as the perfect revelation of the Godhead.

The way was Christ, but it was also the narrow way of his Gospel teaching, which, as St Benedict pointed out, was, especially at the beginning, a hard and rugged way. It could not be otherwise, for Christ's way was the way of the Cross which was the complete contradiction of the comfortable way of life. 'Our way of life is the Cross of Christ,' said Ailred. He meant that the monastic way with its worship, vigils, abstinence, doing the will of another, bearing patiently one another's weaknesses, was the way by which a monk carried not simply his own cross but shared in the Cross of Christ; and was inserted, as it were, into the saving act of Calvary which redeemed the world. He did not use the phrase 'Paschal Mystery' but he was speaking of the working out of the Paschal Mystery—the Passion, Death and Resurrection of Christ in our daily lives, just as his fellow-countryman Langland was to do two centuries later.

But all this could not be done on one's own: Ailred taught that just as the Jews needed Moses as their mediator, so monks needed Benedict. He is more than a mediator, rather a Father who has begotten us in Christ, and who obtains for us by his mediation the grace and spiritual power to put his teaching, which is simply that of the Gospel, into practice. Ailred points out that as a father Benedict has transmitted life to his sons, the life which he himself had received from above, so that as his monks grow in monastic virtues and in prayer, so too they grow in the likeness of Christ.

To live the teaching of the Gospel is certainly not the prerogative of monks. It is the ideal of every Christian. It is simply that there are different ways of doing this. All are called to holiness—to union with God; from every vocation in life there is a doorway leading to the heart of God; so, for instance, the parent who accepts his life and gives his life as a parent, grows and becomes holy as a parent and his parenthood will give him an insight into the ways of God who is the Father of all.

The monk is called to a rather special way of life, which is his form of Christian living; his maturity and identity will depend on how he lives this life in its fulness. When we look at this life in detail as it was lived at Rievaulx and other Cistercian abbeys in England, we see that it fell into three main areas: work, reading and prayer. These were not three separate compartments in a monk's day. It is true that there were specific times for each of these activities, but they blended together to form an integral whole. The thoughts gained from a monk's reading carried over into his prayer and his work; the fruits of his prayer affected his work and his dealings with others; and work done conscientiously in silence could lead to compunction or contemplation in prayer.

The Cistercians wanted to earn their own living, to be self-supporting and have something over to give to the poor. The labour for this was to come from the monks, lay brothers and hired workers. Lay brothers had been introduced in the very early years at Cîteaux, when the monks found it almost impossible to give the required amount of time to the services in choir and reading, and also spend sufficient time on the land, especially when their fields were at some distance from the monastery. So they introduced lay brothers, men under vows like themselves but who were given a form of prayer that was simpler than the Office in choir. Once trained, they were skilled and competent in helping to build, develop and maintain a Cistercian abbey, and many were men of deep contemplative prayer. The Cistercians were not the first to think of the idea of a lay brotherhood, but they were the first to develop it on such a scale; it is a good example of how they were prepared to innovate in order to keep not simply the letter of the Rule but also its spirit. The lay-brother vocation opened the monastic life to many for whom it would otherwise have been closed; when Ailred was abbot, there were between four and five hundred lay brothers at Rievaulx, and on Sundays and great feasts when they came in from the granges they filled the Church 'like bees packed in a hive'.

Serfs—almost the equivalent of slaves—were forbidden, as were ecclesiastical revenues, likewise the system by which mills were owned and run as a source of income. Gradually, however, serfs began to be acquired either by purchase or by gift with grants of land that included the serfs living there. And as early as 1157 the General Chapter at Cîteaux had to make legislation regarding the evasion of rules concerning mills, and later issued prohibitions

Plate III: High altar and rood, Ampleforth Abbey (York).

Plate IV: Organ loft and entrance to Choir, Stanbrook Abbey
(Worcester).

against the possession of churches with their incomes, a practice which was involving the monasteries in lawsuits and rivalries. Gradually the changing economy of the surrounding countryside had its effect on the White monks—the disappearance of the serf class and the rise of the small farmers lessened the number of vocations to the lay brothers, but though they did the same kind of things as any other monastic group of the time, it might be argued that the Cistercian economy always remained less complicated than in some of the Black-monk houses.

Primarily the Cistercians were farmers; in England the cultivation of grain crops was normal and basic to their system. But some houses like Sawley and Jervaulx were situated in cold, damp districts where the crops would not ripen, so such houses developed their livestock. Rievaulx had horses and in the twelfth century received a single pasture for sixty mares with their foals—Dieulacre had at least seventy mares—but Jervaulx was most famous of all for the quality of its horses; a reputation which was maintained right down to the Reformation, and even some twentieth-century bloodstock goes back to the Jervaulx line. Pig-farming was another Cistercian activity; the outlay was cheap and the returns good, especially where the monastery had access to woods with acorns and nuts; the pig meat was sold, while the grease was invaluable for the softening and waterproofing of leather boots.

But it is as sheep farmers that the great Cistercian abbeys of the North are best known. Their situation near moorlands and wolds with large areas for free-range grazing, their system of granges run by lay brothers, all helped to make sheep farming with its annual wool crop a profitable enterprise. It was largely through their work that their high quality wool crop became one of the assets of the country and the abbey of Fountains an important clearing centre. Cistercian abbeys were usually built near a river and the monks were skilful in diverting water for all necessary domestic purposes. Rivers were valuable too for fishing, as sources of power for mills, and also for transport. Tintern had its own harbour on the river Wye and Furness and Holmcultram both owned ships—presumably for buying grain from Ireland. Netley and Beaulieu had them too, and sent grain to France and brought back wine and other provisions. Sometimes abbeys were close to areas of mineral deposit and these resources were soon exploited. Rievaulx, Kirkstead, Sawley and Byland were running iron furnaces from the twelfth century—but the greatest producer was Furness which had forty in operation in the thirteenth century. Salt, so necessary for preserving food, was produced at many abbeys; Newminster and others had salt works quite early in their history.

7

There were probably other smaller industries as well and we get a hint from Ailred's letter to his sister that flax was grown and made into linen at Rievaulx. (Structural evidence in the oldest part of the ruins would suggest that there was also a tannery in Ailred's time.) As a practical administrator ultimately responsible for the temporal as well as the spiritual welfare of his monastery, Ailred was interested in all that was going on around him, and in his sermons and treatises often used illustrations which would be familiar in the day-to-day life of his monks and brothers. The work at Rievaulx was heavy and demanding; as a novice he sometimes fell asleep over his reading from sheer weariness.

Reading was another important area in the life of a Cistercian, the *lectio divina* of Benedict's Rule, holy because its aim and purpose was to lead the reader to a deeper communion with God. Holy also, because most of a monk's reading came from Holy Scripture and commentaries on the sacred text. It was a slow meditative reading which sought not simply information for the mind, but rather the formation of the whole person to the likeness of Christ; not simply knowledge about God, but that loving knowledge of him as a person which the Bible describes in terms of the union between husband and wife. Ailred taught that the monk was not simply reading about God's dealings with men in the past, and events in Christ's life that were over and done with. Rather, by prayerfully reflecting upon and 'ruminating' what he was reading, the monk was brought into contact with that same God, present now in his soul. He could enter by faith and love into these same mysteries of Christ's life on earth, and make his own in 'the here and now' the special graces offered by each mystery, by each saving event.

This remembrance, this *memoria*, which made God present in a new and life-giving way, was the monastic way of reflecting on the message of revelation, the monastic way of doing theology. It differed from the more speculative and analytical methods of the later 'schools'—methods which could be independent of the moral and spiritual life of the student, and which were based more on philosophy and metaphysics than on Scripture and the writings of the Fathers. For the monastic method, asceticism, humility and prayer, which led to purity of heart, were needed to prepare the way for this contact with the living God; and so it might be called a kind of 'living theology'. It was a theology often expressed in terms of symbols, parables and allegories, but its best exponents like Bernard and Ailred never allowed it to remain in the realm of the symbol. It had to be linked with reality and applied to the individual; just as the prophet Nathan, after recounting his parable, could point to King David and say: 'You are the man.'

In his *Letter to his Sister* and the little treatise *On Jesus at Twelve Years Old* Ailred suggests the same way of meditation—inserting oneself into the Gospel—as Bernard did in his Rule for the Knights Templar; a way that Ignatius was to develop, perhaps as a result of reading the life of Christ by Ludolph of Saxony. And it has been suggested that Ludolph himself was influenced by the meditations of Ailred. Today, as men of our time, we cannot ignore the 800 years of development in methods of study, and new scientific ways of thinking which separate us from Ailred. But even so, Ailred and his contemporaries have much to teach us about the way our reading should not only inform, but form us. Perhaps their method should complete and fulfil our modern ways of reflecting on the Christian mysteries.

The third area of a monk's life, one that should permeate the rest of it, was that of prayer. The Divine Office, the work of God to which Benedict said nothing should be preferred, formed a background for personal prayer. Verses from the psalms and readings would come to mind during the day and these the monk could make his own; and Ailred's sermons are full of little phrases from the Office. He was very conscious of the way the Office was performed in his Abbey, and once remarked that visiting Abbots were checking the weight of the portions of bread in the refectory whilst missing the fervour with which the Office was being sung in choir. He had strong views about the way monks should sing. 'What are we doing,' he writes, 'with the thunder of organ music, the clash of cymbals and elaborate part-settings for different voices? We hear monks doing all sorts of ridiculous things with their voices, plaguing us with womanish falsettos, spavined bleatings and tremulos. I have even seen them waving their arms about, beating time to the music and contracting their bodies in all directions . . . and the mere sound of singing is preferred to the meaning of the words that are sung. Sense and sound together are meant to stir us to devotion, and so the sound of our music must be sober and moderate . . . and not trespass on the words so that our minds are distracted from their meaning.'

He was also in the Cistercian tradition when he wrote that 'the man who has found Jesus' company within his own soul . . . is happy enough to say his prayers in a little chapel of rough unpolished stone where there is nothing carved or painted to distract the eye, no fine hangings, no marble pavements, no blaze of candles, no glittering of golden vessels'.

The point of this simplicity was to remove distractions which could stimulate the imagination instead of quietening it, in preparation for the quiet, almost wordless, prayer of the heart, a form of prayer that goes back beyond the Rule to the early monks of Mount Sinai. It is the prayer of centring—a prayer that is as old as the hills. It is for this kind of prayer that monks need leisure, in the sense of being free from business. It means being empty, disengaged, free, not tied down by created things, so that one is available for God. It means entering into the 'rest of the Sabbath'. It is no idle rest, for, as Ailred explains, it is filled with a contemplative gazing on the Lord. It is this gazing, this being with Him, that gives us a share in his peace and in his dynamic rest, because it unites us with Him.

Words like 'leisure', being 'empty', 'idle' or 'at rest', have a rather negative sound for us today, but the content of the leisure was a very positive making-oneself-available for God so as to be capable of enjoying Him; and in its wider sense this covered the whole meaning of the monastic way of life. Apartness from the world, asceticism, meditation on the Word that was life, all this orientated the life of a Cistercian towards contemplation. It was the response to a call that could only reach its fulfilment in Heaven, when our longing would no longer be bound by the limitations of the flesh and we should see Jesus Christ as God. Being drawn into his glorious light and lost in his unbelievable joy, this will be the Sabbath of Sabbaths, when we return to our Maker to whom we belong, and who is Himself our greatest possession. We shall have received the Holy Spirit with the very perfection and fulfilment of all He can give, and with Him the outpouring of that love beside which servile fear is no more. This is the Sabbath of Sabbaths—the goal of St Benedict's Rule—and from what his biographer tells us, Ailred had at least a foretaste of this towards the end of his life as he prayed in his little oratory. The monastic life with its call to a close union with God is basically a contemplative life. But it seems that the invitation to the mystical life was preached in Cistercian houses in a way that was not to be found in other monastic reforms of the time.

In 1147 Ailred was elected abbot by the community at Rievaulx. Not far away at Byland Roger was abbot, while Fountains was in the care of Henry Murdac. Both these men were friends of Ailred— Roger, twenty years later, gave him the last sacraments and was present when he died. He had been sent from Furness, a Savigniac house, in 1134 as one of the group to make a foundation at Calder. This new monastery was destroyed by the Scots, so the community returned to Furness for shelter, where however they were unwelcome and were sent off again. Their wanderings were manifold; they moved to Old Byland, where they were so close to Rievaulx that the bells of the two monasteries caused confusion, then again to Stocking and finally to a site near Cuxwold. Roger, like Ailred, had great sympathy for the young, understanding their weaknesses and hesitations as well as their ideals and generosity. Ailred was called on to arbitrate in a dispute about jurisdiction over Byland. He decided in favour of Savigny.

Also in 1147 Henry Murdac, abbot of Fountains, became archbishop of York. His dissimilarity in character to Ailred did not prevent the two men becoming friends. Henry, sent to Fountains by Bernard, brought with him the full Cistercian observance in all its austerity. The community rose to the challenge with enthusiasm. But Henry was a stern man and so unafraid to speak his mind that once the citizens of York went out to Fountains intent on destroying the monastery and killing the abbot. They did indeed set fire to the church, but overlooked Henry lying prostrate before the altar. Often he was involved in controversy. He acted from a deep sense of duty and conscience; though intransigent, he was basically humble. As archbishop he retained a constant interest in his monastery, where he was succeeded as abbot by two of Ailred's monks from Rievaulx in succession. Ailred regarded Henry as a saint and kept for many years a cross which had belonged to him.

Ailred's contacts were not limited to neighbouring abbots and members of his own Order. Walter Daniel tells us that he wrote letters to the pope, to the kings of England, France and Scotland, to most of the bishops and many of the great men of England. It is tantalizing to find just references to these letters, which survived at both Reivaulx and Margam in the later Middle Ages. Their loss is particularly disappointing because Walter Daniel commented that in them are to be found the spirit and the living image of Ailred.

Gradually he became a man of considerable influence, specially but not exclusively in the North of England. He had to make regular journeys on visitations to the daughter houses of Rievaulx, two of which, Melrose and Dundrennan, were in Scotland. He was also called in often as an adviser in disputes of various kinds. His great common sense, his flair for penetrating to the crux of the dispute, together with his obvious sincerity and the way he expressed his decisions, made him specially acceptable as an arbitrator. By nature he was a peacemaker, but remained always a man of his time, taking for granted that twelfth-century justice required harsh penalties.

He was well known to King Henry II, whom he persuaded to support Alexander III against the anti-pope Octavian. He was also a friend of the earl of Leicester, who became justiciar of England, and of Gilbert Foliot, bishop of London and critic of Thomas Becket.

One of the first acts of Alexander III after his recognition by Henry II was to canonize King Edward the Confessor. At the request of his kinsman Laurence, abbot of Westminster, Ailred rewrote the

Life of the Confessor by Osbert of Clare. This became widespread and popular. He also wrote a homily on the new saint which he preached at Westminster Abbey when the relics of St Edward were translated in 1163, a ceremony presided over by the new archbishop of Canterbury, Thomas Becket. It was an event which gave Ailred great pleasure because an Anglo-Saxon king was venerated for his holiness in the presence of a descendant of the Norman conqueror.

Ailred had dedicated to this descendant, now Henry II, his work *The Genealogy of the Kings of England*. For Henry was not only of Norman descent, but through his grandmother (the daughter of the justly famous queen, St Margaret of Scotland) he was related to Edmund Ironside and the old Anglo-Saxon kings of England. Thus he was a sorely-needed centre of unity for the country after the troubled reign of Stephen. Those fifteen years, the time of the Cistercian implantation in England, had seen the civil war with Matilda and the lawlessness of the Barons. They had been full of violence, terrorism and hardship for some monks as well as for ordinary people; in some parts of the country fighting and devastation were followed by famine.

At the accession of Henry II all looked forward to a return to normality; a period of enthusiastic expansion and monastic building began, which however was to lead many monasteries into debt. In the next century when the lovely Gothic choir was built, even Rievaulx suffered in this way.

Ailred was interested in history as part of his humanistic outlook, but it was particularly the people of the past rather than events which interested him. He wrote of St Cuthbert for whom he had a deep personal devotion, always committing himself to his safe-keeping while on his journeys. He wrote of the saints of his native Hexham and, in his treatise on the Battle of the Standard, of his friends who were fighting on opposite sides. Yet surprisingly, it must be admitted that these writings often lack the verve, vivid detail and pungent phrase of the old chroniclers, such as Jocelyn of Furness in his life of Ailred's friend, St Waltheof.

However, Ailred's real greatness lay especially in the kind of man he was, the kind of person he became. For one can sense a growth, a transformation over the years. The young man who entered Rievaulx was handsome, debonair, with an attractive friendly personality, a good mixer who could enjoy the company both of monks and of Walter Espec with his friends at Helmsley castle. He was not strong physically, and as the years passed he suffered intensely from gallstones; to this was added the agonies of arthritis, which at times were so great that he had to be carried by four men holding the corners of a linen sheet, and a mere touch would make him cry out in pain. The General Chapter gave him permission to live in the infirmary and to attend choir and Mass just when he was able. He was also left perfectly free to attend to the business of the house, the estate and its granges in the way he thought best and according to his health.

About ten years before his death he decided to have a little cell built near the infirmary where the brethren could visit him. This they did, twenty or thirty at a time, walking about the room, sitting on his bed, talking together, and Ailred would say: 'My sons, say what you like—only let there be no unseemly word, no detraction, no blasphemy.'

In this cottage, with its little oratory where he spent much time when he was well enough, he did most of his writing. Here he composed his treatises, his sermons and his letters.

About four years before his death he underwent a second conversion; he increased his austerities—dropping, not superfluities for he had none, but even things that were necessary for him in his weakness. He spent more time in prayer and vigils; and shut away in his little oratory often forgot all about the times for his meals. He gave more time also to reading and he returned to the books which had been his guide and inspiration when he first left the world, especially the *Confessions* of St Augustine. It was as if he had had some fresh insight regarding his commitment to Christ, which resulted in a renewal of his desire to give himself utterly; this found expression in greater self-denial and a deepening of his life of prayer. This renewed presence of the Holy Spirit, if we may call it that, this fresh impulse of the life of Christ in his soul, showed itself especially in the gifts of prophecy and discernment of spirit that he received, and which were experienced by the community in his day-to-day dealings with them, and in his comments in Chapter. But also there was a renewal, as it were, in his personality which could be felt and recognized by others, even though it was difficult to put into words.

He was now living out the doctrine which he had begun to write about so many years before in his *Mirror of Charity*. He saw the monk as a true Christian, whose baptismal consecration was deepened and enabled to flower by monastic profession. It was no accident that the exodus theme was at the heart of his spirituality, because it was also the theme of Christ's life. Benedict was his leader, but only because he was following in the footsteps of Christ. There was no dichotomy between the monastic life and the Christian life, and all the monastic observances were geared to the following of Christ which was the only thing that mattered. It was a journey, like that of the Israelites through the desert; there were long periods of aridity and dryness, but there were oases too. The desert was a place where the monk struggled with temptations, but it was also a place where he encountered the Holy Spirit. Drawn further and further away from Egypt and its security, he was taught to depend on God alone —on the water which He provided in situations where it could be least expected—on the strength which came from the manna given day by day and which could not be collected and stored. It was a perfect allegory of the monastic/Christian life with its times of dryness and weariness, when there was the temptation to grumble and murmur, to make idols of work, study or something other than God who so often made Himself felt by His seeming absence. But there were times also when the monk came to an oasis and felt he was being cared for and carried by God as a man carried his little son with his cheek close against the child, or like an eagle leaving her nest and teaching her young to fly and catching them on her wings. If he was invited to enter the promised land, to seek a closer union with the Lord, he had to be courageous and trusting, ready to go forward into the unknown—unlike those Israelites who remained in their tents and sulked, afraid, refusing to put themselves into the hands of the God who had done so much for them. All this demanded not only faith but love. Ailred like other Cistercians of his time saw the true monk/Christian as a lover, as a person whose capacity to love was completely fulfilled, both with the commitment-love for God, and the merciful-compassionate love for others. He tells his sister (for the journey was the same for women as for men) to bind all the world into her heart with a bond of love and pity; her heart had to be a kind of Noah's ark in which there was room for everyone with their needs.

Like Julian of Norwich two hundred years later, Ailred saw that the meaning of the Christian life was love, love for God, for oneself and for one's fellow men. Love was not something sentimental or emotional, which resided only in the feelings and could change with the weather. It also had to do with the will and with the powers of reasoning. There could be a good love and a bad love—one that led from created things and swept upwards to God, and one that was selfish, possessive and turned away from God.

Like his master Augustine he saw that there were three human acts involved in love. Firstly there was the choice of what was to be loved and this involved a judgement of the mind, because some-times our feelings could deceive us. We had to avoid choosing something that would lead us away from God, or something that was not for us because of our particular vocation in life. Choice was at the beginning of love, whether it was good or bad love. It was by his choices, by saying Yes or No, that a man became mature. But usually such choices were not made simply by cold reflection, for one's desires, needs, and feelings were involved as well. Then secondly the will had to move the person to act more positively to attain what was loved. Finally it rested in the possession and enjoyment of the object loved. The process was really a collaboration between reason, feelings and will, for it had to do with the whole person. Everyday experience showed that there were temptations to selfishness, and strong emotions could sway the whole personality; so there was need not only of God's help of guidance and discernment, but also of his creative power to carry out a right decision once it had been discerned.

True love, which is the charity spoken of in the New Testament, means that we have chosen something that is permitted for us in our particular way of life, that we have set about attaining it in the right way, and that we enjoy it in the way God intended and meant it to be enjoyed without grabbing or greed. It implies a complete turning away from sin, but leads to the true human happiness and peace of soul that come with a clean conscience. Charity is the soul's true Sabbath—the day on which it enters into the rest and enjoyment of God.

Love has to do not only with God, but also with ourselves and other people. Knowing and loving others, taking joy and delight in them is what we call friendship. Ailred himself tells us that as a boy he wanted only to love and to be loved. It was a trait that remained with him all his life for he was a man who was born for friendship; finally in his full maturity, about seven years before he died, he wrote a treatise on spiritual friendship. As a boy and a young monk he had read Cicero's book on friendship and it made a deep impression on him. His own treatise follows Cicero in that it takes the form of a dialogue, and this enables him to express the fruit of his experience in a personal, intimate and informal way; but his characters are much more vivid than those of Cicero; we feel they are real people carrying on a real discussion, and Walter Daniel especially comes alive. Ailred is not looking at friendship from the purely human point of view, he is more concerned with its spiritual benefits, and so, much of his teaching and examples are taken from the Fathers and from Scripture. He takes examples of all types of friendships from the Old Testament; and uses the Wisdom books to discuss the qualities of friends, how one should choose them, and how one should develop the different types of friendship—for all friendship is not on the same level. But it is in the New Testament that he finds the supreme example of friendship in Jesus himself who gave the uttermost proof of his love by laying down his life for his friends, and by giving himself to them, to be assimilated into their very substance, in the Eucharist.

It was union with Jesus that he saw as the basis of all Christian friendship, and he found it exemplified in the early Church where the believers were the followers of Christ and shared in the breaking of the Bread, the prayers and the joy of the Holy Spirit, and had but one heart and one mind. True friendship must be founded on virtue, he said, for friendship is a form of love and love is of God. It does not exist to satisfy the lower passions of people; this is not true friendship for it takes no account of the respect that a person must have, both for himself and for the other as members of Christ's body. 'A man who does not love himself cannot possibly love another, for the love he offers his neighbour must be framed on the kind of love he has for himself.' It is evident he does not love himself if he commits base and immoral acts for himself. So truly Christian friendship never involves only two persons, Christ is always the third—and as soon as anything is said or done that would drive away Christ, then it ceases to be a Christian friendship. Ailred may be called the patron of friendship, but he will have nothing to do with friendship that uses other people simply to satisfy a personal need.

He speaks of the care with which one should choose one's friends, of how one should test them to see if they are worthy of confidence, because friendship involves a sharing of personal thoughts, an opening of the doors of heart and mind. This is something one cannot do fully with everyone and so friendship is of its nature 'particular'; it also involves a certain constancy and stability. A man does not change his friends, he says, as a child changes his toys. The great enemy of friendship is mistrust; though the loyalty which is its opposite does not mean that we should be blind to the faults and defects of our friends. It is here that true charity is needed; not simply to destroy the defect in our friend but to draw out and develop what is good in him. For that good was placed in him by God, and our love must always build up. Often we are at first drawn to others because of similar interests and ideals and then as we get to know them better we become aware of the differences between us. We realize that our friend is 'other', that he is not simply a reflection of ourselves. This is the time to adapt, to accept him as he is, as a person in his own right; and then the friendship becomes enriching on both sides.

Human friendship involves loyalty, generosity, patience, under-standing and unselfishness—all elements of that charity which is the gift of the Holy Spirit, the Spirit of Jesus. So, if these things are practised, then there is a growth in that charity which is of God and a gradual transformation into the likeness of Jesus. Ailred points out that friends pray for each other; but the essence of prayer is not attention and preoccupation with what one is praying for, but a communion and being-with the person one is praying to. And thus in prayer a man passes from the love of his friend and from the union of wills that exists between them, to the presence and love of Christ. And thus, beginning with the love with which he embraces his friend and rising to the love with which he embraces Christ, he will come to that complete security where he will rejoice in the ever-lasting presence of the God of all goodness. Then this friendship to which on earth he can admit only a few, will be extended to all, and by all will be extended to God, since God will be All in all.

'The day before yesterday,' Ailred wrote, 'as I was walking round the cloisters, all the brethren sat together . . . and in the whole of that throng I could not find one whom I did not love, and by whom I was not loved, and I was filled with such great joy . . . that I felt my spirit was transfused into them and their affection was flowing back into me.' This does not mean that Ailred never felt strong emotion like anger, but he tells us that he never allowed the sun to set upon his anger. It does not mean that he did not have his critics —it was to answer some of these that Walter Daniel wrote his biography and the *Letter to Maurice*. It does not mean that his monks were never angry with him—one of them once picked him up as he lay in his cell and threw him on the embers of the fire. But it does mean that as he lay dying he could say: 'God who knows all things knows that I love you all as myself, and as earnestly as a mother does her sons.' It was in his relationship with his community, and in the kind of monastery he wanted his abbey to be that we find the best expression of his character and spirituality.

Without question he had a great love for Rievaulx itself. He knew those days when the driving rain swept across the valley, leaving an icy cold in the stone buildings, but he also enjoyed those times when the warm sun was caught and trapped in the large cloister garth. He said he had always loved peace and inward quiet and he especially loved the quietness of the valley broken only by the sounds of the rooks nesting in the tall trees on the ridge, and the wood pigeons in the woods on the slopes, the bleating of the sheep, and in the spring the incessant cries of the young lambs; and then during the working hours the sounds of building—for much building was done while he was abbot—making a background of chip-chip as the masons cut and shaped the stone. But he made Rievaulx more than a place of outward quiet and peace; we are told that he 'turned the house into a stronghold for the sustaining of the weak, and the nourishment of the strong. Who was there, however despised and rejected who did not find in it a place of rest? Monks in need of compassion and mercy, men to whom no other house gave entrance came to Rievaulx the mother of mercy, and found the gates wide open.' He would remind the brethren that it was the special and supreme glory of the house of Rievaulx that above all else it taught tolerance of the infirm, and compassion with others in their needs; it was a holy place because it brought forth for its God sons who were peacemakers.

Ailred was above all an Abba—a father to his community—and we find the quintessence of his life as Abbot spelled out in his 'Pastoral Prayer' addressed to our Lord, the Good Shepherd. He asks: 'What have I undertaken? Is not this your family, your special people, created and redeemed by you and gathered together from far and wide, souls dear to you put in my charge. Lord, since you have put me in this office or at least allowed others to put me here, you have an obligation to look after those entrusted to me.' Then, just as a priest is bound to offer sacrifice first for his own sins, he prays for his own needs. He asks God to look at his soul and to see him as he really is, and then to heal him like a good physician, correct him like a kind mother, forgive him as a forbearing father. He asks for his own needs, but also for what he needs for those entrusted to him. He wants to be a power for good rather than merely a superior. Solomon had asked for wisdom to rule his people; Ailred's people are 'those redeemed by the amazing love you showed on the Cross'. 'My God, you know what a fool I am—I ask for nothing, only that you would send me wisdom to be with me, work with me, act in me, speak in me, to order all my plans—do this for their advancement and my salvation.'

He prays for the good of all: 'Whatever you have given me, Lord, I want to give entirely to them—my work-time, my leisure, my activity and thinking, when things go well and when they go wrong, let all be spent on those for whom you deigned to spend yourself.' He asks for patience to bear with their shortcomings, sympathy to share their griefs, and the power to speak the truth plainly in a way that will be acceptable to the character and understanding of each.

He wishes the Holy Spirit to protect and shield them, to keep them united within themselves, with one another and with himself, to keep them chaste and humble, to cheer them up and help them in all the troubles of life. In their fasting, work, silence and repose 'let each one know that this Holy Spirit is with him in all his trials and temptations'. He asks for what they need in temporal matters, and that he may be a good steward distributing wisely and fairly whatever they have, be it much or little. And so may they persevere with gladness in their holy undertaking until they attain to everlasting life and the presence of their Lord and Helper.

It is a moving little document and taken together with his Sermons it shows his great perception and understanding of men, together with the insights he had in the subtle dangers and difficulties of community life. He saw more clearly than most men that if a community is a little mystical body then each has something different to contribute for the good of the whole, whether it be of work, prayer, artistic talents or simply gifts of character. This in itself meant accepting a certain form of plurality, and yet often members of a community expect all to be contributing the same things. He told those who were tempted to opt out from full community life, that to withhold one's talents is a form of avarice, and is to defraud the community. The community must be close-knit like a coat of mail because through the weakness of one or two links the enemy could wound the whole body.

Throughout the last year of his life he was so weakened and wearied by his various infirmities that he would lie as if unconscious on his pallet—a tiny figure shrunken and dried up like a leaf of parchment. On the morning of Christmas Eve 1166, he spoke to the brethren in Chapter and told them of his longing to depart and be with Christ. He went to Vigils and preached in Chapter on Christmas Day, attended Mass and Vespers sitting near the presbytery steps not far from one of the great square Norman pillars in the church he loved so well. He was carried back to his cell where he lay exhausted, and as the days passed he grew weaker and weaker. On 3 January 1167 to all his monks around him he bade farewell and asked their prayers as he had done so many times before when setting out on a journey. He made no will for he had nothing of his own—and he gave them back his psalter, the *Confessions of St Augustine* and his copy of St John's Gospel, together with the little cross which had belonged to Henry Murdac, and some relics of the saints. On 5 January he was anointed by Roger of Byland and the community came to see him, now twelve, now twenty, now forty, now a hundred gathered about him. He lingered on for three days more, murmuring from time to time: 'Hasten, for the love of Christ, hasten.' The day before he died Richard of Fountains, Roger of Byland and two other abbots with nearly all the monks were with him while one of them read the Passion. Walter Daniel held his head and whispered: 'Lord, gaze on the Cross: let your eye be where your heart is.' Ailred raised his eyes and said: 'You are my God and my Lord. You are my refuge and my Saviour. You are my glory and my hope for evermore. Into your hands I commend my spirit.'

But though he did not speak again (and died about 10.30 p.m. on 12 January 1167), his spirit lived on. And today his spiritual sons have a deep desire to interpret for their own times the traditions and spirituality which he and his contemporaries in the Order of Cîteaux first lived and then handed on. Their vision persists that the

Rule of St Benedict was a practical way of living out the Gospel—
that it was a Rule—a way—pervaded by the sense of the transcen-
dence of God and the lordship of Christ, permeating the life of the
Cistercian monk, making it a search orientated towards an experience of the living God. This search for God was the soul of the Office
in choir, their reading and their work. The environment was poor
and penitential and apart; but it was intended to form a community
of love suffused with the joy of the Holy Spirit in nearness to God.
The call and the mission are the same today as in the twelfth century;
one which demands as a response the commitment of one's whole
life: 'To give,' as Pope Paul VI expressed it, 'clear witness to that
heavenly home for which every man longs, and to keep alive in the
heart of the human family the desire for this heavenly home, as we
bear witness to the majesty and love of God and to the brotherhood
of all men in Christ.'

by Dom Paul Dienier

BIBLIOGRAPHY

Walter Daniel, *The Life of Ailred of Rievaulx* (ed. and trs. by F. M.
Powicke, 1950).

D. Knowles, *The Monastic Order in England* (2nd edition, Cambridge
1963).

A. Squire, *Aelred of Rievaulx* (1969).

Ailred's works are printed in J. P. Migne, *P.L.* 195 and by C. H.
Talbot, *Sermones Inediti* (1952): translations into English of his
Christian Friendship (H. Talbot, 1942), *The Mirror of Charity* (G.
Webb and A. Walker, 1962), *St Aelred's Letter to his Sister* (G. Webb
and A. Walker, 1955) and into French of his *Quand Jésus eut
douze ans* (A. Hoste, Paris 1958). See also *Analecta S.O. Cisterciensis*
vii (1951) and *Cistercian Studies* iv (1969).

St Godric of Finchale and St Bartholomew of Farne

In his Rule St Benedict refers to the life of the hermit, that is, of the individual who chooses to lead the religious life in isolation, as being more challenging than that of the monk, surrounded by his fellows in the monastery. In later centuries this view of Benedict's had two consequences. A small number of monks, to begin with, felt impelled to leave the security of the religious house either temporarily or permanently to struggle on their own with the problems of a life devoted to God. Monasteries, secondly, when given the chance to associate themselves with those who had chosen a life of such difficulty and such distinction, were only too glad to do so. Both consequences, it must be admitted, are but a minor aspect of Benedictine life as lived in this country, but the Middle Ages can furnish a number of significant examples, such as the numerous hermits in twelfth-century Cluny. St Bartholomew of Farne is one of a number of professed monks who left their houses and became hermits; St Godric of Finchale, originally an independent recluse without recourse to a monastery, was patronized by and finally assimilated into a community of monks. Both lived as hermits in the same period, the twelfth century, and both were attached to the same house, the wealthy and powerful northern monastery of Durham.

St Godric was the younger of the two men, being born perhaps about the time of the Norman Conquest or, more exactly, between 1065 and 1071. Aeilward, his father, and Aedwen, his mother, were both of English descent and they lived not far from the Wash, in what was then the Norfolk village of Walpole. The family was completed by Godric's younger brother and sister, called William and Burcwen respectively. It was a peasant family and so poor that the land it held may well have been insufficient to support it.

The poverty of his relatives may well have been the stimulus that led the young Godric, perhaps while still in his teens, to choose a career in trade. Basing himself in Lindsey, the northern part of Lincolnshire and an area noted for its vigorous commercial activity, he began work as a pedlar, walking along the country roads that linked farmsteads and villages. He then progressed to the more ambitious dealings that took place at markets and fairs. After four years, perhaps in 1089 or 1090, his career took another major step forward and he travelled overseas for the first time, visiting St Andrews in Scotland and Rome. Denmark and Flanders were subsequently added to his destinations and his cargoes no doubt ranged from humdrum goods such as corn or wool to more exotic eastern products such as perfumes, dyes or spices, brought to western Europe via Italy.

His journeys abroad developed a new skill in Godric: he became a capable sailor. His exceptional ability in forecasting weather conditions became well known, so much so that he was given the job of sea captain. With success of this kind came financial rewards and he acquired a half-share in one merchant ship and, at another time, a quarter-share in the profits of a second.

Mingling in Godric's character, however, with a desire for worldly achievements was a marked strain of piety. His parents were devout, and religious considerations seem never to have been totally absent from his mind. Indeed the dangers of sea travel made him value more highly the intercession of the saints, while his voyages provided an opportunity to visit their shrines. Two places in particular seem to have made a great impact on him: Lindisfarne or Holy Island and the Inner Farne, both off the north-east coast and both rich in associations with the saintly monk and bishop, Cuthbert. It was on the Inner Farne in fact, where Cuthbert had lived as a hermit, that Godric first conceived the idea of leading the solitary life himself. From that point onwards he regarded his commercial work less highly and he may have taken steps to correct some less than moral features of his way of life.

Perhaps about 1101 or 1102 Godric had spent sixteen years in trade. He now decided to use the wealth he had acquired to finance a pilgrimage to the Holy Land. While there, he may well have become involved in the politics of the newly established crusader kingdom of Jerusalem as he was probably the 'Guderic, a pirate from the kingdom of England' who helped the king, Baldwin I, escape capture by the Muslims. On the way home he visited another major shrine, that of St James the Greater, the brother of St John the Apostle, at Compostella in northern Spain.

When he returned to England he did not resume his work in commerce, but became the steward of a wealthy household, perhaps in Norfolk. Having decided to abandon the world of trade by now, he may have wanted time to reflect on the precise form his future would take. The younger servants of the household were interested only in their own advantage, however, and had previously stolen and damaged their master's possessions. With the arrival of Godric they merely transferred their attentions to the property of his neighbours, specializing in carrying off sheep and cattle and serving the meat at lavish feasts. The steward unwittingly participated in these until he discovered the truth. He then fled the household and, appalled at what had happened, decided to go on pilgrimage to atone for what he had done. He visited St Gilles in Provence, the shrine of an early hermit, and travelled again to Rome.

Once home again he was still in doubt as to his future and he decided upon a third journey to Rome, hoping that St Peter and St Paul, whose shrines were there, would help him come to a decision. Although by no means young, Aedwen, his mother, decided to accompany him on the arduous journey which was made on foot. She deliberately added to its rigours by travelling most of the way without shoes.

St Peter and St Paul seem indeed to have helped Godric make up his mind as he arrived home with a firm resolve to become a hermit. He now disposed of what remained of his wealth and embarked on the search for a suitable hermitage.

We can perhaps suggest some reasons, in addition to the inspiration derived from his visit to Rome, that prompted Godric to decide on this way of life. His existence had always had a spiritual dimension, as we have seen, and with encouragement this became increasingly important until all other aspects of his life were excluded. Encouragement may well have been provided by disillusionment with his work in commerce and by a guilty conscience. His disillusionment probably sprang from the knowledge that the traditional peak of a merchant's career was not within his grasp. Before the Norman Conquest a trader who went abroad three times in his own ship was entitled to the rank of nobleman. It is probable that Godric had amply met this requirement, but what hope had he, an Anglo-Saxon, of entering the French-speaking aristocracy then controlling England? His commercial career may well have begun to trouble his conscience also. He had dedicated himself to the accumulation of earthly profit, he had lied, cheated and committed the sin of usury, together with other sins associated with a life based largely on secular values. He no doubt felt that the remainder of his existence should be devoted to God and, in the light of his extreme guilt, that the conditions should be as harsh as possible. The obvious answer was the life of a hermit.

In his search for a suitable location he travelled northwards and soon, perhaps in 1104 or 1105, he came to Carlisle. Here, where he knew no one, he was able to live a life of strict and isolated piety until he discovered that he had a blood relationship with some of the inhabitants. One of them gave him a copy of the *Psalter of St Jerome*, an abridged version of the psalms which he was to treasure for the rest of his life, but on the whole he found the attention of his relatives a nuisance. He moved on again, this time into the forest, where he wandered from place to place, providing himself with no base of any kind and living on wild fruit, honey and other natural foods. Much of his time was devoted to prayer.

He may have spent several months in this fashion and he certainly crossed the Pennines at this time as he found himself next at Wolsingham, in the bleak country near the upper reaches of the river Wear. Here, perhaps in 1106, he came upon another hermit, an old man by the name of Aelric, who had spent his youth in the monastery at Durham. Aelric agreed that Godric should become his companion and so for a time the future saint lived at Wolsingham, apprenticed as it were to someone with greater experience of the solitary life. The association was significant, for the lessons Aelric taught him were no doubt coloured by what the elderly hermit had learnt many years before at Durham and for a long time they remained Godric's sole and tenuous contact with the life governed by St Benedict's *Rule*.

After a year and nine months, however, Aelric died and Godric, apparently dazed by this turn of events, was uncertain what to do next. He believed that St Cuthbert then came to his assistance in a vision, urging him to make a second pilgrimage to Jerusalem and on his return to live as a hermit at a place near Durham called Finchale.

Godric's last journey overseas, undertaken perhaps in 1108, was conducted under the harshest conditions. His diet consisted of dry barley-bread and water. He wore a hair shirt and did not wash until he had reached his destination. On his arrival in the Holy Land he bathed in the Jordan and, removing his shoes, swore never to wear shoes again. In and around Jerusalem he visited the church of the Holy Sepulchre, the Dome of the Rock, held in veneration as it was close to the site of Jesus's presentation in the Temple, the Mount of Olives and other places associated with Christ. He also sought out the hermits who lived in the area and for several months nursed sick pilgrims in the hospital of St John.

On his return to England he seems to have given no thought to Cuthbert's directions for Finchale, as he resumed his search for a hermitage, supporting himself by trading in low-priced goods. In perhaps 1110 or 1111 he came upon Eskdale, very near to Whitby in North Yorkshire, and, deciding to settle here, he had soon built a home for himself out of unfashioned wood and green turf. After a year and some months, however, the harassment of local landowners forced him to move again and so he travelled northwards to the city of Durham.

Here, some time in or after 1112, he attached himself to the church of St Giles, in a suburb of the city, where he was given the post of sexton or bellringer. He then transferred himself to the church of St Mary, within the city walls, where he attended a song school, the equivalent of a modern primary school. No doubt looking rather incongruous among the children, he used this opportunity to learn by heart a number of psalms, hymns and prayers, used in school as reading and singing exercises. He may also have extended a rather limited ability to read. Another occupation was praying in the cathedral, whose magnificent Norman structure was far from complete at this time.

He also began to search the area around Durham for a suitable hermitage and one day he overheard a shepherd refer to Finchale. He was obviously reminded of the vision of St Cuthbert, as he paid the man a halfpenny to show him where Finchale was. A difficult journey followed, during which Godric encountered an enormous wolf which he believed could only be the devil bent on hindering his sacred purpose. Surviving this danger, he pressed on and found himself in a place altogether suitable as a hermitage. Having obtained the permission of Finchale's owner, the bishop of Durham, he began, probably in late 1112 or early 1113, to live as a hermit there.

Thanks to one of his biographers, Reginald of Durham, who knew the saint well and describes his life in great detail, we possess much information about Godric's appearance and character. He was short, but broad-shouldered and strong. His face was long, and above sparkling grey-blue eyes were hairy eyebrows, which almost touched in the middle. He had a long nose, rounded at the bridge and curved at the end. A mouth with full lips gave way to a thick and lengthy beard, black like his hair in youth, but turning white in old age. His neck was short and fat, with prominent sinews and blood vessels. He had a barrel chest with a hollow, that appeared with age, at the bottom of the rib cage. His stomach was flat. Godric had short legs and in his early years at Finchale his knees bore hard calluses, the result of many hours spent in prayer. His feet were small and the skin was hard because, as we have seen, the hermit wore no shoes. His hands were broad, with long fingers; in time he lost the use of one of his little fingers which was bent towards the palm.

Godric's early career indicates that he possessed the qualities needed by a successful sailor and merchant: practical skills including an understanding of weather conditions, a love of adventure, business acumen and no doubt a certain lack of scruples. What probably underlay his wordly success was sheer native wit. There are other indications that he had an alert mind: without help from others he had learnt something of reading, he had picked up a smattering of French and Latin and he came to possess a wide knowledge of Christian doctrine. Common sense, a quality indispensable in one who, like all hermits, forced himself to the limits of his strength and endurance, was also to be found in his character, as was humility. He did not lack warm human feeling, as the assistance which he later gave to the visitors to Finchale shows and often, it was believed, this assistance involved the use of exceptional powers. These consisted of both the gift of 'prophecy'—the ability to see events which occurred at a distance and to foretell the future—and 'supernatural' powers of healing. This side of his personality was also revealed by the many visions he experienced, apparently both demonic and divine in origin. The diabolic visions took many forms ranging from a devil called Corinbrand, who vomited flames, to the demon of avarice, who appeared in the shape of a goldsmith, complete with tools, gems, rings and necklaces. By way of consolation he was visited, or so he believed, by Christ and the Virgin in person; John the Baptist frequently appeared to him and he once participated in a lengthy conversation with St Peter. Also regarded as 'supernatural' by his contemporaries was the relationship which Godric had with animals. Indeed he does seem to have had a special sympathy for them as, when he first came to Finchale, he shared his home with the local snakes who coiled themselves round the beams and warmed themselves by his fire. A hare, in addition, who was caught raiding Godric's vegetable patch, was punished but went on his way with some of the green stuff tied to his back.

Certain other, more idiosyncratic, features of the saint's personality help us to see him as a living individual. During his early years at Finchale he seems to have revealed an unattractive strictness and severity, bordering on fanaticism, which eventually gave way to a mellower and more moderate outlook on life. It was very pleasant to converse with this older, softened Godric, partly because he was cheerful by nature. In extreme old age, however, he became rather irritable with those around him and he suffered from bouts of severe depression. He was, finally, extremely musical, being frequently heard to sing and was responsible for the earliest songs, complete with English words and music, that have come down to us. The songs, revealed to the hermit in visions, consist of hymns to the Virgin and St Nicholas and the lines sung by Godric's sister, Burcwen, when she appeared to him after her death.

Before he came to Finchale the area had not been entirely neglected. The site of a farmstead or villa during the Roman occupation of Britain, it had been uninhabited for many centuries— some said because of the snakes—but it was used by the local peasantry for pasturing their animals and by the bishop of Durham as a hunting ground. When the saint first came to live there he probably did not occupy the area now associated with him and he may have settled on the plot of land still called St Godric's Garth, about a mile above the present Finchale site. The Garth is raised high above the river, a factor which may have led Godric to move after a short while.

The location of the saint's permanent home at Finchale, and the site of the Benedictine priory which grew up after his death, is three and a half miles downstream on the Wear from Durham. A beautiful but somewhat bleak place, where a chill wind seems to blow even in summer, it has changed relatively little since Godric's time. Indeed it is still the home of the finches who originally provided it with a name. The small, flat area where the hermit settled is in a dip and surrounded on three sides by the river. The opposite banks are sheer, rocky and covered with trees. In the twelfth century the spot could only be approached from the fourth or south-west side and the journey was made difficult by the thick, trackless forest which surrounded the place.

Once Godric had moved to the present Finchale site, he set about erecting buildings to make it habitable. The first structure, a little house with an earthen floor and a turf roof, was soon followed by a wooden oratory dedicated to the Virgin. Somewhat later the church of St John the Baptist was built from local stone. It was small and narrow, as its foundations, which still exist, indicate. A cloister of wattle with a thatched roof joined the door of the church to that of the oratory. Another building on the site came to be known as the guest-house.

Before long the surrounding land was fenced in and brought under cultivation. One area was turned into fields; another became a vegetable garden. Godric also had two orchards. In the river a fish-weir was set up, consisting of a framework into which nets and fish-traps could be lowered. Excellent salmon were often caught in the weir, even in the height of summer when the river level was low, occurrences which contemporaries regarded as miraculous.

Compared with the years before he came to Finchale, Godric's life in the hermitage must have seemed monotonous in the extreme, but this of course was what was intended. A few events and developments disturbed the peace of the settlement, however, and modified his way of life.

His early years at Finchale were marked by an extreme un-sociability—he would hide in the depths of the forest if anyone approached—but even at this stage he made a point of giving alms to the poor. Gradually his intolerant attitude softened and about this time the surviving members of his family—his mother, brother and sister—decided to move north to join him. Indeed Burcwen came to Finchale to lead the solitary life in a cell not far from her brother's home.

About 1122 the hermit modified his isolation somewhat by accepting the young son of his brother William as his servant. That a person as humble as a solitary should acquire a servant may strike us as odd, but the arrangement relieved the hermit of some of his mundane responsibilities and enabled him to devote more time to God. Thereafter servants were always to be found at Finchale.

The first three decades at the hermitage almost certainly formed the most energetic period in Godric's life there. This was the time of his hardest work, claiming land from the surrounding forest, a task which he pursued even at night so that the sound of his axe-blows could be heard for miles around, and producing food. It was also the time of his most spectacular acts of asceticism, which will be discussed below. During these years, in addition, he experienced repeated and potentially devastating floodings of the Wear and, probably in 1136, an attack by marauding soldiers belonging to King David of Scotland's invading army. They believed, wrongly, that he was concealing treasure from them; he suffered a lengthy beating and barely escaped with his life.

One of the most important changes in the hermit's life at Finchale took place in the years after 1138. During this period he became friendly with the monks of Durham and was subjected, for the first time, to the full impact of the Rule of St Benedict. This major development will be dealt with more fully below.

By this stage the hermit was becoming elderly and old age brought its usual problems, including physical weakness and ill-health. About 1162, when Godric must have been in his nineties, he retired permanently to his bed. Now totally dependent on the help of others, he was unable even to roll over in bed without assistance. At this time he lived in the stone church of St John the Baptist, his bed standing by the north wall near the altar.

In spite of the contact, through the hermit Aelric, that Godric had already had with the Benedictine life, his existence at Finchale bore little relation to what was described in the Rule until he was befriended by the Durham monks. Admittedly from an early date his life was organized according to the traditional pattern of prayer, meditation and manual work. Thus during the early years at Finchale he spent long periods—the whole night or even twenty-four hours—on his knees in prayer. After a while he composed an 'Office' for himself from the psalms and prayers that he knew and this personal version of the canonical hours was sung at the regular times. He possessed an aid to prayer in a set of beads which probably resembled a rosary and indeed part of his mind was always devoted to this activity whatever occupation he appeared to be engaged in. Much time was also taken up with meditation, in which words are read aloud, learnt by heart and their full meaning absorbed. The third element in Godric's routine was manual labour and here a variety of activities, the best corrective to boredom and monotony, presented themselves. The hermit worked at clearing the forest, labouring in his fields, grafting shoots on to trees, constructing fish traps for his weir in the river and growing vegetables. This sensible three-fold division of the time, while finding a place in St Benedict's Rule, cannot, however, be regarded as specifically Benedictine; it had also been employed by the earlier hermits of the Egyptian desert.

The saint cultivated two of the major spiritual virtues, poverty and chastity, recommended by St Benedict. Thus his meagre possessions consisted of his cooking pot, his agricultural implements, his cup—treasured since he had dipped it in the Jordan on his second visit to Palestine—the beloved *Psalter of St Jerome* and another book, possibly a missal. At one point he also owned a cow and, at a later date, sheep and cattle, the latter probably intended to assist him in feeding the poor. Although, in addition, he came to welcome the attention of spiritually-minded women, his concern for chastity led him to recoil in horror from the visitations of female demons who claimed to long for his embraces while spurning those of kings and earls. Obedience, the third great spiritual virtue recommended by Benedict and one of the pillars of the life described in the Rule, formed no part of Godric's existence, however. Until he was be-friended by the monks of Durham, his life was governed solely by his own precepts.

A second great omission in the hermit's life, of equal significance, was the sense of moderation which is such a marked feature of St Benedict's Rule. In many aspects of his existence Godric went to extremes, a typical example being his acts of asceticism, which seem in many cases to have touched the limits of human endurance. Thus he undertook severe fasts, sometimes up to a week in length and slept in conditions of great discomfort, for example, leaning against a wall. At night he prayed for long periods immersed in cold water, either in the Wear where a hollow stone on the river bed acted as a seat or in a barrel buried in the floor of the oratory. He wore a succession of hair shirts and coats of mail, and 'treated' a skin disease by rubbing the inflamed areas with salt and straw. When particularly assailed by physical temptation he applied thorns and brambles to his naked body.

His food, likewise, was not very appetizing. In the early years he lived on the roots and foliage of wild plants. He then decided to cultivate the soil and produce bread. Made of oat- or barley-meal mixed with ashes, it was eaten only when dry and mouldy. With it were consumed balls of vegetable matter derived from wild plants which had been cooked and then left to soak and rot. Water was the only accompaniment to these foods, as Godric ate no cheese, honey, butter or flesh of any kind at this time. Eventually he came to grow vegetables but there is no way of knowing if they were prepared in a more attractive fashion than the wild plants. He probably relaxed his rigid vegetarianism later as he survived on a little milk at the end of his life. Such extreme practices in the fields of asceticism and diet find no counterpart in the Rule; neither the detailed provisions of St Benedict nor the spirit which informs his work corresponds with these features of Godric's life.

This great discrepancy between the hermit's existence at Finchale and the life of the Rule was modified somewhat when he came under the influence of the monastery of Durham. It was probably the monks, anxious to associate themselves in the spiritual prestige of the hermit but also covetous, in all probability, of his land and any offerings which might be made at his tomb, who took the initiative. In particular Roger, prior of the house from about 1138 to 1149, became friendly with Godric, who was persuaded to accept the monk as his religious superior. This arrangement was probably relaxed and informal. The hermit was then taught that obedience was of fundamental importance in a life devoted to God; after Roger's death, instead of reverting to independence, he subjected himself and all his possessions to the authority of the prior's successors. He was probably glad of the security this would provide as he faced the helplessness of old age. This act of submission, made after 1149, probably marks Godric's formal assimilation into the community. He was almost certainly never professed, as was conventional, but was associated with the monastery by a decree promulgated by the full community sitting in chapter. Subject to the authority of the house, but an 'associate monk' rather than a professed one and remaining at Finchale, he probably occupied a position that was unique.

The Rule of St Benedict was soon exerting an influence over the old man. Most significantly, in the latter part of his life he abandoned the extreme austerities of earlier years and began to develop the attractive moderation and mellowness which characterized him in this period. One factor here was almost certainly old age, but the Rule was no doubt another. Of equal importance was the new acceptance of obedience, and the tight control of the prior over him can be seen in operation; for a time he would speak only to visitors who brought with them a wooden cross from the prior to indicate his consent to the conversation.

He was also introduced to the monastic discipline of silence, which, in spite of the changes in outlook that he was undergoing, he could not resist taking beyond the provisions of the Rule. Thus silence was maintained at night, as St Benedict suggested, but Godric would also speak to no one on certain days of the week, frequently on feastdays, and during periods which covered Advent, Lent and Pentecost. This practice caused him to invent a system of manual signs and nods, which he taught to his servants and by means of which he could communicate with them.

The association with Durham brought Godric into closer contact than hitherto with the ceremonies of the Church. He seems to have heard Mass rarely during his years of independence, though he may have given communion to himself, the Eucharist being kept in his oratory. Now the monks said Mass for him regularly and heard his confession. Indeed when he was close to death he received communion every second or third day. The canonical hours in their official form were also said by the monks, in contrast to the personal version which Godric had used before. No doubt the hermit was deeply influenced by the frequent presence of Durham monks at Finchale. At first they merely paid him visits but as he became more infirm one or more of them, and especially Reginald, his biographer, came to live at the settlement. They organized worship, as we have seen, took part in spiritual discussions, gave Godric instruction and nursed the declining old man.

It is impossible to say how far the life of the saint can be described as Benedictine. Strictly speaking, no hermit can be a complete follower of St. Benedict who was concerned with a life lived in common with others. This particular solitary, in addition, had established most of his habits and rules of life before the monks of Durham made contact with him. They no doubt modified his practices, but it is obvious that some at least of their regulations had been relaxed by the end of Godric's life. Probably the hermit was influenced more by the spirit of the Rule than by any of its specific provisions; in particular the stress it laid on moderation helped to smooth out harsh elements in his way of life and indeed in his character.

For one who claimed to live alone, Godric came into contact with a large number of people. Probably as early as the 1130s he was an important figure in the local area and for a substantial part of his life as a hermit crowds of visitors were a common sight at Finchale. Many of those who came needed assistance and he dispensed relief of various kinds, ranging from reassuring predictions about law suits to cures for sterility. The tricks of the devil, in addition, were exposed, dreams were interpreted and hidden sins, such as that of a local man who, returning home tired from a day's work, had beaten his nagging wife, brought to light.

Various individuals stand out among the hundreds who no doubt visited Godric or had contact with him. Some were based in Durham or the surrounding area, including Bishop Ranulf Flambard (1099–1128), the cynical minister of William Rufus and Henry I, but the hermit's original patron nevertheless. Perhaps recognizing in the reformed merchant and double-dealer a man not so dissimilar from himself, he granted Godric the land on which to live. Another Durham friend was the monk Reginald, who wrote the life of the hermit and more than anyone nursed the rather cantankerous old man. Other monastic friends belonged to the strict Cistercian Order. They included the saintly Robert, abbot of Newminster from about 1139 to 1159 and Ailred, abbot of Rievaulx, one of the most sympathetic figures of the twelfth century.

Bishops and abbots were far from insignificant figures, but some of the hermit's other contacts were even more eminent. Three kings took an interest in the saint, probably because they believed in the particular efficacy of his prayers. Malcolm IV, king of Scotland from 1153 to 1165, made a grant of land to Godric, while his successor, William the Lion, visited the old man at Finchale in 1170 and was known as his friend. The hermit had also been brought to the attention of King Henry II of England, who granted land in Yorkshire to him. Godric was, furthermore, in communication with two of the major ecclesiastical figures of the day. He exchanged a number of messages with Archbishop Thomas Becket, enmeshed at the time in his quarrel with King Henry; the saint offered encouragement and prophesied the archbishop's martyrdom amongst other things. The hermit, finally, received a personal letter from Pope Alexander III. In June 1168 or 1169 Alexander sent Godric his blessing and asked for his prayers for both the Church and the pope. He said that in his turn he would remember the hermit in his prayers.

Godric died at sunrise on Thursday, 21 May 1170. He must have been about a hundred years old and had been at Finchale for almost sixty. He was buried, in a stone tomb which he had prepared for himself, in the church of St John the Baptist. His visions and clairvoyance ensured that he was regarded as a saint before his death and a collection of over two hundred posthumous miracles, made by Reginald and consisting largely of cures, confirmed his sanctity. Although never formally canonized, he was regarded with veneration in many parts of England and beyond, but especially at Finchale and Durham, until the end of the Middle Ages.

Paralleling Godric's life in many instances is that of his contemporary, St Bartholomew of Farne.

The future hermit and monk was born in Whitby and was given the Scandinavian name of Tostig by his parents. The name caused him to be mocked by other young people, who were perhaps French-speakers as it was changed to the Norman one of William. Like Godric, his youth was worldly, but he engaged in no systematic accumulation of wealth, rather giving himself up wholeheartedly to pleasure. Indeed a vision of Christ and the Virgin themselves was insufficient to turn the playboy immediately from his course. Not surprisingly he was unsettled at this time and he chose to travel abroad, curious to investigate other countries and other ways of life. As the vision suggests, however, and as was also the case but to a greater degree with Godric, a pious germ existed within him. On reaching Norway he attached himself to a local priest and became first a deacon and was then ordained himself. In spite of taking orders, however, he became the object of some romantic scheming: a local man wished to marry him to his daughter, who was agreeable to the match. Although strenuous efforts were made to win him over, Bartholomew declined the offer. After three years in Norway he decided to return home and, settling at a church in Northumbria, worked as a parish priest for some time.

The memory of his earlier vision now recurred to him and, perhaps because he had begun to regret his early life like Godric and wished to atone for it, he immediately decided to leave the world and enter the monastery of Durham. A vision of the figure on the cross at the ceremony of profession indicated the rightness of his choice. It was at this time that he received the name in religion of Bartholomew, the choice of his fellow-monks. While living in the monastery he cultivated the virtues of humility and obedience, and always discharged his part in the Office with great care. He does not seem to have been totally satisfied with the monastic life, however, and aspired to a solitary existence, perhaps feeling that the rigours of the latter would be more likely to wipe out his earlier sins. At this stage St Cuthbert, who had inspired Godric at a similar time, appeared to him, or so he believed, and in a vision showed him round the island of Inner Farne. After such an experience he was unable to contain his enthusiasm and he revealed his hopes to Lawrence, prior of Durham from 1149 to 1154. Perhaps aware of his earlier instability, Lawrence had misgivings about Bartholomew's plan, especially as he had not yet spent a year in the monastery,

Eventually he gave in to the monk's ardour, however, and Bartholomew sailed to his new home late in the year 1150.

He had chosen a location even more bleak and isolated than Finchale. His home was one of the Farne Islands, a group of about twenty off the coast of Northumberland, five miles south of Lindisfarne. The largest of the group and the closest—one and a half miles —to the shore, the Inner Farne is treeless and relatively barren. On the south side are cliffs and there is only one small place which can act as a landing ground. Epitomized best by the cries of its natural inhabitants, birds, especially eider-ducks, and seals, the island suffers a continuous buffeting by the waves and is cold at most times of the year. Bartholomew no doubt chose it because St Cuthbert had once lived there as a hermit, leaving a permanent memorial in the buildings he had erected, and it was this same island that had inspired Godric to lead the solitary life.

Not long before the monk's arrival it had been in a state of disorder, animals being pastured there and taking shelter in the oratory in bad weather. A man from Lindisfarne had restored it to a suitable condition and in Bartholomew's time the oratory, and the little hut of unshaped stones and turf, which stood next to the landing ground and acted as a guest-house, were both in use. A narrow path led from one to the other and fresh water was provided by two springs. A flat area, covered in grass, was used for growing barley and pasturing the hermit's animals. Other islands supplied the Inner Farne with hay or fuel and one furnished the dead sailors brought to the hermit with a burial ground.

When Bartholomew first went to the island he found another Durham monk, Aelwin, already living there as a solitary. The latter did not react favourably to the newcomer's arrival and indeed subjected him to a campaign of hostility. He failed to alter Bartholomew's determination to live on Farne, however, and when he realized this he withdrew himself.

The new hermit lived alone until 1163 when Thomas, formerly prior of Durham and driven from office because he had opposed the bishop's will, came to join him. By now Bartholomew himself seems to have become inflexible as a disagreement soon arose over the type of food the two should eat and the length of mealtimes. On this occasion Bartholomew withdrew to Durham, but after a year he returned and the hermits lived together in harmony for the remainder of Thomas's life.

Like Godric, Bartholomew was aware of the dangers of monotony and occupied himself with a range of activities. His life was no doubt organized according to the traditional threefold pattern of prayer, meditation and work, though a particular emphasis was placed on prayer. He regarded the chanting of the whole psalter once, twice or even three times in twenty-four hours as the bare minimum and spent much time on his knees, including at night. He also read and no doubt meditated, and occupied himself with manual labour, which included writing. His relaxation was walking round the island.

Bartholomew loved poverty and praised the freedom from anxiety and acquisitiveness that it conferred. He possessed only what was strictly necessary, such as vestments for services, books, and sheep, which provided both food and clothing. His diet consisted of bread, vegetables, milk products and, during the first few years at Farne, the fish found so plentifully in the sea around the island. After a while he gave up fish and he never ate meat. His drink was water and sometimes milk, but he never touched alcoholic beverages in any form. Only a little time was devoted to meals and he ate sparingly. It is possible that Bartholomew, like Godric, had servants to perform some of the mundane tasks which hindered his concentration on God.

The hermit had received a formal training, albeit of short duration, in the monastery at Durham and no doubt much of his life bore the imprint of the Rule. Such aspects of his routine as have already been described are broadly consistent with St Benedict's directives. He had deliberately abandoned a communal existence, however, and the time he spent on Farne revealed much of the hardship and rigour traditionally associated with the life of a hermit.

To a greater extent than Finchale, the Inner Farne provided conditions amounting to an ascetic exercise in their own right. Indeed one of Bartholomew's contemporaries referred to it as 'a purgatory on earth'. Barely furnished with the necessities of life, bitterly cold and damp—ideally suited to the exacerbation of psychological stresses—it was also at the mercy of North Sea storms and the sea-raiders who used it as a haven.

Other forms of self-mortification included a hair shirt, which Bartholomew wore for five years, and a bed in which the saint lay on a concealed wooden cross so that there was no chance of being comfortable. When Thomas, the former prior, arrived on Farne these practices were abandoned lest Thomas should become aware of them and lest the sweat produced by the hair shirt should offend him. After this Bartholomew used no bed, not even in his final illness. As his death approached and no doubt because he felt that little time was left to expiate his sins, his ascetic exercises became more extreme. It was believed that he drank nothing during the last seven and a half years of his life and in addition ate nothing during the last seven weeks. Apart from the latter rigours, however, his spiritual practices do not seem to have been as harsh as those of

Godric. The sense of moderation derived from the Rule probably held him back from the most severe forms of self-chastisement.

Our knowledge of the hermit's appearance is limited, though it is recorded that he was strong and healthy-looking with rosy cheeks, but at the same time created a venerable impression. He dressed in a monastic tunic, made of a mixture of wool and linen, and a cowl. The tunic was worn until it was black with sweat, a practice he maintained even in the face of criticism. Covering the tunic was a black cloak lined with fur of the same colour, while his shoes, which once put on were never removed, were of sheepskin. Like Godric, Bartholomew was of a cheerful disposition, and he believed sadness to be a crime. His humility was also noted by contemporaries. He was compassionate towards those who came to him with problems—urging compassion also on others—and was full of generosity to those who were marooned on Farne in bad weather. Like Godric he had a particular sympathy for animals, especially the pet bird who took food from his hand and came each day to feed at his table. A mother eider-duck, in addition, seems to have known she could rely on his help when one of her chicks fell down the side of a rock. It was perhaps because of his interest in animals that the demonic visitations he believed himself to experience tended to assume animal forms. When not taking the shape of a lion, bull, bear or mouse, the devil would remain invisible but reveal his presence by making mysterious and alarming noises. The hermit also felt that saints visited him, including St Cuthbert who said Mass with him early one Christmas morning. Apart from the ability to see such visions, Bartholomew was also credited with the gift of foretelling the future, especially, and most appositely, changes in the weather.

In spite of his isolation the hermit obviously remained in close touch with his fellow-monks. They came to Farne to speak with him and commend themselves to his prayers, while he would provide them with such spartan meals as his island could supply. He would also tell them stories, which no doubt included a number of miracles of St Cuthbert, derived from Bartholomew, that have come down to us. The monks, who included Godric's biographer, Reginald, came from the hermit's former home at Durham, but also from its dependencies at Lindisfarne and Coldingham. Non-monastic visitors also came to Farne, though one would imagine that fewer people journeyed to the rocky island than to Finchale. Both the wealthy—whom Bartholomew rebuked and urged to mend their ways—and the poverty-stricken came to see him and he advised and consoled his visitors. Some came from a great distance, like the woman from Flanders who foolishly defied the ban on admitting females to the oratory and received an instant punishment. He also ministered to those who came to the island to pray to St Cuthbert. At one point the number of visitors led him to consider adopting the enclosed life of the anchorite but, aware of the spiritual value of what he was doing, he decided against the step.

Nine years before his death Bartholomew was aware of when the event would occur. His death was preceded by a lengthy illness which included an internal abscess. He died on 24 June 1193 after living over forty-two years on the island. He had prepared a stone tomb for himself, again like Godric, and his body, placed within this, was buried outside the southern wall of his oratory. Cures were soon reported at the tomb and he long enjoyed a modest reputation for sanctity in Durham and the north-east.

In terms of their personal histories and their characters—sharing in particular the toughness that enabled them to survive under harsh conditions for many years—the two saints were not dissimilar. A significant difference, however, is the point in their lives when the Rule of St Benedict exerted an influence on them—in Bartholomew's case, before he became a hermit and in Godric's, long after he had established himself in the solitary life. In both cases, however, the Rule had encouraged a marked degree of moderation, even in the context of the traditionally far from moderate life of the hermit.

by Victoria M. Tudor

BIBLIOGRAPHY

St Godric

Reginald of Durham, *Libellus de vita et miraculis S. Godrici, heremitae de Finchale*, ed. J. Stevenson (Surtees Society 20, 1845).

Geoffrey of Durham, *Life of St Godric* in *Acta Sanctorum Bollandiana* (3rd edition, Paris, 1863–), May, vol. V, pp. 70–85.

William of Newburgh, *Historia Rerum Anglicarum* in *Chronicles of the Reigns of Stephen, Henry II, and Richard I*, ed. R. Howlett (Rolls Series 82, 1884–90), vol. I, pp. 149–50.

——, Record of Godric's songs: *English Medieval Songs* (*Music of the Middle Ages*, vol. V, Expériences Anonymes EAS-29, New York).

St Bartholomew

Geoffrey of Durham, *Vita Bartholomaei Farnensis* in *Symeonis Monachi Opera Omnia*, ed. T. Arnold (Rolls Series 75, 1882–5), vol. II, pp. 295–325.

Reginald of Durham, *Libellus de admirandis beati Cuthberti virtutibus*, ed. J. Raine (Surtees Society 1, 1835).

H. H. E. Craster, 'The Miracles of Farne', *Archaeologia Aeliana*, 4th series, 29 (1951), pp. 93–107 (a collection of stories recounted by Bartholomew).

Thomas de la Mare and Uthred of Boldon

The abbey of St Albans in the South and the cathedral priory of Durham in the North were centres of monastic distinction during the Middle Ages. The first claimed to have been founded by King Offa (d. 796); it certainly joined the reform of Dunstan and Ethelwold in the tenth century. It was fortunate to have Lanfranc's nephew Paul as its abbot after the Norman Conquest. The only English pope, Adrian IV, was educated there. It gradually grew in wealth and prestige until it was reckoned as the premier abbey of the whole of England. For this position it had its strategic geographical situation to thank, as well as the many notable monks who chose it as their home and the kings and magnates who frequently stayed in its guest house. The purpose of this essay is to recall the memory of one of its most distinguished abbots, together with that of one of England's most important 'University monks'. Each knew and respected the other; each provided an example of the perennial vitality of the Benedictine ideal in a context often regarded as unhelpful or even decadent.

Each of them was conscious of being a representative of a tradition greater than themselves. Thomas de la Mare, who was born in 1309, came of a notable aristocratic background. He was one of a large family, of whom three brothers and one sister also became religious. He joined the monastery at the age of seventeen, but was sent for his novitiate to the dependent priory of Wymondham in Norfolk. The reason may well have been to spare him from too frequent visits from friends and family. However this may be, he was recalled to St Albans nine years later, in 1335. He became in succession abbot's chaplain, kitchener and cellarer.

By this time St Albans had been a large community for many years. It numbered 100 monks in the late twelfth and early thirteenth centuries. It had also been distinguished for its artistic and literary work. Some of this was centred on the local saint, whose cult was the only one in the country which had continuity since Romano-British times. In the scriptorium were produced varied and often very beautiful manuscripts. Matthew Paris was a historian and writer of the abbey whose enormous range, output and indefatigable energy were combined with outstanding artistic gifts and an insular partisanship with regard to national and ecclesiastical affairs. He however had died long since, but his manuscripts were still in the abbey library, an impressive monument to the medieval, as to the modern viewer. They reveal great industry and learning, enlivened by numerous marginal sketches.

From the rich life, liturgical, artistic and literary of St Albans Thomas was sent in 1340 to be prior of the distant cell of Tynemouth. This monastery, the object of prolonged litigation with Durham, had belonged to St Albans from the late eleventh century. It housed the shrine of the Anglo-Saxon St Oswin, never of the first importance. Its immense distance from the mother-house brought it difficulties of several kinds. It was never large, its highest recorded community number being eighteen, but this dates from after the Black Death, so one might conjecture that it numbered twenty to thirty when Thomas de la Mare became its prior. It had for long been used by St Albans abbots as a destination for trouble-makers in the community or for those who were, in one way or another, misfits. Such houses had their economic importance as the base for administering distant community lands, but also, as is less often stated, as a legitimate and dignified home for those monks who, in an age which did not recognize the validity of dispensation from vows, found the normal life of a large abbey, for various reasons, frustrating or intolerable. Thomas's skill as a superior must have been tested in these conditions. Among the community he ruled was John of Tynemouth, the famous compiler of saints' Lives whose work underlies the collection called *Nova Legenda Angliae*, usually but inaccurately ascribed to Capgrave. Like other abbots and priors of his time, Thomas was litigious; he was always prompt to vindicate in the courts any of his houses' claims which he considered just. More admirable characteristics which won him respect in the North were his urbane hospitality, his prudent administration and his care for high monastic standards of his house.

An unexpected catastrophe however was just round the corner. The Black Death, bubonic plague carried by flea-infested rats, reached England in 1348. It struck St Albans and struck it hard. About Easter in 1349 the abbot, Michael of Mentmore, friend of kings and patron of monastic scholars, died of the plague. With him perished also the prior, the sub-prior and forty-six monks, not counting those in dependent cells. The community was thus reduced to half its accustomed number in a few days. Although the abbeys as a whole recovered to a large extent from this disaster after some years, some suffered more than others; for those monks who actually lived through those critical years, the experience must have been terrifying indeed.

The most urgent task at St Albans after burying the dead was to

8

choose a new abbot. The first candidate elected was the prior of Wymondham, but he refused. The electors set to work again and chose Thomas de la Mare. He was about forty years of age. He remained abbot for forty-seven years, the rest of his unusually long life.

His public life, his litigation, his friendship with royalty, his conflict with the townsmen of St Albans at the time of the Peasants' revolt; all these were consequent on the social position of one of the richest abbeys in England. What is more to our purpose here is to sketch the characteristics of his internal rule and see how it was still possible for a fourteenth-century abbot, in spite of many conflicting claims upon him, to live a community life according to the Rule of St Benedict.

His external achievements were considerable. The great gateway and much of the guesthouse were built by him. But his first care was for his monks. The cloister was glazed and provided with seats, studies allocated for chaplains and monk-students; furniture, chests and books provided. In the church the shrine of St Alban was enriched with a silver-gilt eagle, the sacristy with vestments, service-books, lamps and tapestries. It was indeed both an example of princely magnificence and also of the *luxe pour Dieu* beloved both by Cluny and by Abbot Suger of Saint-Denis. Cistercian austerity in Church furnishings had no place in the St Albans of Thomas de la Mare. St Bernard would certainly not have approved of the expensive pictures which came from Italy, still less of the fine new clock which still survives.

But Thomas's hidden life was unexpectedly impressive. He had but one meal a day, he slept on a hard bed and rose before midnight to say extra prayers, he not only said Mass, but heard others as well. He would privately recite the Office of the Dead on journeys or between business. He wore a hair shirt and observed the times and places of monastic silence. Visitors were not allowed to take him away from the recitation at the right time of the Divine Office. In most of these ways his practices were like those of St Wulfstan or St Hugh of Lincoln before him.

He loved his community; their voices in the Divine Office pleased him more than any other singers. He reformed the domestic liturgy by insisting on slower recitation, but introducing extra chant to increase devotion; with the same end in view he eliminated some of the extra additions. Such reforms reveal a mind concerned more with the quality and reverence of prayer than with the material fulfilment of an external duty. He also showed special care for his sick monks, performing himself, rather than by deputy, the ordinary nursing service of an infirmarian. He specially enjoyed the company of the brethren when they were on convalescence or short holidays in his manor of Redburn, but he took care of the Liturgy there also, insisting on singing the Masses on Sundays and feastdays and prescribing the singing of the *Salve Regina* after Compline.

Like his predecessor, he exercised for many years the office of president and visitor of the Congregation. He was also appointed visitor of monasteries such as Eynsham, Battle, Reading and Abingdon which for one reason or another were considered to be royal. Sometimes he took difficult monks from elsewhere into his own community for a time and charged nothing for their keep. Yet another example of his charity was revealed in his compassionate treatment of fugitive monks, whom he received back with both mercy and joy. He also allowed some of his own monks to be transferred to other houses.

His Constitutions in various General Chapters from 1351 onwards are full of interest, but too long for adequate treatment here. Suffice it to say that they are conspicuous for care taken in the performance of the Divine Office, in the training of the novices, in the keeping of enclosure and silence and the occupation of the monks in reading, writing, correcting, illuminating and binding books. The duties of the various obedientiaries are outlined, as well as those of confessors, almoners and infirmarians. The monastic duties of fasting and abstinence are recalled, stricter than for the laity and including a fast on every Friday, abstinence on every Wednesday and throughout Advent and Lent, Sundays included. Although these prescriptions were less severe than those in earlier days, Thomas de la Mare took good care to see that all was well observed. It is perhaps not fanciful to see here a Cluniac care for order in monastic life, comparable to the Cluniac devotion and reverence which he insisted on in the performance of the Divine Office.

He enjoyed the favour of the kings of England and France, of the Black Prince and of a series of Popes, who highly valued his integrity and energy. With approaching old age and the ill-effects of a later outbreak of the plague to contend with, he wished to resign his office. His community however refused to allow this. With the passing of the years he was appropriately nursed with devotion by his monks and eventually his sight began to fail. To these years belong a manuscript from his manor of Redburn written in huge letters appropriate to one in his condition. It contains a short spiritual work by his contemporary, Uthred of Boldon, monk of Durham. This *Devout Meditation* was arranged (or even initially written) for him by its author, described below, who happened to die in the same year, 1396, as the thirtieth abbot of St Albans.

Thomas was a figure of national importance, involved in business and litigation of all kinds. But in exercising the functions of a feudal abbot, in vindicating for his abbey the rights which were its due in the House of Lords, in waiting on the king at court, he never forgot what he was and why he was there. He at least among his contemporaries gave a fine example of a life dedicated to the Rule of St Benedict, both as monk and as abbot. We do not know how many late medieval abbots shared his ideals or scale of values, or how many practised as he did the traditional monastic austerities amid the splendour by then inseparable from his office. One hopes that his inspiration was widely followed.

Uthred of Boldon, monk of Durham, was born in Northumbria in 1315 and spent much of his life there. But he was resident at Oxford for twenty years (1347–67) and took a prominent part in some of the theological disputes of the day. He is often considered the most impressive of the university monks of the fourteenth century: Leland, in the sixteenth, declared that there was never a monk of Durham more learned than he. His theological works have often been studied; here our aim is to see rather what his monastic and devotional writings can tell us about him.

The memory of the Anglo-Saxon past of Northumbria was a powerful inspiration to the monks of Durham; it was made concrete, so to speak, by the presence of the relics of both Cuthbert and Bede in their cathedral. Durham indeed was such a magnet to pilgrims that it was called the 'English Sion'; its monks were, by definition, the servants of Cuthbert, the most popular saint of the North. His gentle personality on earth contrasted with his posthumous reputation of an avenger of all who violated his property or attacked his community. The progressive enrichment of his cathedral during the later Middle Ages was matched by a corresponding, less tangible, enrichment in the life of the monastery. This was seen not only in the fine monastic buildings (many of which survive) but also in notable increases in the library. Indeed the Durham monks' assiduity in study remained until the Dissolution, when it was commented on by the eloquent and articulate author of *The Rites of Durham*.

Uthred's rise to fame was very slow. It is likely that he was one of those promising boys born on or near the abbey estates, noticed by one of the community and encouraged to join it in his turn. Many of these novices were of comparatively humble social status. He was professed at the age of eighteen. Five years later he was sent to the priory's college at Oxford (now part of Trinity College). This had been founded for eight monks and eight secular students.

It was one of three Oxford Halls which housed monks: the others were Canterbury Hall (now part of Christ Church) and Gloucester Hall (now part of Worcester College) which was supported by several abbeys in the south and west. Monks were in Oxford not only because the Holy See encouraged the monasteries to send them, but also because the abbeys were enlightened enough to see that the intellectual training of their gifted members, especially in theology, would improve the quality of life of the community as well as enrich the individual concerned. Durham indeed was outstanding in its support for this policy: during the last century and a half of its existence between a third and a half of its monks resided at Oxford at least for a few years.

It was important that the right scale of values should be kept by the monks in this rather different environment. It should be remembered, though, that Durham monks often spent considerable number of years in one or other of their cells in different parts of northern England. A famous saying of Uthred, repeated and made his own by the later prior of Durham, John Wessington, was however primarily intended for monks who were students:

> It is not good to lose the substance for the sake of the accidents. The substance is to say and hear Mass, to recite the Divine Office at the proscribed times and to fulfil in the first place all the other things which belong to monastic life: then and only then, as opportunity allows, should one study books and theology.

Such a statement was appropriate for all seasons and has lost none of its value down the centuries. Monks at universities have always needed to safeguard their priorities and to ensure that various attractions do not lead them astray from their proper vocation in the Church. This is to safeguard the essentials rather than to promote novelty or experiment. Elsewhere in this volume it has been suggested that the Benedictines would have done better to concentrate on their scriptural and patristic inheritance rather than become second-rate purveyors of decadent scholasticism. There is much to be said for this viewpoint. Uthred however, like every other theologian at Oxford, studied theology in the idiom of the time. This was a scholastic one and in contemporary Oxford the Friars, both Dominican and Franciscan, were in the vanguard, while some secular masters were also prominent. Few monks were really outstanding theologians in fourteenth century Oxford.

Uthred's controversies with the Friars, when he had been there for about twenty years as student and teacher, were varied and acrimonious. It seems that he gave as good as he got, that Benedictine peace had not yet completely permeated the soul of this energetic and outspoken Northerner. The details of the controversies do not concern us here, except insofar as Uthred can be claimed as a pioneer about the eternal destiny of the unbeliever. Students of St Thomas Aquinas know of this great Doctor's preoccupation with the fate of those who had never heard of Christian Revelation; towards those he called *nutriti in silvis* he showed himself compassionate, and optimistic about their fate. Uthred showed similar qualities at a time when relatively few knew or cared about extra-European and non-Christian humanity. In our own days, when interest in comparative religion is regarded often as essential in any religious education, it is difficult to understand the particularism of most medieval people. Uthred was a welcome exception. The problem he faced was how to provide for the salvation of unbelievers when it was taught that baptism and faith were necessary for salvation. But he did not stand alone in his efforts to solve this problem.

The fact that Uthred made mistakes should not blind us to his achievement. His view has been restated, with necessary modifications, by theologians of our own time. Essentially he believed that all human beings, whether Christians, Jews, Saracens or pagans, whether adults, children or still-born infants, enjoyed at the moment preceding death a clear vision of God. In the light of this, the individual chose or rejected God for eternity.

Although at first sight the hypothesis was attractive, on closer consideration it was open to severe criticism. This it received from the Friars, notably the Dominican William Jordan. In the event the Benedictine archbishop of Canterbury, Simon Langham, after an acrimonious controversy, imposed silence on both parties, censuring thirty propositions, of which twenty-two were drawn from Uthred's works and the remaining eight from his opponents'.

Perhaps the most fundamental criticism which could be made of Uthred's view was that it seemed to render revelation and the supernatural life unnecessary. Moreover it appeared to make faith and baptism superfluous, but the need for the latter rests on divine, and not only ecclesiastical authority. Also Uthred in fact called into question the fate of both baptized and unbaptized children; he excluded the possibility of 'limbo'; his theory also rendered original sin virtually meaningless. Recent restatements of what is best in Uthred's original intuition have avoided these serious deficiencies.

One important effect of the controversy was that Uthred was withdrawn from Oxford. In 1367, at the very time when he was under attack, but just before Langham's commission imposed silence on the parties, he was appointed prior of Finchale. This was an agreeable position, but not one of the first importance. The setting of Finchale had scarcely changed since the days of St Godric, but the status of the house and the physical extent of its buildings had done. After Godric's death in 1170 and the rise of his cult, centred round his tomb there, Finchale developed in importance during the thirteenth century, particularly when two of its priors in succession became bishops of Durham. Regarding it more as a possible rival than as a daughter, the Durham monks reduced its status to that of a holiday house for its monks and pulled down considerable sections of the monastic buildings, now no longer needed. When Uthred became prior, Durham monks went there four at a time for a week or more and the resident community numbered another eight.

The condemnation of some of his theological opinions did not spoil the monastic career of Uthred. He was either subprior of Durham or else prior of Finchale for the rest of his life. He was also much in demand as a Visitor for the monasteries of Whitby (then in a deplorable state), of St Mary's York, of the churches of Howdenshire and, in the entourage of the bishop of Durham, of his monastic priory itself. Later he visited the northern monasteries on behalf of the chapter in 1380–1. Already in 1373 he was chosen as a member of the royal embassy to Avignon to negotiate about papal subsidies and may have been one of a group of theologians questioned by the Black Prince about papal power in temporal matters. Such confidence in him far outside his monastic family is a tribute to his good judgement, learning and prudence: he was the only Benedictine who was not an abbot to attain such widespread offices.

Instead of the vexed questions of grace and predestination, Uthred chose to write later in life on monastic origins. We can see in this definite change of subject something of his deeper monastic scale of values coming to light. It is true to say that these treatises were occasioned by controversy, again between the various religious Orders, on the subject of their comparative antiquity and intrinsic worth. In the seventeenth century much ink flowed in the pursuit of rival claims to antiquity by the universities of Oxford and Cambridge. These had been preceded by similar rival claims between different Benedictine abbeys, for example Glastonbury and Westminster. Such controversies often engender heat rather than light. In the fourteenth century the Carmelites, for example, claimed that their Order was the oldest because it had been founded by the prophet Elias: some Dominicans however answered that the patriarch Jacob was their founder. Into this context came Uthred's two treatises *De substantialibus* and *De perfectione vivendi*. They rose above the level of current controversy and one of them, in the words of Dom David Knowles, 'became an extremely reasonable, persuasive-and historically accurate account of the development of the monastic ideal, as seen first in kindred endeavours in the Old Testament and by St John the Baptist, and traced from apostolic times through Cassian and the monks of Palestine to the Italian monks of the age of St Benedict.'

In it may be seen the attempt to come to grips with the relationship between Christian monasticism and that of the Old Testament: such consideration can help in contemporary dialogue about Buddhist monks of the present day or about the semi-monastic movements revealed by the Dead Sea Scrolls. Equally interesting is the stress laid (under Aristotelian influence) on the reasonableness of monastic life: some kind of restraint in the use of goods, in food and sexual pleasure and in the choice of rational obedience is incumbent on all men.

But the monastic life is in its full form is a regime of grace. As the Christian religion existed from the beginning of time, so also did the monastic rule and religious way of life exist from the beginning of monasticism, although only later did it receive the name of Benedictine. This monastic way of life is not (as Erasmus later asserted) based on ceremonies, but on obedience according to the Rule of St Benedict: the observance of Christ's law of charity is the end towards which different forms of religious life are ordered. The worship of God indeed is also the end, towards which different means lead: these include corporal observances, which are sometimes expendable if charity demands it. But true religion must be founded in both interior virtue and in some corporal observances. In short, Uthred reasserted the traditional monastic teaching, habitual since the time of Cassian, whose insistence on the two-fold meaning of *puritas cordis* as both worship and charity became classical in monastic thinking. He sees the Benedictine life not as adding a new perfection to Christ's teaching, but as helping the observance and fulfilment of the gospel.

In his second treatise *De perfectione vivendi*, possibly written for novice-masters, there is consideration of the arguments about secular and regular life in view of Christ's invitation to the young man in the Gospel and the life of the Apostles with Him. Then follow distinctions and definitions concerning perfection and its different kinds. The traditional distinction between active and contemplative lives is outlined. A man may be perfect in any state of life, and he will be more or less perfect insofar as he practises the three theological virtues. This is important in the consideration of personal, individual perfection; but there is also dispute about the perfection of different approved ways of life in the Church. Here the supreme criterion consists in the following of Christ. In the early

Church, as nowadays, cenobitic and contemplative life is necessary and holy, but the apostolic life, as lived by Christ, is the most perfect of all. He then shows genuine appreciation of the many different vocations in the Church as shown by the Lives of Saints, and places the monastic Order in the context of pseudo-Denys' hierarchy of perfection. He concludes that the monastic way of life is the first among the Religious Orders, that it is the most sacred and the highest in the Church. This conclusion follows considerations of it being necessary to complete the work of the ecclesiastical hierarchy, of monasticism's antiquity, purity and excellence, its harmony and unity, its renunciation of secular things and its contemplation of divine mysteries. It can never be destroyed, nor is it defiled by the defection of unworthy members any more than the angels are defiled by the apostasy of Satan and his followers. Moreover, its excellence can be shown by its many eminent members: pastors, teachers, contemplatives. A list of such monastic saints and writers was originally appended to the treatise: surely Uthred would have approved of this present volume which in some ways overlaps with his.

If Uthred's treatise is characteristic of late medieval English monasticism, it reveals a very different state of affairs from the caricatures of Wycliffe and Erasmus. Although the structure of the treatise reflects the scholastic technique and has a somewhat arid appearance for this reason, his balance and restraint are in strong contrast with some contemporary controversies, including some of his own earlier efforts. Even more important, they show him as a profoundly traditional writer insisting rightly on the internal virtues, especially charity, as constituting perfection of monastic life; there is no question for him of a monasticism consisting in merely external observances: formalities, ceremonies or superstitions. By sending Uthred to Oxford, Durham assured a restatement in terms appreciated by contemporary theologians, of the value of monastic life in the Church.

Another fruit of his reading was the short treatise called the *Devout Meditation*. This also was a traditional kind of spiritual writing; it revealed his personal convictions and his personal religion. Reading it is almost like hearing him thinking aloud on his knees. It is a devout consideration of some of the most fundamental spiritual truths: the sinfulness of the individual and his complete dependence on God, who has both gratuitously chosen and mercifully forgiven him. The tone of it is both personal and doctrinal. It begins with a paraphrase of one of St Anselm's Meditations: the words are to be read slowly and quietly, from the depths of the heart when the soul is raised towards God high above all worldly and carnal thoughts. The reader should not necessarily read it all at a sitting, but only as much as will inflame his heart.

The words of the meditation are frequently biblical or else inspired by the Liturgy or, significantly, the words of St Anselm. A few extracts may suffice to provide an idea of its general quality.

To the infinite favour of my precious Redemption God has added the immense benefit of his merciful guidance. Without any merit of mine he called me to the grace of baptism which cleansed me from all my previous sins, adopted me among the sons and heirs of God, removed the strength and power of my enemies, diminished my tendency to sin and my impure desires, and gave both the grace to act with virtue and the strength to complete such actions. God brought me up in the Christian religion, in which I received the sacraments of the true faith, as it were naturally, through its continual practice, in which I learnt the worship of the one true God by assiduous teaching and the example of the faithful; moreover he called me personally out of the world, so that I might rise to his familiar service.

God kept me free from innumerable repulsive sins, into which my enemies the world, the devil and the flesh tried hard to make me fall. He kept me safe from innumerable bodily dangers, of water and fire, journeys and robbers and countless evil fortunes which occur in this life. As I slept and when I was awake, he kept me from the attacks of the devil and the importunities of evil spirits.

God gave me a mind and understanding, perceptiveness and ability to reason together with other powers and endowments of the soul. He gave me proportion and elegance in my bodily members, sufficient food and clothing, also the appropriate external strength and adaptibility. God also gave me time for coming to maturity, not to be cut down after three or four years like the barren fig-tree, but waiting a considerable time and encouraging me daily with fresh gifts so that I might use these and his other gifts fruitfully for his glory. In so doing I would be spending them also on my own advantage, because this exercise would bring me the reward of eternal happiness.

After accusing himself of ingratitude and revealing true compunction of heart for past sins and their consequences, he invoked God's mercy, recalling the principal biblical examples of sin and repentance. He continued:

Inspire me Lord with thoughts to deter me from yielding to my sins and to excite me to fulfil your commands so that, going outside with the apostle Peter, I may no longer return with consent to the enticements of the flesh, or the false values of the world or to the deceitful suggestions of the devil. Instead with St Peter I would weep bitterly for my past sins, recalling every day all my years in the bitterness of my soul, fearing no longer the adversity of fortune, but willingly suffering for the purgation of my sins and the increase of merit. . . . Instead I would praise you without ceasing, glorify you with all my strength, thank you with every faculty for your immense mercy for the benefits of creation and redemption . . . and for the wonderful gift of your secret inspiration which you imparted to my soul. This enabled me to recognize my dependence on you and rejoice to praise your supreme gift of predestination, by which you have, I hope, chosen me from the beginning for your eternal glory.

May the Holy Trinity grant this, Father, Son and Holy Spirit, by the intercession of the glorious Virgin, St Cuthbert and all the saints. Amen.

In the copy sent to Abbot Thomas de la Mare, Uthred substituted for Cuthbert the saints of St Albans, namely Alban and Amphibalus, Oswin, Thomas, Benedict, Mary Magdalene and Katherine. On the vigils of the last two Thomas de la Mare was accustomed to fast through devotion.

It may well be asked: Did Uthred stand alone? The answer is No. There was at least one prior of Durham of his time who wrote a commentary on the Rule; a later prior, Wessington, both encouraged and himself wrote works of edification and of domestic history, while at least one other monk of Durham, also contemporary with Uthred, retired to the island of the Inner Farne, where he wrote a voluminous series of meditations, which survive in but one manuscript and have been published some years ago. Uthred's shorter work, however, enjoyed a much wider diffusion: surviving manuscripts show that it was read at Durham and its dependencies, St Albans, Reading and Canterbury and in houses of Carthusians and Brigittines. Certainly late medieval Benedictine monasticism did have its weaknesses, but it seems likely that further evidence could well reinforce the good impression given by the lives of both Thomas de la Mare and Uthred of Boldon.

One amid the splendour of his office remained a monk and abbot in St Benedict's mould; the other, after exciting controversies as a university monk, settled to the enrichment of study of monastic origins and devotional life and proved his reliability and judgement, like de la Mare, in the exacting task of monastic visitor. Finchale and Redburn were both small houses : perhaps we may appropriately take our leave of both these fine monks as they cared for the brethren who were ill or tired, depressed or anxious. Perhaps each of them was specially at home in a small community. Uthred was buried, almost unknown today, in the sanctuary at Finchale, but Thomas de la Mare is commemorated by one of the finest Flemish-style monumental brasses in the country. Each contributed powerfully to the maintenance of monastic values in English monasteries of the fourteenth century: one in a long line of monastic superiors which included men like Lanfranc, Ralph of Battle, Hugh of Cluny going back to St Benedict, and the other as an example of the series of monastic scholars which goes back through Eadmer and William of Malmesbury to Bede. Each of these types of Benedictine distinction can also be traced forwards to our own days.

by D. H. Farmer

BIBLIOGRAPHY

H. T. Riley, *Gesta Abbatum monasterii S. Albani* vols. II and III (Rolls Series 1867–69).

W. A. Pantin, *The English Church in the Fourteenth Century* (Cambridge 1955).

'Two Treatises by Uthred of Boldon on the Monastic Life' in *Studies in Medieval History presented to F. M. Powicke* (Oxford 1948), pp. 363–85.

D. Knowles, *The Religious Orders in England,* vol. II (Cambridge 1955).

'The Censured Opinions of Uthred of Boldon' in *Proceedings of the British Academy* xxxvii (1951–3), 305–42.

D. H. Farmer, 'The Meditacio Devota of Uthred of Boldon' in *Analecta Monastica* xliii (1958), 187–206.

The Monk of Farne (London 1961).

R. B. Dobson, *Durham Priory 1400–1450* (Cambridge 1973).

The last Abbots of Glastonbury, Reading and Colchester (died 1539)

The cult of the last abbots of Glastonbury, Reading and Colchester, Richard Whiting, Hugh Cooke and John Beche and their companions, was confirmed by Pope Leo XIII in 1895. The decree of their beatification declared it was proved by certain, indisputable and well-known evidence adduced that all these latter martyrs . . . had rendered their obedience to God and not to man, even to the shedding of their blood. Their feast has been celebrated on 1 December ever since.

Doubt however has been cast by certain historians on the true reason for their deaths. Is the narrative evidence on which the 1895 decision is based really supported by record evidence, now available? Did these abbots give clear and consistent indications that they died, like More, Fisher and the Carthusians for the papacy being of divine institution in the Church? Or were they simply victims of injustice, like many political prisoners in Tudor times as well as in our own? Is there a case for refusing them the name of martyr in the true and proper sense of this word? If the present evidence does not allow us to affirm unequivocal answers to all these questions, at least it enables us to see where the convictions of these men lay. In spite of hesitations and inconsistencies on their part, it seems probable, if not certain, that they did indeed die for Christ and that their deepest convictions were revealed by the fact of their painful deaths.

The most famous of them was Richard Whiting, abbot of Glastonbury. Like St John Fisher he died on the scaffold at an advanced age. The antiquity and the wealth of his abbey were unique: it was both the oldest and the richest in the country. Glastonbury's roots were deep in the remote past. It was the oldest known centre of Christianity in England; it existed even before the coming of the Angles and Saxons. The full development of the myth of Glastonbury took place in the later Middle Ages, partly to resist pressure from the local bishop and partly through rivalry with other monasteries. These legends were (and are) believed by many. Historical evidence, on the other hand, reveals the close connexion between Anglo-Saxon kings and Glastonbury. Ina of Wessex (688–726) was an early benefactor, giving, it was said, lands, gold, silver and precious stones. The most famous saint connected with Glastonbury was St

Dunstan. Born nearby in 909, he received his early education from Irish exiles who then formed part of its community. Later he took the Benedictine habit and returned there to live as a hermit, dividing his day between prayer, study and manual labour. He made bells and sacred vessels for the Church, illuminated manuscripts and played the harp. In 940 King Edmund appointed him abbot of Glastonbury: from that day until 1539 Benedictine life had continued there uninterrupted. Normans and Plantagenets too had enriched this unique monastery.

In the sixteenth century the abbot of Glastonbury administered vast estates; in his princely lodgings 'fit only for the King's Grace', five hundred guests and pilgrims could sit down together at his table. All through the year some of these visitors were there; on every Wednesday and Friday food was distributed to the poor of the neighbourhood; here too were educated the sons of the local nobility. The innumerable offices and outbuildings made the monastery look like a small town.

Who could imagine when Abbot Richard Bere died in February, 1525, that this famous sanctuary, with its unique place in the people's history, now apparently overflowing with vitality, would in his successor's time, at a word, and almost without protest, collapse and be left in ruins?

On 11 February, 1525 the forty-seven monks of Glaston met to elect Abbot Bere's successor. According to ancient right, the Chapter decided to give up their power of choice to a distinguished prelate, and the one they selected was Cardinal Wolsey. After enquiry, his choice fell upon Richard Whiting, the Chamberlain of the monastery. The Cardinal's Commission announcing the choice described Dom Richard as an 'upright and religious monk, a provident and discreet man, and a priest commendable for his virtues and learning.' Among those who signed the Commission was Thomas More. In March 1525 the announcement that Richard Whiting had been chosen, was made in the great Abbey Church to a large gathering of people from the Glastonbury estates. But Whiting himself had misgivings about accepting, and retired to the guest-house, or 'hostryre', for prayer and thought, and for some time could not be persuaded to consent. However after more consideration, he declared himself 'unwilling any longer to offer resistance to what appeared to be the will of God.' At length on 28 March, he received his solemn Blessing in the Abbey Church from Dr William Gilbert, abbot of Bruton, bishop of Mayo in Ireland, then acting as Suffragan to the bishop of Bath and Wells.

Whiting's family was west-country, and Richard was born about 1460 at Wrington, where the family were tenant holders of land in a fertile valley belonging to the Abbey of Glastonbury. The boy grew up during the excitement and troubles of the Wars of the Roses. He received his early education in the cloister school at the Abbey, as did many boys from the Abbey estates and further afield, both poor and well to do. While still a youth he joined the monastic novitiate. From Glastonbury the young man was sent on to Cambridge, probably to 'Monks' College', later Magdalene, and his name appears among those who took an M.A. degree about 1483. At Cambridge he would very likely have met or even come to know the young John Fisher, who like himself was a student at the time, and like himself, a future martyr. After his degree Dom Richard Whiting returned to Glastonbury to take part in teaching in the abbey and in the ordinary life of the monastery. He was ordained priest at Wells in 1501, and in 1505 returned again to Cambridge and took his final degree as Doctor of Theology.

We know very little of Dom Richard's life and activity during the next twenty years; no doubt he would have succeeded to various offices in the monastery, and his would have been the monk's daily round of prayer and work. We do know that for some years before 1525 he held the office of Chamberlain of the monastery, which placed him over the numerous officials and servants in the immense establishment, and he was holding this office at the time he became abbot.

When Whiting took over this vast inheritance from his predecessor, the life of the great abbey appeared prosperous and peaceful in its daily round of choir service and labour. The abbot went quietly about his duties of administration in his competent and business-like way. He was one of the most important prelates in the land, a peer of the realm with a seat in Parliament, and his name appears in many State Papers of the time. Yet already in the year before Abbot Bere died clouds were gathering on the horizon, for Anne Boleyn had been summoned to Court by Henry VIII to be one of Queen Catherine's Maids of Honour, and was soon to attract the affections of the king. But who then could tell what a storm was gathering of revolution and change? Even the far-sighted More could hardly have guessed, though he, even in the heyday of the king's favour, understood his master's character well: 'Could my head secure him a castle in France,' he said, 'it would go!'

For about five years the abbot's life at Glastonbury went on much as usual, then in 1530 came Cardinal Wolsey's sudden fall from the king's favour: he had been unable to obtain from the pope the divorce from Queen Catherine which the king desired, in order to marry Anne Boleyn. Wolsey's fall paved the way for the rise of Thomas Cromwell—a skilful but unscrupulous man, subservient

to the king's every whim. He may well be called Henry's evil
genius. He paid no attention to More's wise words: 'Mark, Cromwell, you are now entered the service of a most noble, wise and
liberal prince. If you follow my poor advice, you shall in your
counsel given to His Grace, ever tell him what he ought to do, but
not what he is able to do. For if a lion but knew his own strength,
hard were it for any man to rule him.' It is said to have been
Cromwell who first suggested to the king the throwing off of the
ecclesiastical authority of the pope, as the reformers had done in
Germany, for Cromwell himself had much sympathy with the new
learning from the Continent. Henry let the idea mature in his mind.

The king, following Cromwell's astute advice, gradually mastered
Parliament and paralysed Convocation, and since Friday, 7 February
1531, had been recognized by the English Clergy as 'Supreme Head
of the Church in England.' The clergy had struggled for a time, but
eventually gave way, after the qualifying phrase, 'in so far as the
law of Christ allows', had been added to the Statute.

On 25 January 1533, Henry was secretly married to Anne in a
garret, at the west end of Whitehall, by Dr Rowland Lee, one of
the royal chaplains. In February the same year, Thomas Cranmer,
a King's man, was made archbishop of Canterbury, and in March
pronounced Henry's long desired divorce. On 1 June Anne was
solemnly crowned as queen—the only one of the king's wives,
apart from Catherine, to be so.

The Act of Supremacy was publicly proclaimed on 9 June 1534,
and was passed by Parliament in the following November, and a
second Statute made it treason to deny the royal prerogative. Few
were found courageous enough to express their conscientious doubts
about the matter, or clear-sighted enough to see that they were
also rejecting the spiritual jurisdiction of the pope. To many it all
seemed just a matter of words. Fisher indeed spoke out boldly
enough, with dire consequences, but the day was lost.

Meanwhile the Oath of Supremacy was being tendered to
selected persons throughout the country—as a rule it was taken
wherever demanded.

The Oath was proposed to the religious in a more offensive form
than that which Fisher and More had refused to take. It was hoped
that by making the oath intolerable, the religious would refuse it,
and so provide a pretext for falling on their houses and property.
But this hope failed as the oath was taken in almost all the Chapter-
Houses of the land. The abbot and monks of Glastonbury, Colchester, and probably Reading were no exception.

It is not difficult to see the reason for the monks' compliance with
the oath—it was being taken all around them—its intricacies

would be hard to understand. Bishops who had taken it exerted pressure on others to do the same. To many the possibility of a final separation from Rome seemed incredible. It would hardly have occurred to them in any case that the Act could possibly mean the king's jurisdiction in spiritual matters, not only in temporal ones. The pope was now to have no more temporal jurisdiction than any foreign bishop in his own diocese. They would remember how the king in his early years had often heard three or even five Masses a day, (although perhaps bent on a hunting expedition); they would remember how he had written against Luther, how he was the 'Defender of the Faith'; the whole affair seemed only a passing aberration.

On 1 June 1534, the Commissioners arrived at Glastonbury, and Abbot Whiting, Dom Nicholas London, the Prior, and the Community, fifty in number took the Oath, and on 19 September attached their signatures to the declaration.

In 1535, Cromwell was appointed the king's Vicar General for Ecclesiastical affairs, and in the same year planned a Visitation of all the religious houses in the land. He knew the king as extravagant, and always short of money for his needs, such as keeping up his army and fortresses. He was in great want of financial aid, and he looked to the suppression of some of the lesser monasteries to help fill the king's coffers. By the Visitation Cromwell hoped to find sufficient reasons and accusations, which might be used to disguise a general attack upon the monasteries, described as an 'enormous scheme for filling the king's purse.'

On 1 August, the Commissioners arrived for the Visitation at Glastonbury, and later reported with regret, that the brethren were kept in such good order, that they could not offend, and the monks were assured that nothing was intended against them. Indeed, as an Anglican bishop wrote later: 'the monks lived apart from the world religiously and in peace, wholly given to study and contemplation; noted for their maintenance of common life, choral observance and enclosure.' As regards learning and study, Leland, the antiquary, had visited the Abbey in earlier years in search of ancient manuscripts and Whiting, whom he describes as 'a man truly upright and of spotless life', himself showed him the great Library of the abbey. Leland was amazed at the great treasures it contained. 'No sooner did I pass the threshold, than I was struck with awe and astonishment at the mere sight of so many remains of antiquity,' and he spent some days examining the shelves and the many wonderful books he found there.

As a result of the Visitation, it was asserted in Parliament, that, 'in the great and solemn monasteries, religion was right well kept and observed.' Dr Richard Layton, one of the Commissioners, so far forgot himself as to speak in praise of Abbot Whiting to the king, a fact he was later to regret. 'I understand you marvel I praised to the king at the Visitation the abbot of Glaston, who now appears to have no part of a Christian man . . . I cannot know the inward thought of a man, fair of outward appearance, but inwardly cankered—although they all be false, feigned, hypocrite knaves,' he wrote to Cromwell, regretting his *faux pas*. Of Layton's character this speaks for itself. Under the pretext of 'reformation' certain impossible and unpractical 'injunctions' were laid on all the houses visited. So we find the abbot, through his steward, complaining to Cromwell of their hindrance to the good order of his monastery. This clever device of Cromwell's was intended, as indeed it did, to upset the equilibrium of monastic life. It gave individual members of the Community the right of complaint to the Vicar-General against the abbot and the other monks where the injunctions were not kept, despite their being quite unworkable. So trouble was fostered for a later occasion, as Cromwell had foreseen. But for a time Abbot Whiting and Glastonbury were safe.

When the Act of Dissolution of the lesser (or poorer) monasteries was passed in March 1536, there was little or no opposition in Parliament, for its moderation made it acceptable to the Parliamentary abbots; reasonable means, such as pensions or places in larger houses for the religious who wished, gave them some security. In the event some priories and monasteries who appealed to the king, were granted a reprieve for a time. The suppression of smaller and decaying convents was not of course an original idea, or without precedent. With papal dispensation, Bishop John Fisher had done so, and had so been able to endow his College of St John at Cambridge. Wolsey too, in the 1520's had done likewise to secure his college at Oxford, Cardinal's College, later Christ Church, and also his Grammar School in his native town of Ipswich. The object of these earlier suppressions, however, was ecclesiastical or educational improvement, not, as was Cromwell's, to loot, and so fill the royal treasury.

By the autumn of 1536, most of the work of suppression of 243 smaller abbeys and priories was completed. There certainly does seem to have been some justification for the closure of a number of these ineffective houses.

We may easily imagine how all these proceedings must have filled Whiting's mind with doubts and forebodings, but about March, 1538, he was again reassured by Cromwell, that the king had no intentions against the greater religious houses. 'You may therefore repose yourself to God to serve devoutly, to live like true subjects of His Majesty, and provide for the relief of the poor, with hospitality, without the wilful waste and spoil that has lately been made in many abbeys, who imagined they were going to be dissolved.' In the sequel this was an ominous sentence for Abbot Whiting, and hardly likely to reassure him.

However, by 13 May of the same year the policy of partial dissolution was given up in favour of total dissolution. The wealth which came to the Crown from the smaller monasteries made Cromwell and the king look eagerly to the greater houses. 'All the wealth in the world would not be enough to satisfy and content his ambition,' wrote the French Ambassador. Little by little the greater abbeys were being drained of their resources by the demands of Cromwell for pensions charged on the monastic lands and so forth. None could be denied; all were anxious to keep on good terms with the Vicar General.

The Act of Parliament of April 1539, a Parliament which the aged Abbot Whiting excused himself from attending on account of ill-health, gave the king the abbeys which should happen to be 'dissolved, suppressed, renounced or relinquished, forfeited, given up, or come unto the king's Highness, by attainder, or attainders of treason', another ominous sentence which brought the king the free or persuaded surrender of a large number of the monasteries.

It would, well before then, be known through timorous traitors in his own monastery, and the talk of servants, tenants and others, what the abbot's real convictions were about the King's Supremacy, and the right and justice of dissolving so many of the religious houses. The precedent of 'free surrender' of a number of these, carried no weight with Abbot Whiting, and he was now determined at all costs not to surrender what he deemed to be a spiritual inheritance, to which the king could have no right.

Looking back as we do, with the certainty of hindsight, it is hard to fathom how the abbots could have signed Henry's earlier letter to the pope, petitioning for the divorce, and could have taken the later, repellent Oath of Supremacy. They certainly lived in bewildering times of upheaval; they would naturally hope for a return, in time, to a more conservative way of life, and it would be hard for them to see clearly where their path lay. It needed men of the calibre of Fisher and More, and rare religious such as the Carthusians, to see the future with clarity of vision. But whatever sad mistakes may have been made earlier by the abbots, it is fairly certain that at this juncture, they were firmly set on holding to their genuine convictions.

Between the passing of the Act in April 1539 and the following September, it is clear that the abbots of Glaston and Reading had been sounded, and that a free surrender was not to be expected from them. Now it was necessary for Cromwell to devise some way of having them accused of treason, that being attained, the property of their abbeys and possessions would become forfeit to the Crown. So we find in Cromwell's 'Remembrances' or book of reminders for September, 1539: 'Item. for proceeding against the Abbots of Reading and Glaston.'

On Friday, 19th of the same month, three Commissioners suddenly appeared at Glastonbury about ten o'clock in the morning. The abbot, having had no warning of their coming, was absent at his grange of Sharpham, about a mile from the monastery. They hurried there 'without delay', and telling him why they had come, began to badger the old man 'with certain articles' set out by Cromwell, and urging him 'to mind what he had forgotten and tell the truth.' They then carried him back to the abbey.

During the night they proceeded to search the abbot's papers, and ransack his apartments. It seemed they were searching for treasonable correspondence with the abbot of Reading and others, but nothing was forthcoming. They found, however 'a book of arguments against the King's Divorce, secretly laid, which we take to be a great matter, as also divers pardons, (indulgences), copies of (Papal) bulls, and the counterfeit life of Thomas Becket, but could not find any letter that was material'. Having found this evidence of the abbot's mind, in the morning they questioned him again on the 'articles received from your Lordship.' The abbot's answers having shown 'his cankered heart and traitorous mind against the King's Majesty and his succession', the Commissioners made him sign his name to the answers they recorded. These answers would be revealing if they were to come to light. Then 'with as fair words' as they could, 'he being a very weak man and sickly,' they sent him up to London, to the Tower, to be examined by Cromwell.

Some days later Cromwell's Glastonbury trio had secured depositions alleging treasonable conduct on the part of Abbot Whiting, which they called 'a book of evidences' of 'divers and sundry treasons.' It has to be remembered, that by the Treasons Act of 1534, 'misprision of treason' was liable to be charged as 'treason', and it was not difficult therefore, to extort declarations from servants, tenants and others, always ready to report to the agents for gain, and fearing reportings on themselves, if they withheld what they knew or had heard. Names were put to all the accusations, 'which we consider to be very high and rank treasons', and the 'book' sent up to Cromwell, who doubtless made good use of it while questioning the abbot in the Tower. The details of these questions are not certainly known.

Meanwhile the Commissioners were not idle at the abbey. Their first letter to Cromwell shows that they were enraptured with the beauty of the place: 'It is the goodliest house of the sort we ever saw, meet for the King and no man else.' The abbot being gone, it was taken for granted, he being guilty of treason, the house was now the king's property, and they proceeded to despatch the monks with as much celerity as possible. However they retained the Treasurer and the Sacrist, and at once began a thorough search for the great treasures known to belong to the monastery. But to their consternation, when they entered the treasure-house, they found it almost empty. Yet this house was reputed the oldest, the most magnificent, and richest in the country with an income of £3,000, manors innumerable, four parks, furniture, jewels and ornaments of priceless value. However after a more careful search they found money and plate walled up in the vaults, and secreted around the monastery. They eventually found enough precious stuff 'as would have sufficed for a new Abbey'—and more, they found, had been carried off to the country estates. The two monks, John Thorne, the Treasurer, and Roger James, the Sacrist, were now imprisoned to await the king's pleasure.

On 24 October 1539, the riches of the great house were in the hands of the royal treasurer, as among the possessions of 'attainted persons and places.' Among the treasures is noted 'a cross of silver gilt, garnished with a great, coarse emerald, and two sapphires, a superaltar garnished with silver and part gold, called the "great Sapphire of Glastonbury" '.

It is, unfortunately, not known what took place in the Tower, where Abbot Whiting lay from September until about 10 November, but it is certain that he was examined by Cromwell and others, and was there driven to the confession of more concealments of gold and silver. As Glastonbury was already considered to be Crown property, the crime of sacrilege for robbing Glastonbury Church was therefore to be laid to his charge as well as that of treason.

According to law, Abbot Whiting and the abbots of Reading and Colchester, being peers of the realm, should have been arraigned before Parliament, but Parliament was not sitting at the time, so Cromwell took the law into his own hands and noted in his *Remembrances*, 'Item, the Abbot of Glaston to be tried at Glaston and also executed there, with his complyces.' His execution was decided upon before his trial. Cromwell himself acted as prosecutor, judge and jury. He reminded himself to see 'that the evidence be well sorted and the indictments well drawn.' At some point Cromwell seems to have changed his mind about a 'trial' at Glaston and decided to have the mockery take place instead at Wells, perhaps to give it more publicity. Maybe at this time he had also decided to base the condemnation on robbery.

It was on Friday, 14 November, that the abbot reached Wells. With no time allowed for rest, the old man, nearly eighty, was hurried to the Bishop's Hall. Here everything had been well prepared for a mock trial, and Lord John Russell, now in charge of the proceedings had procured a suitable jury, 'very diligent to serve the Kyng.' A great crowd of people had gathered around to see and hear what was to be the fate of the abbot they had revered for his blameless life and who had been loved by all who knew him. It seems that the whole affair was a speedy one; the uncommonly 'worshipfull' jury knew their business—the verdict, as we have seen, had already been settled by Cromwell in London, where it was said there had been an arraignment in the 'Counter'. The capital charge on which the verdict was found was that of robbing Glastonbury Church. The abbot was to be hanged as a traitor for robbing his own Church—the irony of the verdict did not seem to register with Lord Russell, and no defence had been allowed. Later there seem to have been more interrogations, but the old man would accuse no one but himself, nor would he confess more gold or silver than he did before Cromwell in the Tower.

With the abbot were condemned on the same charge his two monks, John Thorne, the Treasurer, and Roger James, the Sacrist.

On the following day, Saturday 15 November, the abbot and his monks were brought back across the moor to Glastonbury. The abbot asked permission to enter the monastery and give his blessing to his monks for the last time. His captors had not troubled to tell him that the abbey had been taken over by the king, ransacked, and the monks dispersed—his request was not granted. From the abbey gates he was dragged on a hurdle over the stones of the town, and up the steep Tor Hill, which had been chosen as the place of his cruel death. Here below the tower of St Michael, the old man was hanged, cut down and mutilated. By nightfall, his head was fixed over the great gateway of the abbey—a ghastly warning to all who withstood the royal will.

The abbot was not allowed the consolation of having his two monks near him at his death. He was intentionally executed alone. Next came the turn of Dom John Thorne, the treasurer of the Church, a man of mature age, and Dom Roger James, the sacrist, a much younger man, both condemned and executed in the same manner as their abbot for robbing Glastonbury Church—considered the rightful property of the king. We are told that both the abbot and the monks 'took their death very patiently, begging forgiveness of all they might have offended'.

To the present time, the Tor, the scene of their martyrdom, and the tower of St Michael, still standing, are looked upon as the monument to the memory of 'good Abbot Whiting'.

Abbot Whiting's indictment has not so far been found. From the evidence we have, although he was apparently condemned for withholding and concealing the property of his own monastery, termed 'robbery' by his accusers, the Commissioners were earlier looking for other treasonable causes for condemning him. Glastonbury was known to be a Papal enclave, and the abbot would have no preacher of the new doctrines in his Church, but only those who upheld the Papal Supremacy and the old ways. At present we can only surmise that his actual indictment was similar to those of Abbot Cooke and Abbot Beche.

Professor Knowles writes of Abbot Whiting's last moments: 'The Statesmen and public servants of the early Tudors had little sense of the tears of things, or of the rich historic past preserved in the book they were closing forever. . . . The old man's eyes, as he stood beneath the gallows would have travelled for the last time along the slopes of the clouded hills, and over the ridges to the south, and over those to the north, once hallowed, so the story ran, by the footsteps of the "beauteous Lamb of God." No other landscape in all England carried so great a weight of legend. . . . Below him lay now the majestic pile of his Abbey, desolate, solitary, and about to crumble into ruins. . . . We know only that the Abbot and his companions took their deaths very patiently, and that Abbot Whiting's head was set up over the gateway of the Abbey which he had robbed, not before other hands than his had stolen hence the life of the building.'

Reading Abbey, of which Bd Hugh Cooke (or Faringdon) was the last abbot, though not so ancient as Glastonbury, is still of much historical interest. It was of Norman origin, having been founded by King Henry I in June, 1121, on a site between the Rivers Thames and Kennet, where there had been an earlier Saxon foundation. King Henry had richly endowed the monastery for two hundred monks, and in 1125 added more land and privileges, and the abbots had special juridical rights. These included creating knights, provided the solemnity was performed in the clerical habit, while the abbots had the same power in the monastic forests and woods as the King in his own. Finally in 1133, Henry bestowed on the abbey the relic of the hand of St James the Apostle, which had been brought to him from Germany by his daughter, the Empress Matilda. When Henry died near Rouen in 1135, the first abbot of Reading, Hugh of France, attended him on his deathbed, and the great church was

far enough advanced for the king to be buried before the High
Altar. In 1164 the church was solemnly consecrated by Thomas
Becket in the presence of Henry II.

Kings frequently confirmed the abbey's Charters and liberties,
and there were large grants of land from further afield. King John
assigned a mark of gold to cover the hand of St James.

Henry III was often at Reading; he allowed the abbot's boats on
the Thames, on payment of a fee, to be free of the customs demanded
at Windsor; the right to farm forty acres of land in the New Forest;
and an unusual right, probably little used, to mint coins. Such
coins are extremely rare, and none have been found after the reign
of Edward I. The wedding of John of Gaunt and Blanche of Lancaster took place in Reading Abbey Church, and many notable
people were buried there.

Reading was an important abbacy, ranking next after Glastonbury and St Albans; the abbot had a seat in the House of Lords and
in Convocation; he was also a County Magistrate. Several Parlia-
ments had been held at Reading, probably in the monastic refectory.

Hugh Cooke, often known as Faringdon from his birthplace in
Berkshire, is thought to have belonged to the family of Cooke, well
known in Kent. Of his early years we have no information at all,
nor do we know where he was educated, but it seems very probable
that he went either to the Grammar School at Reading or to the
abbey, where he later became a monk. He is described as a man of
learning, and his 'Epistles to the University of Oxford' remained on
the register of the University, and show his zeal for the Catholic
faith, and his disgust with the new Protestant teaching, which had
gradually begun to spread in the country, especially in the centres
of learning. He was interested in the education of the young, as can
be seen from letters between himself and Lord Lisle, whose little
stepson was in the Abbey School. A letter to Lady Lisle says, 'My
Lord of Reading begs my Lord and her, not to mistrust him about
the keeping of Mr James. He is as tender of him, as if he were the
King's son; he makes much of him, and pliath him to his learning
both in Latin and French.'

Dom Hugh Cooke was sub-Chamberlain of his monastery, when
in July 1520, he was elected to succeed Abbot Thomas Worcester.
The election was confirmed by Henry VIII on 26 September, and
not long after the king visited Reading, and was the abbot's guest
on 30 January 1521.

Abbot Cooke like Abbot Whiting, seems to have been a man of
attractive character, courteous and easy in manner, and, with his
learning and wit soon won Henry's special friendship. The king
would refer to him as 'my own abbot' and invited him to some of

his shooting expeditions. In 1532 Henry sent the abbot a New Year's gift of £20, (a considerable sum) in a white leather purse. The abbot, in his turn, would send the king presents of trout caught in the Kennet, or of hunting knives, when he knew him to be hunting in Windsor Forest. There is a story told, said to be authentic, that on one occasion, Henry while hunting descended on the abbey at dinner time incognito, 'much for delight, to see unseen', pretending to be one of the king's bodyguard lost in the forest. He was hospitably entertained, and invited to the abbot's table, where a large sirloin of beef was set before him; the king ate lustily, as would such a large bodyguard. 'Well fare, my heart,' said the abbot, 'and here in a cup of sack, I remember His Grace your Master. I would give £100, on condition I could feed as heartily on beef as you do! Alas! my weak stomach will hardly digest a small rabbit or a chicken.' The king pleasantly pledged the abbot, and heartily thanked him for his good cheer, and departed, undiscovered, as he came. Some weeks later the abbot was sent for to London and clapped in the Tower, and kept a close prisoner, being fed for a short time on bread and water. His mind was filled with fears as to how he could have incurred the king's displeasure. At last a sirloin of beef was placed before him, on which the abbot was feeding hungrily, when out sprang the king from a hiding-place, where he had been an invisible spectator! 'My Lord,' said the king, 'presently deposit your £100 in gold, or else no going hence all the days of your life! I have been your physician to cure you of your weak stomach, and as I deserve, I demand my fee!' The abbot paid up, and so returned to Reading, lighter in purse, but easier in mind than when he came. It is not quite certain to which abbot the story refers—there had been two others earlier in the reign.

Abbot Hugh took his part in the public life of the country, and sat in Parliament from 1523 to 1539. In November, 1529 he attended an important Convocation, held at old St Paul's, for the purpose of reforming current abuses. This Convocation met at the same time as Parliament, which was itself already dealing its first assaults against the liberties of the Church.

While Henry was searching everywhere (in England and on the Continent) for support for his matrimonial 'scruple', Abbot Cooke sent him a catalogue of his library, and later lent him books which he thought might be helpful for the king's case.

In July, 1530, we find Abbot Cooke, as well as Abbot Whiting and others, attaching signatures to the letter, which Henry wished to send to the pope, about the evils likely to result in delaying the divorce the king desired.

However in April, 1533, Abbot Cooke was one of the sixteen

theologians, who had the courage to hold to the opinion, that marriage with a dead brother's widow was permissible, for a papal dispensation could remove an impediment of affinity. Abbot Hugh has been described as a wholly upright and courageous man.

There is no direct evidence that Abbot Cooke and his community took the Oath of Supremacy in 1534, when it was demanded of all religions throughout the kingdom, but there seems little doubt that it must have been taken, for had it not been, the abbot would hardly have continued so long in the king's favour. The Oath was certainly taken the following year at Cromwell's Visitation, probably under some form of compromise, for few understood clearly the real significance of the Act of Supremacy.

As a result of the Visitation, Dr London, Dean of Wallingford, the Visitor, reported to Cromwell, that discipline was well maintained at Reading. 'They have a good lecture in Scripture daily read in their Chapter-House, both in English and Latin, to which is good resort, and the Abbot is at it himself.' We hear too from an anonymous, unfriendly writer, probably Latimer, Bishop of Worcester, that the abbot 'was ever a great student and setter forth of St Benet's rules, and said they were rules right holy and of great perfectness,' and, ridiculing the abbot, 'thought it both heresy and treason to God to leave Matins unsaid, or to speak loudly in the cloister!' Cromwell was on his guard in his dealings with Abbot Hugh, knowing him to be in much favour with the king.

In 1536, Abbot Cooke signed Convocation's Articles of Faith, which though adhering in most particulars to the ancient Faith, virtually acknowledged the King's Supremacy over the English Church. It was known that the abbot 'could not abide' the preachers of the new doctrines, whom he called 'heretics and knaves.' On this occasion he must have acted with a heavy heart, full of forebodings for the future. In this same year the dissolution of the lesser religious houses was completed.

We find him still in the royal favour at the end of 1537, for on Sunday, 4 November, he took a prominent part in singing a solemn Requiem in the presence of the body of Queen Jane Seymour, and on 12 November he read one of the lessons at the Dirge, and assisted at her magnificent funeral in St George's Chapel, Windsor.

However trouble was brewing, for on 12 December a rumour had spread that the king was dead, and Abbot Cooke wrote to Cromwell: 'There is sprung up in our country the most lamentable tidings that ever was, that the King and the Lord Marquis of Exeter are dead.' This rumour seems to have spread all over the south of England, and Cooke passed on the news to the abbot of Abingdon. Such rumours could be interpreted as indications of a

treasonable disposition, especially so soon after the Exeter con-
spiracy. An investigation took place on 24 December. The abbot
however was pardoned, but it was later brought up against him.

By May, the following year, 1538, the total dissolution of the
monasteries had been decided upon, and from 31 August to 10
December, we find Dr London again in the midland counties
bringing ruin and desecration everywhere, relentlessly sweeping
relics out of churches and monasteries. At Caversham he demolished
the famous shrine of Our Lady, sending the image, 'platyd over with
silver' in a nailed box 'by the next bardge that cometh from Reading
to London.' Dr London arrived at Reading on 17 September, and
on 18th wrote to Cromwell, 'I have required of my Lord Abbot the
relics of his house, which he showed unto me with a good will,' and
these he locked up behind the High Altar. The Inventory of the
Relics of the House of Reading is still extant.

One of Cromwell's 'Injunctions' left at the Visitation of 1535,
forbade the monks to leave their enclosure, but a method of communication between the abbots of Reading, Glastonbury and the
other monasteries left standing, was found by means of a blind
harper, named William Moore, whose sad condition and musical
skill had brought him under the kindly notice of the king. He was
himself a firm believer in the old ways and loyal to the pope, and
being a trustworthy man, would be a completely unsuspected agent.
He travelled from monastery to monastery, entertaining, and receiving in return, shelter and food, and for a time was able to act as a
messenger between the anxious abbots, who were thus enabled to
encourage one another to stand firm and not to surrender their
abbeys.

At the end of April, 1539, Parliament, as we have seen earlier,
met to give the king the greater monasteries, which should come
to him by surrender or by attainder of treason. Cromwell took care
'to bring all things so to pass, that your Majesty had never more
tractable Parliament'.

Eighteen abbots were present at the first reading of the Act of
21 April; none of them opposed it or apparently voted against it,
and all were shortly brought to surrender their abbeys, with the
exception of the abbot of Woburn and our three abbots, who could
not be persuaded for any reasons to do so, and so were accused of
treason and executed.

However, as late as 14 August, Abbot Cooke was still in his
monastery, and was said to be selling off sheep, grain and timber,
but on 8 September Commissioners were at the abbey drawing up
an inventory for Cromwell. So it is evident that the abbot must
have been arrested early in September, charged with treason and

sent to the Tower, that the abbey might be considered as forfeited to the Crown by attainder.

While the Commissioners were at Reading, the correspondence between the abbots, by means of the blind harper, had been discovered, and we find William Moore's name amongst the prisoners in the Tower on 20 November 1539. Perhaps it is he who is referred to as on '1st July, 1540, a Welchman, a minstrel, was hanged and quartered for singing of songs, which were interpreted to be prophesying against the King.'

The abbot himself remained in the Tower for about two months, where he underwent examination, and to all intents and purposes, condemnation without trial, before being sent down to his 'country to be tried and executed,' by a Commission appointed on 27 October. Several others from Reading had been arrested at the same time as Abbot Hugh: among them were two priests, (one from St Giles Reading and the other lived in retirement at the abbey) John Eynon and John Rugg—the latter was indicted for saying 'the King's Highness cannot be Supreme Head of the Church in England'. Asked what he did to soothe his conscience, when he had taken the Oath, Rugg replied, 'I added this condition in my mind, to take him for supreme head in temporal things, but not in spiritual things,' which seems to be what had been done by many others in the same predicament. Books against the King's Divorce and his Supremacy had been found among his papers. Both priests acknowledged that they were guilty of treason in that they rejected the Royal Supremacy, but both protested that they were none the less the king's loyal subjects. These two were brought down to Reading with the abbot for the mockery of a trial, at which all three were condemned, as had already been decided.

On 14 November, the day after Abbot Whiting had suffered at Glastonbury, Abbot Hugh and his two companions, were laid on hurdles, and dragged through the streets of Reading to the great gateway of the abbey. Here a large crowd had gathered to witness the awful executions. The abbot spoke to the people for the last time, telling them that he and his companions were about to die for their fidelity to the Roman Pontiff, which was 'the common faith of those who had the best right to declare the true teaching of the English Church.' He instanced archbishop Wareham of Canterbury, and bishop Stokesley of London, men, he declared, guilty of the same treason as himself. He said this, 'not out of malice,' for the abbot 'as heartily loved those holy fathers as ever he loved any man in his life.'

And so the tragic story ends: the three were hanged and mutilated, and by evening their heads were to be seen over the gateway of the abbey, to strike terror on all around.

In recent years the indictments of Abbot Cooke and Abbot Beche have been found in the Record Office: these clearly state that they were charged with supporting Papal Supremacy, and it was for this that they were found guilty and executed—this was treason in the eyes of the law, quite apart from their unwillingness to surrender their abbeys, which is not mentioned in the indictment.

This however quotes Cooke's words as follows:

1. 'The king is not supreme head of the Church in England. And I trust to see the Pope bear as great a rule in England as ever he did, shortly. And I will say Mass every week for him. I will say that there is a Pope as long as I live.

2. On being questioned whether the bishop of Rome shall ever have to do here in this realm after his old accustomed fashion or no, he answered: Truly, or else I will never believe God to be God.'

The Abbey of St John the Baptist, Colchester, was, like that of Reading, a Norman foundation, made by Eudo, a Court Steward; the foundation stone was laid by Henry I and the church consecrated on 10 January 1104. The abbey was endowed through the centuries with many privileges, among them that of sanctuary, and its abbot was one of the twenty-eight who sat in the Upper House of Parliament.

John Beche, sometimes known as Thomas Marshall, (Marshall was an alias and Thomas probably his name in religion) seems to have been a monk of St Wereburg's, Chester. He had been educated at Oxford, where he attended St Benedict's or Gloucester Hall for several years, and obtained his B.D. in 1509, and his Doctorate in Divinity in April, 1511. He became abbot of St Wereburg's for some period between 1511 and 1530. He was described as excelling many of the abbots of his time in devotion, piety and learning, and perhaps it was this reputation which led to his election on 10 June 1533, to succeed Abbot Barton as abbot of St John's, Colchester.

Abbot Beche thus took up his new burden, at a time when many difficulties had to be faced. At first he was unable to obtain the temporalities or income due to his monastery, which would normally follow the king's approval of his election. However, after an appeal to Cromwell about the financial state of the monastery, and the payment of £200 for the king's use, his temporalities were restored to him on 23 January 1534.

Abbot Beche was evidently known to be a strong conservative and an opponent of the king's new religious policies, as were his community at Colchester, but, even so, the Oath of Supremacy was taken in the Chapter-House of St John's in 7 July 1534, no doubt with certain mental reservations regarding 'spiritualities', which few could really in their hearts allow to the king.

The sad events of the executions of Fisher and More in 1535, afflicted Abbot Beche deeply, for they seem to have been his personal and loved friends; he would often speak of them with great admiration, and, after they had been put to death, declared them to be true martyrs. He 'made his friends partakers of his grief,' adding 'he marvelled what cause of complaint the King could have found in men so virtuous and learned, the greatest ornaments of Church and State, as to deem them unworthy of longer life, and to condemn them to a most cruel death.' The abbot would speak so to his guests whom he had invited to his table, some would gladly agree with what he said, others would remain silent. It appears that on one occasion a guest, enjoying his hospitality, prevailed on the abbot to talk about the late martyrs, so that he might entrap him into what could be regarded as traitorous speech, and later reported what had been said to the king's agents. There was little doubt that trouble was in store for Abbot Beche.

The abbot, in spite of the perilous times, was not at much pains to hide his real opinions. At the time of the Northern Rising, he had been heard to say: 'I would to God the rebels in the North Country had the Bishop of Canterbury (Cranmer), the Lord Chancellor (Audley), and the Lord Privy Seal (Cromwell), amongst them, I trust then we should have a merry world again, for they are all arch-heretics!' On 16 December 1536, we find two neighbours Sir William Pyrton and Sir John Seyncler reporting to Cromwell that they had been invited to dine with the abbot on the previous day, when Marmaduke Neville and others from the North had come in. Sir John said: 'How do the traitors in the North?' 'No traitors', replied Neville, 'for if you call us traitors, we will call you heretics.' Neville went on to say that the king had pardoned them, or they would not have been at Colchester, and he was sure my Lord Abbot would give him good cheer, for 'we have set up all the abbeys again in our country, and though it was never so late, some sang Matins the same night!' and he had added they were 'plain fellows' in the North, and Southern men, though they thought as much, dare not utter it!' Seyncler wrote, 'My Lord, I like not the Abbot, I fear he hath a cankered heart, for he was accused but of late of traitorous words, by one William Hall, but he had no witness.'

We have very little factual knowledge about Abbot Beche between 1536 and 1538, when in the April of that year, the dissoluton of the greater abbeys was decided on, either by surrender or attainder of treason. On 6 November 1538, a commission was issued to dissolve the abbeys of Colchester and St Osyth's, although the Chancellor, Audley, had petitioned in the summer that at least one of them might be spared, perhaps as a college, as there were numerous poor people around Colchester who were relieved at both these abbeys, but he pleaded in vain. Hearing that Abbot Beche was determined not to surrender freely, Cromwell sent Sir John Seyncler to see him, and on 21 November Sir John wrote: 'Yesterday 20th, I was with the abbot of St John's, Colchester, who asked me what the abbot of St Osyth's did as touching his house, for the bruit was the King would have it. To which I answered him, he did like an honest man, "I am the King's subject, and I and my house are all the King's; I, as a true subject, shall obey without grudge." To which the abbot of St John's answered: "I will not say so, for the king shall never have my house, but against my will and against my heart, for I know by my learning that he cannot take it by right and law; wherefore in my conscience I cannot consent, not shall he have it with my heart and will." ' Such words to Cromwell already sealed the abbot's fate.

We know no more of the abbot until the following year, 1539, when in October he was arrested and sent to the Tower on a charge of treason; the abbey was dissolved and investigations concerning the abbot were set on foot. The Commissioners were in Brentwood examining witnesses from 1 to 4 November. It was not a difficult matter to find charges of treason against Abbot Beche; there were many giving such testimony. His Chaplain and his servants were questioned as were many in the town. Enquiries were made as to what money, plate and jewels he had embezzled. One witness had heard the abbot say that two or three of the Council had brought the king to such a covetous state of mind, 'that if the Thames flowed gold and silver, it would not quench his thirst.' Several times he had been heard to say that the king had made himself Head of the Church so that he could divorce Queen Catherine and marry Queen Anne. Once he had talked of Queen Anne's death, and he hoped Queen Jane would not come to the same. 'That those who made the king Supreme Head of the Church were heretics. The Bishop of Rome is only supreme Head of the Church by the laws of God, immediately after Christ, and none other. That the whole authority was given by Christ to Peter and his successors, the Bishops of Rome to bind and loose. It was against God's laws that any temporal prince should be head of the Church.' Here was much more than sufficient evidence to condemn the abbot.

Meanwhile the abbot was being interrogated in the Tower, and was required to answer six articles, on the accusations made against him. At some point he seems to have been overwhelmed by a terrible fear, not unknown to other martyrs in the face of a ghastly death. A document, written unhappily and signed by himself, came to light about eighty years ago; in this he denied some of the charges against him and tried to palliate his statements on the Royal Supremacy. He was evidently trying to save his life, but there is no reason to doubt the reliable evidence of his genuine and convinced adherence to the old faith and to Rome. For a time weakness and fear had overcome him, and which of us cannot feel compassion for him?

The abbot was sent down to Colchester to be tried by a special commission headed by the Earl of Essex, Sir Christopher Jenny, the judge, and others, the trial to take place on 1 December. After the trial and condemnation Sir Christopher Jenny wrote to Cromwell: 'the prisoner acknowledged himself in substance to be guilty according to the effect of the indictment; he stood somewhat in his own conceit that the suppression of the abbeys should not stand with the law of God, and thereby, and by other circumstances, I thought him an evil man in mine own conscience and opinion, if there had been no more than his own confession.' It does appear that at his trial the abbot's courage had returned. Abbot Beche's indictment was discovered in the Record Office about 1960, and it clearly shows that he was accused and condemned for 'treason', mainly for upholding Papal Supremacy against that of the king. It also reveals that he said that those who killed John Fisher and Thomas More and put down abbeys and thrust out the religious were 'tyrants and bloodsuckers'.

On the same day as the trial, 1 December 1539, the abbot was drawn on a sledge from the town to a hill nearby and executed—a warning to all who doubted the Royal Supremacy.

It is well known that there has been a good deal of controversy regarding these three abbots and their condemnations. From what evidence we have, it certainly appears that they were put to death for their well-known adherence to Rome, as well as for other so-called treasons. However, Professor Knowles' distinction between favourable literary accounts and unfavourable record evidence has not been substantiated by the subsequent discovery of the indictments for the abbots of Reading and Colchester. In view of these the abbot of Reading emerges as the clearest example of the three before us as a martyr for the faith of the Church. The abbot of Colchester, outspoken and indiscreet, tried to escape the consequences of his words. His hesitations and denials, in invoking the theory of a merely human origin for papacy, while very understandable under extreme pressure, can hardly be regarded as evidence for the heroic and constant fortitude usually revealed by martyrs. However, his admission of his deepest convictions at his trial removed much of the fault of his previous failure.

In the case of the abbot of Glastonbury the charge of embezzlement may be regarded as the pretext rather than the reason for his death. It might be compared to certain currency charges brought against prominent Christians in Iron Curtain countries in our own day. More relevant and more ironical is the fact that the king was engaged on an enormous and nationwide spoliation of Church property which made even the sequestration of some of the Glastonbury treasure trifling indeed.

However it must be recalled that all three abbots, on one occasion or more, had formally agreed to take the Oath of Supremacy. Fisher and More had constantly refused to do this, as did the London Carthusians. This makes the abbots' witness less clear than we would really like. Furthermore, no contemporary evidence has revealed their last words on the scaffold. These are known in most of the cases of the Forty Martyrs.

It is highly desirable that more contemporary documents significant to these cases should be discovered. Until that happens, it seems likely that the canonization cause of the three abbots, if taken together as before, will not advance further. The three abbots however were undoubtedly victims of injustice, oppression and religious persecution. There can be no doubt either that they retained their Catholic faith which both inspired them to refuse the surrender of their monasteries and to accept their violent deaths.

by Dame Veronica Buss

BIBLIOGRAPHY

M. D. Knowles, *The Religious Orders in England*, vol. III (Cambridge 1959).

id., *Bare Ruined Choirs* (Cambridge 1976).

G. W. O. Woodward, *The Dissolution of the Monasteries* (London 1966).

J. E. Paul, 'The last Abbots of Reading and Colchester', *Bulletin of the Institute of Historical Research* xxxiii (1960), pp. 115–20.

F. A. Gasquet, *The Last Abbot of Glastonbury* (London 1895).

B. Camm, *Lives of the English Martyrs*, vol. I (London 1904).

9

Three Seventeenth-Century Benedictine Martyrs: John Roberts, Alban Roe and Ambrose Barlow

Deposuit potentes de sede ('He has put down the mighty from their thrones'), sang the thirty Benedictine monks of Evesham at Vespers one day in 1539, at the critical moment when Henry VIII's Commissioners burst in to enforce the surrender of their Abbey. This was but one episode in the destruction of Benedictine monasticism in England which had existed for nine centuries, and uninterruptedly for six. The 'progressive' prophets of the day and men of fashion agreed that monastic life was outmoded, its vitality spent. Monasteries, they thought, were only an obstacle to a national renaissance and a threat to the vision of a Church in which all would be equal in God's sight, able to be saints without any need to join monasteries. Those who excused the wanton destruction of the religious houses and much of their contents by such words did not see that the demolition of buildings did not inevitably spell the demise of the monk or that, in the final analysis, the habit does not make the monk.

One of St Bernard's favourite images of St Benedict was that of the good man in Scripture who stood like a tree beside the flowing waters, yielding its fruit in due season. The tree symbolized permanence and stability. This virtue seemed embodied in the Benedictine strongholds of medieval England, yet the tree was sustained only by drinking from the stream and grew only by adapting itself to the seasons. Stability, then, was harmony through total involvement, as well as peace which included assimilating contemporary currents of thought and conditions. It was an interior virtue, outliving material changes in a monk's life. It stretched from the cave in the wilderness through the restlessness of urban monasteries back to its first home, the desert of the monk's soul. The survival of monasticism in England after the destruction of the abbeys illustrates the continuous adaptation which monks make to the pattern of life while they preserve the spiritual essentials.

The English Benedictine martyrs of the seventeenth century did not have the normal setting for monastic life: they were isolated missionaries, labouring anxiously under the constant threat of persecution. Yet for these men, monastic ideals had a place in their day. They did not apparently show much nostalgia for the outward show or the shortcomings of medieval monasticism, but they hearkened back to the spirit of monks like St Augustine of Canterbury. These martyr monks were among the founding fathers of a new Benedictine growth which sought to apply the wisdom of monastic tradition to the altered circumstances of the time, particularly in England. In the early seventeenth century individuals and small groups of men and women who felt a call to monastic Benedictine life established the English Benedictine Congregation. This included within its ranks a wide spectrum of personalities, ranging from enthusiastic, practically-minded missionaries to gentle, withdrawn mystics. The simple monastic ideal of the search for God remained present in all, so that the great spiritual writers among the English Benedictines could insist that what they called 'contemplation' could flourish even under the most adverse conditions.

Before the English Benedictine Congregation was juridically established, there had been a final attempt to revive a Benedictine monastery at Westminster Abbey in the reign of Queen Mary. Early in 1555 she received at court a small body of monks headed by Dr Feckenham, once a monk of Evesham and now Dean of St Paul's. All these former monks were prepared to surrender their positions in the new religious establishment if the queen would re-establish the Benedictine body in England. Mary heard their appeal with tears in her eyes, for she saw that the return of the Benedictines would help to consolidate her work of restoring the kingdom to obedience to Rome. A permanent monastic restoration was frankly impossible: Protestantism had captured the hearts of many at court during Edward VI's reign, and there was never much likelihood that the new owners of monastic land and property would willingly return their gains to the monks. Mary could only hope that her own example would be followed. She decided that Westminster Abbey should be the centre of the restoration: it was the largest Benedictine foundation nearest the Court, some of its old monastic buildings, including the church, were in good repair, and, above all, it was a 'royal peculiar', that is, the monarch had total jurisdiction over it. On 20 November 1556, a group of sixteen monks returned to Westminster, headed by Dr Feckenham who was soon blessed as abbot. With a steady intake of new recruits, the monastery began, quite optimistically, its brief life. The monastic life was to be again extinguished at Westminster in June 1559 after Elizabeth I's accession and the gradual return of the kingdom towards Protestantism.

Westminster's fragile existence has a place here because it served as the link between old and new. In the first place, its community argued that it was the direct descendant of the medieval English Benedictine body since it comprised monks from older foundations like Glastonbury and St Alban's, and two of the original sixteen had been monks of the earlier Westminster in the 1530s, even though, in a legal sense, this older community was now extinct. Indeed, the new Westminster community seemed essentially backward-looking rather than the harbinger of a revived Benedictine monasticism speaking powerfully to the times and setting the pace for the future. Most of the Westminster monks were already quite elderly when they joined, and many were bookish: so the monastery, in the words of a later commentator, resembled a cathedral close. Thus, when the end came, the monks appear to have acted like gentlemen, begging to differ though packing their bags. Abbot Feckenham, above all, was the epitome of English propriety; there are suggestions that he was rather triumphalist, an abbot after the old manner, courting royal favour by restoring Edward the Confessor's tomb in his church, and burying Queen Mary there when she died in 1558. Still, he was gracious enough to help in giving up his place to the new Dean, and retired into a long and comparatively comfortable imprisonment, maintaining his religious principles until his death in 1584. This neo-medieval Westminster was to appeal to later Benedictines, including our martyrs, because they felt, rightly or wrongly, that it provided a continuity of monastic tradition reaching right back to St Augustine of Canterbury in the sixth and seventh centuries, and because it demonstrated how Benedictine monasticism could quite naturally be part of the fabric of English life and society, sharing the same attitudes and interests.

The Westminster tradition survived in the enigmatic person of Fr Sigebert Buckley who at his death in 1610 was the sole survivor of this community, having been apparently professed there after the abbey's re-establishment. He was to be in and out of prison for twenty years: his main claim to fame rests on his meeting in 1607 with a number of Englishmen who had become Benedictines on the Continent. He affiliated these to the abbey of Westminster, and perhaps even received their vows in the name of the old English Benedictine body. Buckley's name has been immortalized from that day to this. English Benedictines have been quick to point out the symbolism which lay behind the 21st of November, the formal date of the re-establishment of Westminster in 1556, and the same day in 1607 when Buckley performed his patriarchal task. It was also the date of the feast of the Presentation of Christ in the Temple, and it became for later Benedictines, who saw the aged Fr Buckley as a later Simeon recognizing the older dispensation in the new, a *dies memorabilis*.

This meeting of the last survivor of Westminster with his own countrymen trained as Benedictines on the Continent reminds us that the Westminster of Queen Mary's day was not without continental monastic connexions. Had the abbey survived, these would have made it the focus of a lively and vigorous Benedictine reform in this country. The Benedictine martyrs of the seventeenth century were themselves steeped in the effects of this renaissance. Important Italian and Spanish monasteries like those of St Justina in Padua and St Benedict in Valladolid had formed Congregations of monasteries for mutual support, and to preserve their independence from lay control; they practised an austere monastic discipline with much emphasis on personal prayer. Queen Mary had been aided in her attempt to refound Westminster by Cardinal Pole who was not only archbishop of Canterbury, but also the Cardinal Protector of the new Italian Cassinese Congregation. Pole looked forward eagerly to an English Congregation of Benedictines and vigorously persuaded the Westminster monks to elect, reluctantly, Feckenham as abbot for three years only, rather than for life. Pole's grand design for a Cassinese limb in England came to nothing, but Englishmen, trained in Cassinese and Spanish monasteries in Italy and Spain, filtered back into England in the early years of the seventeenth century. They renewed the link with old Fr Buckley, and one story goes that he was prepared to join the Cassinese Congregation following his meeting with these new English monks. The ground was thus prepared for future English Benedictine monks to return from the Continent to preach the Gospel in England according to their own traditions, although monks had not been used as missionaries for some centuries. Our three martyrs were among this group.

Considering the antiquity of Benedictine monasticism, it is surprising that the number of monks who have been canonized is relatively small. Benedictine saints fall mainly into three classes: abbots (or bishops), martyrs or missionaries, with the occasional great scholar like the Venerable Bede forming an exception. Such a phenomenon is perhaps to be expected from a religious tradition which emphasises the hidden life and the personal quest for God, together with the absence of any requirement to maintain a specific work. In conformity to this pattern, the only monks so far canonized in the revived English Benedictine Congregation have been, not its important mystical writers, but its martyrs. These became famous on account of their refusal to surrender their principles. They lived adventurously as missionaries and sacrificed their lives for their ideals. The glory attached to martyrdom also explains why our knowledge of these men is so unbalanced. The story of their trials and their gory deaths is uncomfortably complete, but of their early lives, particularly their life as cloistered monks, we know very little.

John Roberts was the first Benedictine martyr of what has been called the 'second spring', the period of revival of the Catholic Church in England after its decline in the reign of Henry VIII. Though he was firmly attached to English traditions throughout his life, he was in fact wholly Welsh. He came from Trawsfynydd in Merionethshire, a rocky, mountainous region similar to the landscapes the Celtic monastic missionaries of an earlier era had been born in and later sought out. His parents, however, conformed to the religious settlement in fashion, they were only 'Catholic at heart', and John, probably the eldest of five children, must have been of a similar frame of mind when he matriculated at Oxford in February 1593. His college, St John's, had strong attachments to the old religion, and it had its fair share of Catholic martyrs in the sixteenth century. John Roberts shared rooms with another Welshman, John Jones, who was to become a Benedictine himself. He left Oxford for the Inns of Court in London, another strong Catholic centre, and from here he moved to the Continent for what seems to have been an extended holiday.

In Paris John Roberts was received into the Catholic Church, following conversations with an English Catholic exile there. He also met Fr John Cecil, a secular priest from the newly-founded English seminary at Valladolid in Spain. Cecil was to become an informer against priests in later life, but at this time he encouraged Roberts to make himself known at Valladolid. Roberts had expressed the desire after becoming a Catholic to devote his life to God as a missionary in England. On his way to Valladolid, Roberts broke his journey at Madrid, and there met Donna Luisa de Carvajal, a Spanish lady who took a lively interest in English affairs; they were to meet again during his imprisonment. At Valladolid, Roberts' petition for admission to the English College of St Alban 'on account of his burning desire to become a labourer in Our Lord's vineyard' was granted in October 1598.

St Alban's College, like others, was run by the Jesuits, and the life was fairly austere: 'Many fall sick and die by reason of the unwholesomeness of the air and want of bodily exercise, for they have no liberty or recreation . . . neither have they any walks or gardens near their college, and to go forth they are not permitted, save to schools', wrote a Protestant observer about the conditions there. There was also another problem in which Roberts found himself embroiled: many of the secular clergy were totally opposed to the Jesuits' extension of control over the English seminaries and missionary enterprises, and a fierce battle between both parties was taking place. Some dismayed students sought an alternative path between the two combatants, and looked to the Benedictine life as a possible solution. The Benedictines were, as we have seen, undergoing important reforms in many of their houses at this time. Certainly, they provided an alternative spiritual formation to that of the Jesuits, and Englishmen who were inclined towards them convinced themselves that the Benedictines, realizing the missionary labours of monks like Augustine of Canterbury in the past, could be persuaded to co-operate in a second conversion of England.

It was then the missionary spirit of the monks which appealed most strongly to these young English students, rather than a vocation to the contemplative life, and a stream of students from St Alban's College was making its way to the great monastery of St Benedict in Valladolid when John Roberts took the same step in May 1599, despite some opposition from his Jesuit superiors. This royal monastery had been founded at the end of the fourteenth century, and became the centre of an important reforming movement among the Benedictines in Spain, following the same path as the Cassinese Congregation which we have already met. A vow of perpetual enclosure was a marked feature of the Congregation of Valladolid, but it possessed more interest in missionary activities than did the Cassinese Congregation; a number of its monks specialized in preaching and some of its monasteries cared for the pastoral needs of the area surrounding them. This partially explains why Englishmen, bent on becoming missionary monks, received such a ready admittance into the Congregation. Formal papal permission for English monks belonging to the Congregation of Valladolid to become missionaries in England came in 1602. In the late sixteenth century, the forces of the Counter-Reformation were in full swing, determined both to win back the wide tracts of territory lost in Europe to the Reformers and to open up newly-discovered lands to the Christian gospel. The austere training in new orders like the Jesuits and in reformed religious groups like the Benedictines gave its products a military tenacity and fervent zeal which were to be the hallmarks of many martyrs of the period.

John Roberts was sent, along with other English Benedictine aspirants, from Valladolid to the abbey of St Martin at Santiago de Compostella to enter the novitiate. He was to remain here for four years, until early in 1603 when he at last reached England. During these four years, he was formed in the monastic traditions of the Spanish Benedictines with their strict enclosure and regular periods of silent isolation (similar to what he was to experience later in the prison cell), and trained in the familiar round of conventual duties, particularly that of participation in the liturgical life of a large monastic community. He was clothed in the habit, and made his profession as 'Fra Juan de Mervinia' (John of Merionethshire). Despite some ill-health, he went through to ordination.

These were hidden years, but a significant change occurred in 1601 when an English priest, on his way to Lisbon, called at Compostella and informed the monks of the martyrdom of Mark Barkworth in February 1601. Barkworth was attached to the Spanish Benedictines, and appears to have been clothed in the habit when on the mission. The sight of his tonsured head and the habit which he was wearing at his death, we are told, made a profound impression on the crowd. His death also lit the spark in the hearts of the English monks at St Martin's, for the visiting priest went on to describe the great respect and love the English nation had for St Benedict, and how the conversion of England might best be accomplished by Benedictines, since even the heretics treated these monks with honour. It is noteworthy how often the Benedictine missionary monks, as we shall see, stressed England's attachment to the Benedictines; it was a common inheritance which might serve as a basis in the work of reunion.

Once the pope, Clement VIII, had given the Benedictines 'the faculty of the mission', John Roberts and his contemporary Augustine Bradshaw set out from Spain at the end of 1602. They took their time in reaching England, staying in Paris and elsewhere, and no doubt renewed acquaintances. Spies littered their path and informed the English government of their progress, describing Roberts variously as a 'friar' and a 'Jesuit'. Lewis Owen, the Protestant apologist, says that 'he was the first that had his mission from the Pope and his own Spanish Prelate to go for England, which made him not a little proud that he should be a second Augustine, to convert and reconcile his Countrymen to the Roman Antichrist'. Once in London, he was soon captured, but was fortunate that his arrest coincided with the accession of James I in May 1603. The new king proclaimed an amnesty for priests, and John Roberts was freed, though he found himself banished to the Continent. His stay here was brief, not 'long enough to warm the earth', for he returned to London that summer to care for the victims of the terrible plague which was raging, a work which brought him respect from all quarters.

Roberts was keen to reconcile as many as he could to Catholicism by reviving the Benedictines as a living force in English society. He made sure that his own person attracted attention: 'many resorted to him . . . out of curiosity to see a Benedictine monk once again in England', and 'he begot here many Proselytes or Popelings (and) transported them to Spain to be trained up in the Monastical discipline'. There is also evidence that he encouraged the laity to become Benedictine Oblates. The king soon began to regret his earlier tolerance of Catholics and in February 1604 ordered the exile of all priests. Though not recognized as a priest, Roberts was seized and imprisoned a second time, for a few months, as he was about to cross for the Continent accompanied by some Benedictine aspirants, among them the future martyr Maurus Scott.

After release, Roberts managed to work for nearly a year in London, using a house in Holborn as his base, but throughout this time persecution of Catholics was growing dramatically. It reached its peak with the scare following the Gunpowder Plot in November 1605, and on 5 November John Roberts was taken in the house of the wife of Thomas Percy, in Holborn, which seems to have been a centre for Benedictines working in London. He was taken 'newly entered booted, as having ridden', though another source says he was just about to begin Mass when his captors appeared. Thus began his longest imprisonment, of nine months, in the Gatehouse Prison, close by the old Benedictine foundation of Westminster Abbey. Here he was put into solitary confinement for some months, and subjected to the whims of a thoroughly nasty gaoler who delighted in torturing his prisoners. He deprived them of their allowance, adding maliciously that they could eat the straw from his bed if they were still hungry. Still, Roberts continued his work of conversion in prison until his release and banishment to the Continent in mid-1606.

Fr Roberts travelled abroad for over a year, renewing acquaintances and describing his exploits. 'Santico' (the little saint), the name given to him, shows that his reputation had gone before him. At the end of 1607, he returned, unwearied, to England to recommence his mission but was soon captured in London and found himself, once again, in the Gatehouse prison. Conditions appear to have improved here since his last visit; he was careful to tip his gaoler and was thus able to entertain his friends with a certain degree of freedom. During examination, he admitted to very little, and before very long effected a classic escape from his captors by use of an iron file and rope. He was soon recaptured by his exasperated pursuers who described his manner as 'obstinate', but, thanks to the pleading of the French Ambassador, he was again sent into exile.

The monotonous pattern he had established of jumping in and out of prison was bound to come to a halt before long; even his friends saw that his fearless zeal would cause him 'to go to the pot'. After his final return to the English mission, he worked tirelessly among the plague victims in London again, until he was captured in December 1610 while celebrating Mass in the company of other priests, and dragged off to Newgate prison, still wearing his vestments.

The trial of Fr Roberts before the bishop of London, the Lord Chief Justice and others was held in early December. It was a verbal sparring match between sharp legal minds. The priest would not give an inch; he constantly stressed that it was no treason to be a priest and carry out his mission as such, and that he was following in a long tradition: 'If I deceive, then were our ancestors deceived by Blessed St Augustine, the Apostle of the English, who was sent here by the Pope of Rome, St Gregory the Great . . . I am of the same religious Order, and have been professed of the same rule as St Augustine, and I am sent here by the same Apostolic See that sent him before me'. John Roberts had the same opinion as other Benedictines towards the Oath of Allegiance to the king; he was prepared to swear to any Oath which did not conflict with his faith. Such an attitude was wholly opposed to that of the Jesuits, and it demonstrates yet again how the monks were keen to respect English susceptibilities.

The verdict—guilty of high treason—was a foregone conclusion, but this did not prevent John Roberts turning to his companion at the trial, Fr John Somers, a secular priest, and telling him it was the happiest day of his life. He left the court, pardoning those who had worked for his execution, and promising to pray for the royal family. It seems that he was not in the best of health at this time; the fits of shivering were not helped by the strain of the trial and imprisonment. However, once back in Newgate, he was seen by his old friend Donna Luisa de Carvajal who was a frequent visitor to the Catholic prisoners. She used her influence to have him transferred to the area in which the other Catholics were interned. There, on the eve of his execution, occurred the famous meal, attended by herself and twenty Catholic prisoners, including John Roberts. Not surprisingly, the event has been seen as another Last Supper; attention was focussed on Fr Roberts, and the talk was of sacrifice and endurance tempered with joy and hope.

On a wintry morning, 10 December 1610, Fr Roberts and his companion Fr Somers were tied onto a hurdle with other prisoners, and dragged along the rough streets to Tyburn gallows, three miles distant. Fr Roberts, while physically weak, was in good form, and was not prepared to let this precious moment go by without leaving his mark. He encouraged the sixteen prisoners who were to die with the two of them to be converted to the Catholic faith, and once again acknowledged his devotion to England, 'our sweet country' which owed so much to the Benedictine Order of which he was a member.

He was to die, he said, only because he was a priest; his loyalty to the king remained unimpeachable. As with some of the other martyrs of the period, a wry sense of humour overtook him; pointing to the fire, he said: 'Here is a hot breakfast towards, despite the cold weather', and supposing he was cold, one of the crowd asked him if he wanted a nightcap for his head. Fr Roberts replied: 'Do not trouble yourself about that, sir; I am not afraid that hereafter, I shall ever suffer from headache'. After the rope was put round the two priests' necks, the cart was pulled away from under them, and they were left hanging. Later, the bodies were cut down, quartered, and Fr Roberts' head was displayed on London Bridge. His reputation, founded on his sanctity and zeal, which accompanied him during his life, grew after his death, and was acknowledged in his canonization in 1970.

As the seventeenth century wore on, the confused religious divisions of an earlier time became more clearly defined, and English Catholics came to form an easily recognizable group. To a certain extent, they were favoured by King Charles I, a devoted Anglican, whose wife Henrietta Maria was a practising Catholic. On the other hand, however, Parliament was growing more hostile to the king and more Puritan; it effortlessly assumed that Catholicism meant a political movement which stood for tyranny, foreign domination, superstition and chicanery. The lot of Catholic priests had not, then, improved with time.

The character of Fr Alban Roe is not easily defined. The sources for his life are even more scanty than are those for St John Roberts' story. Furthermore, his personality is not one that fits comfortably into any preconceptions we have of the monastic life; it would go beyond the bounds of truth to describe him as peaceful, sober, steadfast and demure. He was, rather, explosive and unpredictable throughout. Some of the later authors of his life have been at pains to show the slow maturing of a nature that was quick and easily agitated towards the well-disciplined stoicism of the typical monk. This is to push, perhaps, a round peg into a square hole; if he did show strength and courage during his imprisonment and martyrdom, there is no reason why these qualities could not exist alongside other elements in his fiery nature. Alban Roe, then, is a consolation to those monks and nuns who share his reactions to similar situations, but often find themselves misunderstood by their brethren. He is also one among many who provide reasons why the monastic life, seen in relief, must be a misshapen object; it is the fabric itself rather than its pattern.

Bartholomew Roe was born in Suffolk in 1583; his father was a

256   BENEDICT'S DISCIPLES

gentleman, probably from Bury St Edmunds where had existed one of the greatest Benedictine abbeys during the Middle Ages. He was brought up as a firm Protestant in a part of the country where the new religious beliefs had become popular. His brother James was also to be a convert to Catholicism, and, like Bartholomew, was to become an English Benedictine monk, renowned for his fine singing voice in choir.

At some early period, Bartholomew went to Cambridge to finish his education. His first known contact with the Catholic church was while he was visiting St Albans. Here, he tried his hand at bringing round an imprisoned Catholic called David to the reasonableness of the Protestant tradition: 'for he had a sharp and ready wit, and a tongue well-hung, and withal was full of conceit of his own religion, and with false ideas of the Catholic doctrine'. We see something of his characteristic impetuosity here.

It came as quite a shock to Roe's blustery self-confidence to find his opponent had the better of him in this argument: 'Mr Roe soon perceived that he had taken a tartar, and knew not which way to turn himself . . . he left the field with confusion'. The outcome of this defeat was Bartholomew Roe's entry into the Catholic Church, after a series of discussions and debates with various priests whom he encountered. Following his conversion, he made his way to the English College at Douai in late 1607 in order to study for the secular priesthood and return to work on the mission in England.

It was at Douai that Roe soon became a student agitator and created hell for his superiors. The College, like that at Valladolid, had had its troubles in the past, and at this period was tending to drift under weak leadership. Roe's character would not allow him to glide gently through this impassivity; he was spoiling for a fight, if only to liven up College life. Things came to a head in December 1610 when he was expelled by the authorities: 'we consider the said Bartholomew (Roe) is not at all fitted for the purposes of this College, on account of his contempt for the discipline, and for his superiors, and of his misleading certain youths living in the College, and also of the great danger of his still leading others astray, and therefore, we adjudge that he must be dismissed from the College'. Roe, apparently, was a disruptive influence; he encouraged the younger students to laugh punishment off, and tried to whittle down the commands of the major superiors while attempting to cause divisions among them. Above all, he had an offensive manner; one of the authorities removed some cupboards from near Roe's bed, on the President's orders, and Roe turned round and savagely retorted: 'There is more trouble with a few fools than with all the wise; if you pull down, I will build up; if you destroy, I will rebuild'.

It is not surprising that, with his defiance and obstinate tenacity, Roe would not readily accept the President's suggestion that he should leave quietly for England and only return when he had sorted himself out. Instead, he whipped up a campaign in the college among his younger supporters who saw him as a liberating hero, and who demanded to know the real reasons why he was felt to be unfit for the college. In a testimonial which they presented to the President, his supporters bore witness to his good behaviour, and felt there was no objection to his going forward to ordination, since he had been unjustly dismissed for the flimsiest of reasons.

The reasons for Bartholomew Roe's becoming a Benedictine monk are not known. Perhaps, as in John Roberts' case, the Benedictines provided a satisfactory alternative to the chaos in the secular colleges; on the other hand, perhaps they provided more of a challenge, for the English Benedictine communities in which Roe spent his early monastic life were well known for their austerity and disciplined approach. If the latter reason decided Roe to become an English Benedictine, it is an indication that there were hidden depths concealed behind his apparent hotheadedness. Whatever the reason, Roe joined the English Benedictine community of St Lawrence at Dieulouard in Lorraine in early 1613; after his ordination in 1615, he became a founder member of the new English Benedictine community of St Edmund in Paris. His religious name was Fr Alban of St Edmund.

We have no indication that he had a rough passage in the monastery, and there is no hint of the insubordination he had shown in the seminary. However, his natural energy made his move to the English mission certain. Like St John Roberts, Fr Alban worked in London until his capture in 1618. He was imprisoned for five years until he was released at the request of the Spanish Ambassador, Gondomar, and banished to the Continent in 1623. Before very long, he returned to England, and worked in the region of St Albans where he was captured and imprisoned, ironically, the town in which he had first come across the Catholic church. His stay here was mercifully short—he had to endure freezing cold and hunger, and beg from passers-by—for his friends managed to have him transferred to the London prison, the Fleet, where he was to remain for over fifteen years.

In the Fleet, Alban Roe was relatively free; he was able to receive visitors, and even to make the occasional journey outside. His health however was poor and he suffered from stone trouble. His reputation for excitement, and his off-beat manner of life lived on, even at this late stage, for we have a list of 'scandalosi' or evil-living priests drawn up by some sanctimonious critic which mentions that the Benedictine monk, Alban Roe, has a bad reputation because of frequent drinking bouts, and indulgence in games (probably cards) and similar activities. One recalls his earlier popularity among the students here, but such fireworks need to be put alongside a more serious attitude to prayer which he seems to have developed in prison; we know, for instance, that he instructed some of his visitors in the school of prayer and translated some of the great works dealing with this subject.

The Long Parliament, which met in 1640, was strongly Puritan and soon began to tighten up the government's laxity in regard to Catholics. In this process, Alban Roe was transferred to Newgate prison and a much stricter regime in late 1641. His trial followed in January 1642; at its end came the verdict of guilty of treason. Fr Alban took the whole process calmly, even cheerfully, and back in prison, encouraged others to persevere in their faith: 'When you see our arms stretched out and nailed on the gates of the city, think that we are giving you the same blessing that you now receive from us. And when you cast your eyes upon our heads (he was to be executed with the old priest Fr Thomas Reynolds), nailed high up on London Bridge, think that they are there to preach to you, and to proclaim to you that same holy Faith for which we are about to die'.

The journey of Fr Alban and Fr Reynolds to the scaffold was like a triumphant progress. Although they were strapped down to the litter and hauled through the muddy streets, it seemed to them that they 'were riding in the best coach the King had, and that they were going to a marriage feast'. Fr Alban was quite cheerful; he called out to various friends whom he encountered on the way, and threw to them anything he found in his pockets, including his handkerchief, as a souvenir. At Tyburn, his spirits were still high; he comforted his companion and the other prisoners, sympathized with the Sheriff, and attacked the laws against priests, as a result of which he was being hanged. He continued his banter with the crowd, shouting 'Here's a jolly company', and while preaching to them of the meaning of his death, he spotted one of his old gaolers, and called to him: 'My friend, I find that thou art a prophet; thou hast told me often I should be hanged'. As the cart was being pulled from underneath him, he called on the name of Jesus three times, and crossed his hands as if in prayer. Such was his popularity and the impression created by his death, that when his remains were quartered, there was a scramble to dip handkerchiefs into his blood and to pick up the straws, covered in his blood, to treasure as relics.

The life in the monastery and interior devotion of this rugged character is difficult to gauge; let it merely be stated that he became a monk and persevered; that, surely, is sufficient. His fame lived on in a way he would not have imagined; he was an early member of the Community of St Lawrence, now at Ampleforth Abbey, York, and a founder member of the Community of St Edmund, now at Douai Abbey, Reading. After 1970, he was their first canonized saint.

Of the three martyr monks, St Ambrose Barlow is probably the one we can most easily identify with today. Not only are the sources of his life fuller than they are for the other two, but he was such a manifestly good and kind man to all he met, whether Catholics or Protestants, that we cannot but sense an increasing sadness in himself, in his circle, and in ourselves as we watch him go forward to his death.

Edward Barlow was born the fourth of fourteen children of Sir Alexander Barlow and his wife Mary, at Barlow Hall, near Manchester in 1585. Lancashire Catholicism had remained strong despite the Reformation, and Ambrose Barlow, as Edward became known when a monk, exemplified this both in his own life and in his interests. Two of his brothers were also to become Benedictine monks; William, the elder, known as Fr Rudesind Barlow, was one of the greatest English monks of his day.

As in the stories of the two monks described above, so there are, in Ambrose Barlow's early life, very few details known. We know that he served as a page in a Catholic house when he was twelve years old, and probably during this time, he decided to go abroad to train as a missionary priest 'to be of some assistance to his native country'. This decision, in fact, followed a period in which Edward Barlow had lapsed from his faith. With the enthusiasm of his reconversion burning within him he followed his brother William to the English secular College at Douai in 1607. Thus, like John Roberts and Alban Roe, Edward Barlow found his way to the Benedictine monastery through the secular clergy. After studies at Douai and two years at the seminary in Valladolid, Edward Barlow was ordained and left for England in 1613. Here he was imprisoned after being captured in London, but was later freed, and returned to Douai.

By this time an English Benedictine monastery had been established at Douai, known as St Gregory's, thanks to the munificence of Abbot Cavarel of Arras. Edward's brother William, now Rudesind, who had left the secular clergy in Douai to become a Benedictine monk at Cellanova in Galicia, Spain, was now its prior. Probably for a whole host of reasons, close relations with his brother, interest in the monastic life and in the reviving of the English Benedictines, among them, Edward became a Benedictine monk at St Gregory's, Douai, becoming Br Ambrose Barlow.

Besides studying at Douai, Barlow also made his preparation for the monastic life at the other English monastery in St Malo; at his profession he was affiliated to the monastery of Cellanova, like his brother. After his ordination to the priesthood in 1617, he left again, this time as a monk missionary, for England.

At this time, England was certainly a missionary territory and Catholic priests were constantly on the move, covering wide areas, and setting up bases in the houses of the Catholic gentry. Fr Ambrose served on one of these 'riding missions' near Manchester, basing himself at Morleys Hall, in the parish of Leigh, owned by the Catholic Tyldesley family. A contemporary account of his life, known as 'The Apostolical Life', gives us a picture of Fr Ambrose trudging over a circuit which stretched for over twenty miles, but which was dotted with Halls owned by Catholics. In these he said Mass, attended by local Catholics. The resemblance between Fr Ambrose and earlier monk missionaries is striking; monks like Martin of Tours and the Northumbrian missionary Aidan disliked riding horses because they were symbols of wealth. So too, 'As long as Ambrose Barlow was able, he would not ride, but still went about on foot with a long staff on his back, like a countryman, and he took mighty pains because he sometimes had to go to several places in a morning to say mass, and then elsewhere for night mass. This made him very weary'.

There was one particular aspect of Fr Ambrose's life which made him rather different from many other missionary priests, and may well have been common among other Benedictines. This was the extended residency which he allowed himself at his home, Morleys Hall, for we read that it was his custom to spend three weeks at home, and only one on his missionary circuit; thus, there was some monastic stability in the midst of his busy labours. In fact, his home resembled a monastery in miniature. although he was the only real monk there. His servants and the local poor dined at table with him, and on the greater feasts, he entertained all who came: 'he served those at table, and made some of his richer guests do the same. He made his dinner of the left-overs of the rich, and divided the residue among the poor'.

Despite Fr Barlow's example of generous Benedictine hospitality, and his making provision for his guests to board with him, he loved monastic solitude and the traditional asceticism of the monk. We can perceive a fairly clear picture of his character from the words of his biographer; though we need to appreciate that much of his description is stylized, and that he uses Fr Barlow's life as a means of transmitting Christian virtues to the reader for his imitation. Thus, for instance, when we read that Fr Ambrose refused to kiss his mother when he returned home: it is the biographer's intention to single out this event to show Fr Barlow's detachment in general. He had, in fact, the detachment which belongs to a clown, an ability to laugh at the world, but also to be laughed at until a point when sympathy to the helpless became the natural reaction. 'You must not be offended with our clownishness', he said, 'for we are all clowns'. He was moderate in what he ate and drank, and merely took what came. 'If God should send a venison pastie, he would not refuse to eat it', though on Doctor's orders, 'he took a mess of new milk in the morning and a roasted apple at night'. As to his appearance, it resembled that of a 'sojourner' for his beard went untrimmed and his hair grew long: 'his breeches tied at the knees; a band about his neck, like country folk's fashion. . . . Instead of pantoufles, a pair of scurvy old slip-shoes which he wore outdoors'. He refused to wear a sword: 'Indeed, I dare not ware a sword because I am of a chol-lericke nature'. We might associate all this with the rig-out of a modern artist, and we do indeed hear that Ambrose Barlow painted, though his pictures were not too accomplished. In fact, he is said to have best resembled St Thomas More, sharing the latter's cheerfulness in the face of affliction right to the end.

Fr Ambrose appears to have realized that martyrdom would be the consequence of his actions, but that did not deter him. A vision he had had in 1628 of the Jesuit martyr Edmund Arrowsmith on the eve of his execution had a profound effect on him, for the Jesuit had told him: 'I have suffered and now you will be to suffer; say little, for they will endeavour to take hold of your words'. He carried on preaching, regardless, and refused to leave Lancashire in spite of sanctions from the government against priests. His health, meanwhile, was deteriorating, and this encouraged him to meditate even more on the sufferings of Christ, in imitation of whom, Fr Ambrose stretched out his arms while praying in the form of a Cross. On Easter Sunday 1641, the local Anglican rector concluded his service by urging his congregation to go to nearby Morleys Hall to capture Fr Barlow. And so the mob moved off, numbering about four hundred, armed with swords and clubs, with the rector in his surplice at the head. They broke down the Hall's door and found Fr Ambrose preaching—he had just finished celebrating Mass, and had refused to escape into the priest's hiding hole. He was taken, and eventually ended up in Lancaster gaol where for four months he was able to give himself to prayer and reflection.

His trial occurred in late May 1641. Ambrose Barlow freely admitted his priesthood, adding that he had not followed the government's order to leave the country because he was a priest, since that had only applied to Jesuits and Seminary priests, and he was a Benedictine. He was also too ill to travel so far. This allowed the judge to suggest that he might go free if he promised to seduce no more people. Fr Alban replied that he was no seducer, but a reducer of the people to the true and ancient religion. The judge therefore, prompted by the government to deal harshly with any priest in the area because of Lancashire's strong Catholicism, declared him guilty of treason for being a priest: the execution was scheduled for 10 September 1641. He was dragged to his death in Lancaster, clutching in his hand a small cross of wood which he had made in prison. After praying at the scaffold and kindly sending away some clergymen who tried to argue with him, he was hanged, drawn and quartered, dying, as he had lived, quietly and with dignity. His memory however lived on among his brethren on the Continent and on the English mission, and in the hearts of his flock. He was canonized in 1970, and with St John Roberts is revered as an early member of the Community of St Gregory, now at Downside Abbey, Bath.

There were to be no other martyr monks among the English Benedictines after these three, though some of their followers were to die in prison for their faith, or in contracting disease while carrying out their missionary labours, and hence became known as 'martyrs of charity'. But by and large, the Benedictines found little difficulty adapting themselves to the English scene in later years as chaplains, pastors, teachers or preachers. Nevertheless, our three martyrs were recognized as the seed bearing this later fruit, and their memory was preserved by the Benedictine annalist, Benet Weldon, for posterity:

'So extraordinary was the fervour of these men that, as in the Primitive Church Children cast away their books and ran out of School to the place of suffering, such as were scarce born into the Order, were found ripe for Martyrdom'.

by Dom Geoffrey Scott

BIBLIOGRAPHY

W. E. Rhodes (ed.), *The Apostolical Life of Ambrose Barlow* (Chetham Miscellanies ii, Manchester 1909).

B. Camm, *Nine Martyr Monks* (London 1931).

J. Forbes, *Blessed Alban Roe* (London 1960).

W. Phillipson, *Blessed John Roberts* (London 1961).

J. Stonor, *Ambrose Barlow* (London 1961).

R. Challoner, *Memoirs of Missionary Priests* (ed. J. H. Pollen, London 1928).

D. M. Lunn, *From Reformation to Revolution; the English Benedictines, 1540–1688* (forthcoming).

Dame Gertrude More

The name of St Thomas More is rightly associated with the Charter-house where he lived for some years in his youth; his links with Benedictines are less widely known. On 23 April 1530 a letter was drawn up by the Prior and Chapter of Canterbury admitting him and his wife to full membership of their confraternity, making them 'participant of all prayers, masses, fasts, almsdeeds, vigils and in fine of all works of piety which with the assistance of God's grace shall be done by us or our successors monks of the Church of Canterbury for ever'. How confident 'for ever' sounds! Only five years later St Thomas suffered a martyr's death in defence of papal supremacy, and in 1540 the monastic community of Canterbury was dissolved. Nearly a century later, however, four of his descen-dants were to play a part in the re-establishment of Benedictine life for Englishwomen. Three of them were foundation members of the community at Cambray, now at Stanbrook Abbey in England, and the fourth, who entered at Cambray slightly later, was to become first prioress of the off-shoot community in Paris, now at Colwich, Staffordshire.

Outstanding amongst the four was Helen More, known in religion as Dame Gertrude. The seventy years which separated Helen from St Thomas had been eventful ones for England as well as for the universal Church. After the death of Henry VIII, in the two short reigns of Edward VI and Mary Tudor, the religious pendulum of the country had swung first to stricter Protestantism, then back to wholehearted Catholicism. With the accession of Elizabeth I in 1558 came the decisive movement, and England was to rank for centuries as Protestant. The national splendour of her reign seemed to confirm the decision. A slight vibration when James I came to the throne in 1603 caused Catholic hopes to flicker but the Guy Fawkes plot, a year before Helen's birth, aroused against Catholics in general the reaction the plot alone deserved.

Systematically over the years, beginning not long after the martyrdom of St Thomas, the Council of Trent had been planning the Church's inward reformation. Following upon its decisions and decrees came the period of intense religious zeal and effort known as the Counter-Reformation, within which fell the entire lifetime of Helen More.

It was a time of tremendous vitality: fierce persecution matched by heroic endurance and self-sacrifice; missionary expansion supported by depths of contemplation; ancient religious orders renewed to keep pace with the generous initiative of new congregations. The world had more than ever to offer but countless young people were ready to leave all—life itself included—to follow Christ.

Helen More was born in 1606 on a family estate at Low Leyton, Essex. Her father, Cresacre More of Barnborough Hall,Yorks., was the youngest son of Thomas More, grandson of St Thomas through the latter's son John. Cresacre had wanted to be a priest and had spent ten years as a seminarian, but on the death of his eldest brother he was persuaded to return and take charge of the family property. It is interesting to note that Mary Tudor had restored some of the More estates, alienated under her predecessors, but for the most part the family estates were derived from the Cresacre ancestors after whom Helen's father was named. Cresacre married Elizabeth, sister of Sir John Gage of Firle in Sussex. They had a son and two daughters, but Elizabeth did not live long enough to see the children grow up. Helen, the elder girl, was a bright and merry child and as she grew older her father delighted in her company. He kept her at home and educated her almost entirely himself. As a small child she was precocious enough to answer him in words that rhymed, and by the time her education was finished she had attained to a maturity beyond her years. Surely there is a reflection here of the happy relationship between St Thomas and his daughter Meg.

Helen's intelligence was not that of a mere bookworm—far from it. She was lively, full of interest in everything around her and gifted with considerable practical ability. There was no fear of a girl like her ever succumbing to inertia; the danger was that she might become a bit too much of a manageress. But we are assured that she was gentle and good-natured. When she was in her teens people began to wonder: 'What is Helen going to do? Will she marry—or what?' Her Benedictine confessor, Fr Benet Jones, talked the matter over with her father and put before him a plan that was on foot within the newly restored English Benedictine Congregation to found a house on the Continent for Englishwomen who wanted to be nuns. Perhaps Helen might be one of them?

Like Canterbury and all the other monks' monasteries, every house of Benedictine nuns had been suppressed under Henry VIII. Benedictine life flickered up again at Westminster for a brief spell under Mary Tudor, but after that penal laws were once again enforced and conventual life in England was an impossibility. In 1597 Lady Mary Percy, daughter of Blessed Thomas Percy, had already founded a house at Brussels for English Benedictine nuns, but the spiritual direction of that community had been largely entrusted to Jesuits and secular priests whereas it was hoped that the projected foundation would remain under Benedictine influence.

For two or three years Fr Benet Jones and Cresacre More discussed the plan on and off and Helen herself was approached about the matter. Frankly the idea left her cold. Not that she knew much about the religious life, nor did she have any particular desire for secular life, but being a sociable girl she shrank from what she imagined must be the austere solitude of the cloister. Fr Benet was so keen on the new foundation that he perhaps overlooked the fact that Helen's spiritual welfare was not the only interest he had at heart: obviously he was on the look-out for suitable candidates, and the dowry which Cresacre was prepared to provide would make the whole scheme viable. But he probably discerned latent spiritual potential in her.

When Helen was seventeen, it was at last agreed between the three of them that she should try the religious life for a time at least, and if she found herself unsuited to it return home. We may well wonder whatever persuaded such a strong-minded young woman to capitulate at this point and fall in with a plan for her future, which held no attraction for her either on a natural or even, as far as she was then aware, on a supernatural plane. Later she herself was to explain that she had been genuinely fond of her spiritual father and had not liked to disappoint him. Nowadays such an explanation would not be accepted: entrance into religious life entails the free, personal choice of a responsible individual; coercion queers the pitch.

Once the decision had been made, Helen was utterly miserable and withdrew as much as she could from company. It was taken for granted that piety was her motive and even her father never guessed the true state of affairs. A word to him might have changed everything, but Helen said nothing and went ahead with the determination of a More. In the summer of 1623 she and seven other young women set sail for the Low Countries escorted by Fr Benet Jones. The group included two of Helen's cousins, Grace, daughter of John More of Bampton, Oxon., and Anne, daughter of Edward More of Barnborough. At Douay, where they stayed until the autumn, they were joined by another candidate, Catherine Gascoigne from Barnbow Hall, Yorkshire. Their ages ranged from fifteen to thirty-five, the average age of the group being about twenty-two. Young as she was, Helen seems to have been regarded as the leader from the start and we may be sure that she shouldered the responsibility capably. It is interesting to contrast her attitude to the whole venture with that of Catherine Gascoigne, who was burning with desire to dedicate her life to God in a monastic community. When Catherine first applied at the age of nineteen for permission to leave England, she was refused, so it is said, by the Bishop of London, partly on account of her great beauty. But she was not prepared to take 'no' for an answer where her vocation was concerned and she appealed to God in heartfelt prayer. The answer came in the shape of smallpox, which marred her good looks so that she was able eventually to obtain the necessary leave. Meanwhile several years elapsed before everything could be fixed up for her departure, and she was already twenty-three by the time she joined Helen and her companions at Douay. Two of Catherine's brothers were already members of the newly restored English Benedictine Congregation: Dom Michael was professed for the community of St Gregory's, established at Douay in 1606; Dom Placid Gascoigne had been clothed at St Lawrence's, founded at Dieulouard in 1608; both were sent for a time to Paris, where the community of St Edmund's had been inaugurated in 1615. These three communities live on to this day in England under the well-known names of Downside, Ampleforth and Douai.

In the seventeenth century this newly restored congregation was distinctly forward-looking in character. To begin with, it was essentially a missionary congregation whose members were pledged to return to England at the will of their superior, there to labour to restore the Catholic faith at the peril of their lives. At least eight of them were to endure a martyr's death.

And now this same congregation was intending to establish a fourth community, this time one for nuns, and contemplative nuns at that. Does this seem a contradiction? Not at all; the two things hang together: the apostolic efficacy of the contemplative life has never been doubted by men of faith, and the less the monks on the English mission had of the usual supports of conventual life, the more they would rely on the prayers of their enclosed sisters.

While Helen, Catherine and the others were living in Douay in a house belonging to the Abbey of St Vedast in Arras, Helen fell seriously ill. She was never very strong and there now seemed to be some fear of her death occurring before the new monastery had even been founded. However, she rallied and recovered in time to move with the others shortly after Michaelmas to Cambray, where there was some hope of their being able to obtain a permanent dwelling of their own. Meanwhile they were warmly welcomed by Arch-bishop Vanderburgh and offered temporary shelter by the Hospital of St James until they were able to take possession of a house which had belonged to the Abbey of Fémy. It turned out to be only the ruined shell of a house—four cracked walls with no partitions inside; it cost them £500 to make it habitable and even then the workmen predicted that it would not last more than thirty years. At first it was only lent to them, but in 1638 it became their own property.

Every religious has to be trained and no exception was made for these recruits. The monks had arranged for three nuns to come from the English house at Brussels and undertake the formation of the new community. They arrived at about the beginning of November and on the 24 December 1623 they and their nine charges moved into the house which the community was to occupy for a hundred and seventy years. In 1793 the nuns were to be ruthlessly ejected, imprisoned at Compiègne and only after eighteen months' internment allowed to make their way back to England in secular dress. Looking ahead for the moment to this apparent disaster, we catch a glimpse of the workings of God's providence in bringing so many English communities back from exile. At the same time we appreciate the kindly inconsistency of the English people who forgot their prejudices of the past and received victims of the French Revolution with such generous hospitality.

But Cambray was for the time being a haven of security when Helen, now Sister Gertrude, and Sister Catherine, who had retained her baptismal name, received the Benedictine habit along with the other seven on 31 December 1623. The archbishop himself performed the ceremony, though he had generously granted full exemption to this community which belonged from the start to the English Benedictine Congregation. Dom Rudesind Barlow, President of the Congregation, had watched over the group since Fr Benet Jones returned to England, and he was there now at the clothing ceremony in his capacity as superior. One of the three Brussels nuns, Dame Frances Gawen, was to hold the office of abbess until 1629, and the second, Dame Viviana Yaxley, was appointed novice mistress. Together with Dame Pudentiana Deacon they devoted themselves wholeheartedly to the task entrusted to them.

There is no reason to suppose that there was any lack of cooperation on the part of the novices; presumably all nine were out to do their best, but somehow they knew instinctively that they were being nourished on the wrong spiritual diet. The type of formal meditation, which had proved such a powerful instrument of spiritual renewal in the Counter-Reformation and had been gladly adopted by some of the Brussels community, was no help to them at all. With one accord they appealed to Fr Rudesind Barlow to send them a spiritual guide versed in the ways of monastic contemplative prayer. Sister Gertrude, according to her own later admission, was in an especially bad way. She had undertaken to try the religious life and try it she certainly did, but when she received the habit she still had no desire to persevere to profession. Hers was no merely superficial unhappiness, it sprang rather from the integrity of her personality. She knew that the main point of being an enclosed religious was to live a life of interior prayer but, try as she would, she could find no way into this unknown world within. However, she put on a good face and threw herself for the time being into monastic life. She could be the life and soul of the community; whether she ever would be so at a deeper level remained to be seen. Meanwhile none of her companions suspected what mental suffering she was enduring.

Fr Rudesind was sympathetic towards the request of the novices and undertook to do his utmost to find a monk who could really help them. His efforts were singularly successful and in July 1624 Fr Augustine Baker arrived at Cambray where he was to remain for nine years.

Fr Baker holds an important position in the history of English spirituality, for he contributed much towards carrying the medieval mystical tradition over into the post-Reformation reflorescence of monasticism. It was at the request of the nuns of Cambray that a number of his spiritual treatises were composed and they carefully preserved notes of his oral instructions as well. David Baker was a Welshman, born at Abergavenny in 1575, and educated at Christ's Hospital and Broadgates Hall, Oxford. Later he took up law and attended the Inns of Court. The story of his conversion at the age of about twenty-five is a romantic one : it took place at a moment of extreme danger when the horse he was riding got stuck on a narrow bridge high above a rushing stream. There and then he vowed in his heart that if he escaped he would believe in God 'who hath more care of my life and safety than I have of his love and worship'. Immediately horse and rider were brought safely to the bank. From that moment David Baker believed once more in God ; later he was reconciled to the Catholic Church, to which both his parents had once belonged. He abandoned his secular career and was clothed at Padua as a Benedictine novice, taking the name Augustine after St Augustine of Canterbury, Apostle of England. He returned to England where he was professed. With his legal knowledge he was of especial use to his Benedictine brethren in 1607 in ensuring juridical continuity between the community of Westminster Abbey—the only one restored by Mary Tudor—and the newly formed Con-gregation ; the former being represented by a single aged monk, Fr Sigebert Buckley. Dom Augustine felt strongly drawn to a life of contemplative prayer in which he lived through the experience of both rapture and desolation. In 1613 he was ordained priest ; when

the English Benedictine Congregation was formally established by
the Holy See in 1619, he entered it at once, shortly afterwards
choosing Dieulouard as the monastery to which he wished to
belong. About this time he underwent a still further conversion
which confirmed him for the rest of his life in the unswerving
practice of contemplative prayer. Fr Rudesind Barlow was right in
thinking that if anyone could help the Cambray novices, now
increased by the addition of three new arrivals, it would be Fr
Baker.

But there was to be no swift *deus ex machina* solution to Sr Gertrude's
problems; things were to get still worse before they finally improved.
Fr Baker's position at Cambray was anyway a delicate one for he
was neither chaplain nor official confessor, and as for his spiritual
teaching, the novices were free to take it or leave it. At first they
welcomed his help enthusiastically but gradually one after another
followed the example of the novice mistress and fell away—all, that
is, except one, Sr Catherine. She remained his loyal disciple and
practised what he taught until her dying day; it was due to her
example that the community was gradually won back to Fr Baker.
Sr Gertrude did more than simply refrain from consulting him: she
campaigned against him 'with witty tongue and animosity' as he
later expressed it when writing her life. Reading his own life one
can see that he was a man with strongly marked individual eccen-
tricities, and Sr Gertrude may have made the most of them. But his
teaching itself could be misinterpreted and ridiculed, and that was
the greater danger now. To quote another of his phrases: 'from a
kind of foundress she might have become a kind of pestilence'. She
and some others even tried to get him removed from the house at
the time of the general chapter in July 1625.

But deep down in her heart Sr Gertrude had a sound judgement
of spiritual things and she had to admit that anyone who followed
Fr Baker's advice improved noticeably. That was a good thing for
them but it would not do for her! While still a novice, Sr Gertrude
received a letter from her father assuring her that if for reasons of
health she thought she had better leave and return home, he 'would
not love her one whitte the less but farre the more for her so heroical
resolutions'. Whatever she thought right to do, she could always
count on his care and support. That letter must have tugged at her
heart-strings. This would have been the moment to leave and extricate herself from her painfully anomalous situation. Instead, she
replied towards the end of her novitiate year that she intended to
go forward to profession.

But as their profession day approached Sr Gertrude felt worse and
worse about the whole thing. Fr Rudesind Barlow arrived at

Cambray a week or two beforehand, and she kept meaning to go and open her heart to him, but something always seemed to prevent her: either when she did have a chance to speak to him she shirked the issue, or if she felt she really could manage it, then there was no opportunity. Probably most people have experienced that kind of thing. On the eve of the profession day she made a last desperate attempt to catch the President before nightfall, but she was summoned to a council meeting for examination and passed for profession. On 1 January 1625 Sr Gertrude and the other eight pronounced the vows which bound them for life. All Benedictines vow 'stability, conversion of life, and obedience according to the Rule of Holy Father Benedict'. The Cambray nuns added a further clause, pledging themselves to perpetual enclosure. Though the vows of poverty and chastity, made by the members of most religious orders, are not expressed by the Benedictine formula, they are nevertheless implicit in it, since their practice is essential to monastic life. This particular profession day was of special significance as being the official canonical foundation day of the community of Our Lady of Consolation, then sometimes termed Our Lady of Comfort.

It might be expected that once that irreversible step had been taken Dame Gertrude's difficulties would have vanished. The exact opposite was the case: her unhappiness increased. She worried about her profession—as well as she might, for she knew that had she explained everything to the President, he could not have allowed her to take vows in that frame of mind. It should be noted at this point that for her own peace of mind she later got leave to renew her profession privately, so that any fear of invalidity might be dispelled. Meanwhile she was so miserable that she could scarcely bear to hear the name of Fr Benet Jones mentioned, let alone hear him spoken of with appreciation and gratitude or referred to as her friend; for in her heart she regretted ever having had anything to do with him since he was responsible for her present plight. In justice to Fr Benet Jones it should be said that he rendered great service not only to these nuns but to the whole English Congregation. He was a courageous missioner ready to take risks, as we shall see.

Outwardly Dame Gertrude continued to face life bravely during the day, but at night, as she afterwards confided to Dame Catherine, she would give vent to her feelings, 'sighing and groaning to God almighty to help her and moaning her lamentable case'. She began to wonder whether the best thing to do would not be to transfer to another religious house. She thought she might find a more sympathetic superior and that it might be better for her to leave the companions of whom she had grown so fond. About Whitsuntide her father came to Cambray for two or three months and she was able to see him practically every day. It seemed just the right opportunity for negotiating a move and she wanted to discuss the matter with him. However, the same thing happened as with the President before her profession—she simply could not bring herself to speak of her unhappiness. Instead she laid herself out to cheer him up and said not a word about her own problems.

Dame Gertrude honestly tried to find a remedy for these problems: she read every spiritual book she could lay hands on and consulted every wise counsellor who visited the house—all, that is, save the one she had for the time being rejected. Her relationship with the abbess was deplorable; even the novice mistress, of whom she was genuinely fond, was reduced to exclaiming: 'Here is Dame Gertrude: but I would to God Sister Helen were here again'.

Sinking into the slough of despond, Dame Gertrude clutched at one last plank: she could make a general confession. The others had done so before clothing and profession but she, for some reason or other, had not. So she made this special confession now. What was the result? By this time we are beginning to know the pattern: she was more tormented in conscience than ever. In fact she was beaten, the Hound of Heaven had her in his grasp and true liberation was close at hand. But for the moment she thought that there was nothing more left to try: this state would have to be endured to her dying day and she only hoped that would not be too far off.

Some time around All Saints' Day the novice mistress, not knowing what else to propose, suggested that Dame Gertrude should have a talk with Fr Baker. She did, and it proved the turning-point in her life. In a mere five weeks or so she had reached a hitherto unknown serenity of soul. Previously she had written on various occasions to the President complaining about her superior and other things she found difficult; now she wrote to retract what she had said and humbly begged forgiveness.

It would be impossible to estimate what Dame Gertrude owed to Fr Baker, but he was also to receive much from her. Her whole-hearted response to his teaching and the remarkable transformation which it brought about were striking testimony to the validity of his spiritual doctrine which, as we shall see, was later to be called in question. Thanks to Fr Baker's life of Dame Gertrude, it is possible to get an unusually vivid insight into the inward workings of a highly favoured soul. First let us see how Fr Baker analyses her rich personality and then take a look at the guidelines he laid down for her.

The first impression one would get of her would be that of an incorrigible extrovert: 'all the business that the house could afford for all the persons in it were little enough for her to employ her head about them. . . . Nothing concerning the house, that was of any worth, were it little or great, but that her head or hand or both of them was in it, but more the former. . . . None conversed more at the grate . . . none more within doors. . . . None wrote more letters.' This was all true, but Fr Baker discerned something else as well: deep within her was a powerful instinct for the things of God, an ability of the will to tend directly to God alone. So deep was this instinct that she was scarcely aware of it, and yet so strong that she acted according to it in spite of herself. Already we have an explanation of her hitherto paradoxical behaviour.

She had other contrasting qualities as well. Bold and courageous on the one hand, she was a prey to inward fear and scrupulosity; in spite of high spirits and a lively sense of humour she was subject to moods of sadness; naturally full of affection, she could find herself inwardly cold as a stone.

Such was the problem confronting Fr Baker; his solution of it was quite literally simplicity itself. She must turn to God and in all things follow his inward inspiration. God alone can teach each soul to pray, for, as the psalm says, 'He fashions hearts one by one': all are made for him but he draws each in a different way. This complete reliance on divine inspiration was to be the guiding principle of Dame Gertrude's spiritual life. She summed it up in the doggerel motto:

> Consider your call,
> That's all in all.

This was to apply not merely to prayer but to all else besides. The task of an external director was to put souls in touch with the Holy Spirit, their inward guide, and after that merely remain available for consultation on exceptional occasions. As for Dame Gertrude's aversion for formal meditation, that was understandable enough. According to Fr Baker, it is unusual for anyone to advance to contemplative prayer—that is, to a prayer of simple loving attention to God beyond all images and words—without having practised some other sort of prayer first. He suggests four possibilities: vocal prayer, discursive meditation, immediate acts, sensible affections. The term 'vocal prayer' speaks for itself, and we know how close it can lead people to God if such prayers are recited with loving attention. The Divine Office is included in this category. 'Discursive meditation' means applying imagination and reason to some particular subject—perhaps an episode in the life of Christ—with the deliberate intention of stirring up the will. Dame Gertrude had no use for this kind of prayer, because her will tended towards God of its own accord and no amount of thinking made any difference to its instinctive movement. In other words, she did not have to think of reasons for loving God: she simply loved him. 'Acts' in this context are verbal expressions of some inward movement of the will —e.g. an act of contrition or of love. 'Immediate acts' are so called because there is no intervening stage of reasoning; the soul turns directly to God, making acts which refer either to God alone or to the soul's own efforts to love and serve him. This kind of prayer did not suit Dame Gertrude either, because there was still a certain amount of use of the imagination in it. 'Sensible affections' were what appealed to her affectionate nature: these affective acts of love prepared her for genuinely contemplative prayer and buoyed her up through times of darkness and aridity. Such acts would either arise spontaneously within her or else sometimes she would use acts composed by others: she made a point of collecting them. After her death her spiritual jottings were collected by the community and edited by Fr Baker. They were eventually published in Paris in 1658 under the title *Confessiones Amantis* ('Confessions of a Lover').

In them we can see how completely her attitude to religious life was changed, once she had received competent advice about prayer: 'O all ye who think it a burden to be obliged by your profession to tend to great perfection and fear the punishment of our doing the contrary, raise up your hearts and remember what it is Our Lord expecteth of you by this your profession. . . . It is— oh! it is—to love without bounds or measure; it is to leave yourself that you may find God; it is to fly from the world that you may hear Our Lord speaking peace to your soul' (25th Confession). Or again, in another statement quoted by Fr Baker: 'Yea, even in five weeks my soul became so enamoured with the yoke of this my dear Lord, that if I must have made not only four, but even four thousand vows to have become wholly dedicated to him, I should have embraced this state with more joy and content than ever I did find in obtaining that whichever I most of all wished and desired. Thou knowest, my God, by my soul being put into a course of prayer I seemed to have found a true means whereby I might love without end or measure.'

But Fr Baker also made it perfectly clear to Dame Gertrude that there is no such thing as a life of prayer without mortification, the purpose of which is to eliminate self-will so that the will may be unimpeded in its movement towards God. He gave her three simple rules:

1. She was to do everything that she was obliged to by divine or human law, including following divine inspirations.

2. She was to abstain from all that was forbidden by divine or human law, or by divine inspiration.

3. She was to bear as patiently as possible all crosses that came to her in body, mind or soul, irrespective of their source.

There was nothing spectacular about such a programme, but Fr Baker knew that it was sufficient for her or anyone else aspiring to a life of prayer. It had the advantage of concealing from others the fact that she was living a mortified life at all. Fr Baker was very broadminded too about her need for conversation and relaxation as well as for plenty of outward occupation. The soundness of his judgement in this matter was proved by the fact that Dame Gertrude never had any difficulty in concentrating on prayer when it was time for it.

Not surprisingly this inward change in such an influential member of the community affected the whole house and made things considerably easier for the abbess. Dame Gertrude's father happened to visit her again in the spring of 1626 on his way from Antwerp to Paris, and he too noticed the difference in her and went away much happier than after his first visit. They met once more for the last time in the following autumn when he was on his way back to Antwerp. He returned to England in the spring of 1627 and never came back to Cambray. In one of her *Confessions* Dame Gertrude gave vent to her appreciation of all he had done for her from childhood upwards: 'Such was the carefulness of Thy servant, my natural father, who was so careful that I should be kept out of all occasions of sin, that I might (considering also the nature which Thou gavest me) have lived very innocently. But what, through my great fault and negligence, is due to me for my sins, may it be supplied by the superabundance of Thy mercy, which I will from henceforth with all my powers extol. And I beseech Thee, remember Thy true servant, my said father, who through his care prevented my further evil.'

Her father had another sacrifice to make when his second daughter, Bridget, left him in June 1629 to join her sister at Cambray, but by this time he was convinced that the community he had done so much to help was now firmly established and under competent spiritual direction. Dame Bridget was to develop into an outstanding nun and years later was chosen to accompany her abbess on a special mission to reform a neighbouring French monastery. In 1652 she was elected first prioress of the foundation made by the Cambray nuns in Paris at a time of dire economic need.

The year 1629 was a memorable one for other more important reasons. The third general chapter of the restored Congregation was held and Fr Benet Jones elected president. He failed to turn up at Douay to be installed for the very good reason that he was in prison in England under sentence of death. Later he was released and continued to serve on the mission but in the meantime Fr Sigebert Bagshawe had necessarily assumed the duties of president.

By this time the nuns' community numbered over thirty and it was decided that the time had come for one of the nuns professed for Cambray to take over the abbatial office from Dame Frances Gawen. Only two of the nine came in for consideration: Dame Gertrude More and Dame Catherine Gascoigne. Both were under the required age, so application was made to Rome for the necessary indult. In the end it was Dame Catherine who was appointed abbess, possibly because she was six years older. It proved a happy choice, for she was confirmed in her position by a series of quadriennial elections until her resignation in 1673, with the single exception of the occasion when she was needed to assist another monastery. There was something rock-like in the character of the new abbess: calm, quiet and reserved, she pursued her way towards God unswervingly, leading her community by example and ready to rise to the occasion in defence of their spiritual liberty. Dame Gertrude worked closely in conjunction with her, acting as abbess's assistant. In the same year she became cellarer and she also had special responsibility for the lay-sisters. The retired abbess and another of the Brussels nuns remained with the Cambray community till death; the third, Dame Viviana Yaxley, eventually returned to her own monastery.

Another appointment resulting from the general chapter of 1629 was less satisfactory. Though Fr Baker was left with the Cambray community as spiritual guide, Fr Francis Hull was sent as chaplain with the authoritative title of Vicar. As we shall see, this zealous and well-meaning Benedictine was to cause untold suffering to the community, especially to Dame Gertrude. But first one should have some idea of the trials which served to purify and strengthen Dame Gertrude's will and so prepare her for this searching test.

After her great breakthrough, prayer rapidly became her one delight, but that does not mean that she always found it easy to pray or that her soul was constantly flooded with light. On the contrary, she had to endure much darkness and aridity, but she never slackened on that account. That was a lesson which Fr Baker had learned at great cost to himself: earlier in his life, after receiving an outstanding grace in prayer, he found himself plunged into desolation and, imagining that he was rejected by God, he turned back for relief to outward occupations. It was not until twelve years later that he had the courage to set out again wholeheartedly on a life of prayer. He was not likely to allow Dame Gertrude to make a mistake of that sort.

Another trial which caused her considerable suffering was a recurring temptation to go back over her past confessions and repeat them, in case they had not been adequate. She was told to resist this at all costs and she struggled hard to obey. Only once did she yield to the temptation and then, as might be expected, the reiterated confession reduced her to a state of still worse spiritual confusion. Gradually perfect love won the day and fear was cast out altogether. At the end of her life fearlessness in face of death was to be the very mark which confirmed Fr Baker's conviction that Dame Gertrude had indeed reached holiness.

After the appointment of the new chaplain at Cambray in 1629 things went fairly well for about eighteen months, in spite of the fact that Fr Francis Hull and Fr Baker were diametrically opposed in character and outlook. Gradually, however, Fr Hull began to resent the fact that Fr Baker's spiritual influence was so much greater than his own. He especially objected to his hearing confessions and inveighed in his sermons against those who would not obey legitimately appointed authority. He had a point here, for according to the Constitutions it was normal for the Vicarius to hear the nuns' confessions. The community accepted this and Dame Gertrude suffered considerably in consequence.

By 1632 the strained relations between the monks and the resulting tensions in the community had reached such a pitch that the president ordered both monks to represent their views at general chapter in the following year. Furthermore, since Fr Baker's whole spiritual doctrine was to be thoroughly examined, Dame Catherine Gascoigne and Dame Gertrude More were each required to submit a written account of their personal prayer. Every manuscript in the possession of the community had also to be sent in to ensure its complete orthodoxy. This vigilant care on the part of the Congregation is easily understood against the spiritual background of the times. So convinced were many of the zealous promoters of the Counter-Reformation of the efficacy of formal meditation as the great means of inward renewal that sixty years previously the Jesuit Balthasar Alvarez had come under suspicion because of his practice of contemplative prayer: the General of the Society had his case investigated with the result that his prayer was highly commended and recommended to others who could profit by it. Such apparently exaggerated vigilance was seen to be justified later in the seventeenth century when first Jansenism and then Quietism came to the fore, attracted adherents and were condemned. But at the time when Fr Baker's teaching fell under suspicion, Molinos and Fénelon, whose names are associated with Quietism, were not yet born.

During the difficult time before the impending chapter Dame

Gertrude was a tower of strength to the community. Dame Catherine wrote of her: 'It cannot be imagined how great a comfort and encouragement she was to us all in these times of our difficulties; her example and words were so moving and efficacious, and proceeding from a heart so enflamed with the divine love and zeal for almighty God's honour, that if a soul were even so much dejected that she was ready to fall or faint, they were of force to raise her up again and move her to confidence and courage'.

The two nuns produced utterly different documents for general chapter, each following her own natural bent. Dame Gertrude wrote a treatise of seventy short sections on contemplative life according to the teaching of Fr Baker; Dame Catherine, a woman of few words, gave a brief but invaluable account of her own personal prayer. From Dame Gertrude's *Apology* we can gather that two of the accusations brought against Fr Baker were that he undermined obedience to superiors, and that the Cambray community disregarded all books and instructions save his own. She did not confine herself to a mere defence but led the attack into the opposing camp with such comments as the following: 'My confessor would have had me plunge myself into difficulties by reason of his words and threats concerning my miserable state. . . . Spiritual men of this kind would be so absolute that there is no power left in the soul under such to have relation or confidence in God . . . ordinarily they do it under this pretence, saying that there is no way to make this or that soul humble, but to bring her into such fear that she dare neither speak, think, nor do anything without their approbation.' Dame Gertrude had fought so hard with herself to win through to confidence in God, that she was not going to stand by and see the confidence of others jeopardized without a protest. She quotes her own saintly ancestor, St Thomas More, apropos of one bereft of confidence in God: 'The urchin wench goes whining up and down as if nothing she did or could do did please him!' But polemics are the least important part of this admirably positive apology which breaks out into such passages as this: 'O you souls who are capable of prayer, be grateful to our Lord, for it is the greatest happiness that can be possessed in this life! For by it, it is easy to pass through all things, however hard and painful. By it we come to be familiar with God himself and to converse in heaven . . . and in fine, by it we shall praise God and become so united to him that nothing shall be able to separate us for time or eternity from his sweet goodness.'

In very different words Dame Catherine takes up the theme: 'I find myself most drawn and moved to a prayer that tends to unity without adhering to any particular image or creature, but seeking

10

only for that one thing which our Saviour said to be necessary, and which contains all things in itself, according to that saying:"*Unum sit mihi*"—"One thing to me be all", that is, "all in all", and on this depends all. This if I shall have, I shall be content, and unless I enjoy it I fluctuate always because many cannot fill me. What this one thing is I cannot say, I feel myself to desire it, than which nothing is better, nor greater, and neither can be thought; for this one thing is not amongst all, but one above all, my God, to whom to adhere and inhere is a good thing.'

They had both done their best and could confidently leave the rest to God, trusting that he would guide the minds of the chapter fathers towards a right decision. He did: Fr Baker's teaching was completely cleared of the slightest suspicion of anything unorthodox. Dame Catherine received a note of encouragement signed by the two theologians who had examined the manuscripts: 'Go on courageously, you have chosen the best way; we beseech Almighty God to accomplish that union which your heart desireth'. At the same time it was thought prudent to remove both the monks concerned from Cambray and appoint a new chaplain. Fr Baker was recalled to Douay where his teaching proved as helpful to monks, priests and students as it had been to nuns.

But the most important summons of all at the time of this chapter was for Dame Gertrude and it came from God himself: her course on earth was finished; she was unexpectedly struck down with smallpox; before the last session of chapter was over, she was dead.

She already felt ill at the end of July when she spoke to Fr Baker on the eve of his departure to general chapter. The following day she had to be moved to the infirmary and finally the nature of the disease declared itself. It was smallpox in a most virulent form, causing intense pain and resulting in putrefaction. All this she endured with complete serenity and resignation. When Dame Catherine came to comfort her, she found that it was she herself who went away comforted. Dame Gertrude was able to make her confession and receive Extreme Unction, but as the symptoms developed Holy Communion was considered impossible owing to the diseased condition of her mouth and throat.

Not even this deprivation could cause a ruffle in her calm, resting as she did in God alone and his most holy will. A few days before her death, when Dame Catherine warned her of her critical condition, Dame Gertrude showed the same peaceful serenity: 'God hath given me peace in my soul, and what can one desire more, coming to die? . . . Methinks I have nothing at all to do but to leave myself wholly to his disposition and let him do what he pleases.' She also expressed particular pleasure in the fact that all was going well with the house: 'It is a great comfort to me to leave all things at so good a pass'. Dame Catherine adds: 'She discoursed with me for a good space together, in as perfect senses and memory as ever she had in her life; so that although I was almost sick with staying there, yet could I scarce find in my heart to leave her, she spoke so comfortably to me'. From the feast of the Assumption until her death on 17 August it was thought best to keep the abbess and community away from her except for four nuns who nursed her to the end, one of whom was her cousin, Dame Anne More. On the evening of 16 August Fr Francis Hull turned up at Cambray with another monk and it was mistakenly supposed that this was Fr Baker. So a message was sent to Dame Gertrude to ask whether she would like to speak to Fr Baker. 'No' was the answer. Then they asked whether she would like to speak to the former confessor. This time the answer was louder and more emphatic: 'No, with no man'. (Can a trace of the unreformed Dame Gertrude be detected in that change of tone?) Finally they asked if she would have God: this time her answer was 'Yea', and before the night was out she was dead.

A brief life indeed, for she was only twenty-seven, but its very brevity makes it striking. 'You have not chosen me but I have chosen you' resounds throughout. It is an encouraging life, for who after reading it could say, 'Prayer is not for me; I just have not got the right sort of temperament'? Might not Dame Gertrude More lead some despairing religious to think just once again?

Her writings too still carry weight. The *Confessions*, *Fragments* and *Apology* are all contained in the second volume of Weld-Blundell's *The Inner Life and Writings of Dame Gertrude More* (1911), a life compiled from the Baker manuscripts.

Dame Gertrude's two cousins at Cambray survived her for a good many years. Dame Agnes translated a French spiritual treatise by an Augustinian nun. Dame Anne, who nursed Dame Gertrude, added her testimony to the holiness of her cousin to that of the other witnesses: 'It was my good fortune to be with her for the time of her sickness, and by her when her happy soul departed. I beseech Jesus to grant me grace to imitate her innocent life, that I may have so happy a death. Truly she hath left so great edification to us, which are behind her, that my poor pen is not able to express. The pains which I took about her in her sickness are not to be compared to the great comfort which I received to see so great patience in a sickness so loathsome as hers was. Verily I have seen in her Job upon the dunghill, Lazarus with his sores, an angel in paradise, so resigned to the will of God, so willing to die, so ready to suffer more if it pleased God, so firm in confidence with humility in almighty God, always praying, still calling on the sweet name of Jesus.'

Fr Baker never returned to Cambray after general chapter 1633. His time at Douay followed the same pattern as his years with the nuns—outstanding success as a spiritual guide leading eventually to a tense situation which culminated in his being sent back to England in 1638. Three years later he died in London. Some years after his death another witch-hunt was organized for unorthodox passages in his writings, and the Cambray community were put through an even worse ordeal than they had previously undergone.

In 1655 the president of the Congregation suddenly demanded from the nuns every autograph manuscript in their possession, 'not to alienate anything from our convent', as Dame Catherine Gascoigne explained, 'but to purge the books that we might not feed upon poisonous doctrine'. The nuns unanimously signed and sent in a petition begging that the examination of the books might be postponed until the next general chapter. The president replied by arriving in person to enforce his demand. Dame Catherine quietly but firmly stood her ground and refused to give him the manuscripts. Two years later *Sancta Sophia*, a compilation of Fr Baker's spiritual teaching, was safely in print and his interpretation of the wisdom of the mystics secured for posterity.

It is common knowledge that in our own materialistic days there has been a great reawakening of desire for contact with the absolute. Rather than turning exclusively to the East for guidelines to contemplation, some of our contemporaries might be interested to trace their way back to the English mystics through Dame Gertrude More and Fr Baker, or even seek out the living guardians of this heritage.

by Dame Frideswide Sandeman

BIBLIOGRAPHY

C. Jenkins, *Sir Thomas More* (Canterbury 1935).

P. A. Allanson, *History of the English Benedictine Congregation 1558–1850* (ed. P. Spearitt and M. Green, Oxford Microform Publications).

B. Weldon, *Chronological Notes on the English Benedictine Congregation* (London 1881).

H. N. Birt, *Obit Book of the English Benedictines* (Edinburgh 1913).

B. Weld-Blundell (ed.), *The Inner Life and Writings of Dame Gertrude More*, 2 volumes (London 1910–11).

The Benedictines of Stanbrook, *In a Great Tradition* (London 1956).

J. McCann and C. Cary-Elwes (ed.), *Ampleforth and its Origins* (London 1952).

J. M. Sweeney, *The Life and Spirit of Father Augustine Baker* (London 1961).

Records of the Abbey of Our Lady of Consolation at Cambrai 1620–1793 (*Catholic Record Society Publications* xiii, 1–85).

Father Augustine Baker (*Catholic Record Society Publications*, vol. xxxiii, passim).

E. C. Butler, 'Dame Gertrude More', *Downside Review* xxxi (1911).

M. Norman, 'Dame Gertrude More and the English Mystical Tradition', *Recusant History* xiii (1976), 196–211.

Use has also been made of Dom Augustine Baker's incomplete Life of Dame Gertrude More and of the Annals of the Abbey of Our Lady of Consolation, which survive in manuscript at Stanbrook Abbey.

The Benedictine Revival in the Nineteenth Century

The curtain goes up on the nineteenth century with an opening act which, so far as the history of Benedictinism is concerned, seemed to betoken a wholesale clearance of the past. The French armies which were over-running Europe regarded monasteries not just as part of the medieval clutter which must be swept away if the new social order was going to take root, but as organisms whose continuance could be positively injurious to the new outlook on life which the Revolutionaries wanted to spread. And this radical hostility to religious life would spontaneously recur throughout the century whenever those who subscribed to the revolutionary tradition swept to power in France, Italy and Spain. For them a life under vows seemed a renunciation of the sacred principle of Liberty. The monasteries also were so enmeshed with the *ancien régime*, its feudal and hierarchical structure, that their extirpation was imperative for the sake of Equality, and they could not be envisaged as taking on any other form than that of great landlords. And even the most spiritual of monks, or especially when they were so, witnessed all too effectively to a mental framework where the concept of man, his sinfulness and need of a Redeemer, his destiny beyond the horizons of this world, challenged the notions of human perfectibility and indefinite progress, the assumptions of the new society, which coloured the revolutionary conception of Fraternity.

As each country succumbed to the French invaders, no time was lost before its monasteries were suppressed—Belgium in 1796, Switzerland in 1798, the different states of Germany between 1803 and 1806 (all monasteries except the Scottish house of St James, Ratisbon, spared because the community consisted of foreigners), Tuscany in 1807, Naples in 1807, Spain in 1808, the Papal states in 1809. Some monks were allowed to remain as caretakers of Monte Cassino, Monte Vergine and Cava where the abbeys were reconstituted as State Archives. Throughout Europe less than two per cent survived of the fifteen hundred or more Benedictine houses that in 1790 had spangled the landscape. The ease and rapidity of this total clearance is not surprising since the Revolution, so far from doing something new in proscribing the religious life, was in many cases only carrying to completion the work of its predecessors, the Bourbon and Habsburg governments of the late eighteenth century, who had already been thinning out the monasteries of their countries in the name of the Enlightenment and forcing them to undertake parishes, schools and other works of immediate and obvious social utility. Under attack the monks too were rarely heroic, but accepted their pensions and merged with the diocesan clergy; few of them sought to continue their monastic way of life elsewhere, although for Benedictines, whose vows and formation have in view a single local monastic family, this question raises difficulties that other religious orders do not have. Nevertheless it does seem that for some decades the fervour of monastic life had wilted in the atmosphere of the Enlightenment. In the later years of the old regime building projects had escalated but the number of vocations plummetted (the monastery of St Vaast in Arras and a few other large houses in its neighbourhood were outstanding exceptions to this rule). Increasing governmental regulations in France and in Austria had stifled that local initiative which is the very breath of life for Benedictinism. But in its hour of trial and humiliation a few martyrs redeemed the monastic race, notably the Superiors General of the Maurists, the Vannists and the Cluniacs. Heroic too was the prolonged exodus of the community of La Trappe under its novice-master, Dom Augustin de Lestrange which, after fleeing to Switzerland to resume their common life at Valsainte in 1798, was driven by the advancing French armies to Austria, Poland and Russia, thence back to America, with an offshoot settling at Lulworth, Dorset, the awkward guests of Mr Weld.

The abbot was a belligerent and ungrateful character who made exorbitant demands on the charity of his benefactor. In 1817 the community was forced out of England for a variety of reasons, one of them being its refusal to pray for the 'heretical' king, George III. It settled at Melleray in Ireland, from which Mount St Bernard was founded in 1835. Unlike the other English monastic houses of this century, Mount St Bernard became part of the converts' dream-world of re-Catholicizing England and sacralizing its landscape. Ambrose de Lisle Phillips and Augustus Welby Pugin were the chief benefactors of this English foundation. For a few decades this Cistercian house maintained the custom of Mount Melleray in attaching an educational establishment, this time an approved school, to the monastery, though the difficulties of this arrangement soon became apparent. Afterwards and to this day, they followed the more normal observance of the traditional Cistercian contemplative community.

In America Lestrange purchased for a projected monastery what was to be the site of St Patrick's Cathedral, New York. All the time this monastery on wheels, comprising sometimes as many as 254 persons, under the iron rule of Lestrange, aspired to an observance far stricter even than that of La Trappe. This resolute stand was responsible for the early and rapid proliferation of Trappist houses in France and America after the war long before the Benedictine revival had gathered momentum. The success of this rapid increase was tempered by the divisions Lestrange's new severe standards gave rise to, between those houses which followed his regime and those, led by Sept Fons, who did not wish to exceed the customs of La Trappe. This rift was only to be healed in 1893 at the prompting of Leo XIII who was simultaneously confederating the Benedictines.

Less dramatic were the other monastic survivals that managed to weather the storm. Austria, though defeated by Napoleon, was never taken over by him so that its palatial monasteries can still vaunt an unbroken continuity of monastic life spanning the centuries, in many cases reaching right back to their foundation by Tassilo, the Bavarian king who rebelled against Charlemagne. Less impressive than their architecture and pedigree were the realities of their monastic observance at this time, overladen as it was with heavy parochial and educational responsibilities which had been the price that Joseph II's rationalist government had exacted for permitting their survival. The equally venerable and monumental monasteries of Switzerland were allowed to reopen in 1803. But although the five years of their suppression were not long enough to seriously dislocate their history, a number of the smaller houses as well as St Gall never re-emerged, while the survivors would have to live through several decades of harrowing uncertainty and occasional suppressions, dependent as they were on the goodwill of the cantonal governments. So in its great Baroque heartland of Central Europe, Benedictinism was nothing like so assured and fecund as its court-like establishments might suggest.

Very similar was the case of the numerous and grand monasteries belonging to the Cassinese Congregation in Sicily which had been protected from Napoleon by the English fleet. Housed in Spanish magnificence, proud of the noble families who provided their recruits, the Sicilian monks were nevertheless addicted to factiousness perhaps because of their family connexions, and this was compounded by the political divisions over the movement for the unification of Italy. The lives of both Cardinal Dusmet and of Abbot Casaretto let fall many hints, and often plain remarks, that all was far from happy in the Sicilian province of the Cassinese; it could hardly be the well-spring of new life for the Order.

Humbler altogether in its outer circumstances was the life of the English Benedictine monks, now repatriated to a warm welcome from their Protestant fellow-countrymen after two centuries of exile on the Continent. Of their four pre-Revolutionary houses one had capsized never to re-emerge save for an experimental few years at Broadway; that was the house which had been most numerous, wealthy and prestigious, the abbey of Lamspringe near Hildesheim in Germany which had hitherto seemed the most secure of all the English Continental establishments, with its abbot a Prince of the Holy Roman Empire. It had been dissolved not by French, but by Prussian invaders in 1802, and most of its resident community lingered on as individuals living in the village, drawing their pensions or hoping for the abbey's resuscitation. St Edmund's Priory in Paris, beloved of the Stuarts in exile, would have petered out too if the energetic President Brewer had not scratched together a small band of volunteers to re-constitute that community in a new locale, when in 1820 it occupied the buildings in Douai, vacated by the St Gregory's conventus. The latter, successfully transplanted to England, first to Acton Burnell in Shropshire, then to Downside near Bath, had finally decided after much debate not to return to France in the time of peace. The community formerly at St Lawrence's, Dieulouard in Lorraine, had likewise settled down at Ampleforth near York after a long series of temporary resting-places. These experiences could be paralleled in the histories of many communities of Benedictine nuns, formerly at Brussels, Ghent, Paris, Cambrai and Montargis (although this latter, now at Fernham near Swindon, started off as a refugee French community rather than one of the historic English houses in exile). Each resumed the quiet and genteel tenor of its life in new houses deep in the English countryside after the nightmare of the Terror. Numerically the English Benedictine Congregation at this time, in common with the Dominicans, Franciscans and most religious orders, reached its lowest ebb. Its members too had few social or intellectual pretensions, but great tenacity and strength of character which went into the moulding of the next generation to produce a galaxy of sturdy and self-taught individuals, admirably suited for the role of pioneer bishops and missionaries. For the moment, however, the communities of Downside and Ampleforth lived in discreet obscurity, running their modest schools and serving remote mission chapels.

These were the shreds which remained of the former vast and intricate fabric. When the Waterloo dust had settled, there seemed little promise that Benedictine life would share in the general restoration of the *status quo*. Even the victors were unconvinced that that would be a good thing, especially since many of their subjects had enriched themselves on confiscated monastic property. The Catholic Church of Restoration France was firmly Gallican in temper, attached to the alliance of throne and altar, anxious to keep the Pope at bay and to allow the Government a stranglehold on Church affairs, believing in the close regulation of all religious orders—the Revolutionary laws against the taking of religious vows were never revoked—and feeling that Christianity should be re-introduced into France by degrees, with the religious life coming last. In this climate it is not surprising that a valiant attempt by some aged survivors, including one who had been Novice-Master to St Gregory's at Downside, Dom Leveaux, to revive the Maurist Congregation at Senlis in 1816 came to grief. Dom Guéranger too, twenty years later, would have to disarm suspicions that his projected monastic foundation would be infected with the doctrines of Lammenais, with whom Guéranger had been closely associated and who advocated that phobia of all good Gallicans, a free Church in a free State.

So, whether the Governments were of the Left or of the Right, Benedictines could not look for sympathetic consideration in those quarters. One factor, however, would tell in favour of a Benedictine revival, and that would be the unwavering and discreet support of the Papacy. Pope Pius VII (1800–1823) had been a Benedictine monk of Cesena, and his patience, courage and dignity during his imprisonments at Savona and Fontainebleau had rehabilitated the Papacy in the esteem of all opposed to Napoleon's tyranny, whether Catholic or not. This upsurge of sympathy for the tragic Pope was probably the first wave of the Ultramontane tide, a movement that would gather force when he ended the suppression of the Jesuits on returning to Rome at the end of the war. He also restored the Benedictine abbeys in the Papal States, two of which—S. Paolo in Rome and Subiaco—were to become the cradles of the Benedictine revival throughout Europe. In his Concordats with the newly estab-lished Catholic powers Pope Pius required that the former monas-teries be reconstituted, which would belatedly have its effect in Bavaria. Gregory XVI (1831–1846) had been a Camaldolese monk, following the Benedictine Rule, from which possibly he derived that distaste for slavery which led him to support the Emancipation movement, perhaps his solitary 'progressive' manifestation. Having lived for fifty years in a monastery, he gave his shrewd support to both Casaretto and Guéranger. Pius IX (1846–78), discovering that the newly founded Benedictines had a strong attachment to all things Roman and would fight his battles in France and Germany, reciprocated with inexhaustible benevolence, while Leo XIII (1879–1903) sought to invigorate the Order by providing it with stronger central organs. Assured of Papal sympathy, the Benedictines responded by making constant and immediate recourse to Rome their normal method of procedure in all their constitutional developments, long before the Definition of Papal Infallibility in 1870 had inaugurated an era where this practice would be universal. In the *Album Benedictinum* the Pope was always introduced under the title 'Abbot of abbots'.

The first large-scale resuscitation of Benedictines outside Rome took place in Bavaria under the patronage of King Ludwig I (1825–1848). His ambition was to transform Munich from a capital with the homely intimacy of a village to a modern Athens, and to a considerable degree he succeeded. He sought to outshine the Enlightenment by making Munich not only a centre of learning, but also of religious vitality; he did achieve a Catholic renaissance in his kingdom, his mentor being the scholarly bishop of Regensburg, Sailer. Braving the disgruntled opposition of the Liberal ministers he inherited from his father, he projected the restoration of the Benedictine abbeys that were once so thick on the ground in Bavaria, beginning with Metten, whose restoration he decreed as early as 1827. The difficulty would be to populate these houses. Only six monks survived of all the Bavarian abbeys that had been suppressed nearly thirty years previously, and of these only two were fit and willing to resume monastic life. There was, however, a superfluity of secular priests in the diocese of Regensburg, and Bishop Sailer encouraged them to join the newborn monasteries, thus launching a recurring feature of the Benedictine revival everywhere, the high proportion of former diocesan clergy among its recruits and leaders. Ludwig I, however, even after his abdication, was a compulsive founder of monasteries—Augsburg in 1834, Scheyern in 1838, Weltenburg in 1842, St Boniface's, Munich (significantly an architectural replica of S. Paolo in Rome) in 1850, Ottobeuren in 1834, Andechs in 1850, while Schaftlarn would follow in 1866. This rapid pace of expansion must have imposed a severe strain on the available manpower, particularly when it became usual for large secondary schools to be annexed to these monasteries—a concession to the Liberal desire to see some social utility resulting from these foundations and a sign of the academic character of this Catholic revival. The dependence of these houses on royal beneficence and their strong attachment to the folk-culture and home-feeling of the Bavarians might well have confined their influence within these local horizons, were it not for the seemingly maverick enterprise of one of their stormy petrels.

Dom Boniface Wimmer, always at odds with his superiors who nicknamed him 'the Planmaker' and aggrieved at their rejection of his proposal to reopen the former monastery of Mallersdorf, found new scope for his dreams of organization when he became aware of the spiritual deprivations of German Catholic emigrants to the United

States. He became convinced that the answer to their needs lay in the foundation of rural Benedictine monasteries which could christianize wide territories and conduct schools for training future priests, just as historically the abbeys had done in Bavaria. In 1846, with the help of the royal Ludwig-Missionsverein and with a German priest called Lemke as his cicerone, he settled in the diocese of Pittsburg, Pennsylvania, whose bishop was anxious to establish a seminary. This was the origin of St Vincent's Archabbey, Latrobe, which soon became the centre of a flourishing agricultural colony and of a constellation of mission stations. Wimmer had to contend for an activist missionary interpretation of Benedictinism against successive eruptions among his subjects and confreres of demands for a more monastic and enclosed practice. He also had to weather criticism from the Irish-born local bishop who could not understand the time-honoured German practice of associating a monastery with a brewery at a time when Father Theobald Mathew was doing his best to spread temperance in Ireland. He did not find Wimmer the tractable cooperator he had hoped for. In 1855 persistent representation by Wimmer and his influential Bavarian supporters procured from Rome in the teeth of opposition from the Bishop of Pittsburg a decree raising St Vincent's to the privileges of an exempt abbey to become the central house of a new Benedictine Congregation which would first be affiliated to the Italian Cassinese, who rendered many useful services to Wimmer in these transactions. This dimension of a Congregation was to accompany the Roman decrees permitting the establishment of Solesmes and Beuron too, and in nineteenth-century monastic politics and constitutional thinking the congregation would often have the upper hand over the notion of individual houses and their rights to determine their destiny.

Wimmer was far-sighted enough to see that it was in the West that America's future lay. Innumerable frontier bishops petitioned him to make foundations in their dioceses. It has been said that his motto was 'Always go ahead'. In 1856 at the request of the Bishop of St Paul's, Minnesota, he founded St John's, Collegeville, (then named 'St Louis' in honour of the munificent Bavarian king) in an area of German settlement; it needed only ten years to attain abbatial status. St Benedict's, Atchison, Kansas, was also founded in 1856, but had a much harder struggle to make its way. These were the two elder daughters of a great chain of monasteries, each of them fast expanding and evolving, spread over the regions of more recent settlement in America, in the West and even in the conquered South, principally working among the ethnic immigrants, of German or Bohemian origin. Wimmer wrote to King Ludwig: 'We must seize the opportunity and spread, even before we have had time to become thoroughly rooted in one place'. It is possible that Wimmer had learnt this tempo of expansion from Ludwig himself. When the Patriarch of this new Congregation died in 1887, he had founded four abbeys and two priories, which were in their turn to reproduce fast.

These American monasteries, although not yet the gigantic enterprises they were to become, were on the large scale, with sights set on limitless expansion. They were outward looking and highly diversified in their operations. Their only limit seemed to be in 1874 that both their recruitment and their clientele were overwhelmingly German, and with the mentality of frontiersmen. A foundation in Iowa for discontented Irish monks was short-lived. Even the rudimentary architectural style of their monastic edifices bespoke the land of their origins; their long brick churches with twin towers would have nestled only too well into a Rhineland landscape. Wimmer, great go-getter as he was, always maintained close ties with Europe, and his patrons and friends in Germany and Rome sustained him with solid material backing, a continuous stream of priestly reinforcements and a powerful lobby for his causes at the Roman Congregations.

The development of the parallel congregation in the New World, the Swiss-American (now the Pan-American Congregation) was later, steadier and quieter, but otherwise not so very different in the nature and scale of its operations, except for a stronger emphasis on the autonomy of the houses and on monastic observance. In 1854 a house dedicated to St Meinrad was founded in Indiana by a small colony of monks in order to be a possible place of refuge for the community of Einsiedeln which was then being harassed by the government of the canton and the aftermath of Switzerland's religious war, the Sonderbund, in which the Catholic minority was defeated. In 1870 it became an abbey. Two years later, a similar foundation, this time from Engelburg, was made at Conception, Missouri. In 1881 the two houses were recognized by Rome as constituting a congregation in their own right. The observances of this Congregation were more austere than those of the mother-houses in Switzerland, and were greatly influenced by the ideas of Beuron. Other houses emerged—like the American-Cassinese almost exclusively in the West and the South—and by 1904 the Congregation comprised five sizeable abbeys. The great success story of these two transatlantic congregations was a powerful assertion and justification of the missionary strain within the Benedictine tradition. A sharp contrast, but an equally impressive achievement was the revival of monasticism in France under the clear-sighted and combative leadership of Prosper Guéranger (1805–75).

Guéranger was a native of the very Catholic West of France, deeply attached to the small riverside town of Sablé where he grew up, a schoolmaster's son, his imagination haunted by the nearby abandoned priory of Solesmes. His seminary education he enriched by pasturing his mind in libraries and on his contacts with De Maistre, Lammenais, Lacordaire, Chateaubriand and other men of wide horizons. It was the Maurist folios of the Fathers in the library of the Grand Séminaire of Le Mans that awakened his curiosity about things Benedictine, and with a gesture that proves his affinity with the Romantic movement, he paced the ruins of St Martin's abbey of Marmoutier on the night of his ordination. In his short career as a diocesan priest he was the highly valued secretary of an aged bishop who had survived from pre-Revolutionary days and who retained Guéranger's services on his retirement to Paris. Here Guéranger was soon in touch with the foremost spirits of the Catholic Revival, at a time when Liberal Catholicism and Ultramontanism went hand in hand until Gregory XVI's condemnation of this combination in his Encyclical *Mirari Vos*, issued at the behest of the Catholic Governments who wished to keep the Church as an instrument of State. Henceforth Ultramontanism and Liberal Catholicism in its different manifestations would be pitted against each other. Lammenais refused to accept the Encyclical and was soon lost to the Church. He had attempted to found a religious community imbued with his ideas: Guéranger's association with him was to give rise to many suspicions that Solesmes was another Lammenaisian covert.

It was the arrival on the property market of Solesmes Priory which forced Guéranger to give practical shape to his Benedictine aspirations. Unable to buy it outright, he raised enough money to lease the building for three years, then collected a small band of aspirants and went to Rome very soon to obtain Papal approval of the constitutions he had drawn up. The way had been smoothed for him by Montalembert, at that time his enthusiastic supporter, though later there was to be an estrangement. It was a great triumph for Guéranger to obtain permission for life abbots since triennial superiors were the norm for Italian Benedictines. He had wished to call his monks 'Maurists' since continuity with the congregation of Mabillon and Montfaucon might recommend his project in the eyes of the French Government. But Gregory XVI personally dissuaded him from using this title since the reputation of the learned Maurists had been sullied by Jansenist tendencies in their last years. Guéranger was successful in parrying proposals that he should merge forces with the Italian Cassinese Congregation, and indeed his whole conduct of these initial proceedings with the

Papal dicasteries, when he had so little to show for his demands, shows him to be a master of diplomatic finesse.

Having obtained approval of everything, including his right to launch a congregation from Solesmes, he made his own monastic profession before a distinguished audience in the sacristy of S. Paolo fuori le Mure, since the church had not yet been rebuilt after its conflagration of the previous year. The scene of this occasion was almost emblematic of Guéranger's role in the equally devastated monastic landscape of France. He served no novitiate, and would very shortly be an abbot, vexing his bishop by the use of pontificalia. In his monastic life as in so much else Guéranger was an autodidact, with no contact with a living tradition, no long stay in another Benedictine house to observe the life. The wonder is that notwithstanding he acquired a sureness of touch that he could share with others.

Guéranger returned to France and sought to sustain the precarious economy of his foundation by the scanty rewards of literary and historical work. Though personally affable and 'douce', he could not resist controversy not just for the sake of his monastery, but also in the wider ecclesiastical arena, though secular politics had no interest for him. . . . He championed the Roman rites of Missal and Breviary against venerable local usage which he denounced as Gallican, and crossed swords with many prelates, often of high eminence; he entered the lists with the Prince de Broglie over the philosophy of naturalism and with the followers of Dupanloup on the Infallibility question. No Benedictine figure of this time made such an impact outside the monastic world. His literary output was prolific and his most widely circulated books were *Les Institutions Liturgiques* and *L'Année Liturgique* which, though written in haste and never completed by him, brought home to his contemporaries that worship is the highest expression of the life both of the Church and of the monastery. The principle that monastic life should be animated and articulated by the liturgy, which should therefore take on a high relief in the monastic horarium and not be cramped or crowded out by works was Guéranger's unique and inestimable contribution to the recovery of monastic life in our century. Though his particular application of that principle might be criticised or thought to be now transcended, its assertion would influence the practice of all other Benedictines and would constitute the first move in the modern liturgical movement. Liturgical antiquities engaged the scholarly researchers of the Congregation of France, Pitra, Cabrol, Leclercq and Ferotin, while Mocquereau and Pothier would divine the meaning of the plainchant manuscripts.

In its expansion the French Congregation experienced many setbacks. Guéranger was not gifted either in financial affairs or in the choice of men to manage his foundations, several of which came to grief. Ligugé, with its ancient associations with St Martin, was restored in 1853 and was situated in the diocese of Poitiers where reigned Monsignor Pie, France's other great Ultramontane gladiator and preacher of the panegyric over the dead Guéranger. Its speciality was to be research into monastic history. The foundation of the city monastery of Marseilles in 1855 seems almost to have been willed on Guéranger by a determined old local priest who wanted to bequeath into safe hands a flourishing catechetical institution he had built up. Its importance is that a number of young women associated with this enterprise joined Cécile Bruyère, who had been under Guéranger's spiritual direction since childhood, to begin the Benedictine community for nuns near Solesmes, Ste Cécile. Here again there does not seem to have been any thought of asking any long-established Benedictine convent to send some nuns to help with the work of initiation.

Though a Frenchman of the French, Abbot Guéranger's monastic principles radiated far beyond the confines of his own country. The powerful Beuronese Congregation was to be almost a mirror-image of his own. Its founders, the Wolter brothers, were his impressively docile disciples and would settle many questions raised at Beuron or Maredsous by the pronouncement, 'At Solesmes it was always done in this way', and *causa finita est*. The Beuronese Congregation would in its turn channel Guéranger's views and priorities to its offshoots—the Belgian Congregation, the restored Brazilian Congregation and the St Ottilien Congregation for missionary monks—and indeed to the whole order when the Beuronese had the formative influence over the international Benedictine College of Sant' Anselmo, Rome. His ideas percolated into the English Congregation through another enthusiastic follower, Dom Lawrence Shepherd, Chaplain of Stanbrook, who translated his works into English. The expulsions of the monks of Solesmes, along with other religious orders, from France in 1880, 1882 and 1901, led to the founding of monasteries of refuge in England, Spain, Luxembourg and Holland, which, when the expatriate monks returned to France in a more benign era, survived as native houses in those countries, though still belonging to the French Congregation.

This network of influence entitles Guéranger to the central position in the nineteenth-century monastic revival. His portraits do not indicate him to be a man of striking physical appearance: he was short, chubby and homely; only his burning eyes indicate a man out of the ordinary. A devourer of books, he once risked the whole small capital of his infant monastery to purchase a set of the Bollandists. Very susceptible to the charm of historic eras which seemed to him privileged moments in the Church's evolution, it was first the middle ages, 'notre cher moyen âge' as he once wrote to Montalembert, then the early Christian period which seemed to him the model to be copied. The Church Father who meant most to him was St Ephraim. To us the chief defect in his ecclesiastical learning was his remoteness from the Bible. He was an inspirer rather than an organizer; only the tactful persuasion of Mme Cécile could induce him to put some order into his monastery's financial affairs, all in his bumbling hands, in the years before his death.

After his death the force of his personality continued to make itself felt within his Congregation, under his successors, Dom Couturier and Dom Delatte, who had both been formed by him. The Abbess of Ste Cécile became a powerful influence because she was held to be almost an oracle, transmitting Guéranger's mind on any matter submitted to her. But along with this strenuous effort to maintain fidelity to the charism of the Founder, there developed a more cloistered mentality than was Guéranger's, ever active in the wider affairs of the Church in whose life he felt monasticism was central with an apostolate of its own. This shift of outlook was due partly to the external circumstances of monastic life in exile, partly to the effect of Mme Bruyère's influence which at one time incurred the suspicion of Quietism. Furthermore within the monastic world itself, at the end of the century, the trend which prevailed and which was encouraged by the Papacy was towards a greater centralization, from which Solesmes stood aloof and surrendered the role of monastic pace-maker to Beuron.

The Congregation of Beuron was yet another product of a monastic inspiration received by diocesan priests. The two brothers (there would have been a trio if Hildebrand Wolter had not died at Rome in 1859) later to be called Maurus and Placid Wolter, emanated from Bonn where their father was a successful brewer who had married a Protestant and had fourteen children, many of whom became priests or nuns. Rudolf, later to be Dom Maurus, the future founder of Beuron, became Rector of the Gymnasiums run by the diocese, first at Julich, then at Aachen, and showed himself an effective teacher and administrator. Both brothers, however, moved in circles at Bonn which were very much under the spell of Anton Gunther. He was a learned and pious theologian of Austrian origin, determined to fight the Church's Rationalist and Materialist enemies with their own weapons of reason and scientific learning. He carried this so far as to incur Roman condemnation on a charge of 'semi-rationalism' because he upheld the possibility of a full and positive understanding by reason of the Christian mysteries. Gunther himself accepted the Church's decision though many of his followers were to become leaders of the German Old Catholic movement. An implacable opponent of all Guntherians was the archbishop of Cologne, and the Wolter brothers were later to be discouraged by his suspicions of them from founding their first monastery in North Germany, as would be their first instinct.

Gunther was a polymath, and had an appreciation of history as well as of science, and in the heyday of his movement, before its condemnation, propounded a practical programme for the spread of his doctrines in which he expressed the hope that the Benedictine order would rise once more to foster the learned investigations he thought would commend Christianity to the nineteenth century. This aspiration was seized upon by the newly elected abbot of S. Paolo, Rome, Simplicio Pappalettere, who had previously taught philosophy to the student monks at Subiaco and had come into contact with some German Guntherians. This was in 1853. Pappalettere wished to make his monastery the spearhead of the Guntherian movement, profiting from its location at the centre of Christendom and hoping to revive the College of Sant' Anselmo, an academy of the Cassinese Benedictines attached to S. Paolo in the seventeenth century. He promised a welcome to any Germans who would enter his novitiate and help him raise the monastery's level of observance and scholarship. Over the next few years a trickle of postulants crossed the Alps in answer to his appeal, among them the three brothers Wolter. They were sent for their novitiate to S. Pietro, Perugia, and returned to Rome where Father Maurus was appointed Lecturer in Theology. During this time he became acquainted with G. B. de Rossi, the explorer of the Catacombs who was also a friend of Guéranger and who implanted in Wolter that enthusiasm for the Early Christian world of Rome that was always a component in the Beuronese ethos. Another Roman contact of great consequence for the future was with another German resident of the city, the widowed Princess Catherine Hohenzollern who was recovering from her unsuccessful attempt to find her vocation with the enclosed Franciscan nuns of Sant' Ambrogio, Rome, but never abandoned her ambition to use her fortune to found a religious house in which she would find a place.

After a few years the high hopes of the Wolters to be the pioneers of a spiritual and intellectual renaissance radiating from S. Paolo were shipwrecked when Abbot Pappalettere was transferred from S. Paolo to Monte Cassino. His successor, Abbot Pescatelli, the great friend and Roman agent of Abbot Boniface Wimmer, was a resolute and agile ecclesiastical politician who led the resistance to Abbot Casaretto's reform of the Cassinese and had no sympathy for Pappalettere's visions. The German monks at S. Paolo now found

themselves isolated and unwanted. Their abbot did not try to hold
them back when they asked if they could prospect in Germany to
make a foundation of their own. Princess Catherine became an
indefatigable agent in their schemes just as Madame Swetchwine, a
convert from Russian Orthodoxy, was in Guéranger's, except that
the Princess had ready access to the pope and could obtain all the
necessary decrees and permissions. After a few short-lived experiments the Wolters alighted on Beuron in 1862. It was an abandoned
Augustinian house, high up in the Danube valley on territory
belonging to the Catholic branch of the Hohenzollerns. The bishop
of Freiburg im Breisgau was sympathetic, and the Princess Catherine
obtained a papal brief in 1863 recognizing the community as a self-
governing priory, free of all connection with S. Paolo. In 1868, with
the profession of the twelfth member of the community, it was
raised to be an abbey with Maurus Wolter as its first abbot and with
the right to form a congregation.

Monastic life at Beuron in its infancy bore very much the imprint
of Solesmes, or rather of Guéranger personally, and that at a time
when he had reached his full monastic maturity. He sent many wise
and affectionate letters to Abbot Wolter, giving him sound and
humane advice on the manner of abbatial government. The
Beuronese Constitutions were drawn up after a model he proposed,
as footnotes to the Rule of St Benedict. Several of the earliest aspirants to Beuron made their novitiate at Solesmes, and Placid Wolter,
who in 1890 would succeed his brother as archabbot, spent several
years there. The Beuronese nuns were initiated into monasticism at
Ste Cécile, and Princess Catherine at one time sought entrance into
the novitiate there. But in spite of this warm interchange and faithful
imitation there were several significant differences between Solesmes
and Beuron. First, as has already been pointed out, while Guéranger
with his monastic schemes had broken in on history with all the
abruptness of a prophet, the founders of Beuron were spared many
of the pains and mistakes which are the price of pioneerdom, and
sought to nestle in to a living monastic tradition.

Secondly, Beuron explicitly renounced any ordinary pastoral
commitments, like the parishes and schools which occupied the
other German-speaking Benedictines. The Beuronese deliberately
set out to differentiate themselves from the Austrian, Bavarian and
Swiss Congregations in whose territory they were, by striving after a
more absolute form of monasticism. Nevertheless, unlike Solesmes,
the Beuronese were ready for extraordinary pastoral work, preaching
retreats, giving parish missions, especially of a liturgical nature,
editing the Schott missals which would attain a mass circulation. At
Beuron itself they inherited a centuries-old Marian pilgrimage,

which gave the monks much work as confessors and a firm place in the hearts of the devout peasantry of that region. Beuron was thus more integrated into the general life of the Church in Germany, less a pole of contradiction than Solesmes never ceased to be in France. There was a steady flow of recruits who would populate the numerous foundations, and especially of recruits into the ranks of the lay-brothers, whose bearded sanctity would be as conspicuous a feature of the Beuronese scene as it had been in the days of the early Cistercians. It would also be a legacy from Beuron to the monks of the missionary congregation of St Ottilien.

Thirdly, Beuron, to a far greater degree than Solesmes, showed a capacity for expanding outside its native ambient. Very early in its history it was forced to send out swarms to new houses outside Germany because of Bismarck's *Kulturkampf*. In 1872 Placid Wolter was entrusted with the formation of a new abbey at Maredsous in Belgium, whose property and buildings were delivered ready-made to the Beuronese by the family of Desclée, the well-known ecclesiastical publishers. In 1899 Maredsous founded a house of studies in the university town of Louvain which would develop into the abbey of Mont César. The Benedictines discovered almost instant success in Belgium, had no difficulty in attracting vocations from the noble families or in setting up a tradition of industrious and recondite scholarship. After the first World War the Belgian monasteries formed an independent congregation of their own, which would reveal an astonishing creativity both in pioneering many of the movements—biblical, liturgical, ecumenical—that would bear fruit in the Second Vatican Council and in missionary endeavours in Africa, India and China.

In the Habsburg Empire the royal monastery of Emaus in Prague was opened in 1880, and the Augustinian house at Seckau in Styria taken over to become an abbey in 1887. Maria Laach, the Beuronese monastery that was to have most *éclat* in the twentieth century, was founded as late as 1892, when the ancient monastery buildings formerly belonging to the Bursfeld Congregation were acquired from the Jesuits who had been occupying them. This Rhineland abbey was to enjoy considerable support from the Kaiser who would also in 1906 present the Beuronese with the buildings of the abbey of the Dormition on Mount Zion in Jerusalem, where he intended them to act as a German presence. In 1894 the Beuronese undertook the reform and reinvigoration of the Brazilian Benedictine Congregation, which, suffering from the displeasure of the anticlerical governments ever since Brazil had seceded from the Portuguese Empire, had dwindled to only ten monks. Very shortly after, the Beuronese undertook the same role with regard to the sole surviving Portuguese abbey of Singeverga.

These instances show that in the latter part of the nineteenth century the Beuronese were a ginger group within the Benedictine order, setting out to raise the general standard of monastic observance. They were sometimes feared because they were credited with believing that the way to reform lay through increased centralization. They assented more eagerly than did most Benedictines to Leo XIII's plans for closer coordination of the different Congregations within the framework of the Benedictine Confederation which he instituted in 1893, having already united the different branches of the Franciscans and the Cistercians. The first two heads of this Pan-Benedictine body were former Beuronese abbots, the old Papal Zouave and amateur architect, Hildebrand de Hemptinne of Maredsous, and Fidelis von Stotzingen of Maria Laach. Both these formidable men had long incumbencies and under their guidance the international college of Sant'Anselmo, Rome, which they made their headquarters, was subjected to Beuronese customs and ceremonial, while of all Congregations the Beuronese were probably the most generous in providing that college with professors and lay-brothers. Thus the vision of monasticism which had been disclosed to Beuron by Solesmes soon pervaded all Benedictine houses through the channels of this international network.

The third column of the nineteenth century monastic reform movement, alongside the contingents of Solesmes and Beuron, was the body later to be known as the Primitive Observance or the Subiaco Congregation. Once more the leadership of a single personality rather than the discovery by a group of a common consciousness was the fountainhead of the movement. The character of Pietro Casaretto (1810–78) has more than once been described by biographers of his own congregation as 'complex'. He was the sickly son of a Genoese commercial family, settled in Ancona, who entered the Cassinese monastery of Cesena at the age of seventeen, was solemnly professed the following year, and almost immediately began a series of locomotions from monastery to monastery in a vain attempt to find a climate that suited his health. These frequent dislocations not only left him with a lifelong urge for travel but must have damaged what would have been in any case a rather straitened education. Although Casaretto pined after a higher level of observance than he found in the Cassinese houses, the vistas that drew him on were not opened out for him, as they had been for Guéranger and the Wolters, by the study of theology and history, but by the narrow conviction that a stricter asceticism necessarily meant a better monasticism. At one time he tried to become a Camaldolese, but in 1842 was ordered to care for a parish at Pegli near Genoa, which belonged to the Benedictines but was threatened by being taken over by the diocesan chapter. It was hardly a flattering appointment, but it was to be the doorway to future developments. Casaretto loudly lamented his exclusion from monastic community life, but soon along with this querimoniousness displayed that unsuspected resolution and resourcefulness that underlay his physical fragility. He set about transforming the parish house into a monastery, enlisted the novice-master of Subiaco as a companion, obtained the support of King Charles Albert of Piedmont, normally opposed to Benedictine foundations which had not done much to recommend themselves previously in his model nineteenth-century state, and soon recruited a little band of aspirants. Very shortly he was able to move to more commodious quarters at S. Giuliano d'Albaro near Genoa, where in 1844 Casaretto became Abbot, nominated by the Cassinese Congregation which was impressed by the ability he had unexpectedly shown. S. Giuliano had been a monastery abandoned by the Carthusians; another house on the Italian Riviera, Finalpia, which the Olivetans found themselves unable to staff any more, Casaretto took over to be a missionary college, especially for territories where the English language was spoken. In this project, as original in the Cassinese ambient as the seventeenth-century English Benedictine missionaries had been in the Congregation of Valladolid with its strong emphasis on enclosure, Casaretto betrays the influence of his spiritual director, S. Vincenzo Pallotti. So what had at first seemed to Casaretto to be an exile from monastic community in the event enabled him to construct a monastery after his own ideal, which would never have been possible for him in any of the other Cassinese houses.

The rather pedestrian way of life in these venerable abbeys was due above all to the prolonged interruption of their life during the French occupation of Italy, which had closed most of the monasteries for nearly a quarter of a century. Even when restored after the war, the monasteries were in suspense as to their continuance because of the apparently inevitable progress of the Risorgimento with its anti-clerical accompaniments. During the suppression the monks had had to become diocesan clergy or live with their families. In the struggle to fend for themselves during this long interval, they had acquired habits which were hard to shed on their return to the monasteries and which they knew they might have to resume. Instead of living entirely from the community's resources, individual monks retained small reserves of private property, the *peculium*. Family ties counted for a great deal, even within the monastery. Greater store was set by the kind of devotional exercises and pious practices suitable for a parish priest than by the liturgy performed in common. The political divide in Italy between those who welcomed the movement for Unification and those who defended the *status quo* gave rise to factions within monastic communities.

Vociferous supporters of the Risorgimento like Abbot Pappalettere of Monte Cassino and the historian, Don Luigi Tosti, had brought the Cassinese Congregation into disfavour with the Holy See. The future Cardinal Dusmet had been forced out of his own monastery, S. Martino della Scala, by the high feelings aroused there by political developments. Yet in spite of all its weaknesses the ancient stock of this congregation could still give proofs of its vitality; the motto of Monte Cassino was *succisa recrescit*, and not in vain. Each one of the mighty Benedictine enterprises we have so far investigated, even though its impact was outside Italy, had in its faltering beginnings owed a great deal to its contact with the Cassinese. And though small in numbers the Cassinese at this time produced a great array of cardinals and archbishops who were entrusted with some of the principal Italian dioceses, particularly in the South. At S. Paolo it maintained an influential Benedictine presence in Rome, while at the same time out of gratitude for its support during the United Italy campaign, particularly the kindness of the monks at Perugia to the wounded in battle, the Liberal governments which supplanted the Popes tolerated an attenuated survival of the monks at a time when all the other religious orders were being suppressed. A last sign of the undiminished power of the Cassinese to make a contribution to the general life of the Church and the Order in this century is that their noblest son, Cardinal Dusmet, was to be the chief instrument of Leo XIII's plans, first for founding Sant'Anselmo, the international college at Rome for Benedictine students, in 1888, and secondly for organizing in 1893 the Congress of Abbots which, after allaying all fears of centralization and loss of autonomy, agreed upon the *Lex Propria*, the constitution of the new Benedictine Confederation.

In 1850 the Holy See, impressed by Casaretto's success in Liguria, decided to use him for reforming the Cassinese generally. This new mission would be more complex than his previous achievement, which had been to take over and restart empty monasteries according to his own ideas, without any need to placate or win round monks who were already there living the monastic life after their own fashion. In less than twenty years he was to find this task of raising the level of observance in all the Cassinese houses too much for his powers, and would hive off a few of these monasteries to be totally given to the Reform, with a growing independence of the rest of the Cassinese Congregation, an evolution similar to that of the Discalced from the Carmelites of the mitigated observance. But for the moment he envisaged his task differently. In 1850 Pius IX used his Commendatory powers over Subiaco to appoint Casaretto Abbot there. The former inhabitants were summarily ejected to make room for Casaretto's little band of reformers from Liguria. From the start co-existence in the same house seemed unthinkable. The principal elements of the reform were common property, total abstinence from meat and the recitation of Matins in the middle of the night. In 1851 the little cluster of reformed houses was formed into the Subiaco Province of the Cassinese Congregation, a grouping based not on regional location of the constituent houses, as was the case with all the other provinces of the Cassinese, but according to the level of the observance. With rapid momentum other houses were aggregated to this province—the Sacro Speco at Subiaco in 1853, S. Giovanni in Parma in 1854, Praglia in 1857. This rapid advance must have seemed rather threatening to the Cassinese of the older variety, especially since Casaretto had been elected—after the Papacy had gone to lengths to make its wishes clear—President of the Cassinese Congregation in 1851.

A new dimension was added to his Reform when isolated monasteries outside Italy began to be attached to it, chiefly at the prompting of the Holy See. In 1856 he was asked to take under his guidance the Flemish monastery of Dendermonde. In 1859 there was annexed to his organization Pierre-qui-Vire, a community which its saintly and apostolic founder, a secular priest Jean-Baptiste Muard, intended to combine penitential practices with missionary initiatives. In 1862 the great Catalonian monastery of Montserrat was affiliated, after Subiaco had opened up many Spanish contacts through its support of the missionary work of Monsignor Serro and Abbot Salvado among the Australian aborigines. The English abbey of Ramsgate, founded as early as 1856, differed from all these other non-Italian houses in that it was a direct overseas foundation by Subiaco, the first-fruit of its missionary college. The leader of its founding fathers was Wilfrid Alcock.

The French anti-monastic legislation of 1880 expelled the community of Pierre-qui-Vire. One group of these monks, after a short sojourn at Leopardstown, a vast property near Dublin owned by Ramsgate, who had hoped to found there an agricultural college in connexion with Newman's Catholic University but in the event found it a source of much financial embarrassment, moved to England to take over Buckfast. This pre-Reformation monastery had been adapted to be a gentleman's country house. In time these French monks opened at Buckfast a school for boys who aspired to the monastic life; this was soon filled with young men from the devout Catholic regions of Wurttemburg. This explains the change in one generation from a French to a German complexion in that community, which impressed legions of visitors by the different products of the skilled work of its monks. This ranged from building the abbey to producing honey and tonic wine. Buckfast was also to give the Church one of its deepest theologians on Eucharistic doctrine in Abbot Anscar Vonier.

This extension of his organization beyond the Alps to include monasteries which were in their turn to be prolific in foundations, just preceding a time when the new Italian state would suppress Casaretto's Italian monasteries (he wasn't so much *persona grata* with the Government as were the Cassinese, possibly because in all his works he was so much an agent of the Holy See) and force them to seek refuge in adjoining countries, led Casaretto to think afresh on the constitution of his Reform. He no longer saw it as his mission to change the Cassinese by degrees as one house after another submitted to the new observances. Instead he set about creating a separate international congregation of the Primitive Observance, which would be subdivided into national provinces; the Italian houses of his allegiance would separate from the Cassinese to form the Italian province. After an experimental stage this new Congregation was finally approved in 1872. The legendary prudence of the Holy See can be seen in its rejection of a set of Constitutions which Casaretto himself had drawn up and which combined the system of temporary local superiors he had known in his Cassinese tradition with strong centralized rule by the Abbot General. The contours of the scheme he proposed reveal the cast of Casaretto's mind—autocratic, not very original and obsessed with observances. He ended his life rather sadly—sick, dying outside a monastic community, under examination on charges of misusing his Congregation's finances. Yet he had built up a work that would have a wider radiation than he could ever have conceived. The poor and severe life he imposed upon his monks would fit them admirably for the implantation of monasteries in the mission field. Many features of his international congregation anticipated the organization of the Benedictine Confederation.

The reason for assigning to the English Benedictines the postscript in this survey of the history of Benedictinism in the nineteenth century is that in some of its major aspects their evolution followed a course quite the opposite to the one which prevailed on the Continent. The tendency elsewhere to greater centralization, to put the accent on the Congregation rather than on its constituent houses, to throw up some great father-figure whose mind would be mirrored in the development of his Congregation synchronized in England with a hard-fought campaign to dismantle the old structure of the Congregation, derived from Valladolid and Santa Giustina, which invested all power centrally in the General Chapter, to elevate the component houses to the status of abbeys whose autonomy would be respected. And this movement in England did not proceed so much from a single great man's vision as from the spontaneous generation of the same aims in many quarters simultaneously. On the other hand, this same English movement did have in common with its continental contemporaries a quest for a more distinctive monasticity of behaviour, less alloyed by the works a monastery might happen to be engaged in, a more pronounced stress on the liturgy and on scholarly services to the Church and a rapturous response to inspirations found in the Middle Ages. As also on the Continent, so in England too, the Holy See played a decisive part at all the turning-points of Benedictine development, and rarely was its judgement at fault.

For the greater part of this century the three small priories of Ampleforth, Downside and Douai went on conducting homely, unpretentious boarding schools where the teaching was generally by very young monks, who had probably only just left the schools they were running and who had seldom received any education outside the system they were returning to. These young monks were preparing either for ordination or for the call by the Congregation's President to leave their priory and serve on one of the Congregation's 'missions', as the future parishes were still called. There, although radically still attached to the community of the priory where they had taken their vows, they were withdrawn from the jurisdiction of their Prior, and subjected to the authority of one of the President's two lieutenants for administering the missions, the Provincial of York for those in the North and the Provincial of Canterbury for those in the South.

This system, whereby the monasteries were subordinated to the missionary organization of the Congregation, was accepted without serious questioning for many years. It can be argued that during the Napoleonic Wars it was responsible for the survival of English Benedictines at a time when its most autonomous house, Lamspringe near Hanover, died never to revive. There was a period of greatness when the Congregation became a nursery of bishops, giving to England Ullathorne (1806–89) of Birmingham, Joseph Brown (1796–1880) and Cuthbert Hedley (1837–1915) both of Newport and Menevia; to Australia Bede Polding (1794–1877), Bede Vaughan (1834–83) and Charles Davis (1815–1848); to Mauritius and South Africa Bede Slater and six successors.

The casual but sturdy training given within the Congregational system fostered that combination of practicability, broad-mindedness and independence of judgement with a deep unobtrusive piety and a Catholic spirit of obedience which fitted these men to be pioneers and apostles in virgin territory. A Benedictine name regularly featured in the *terna* of those submitted to Rome for the archbishopric of Westminster. And on a smaller scale these same characteristics could be found, multiplied in the numerous Benedictine priests who were pastors of large missions to the Irish immigrants in the raw new towns of Lancashire, Cumberland, Durham and South Wales, the regions where there was the heaviest concentration of Benedictine missions. The heroism of this tradition discloses itself with great poignancy in the memorial in St Peter's church, Seel Street, Liverpool, to the numerous Benedictine clergy who died while ministering during the great cholera epidemic. In the watering-places of Bath, Malvern and Cheltenham fashionable congregations had their own way of making heavy demands on the Benedictine clergy there. Everywhere new schools and churches had to be fought for and paid for, the Catholic poor championed, prejudices refuted and disarmed. A noble record of solid achievement was built up, which would be hard to abandon later on.

But in the later decades of the century many influences combined to give the Congregation a more monastic conscience. The Continental reforming movement was brought uncomfortably into the theatre of the English missionary monks with the arrival of the Primitive Observance at Ramsgate in 1856 and the Beuronese at Erdington, a working-class suburb of Birmingham, where a wealthy parish priest presented them with a fine church and house in 1876. Apart from the important difference of their life together, the monks of both these houses were engaged in parish activities not very differently from their English Benedictine counterparts. But they were a presence, for some an encouragement, for others a cause of fear. Abbot Linse of Erdington gave a retreat at Fort Augustus, a monastery founded in 1876 by the volatile romantic, Dom Jerome Vaughan, with the support of some wealthy highland lairds, and the community was so affected that it applied to join the Beuronese Congregation and maintained its Beuronese affiliation from 1883 to 1910. This move was supported by the Scottish Catholic nobility and bishops, possibly because it seemed to register Scottish distinctiveness, but it was deeply resented by the English Benedictine authorities. Stanbrook, the only convent of nuns in the English Congregation at that time, had Guéranger's fervent disciple, Dom Laurence Shepherd, as its chaplain for twenty-two years, and his spirit ruled there even from the grave. There he translated *L'Année Liturgique*. Some time after his death but still very much under his influence the nuns, led by their French Abbess Dubois, took on constitutions framed on those of Solesmes, notably in that they envisaged superiors elected for life, and profited from the sympathy of Cardinal Pitra to thwart the opposition of the English Benedictine authorities. Dom Laurence Shepherd had also preached Guéranger's ideals at a retreat he gave to the Downside community, which became the bastion of the monastic party in the English Benedictine Congregation. Furthermore the minds of many young monks had been affected by their experience of monastic and liturgical life in the common novitiate of the Congregation which was based at St Michael's Cathedral Priory, Belmont near Hereford (the church doubled up as the cathedral for the Benedictine bishops of Newport) from 1859 to 1917. Although constitutionally the idea of such a congregational novitiate was to be eschewed by the 'monastic party' as an offence against the autonomy of the abbeys, in fact the way of life at Belmont, its liturgical performance and the rediscovery there of Father Augustine Baker and his contemplative emphasis, would make its observance bear comparison with most houses of the reformed variety.

A doughty and often bitter rearguard action was fought by the supporters of the *status quo* against the growing demands of the 'monastic party', which was soon to include men like Cardinal Gasquet and Abbot Cuthbert Butler, for changing the Constitutions so that the old centralized structures give way to more self-determination by the communities and that the parishes be subordinated to the monasteries. Although the so-called 'missionary party' had the upper hand in numbers and senority, in fact the tide of events was flowing against it, and powerful influences outside the Congregation, at Rome and among the English bishops, saw the desirability of the changes demanded.

In the first place, the word 'mission' began to lose a lot of its meaning and motive-power when in 1851 the English hierarchy was restored and the missions became settled parishes. It was not long before the new English bishops, particularly Manning and Vaughan, resented the traditional immunities and privileges of religious clergy in their dioceses. Among the religious Manning singled out as particularly obnoxious the Jesuits and the Benedictines. He wrote to Ullathorne (2 May 1880): 'The Regulars in England may be divided into those who more or less observe their rule, e.g. Franciscans, Capucini, Passionists and Redemptorists. . . . And secondly those who do not observe their Rule, e.g. S.J. and the Benedictines; and these league and are maintaining the contest.' The controversy between the Bishops and the Regulars was decided by Rome in the Bishops' favour in the Bull *Romanos Pontifices* of 1881 which gave the Bishops far more authority over Benedictine parishes. This prolonged contest discredited the 'missionary party' both at Rome and with the English Bishops so that when they came to fight on another front, with the 'monastic party' of their own Congregation, their cause was already well-known and weakened when it came to Rome for settlement.

The poor impression the English Benedictines then made upon outsiders can be seen in a letter from Newman advising Gerard Manley Hopkins not to become a Benedictine, because a recent visit to Downside had brought home to the future Cardinal how much the missions dominated the scene and stunted the growth of that Benedictine life which he had extolled in his famous essay. Earlier, the great Rosminian missionary, Gentili, writing to Rome from Prior Park, had lamented the secular style of life he had witnessed at Downside. Perhaps the most accusing sign of the inadequacy of the English Benedictines to rise to the needs of the age is that virtually none of the flow of converts that issued from the Oxford Movement and its aftermath knocked at the monasteries for admission. The tragedy was all the greater because the last years of the century was a time when monastic life might have reaped an abundant harvest of vocations. A hint of this can be seen in the spontaneous development of religious orders in the Anglican Church. In instance after instance a sisterhood founded in some East London High Church parish on the model of a Roman Catholic active order evolved into a contemplative community, some of them adopting the Rule of St Benedict.

But so far as the English Benedictines were concerned, the last decades of the nineteenth century were a time of missed opportunities, of fierce infighting, but at least the object of the battle was a constructive one. Distinguished outsiders, ecclesiastical and lay, gave influential support to the reforming monastic party. Rome too was discreetly favourable, though preferring that the right solution should emerge from within the Congregation rather than be imposed from outside. And therefore in the Rescript *Cliftoniensis* of 1883 and the Bull *Diu Quidem* of 1890 the English monks were requested to revise their constitutions along more monastic lines. An indication of the direction this would take was given in the Apostolic Letter *Religiosus Ordo* of 1890 whereby the provincial organization for governing the parishes in a centralized manner was abolished, and the parishes were shared out between the priories. In 1900 the struggle was concluded when the final revision of the Constitutions was approved by Rome: the priories were raised to be abbeys, deciding their own destinies, loosely federated in a Congregation, with abbots elected for terms of office of eight years.

The restructured English Congregation now faced the onset of the twentieth century with its constituent monasteries as the engines of power and the sources of initiative. Each of the abbeys had responsibility for a small empire of parishes which in some cases might be felt to narrow the choices available for future development. The Benedictines still took second place to the Jesuits in respect of the size and social standing of their schools; the great days of the Benedictine public schools would be after the First World War. For a brief period before the onset of this development, Downside had a halcyon era as a community of scholars, formed and inspired by the shy civil servant and liturgical autodidact, Edmund Bishop, whose hope was that its monks would be Edwardian Maurists.

Rome began to think of the Benedictines as an 'Order' which could serve the Church better if they were as much like the other centrally organized Orders as possible. This would be all the more apparent in the early years of the next century when the Holy See would ask the Benedictines *as an Order* to undertake such works as the revision of the Vulgate, the administration and teaching of the Pontifical Biblical Institute and the Pontifical Oriental Institute as well as of their own central College of Sant' Anselmo in Rome.

Nor was it yet the time to chronicle the history of Anglican Benedictines. 1893 saw the foundation by Aelred Carlyle, a young medical student of ritualist inclinations, of the Anglican Benedictines who were subsequently to migrate to Caldey and to count both Nashdom and Prinknash as their descendants. At this time they were taking their first steps in monasticism in the unlikely surroundings of the Isle of Dogs in London's dockland. It would have been difficult then to foresee the long and fruitful history that lay ahead. At first it must have seemed as quixotic a venture as that of Father Ignatius of Llanthony thirty years earlier, who tried to bring back monks into the Church of England by a combination of ascetical extremism in the Black Mountains and revivalist mass meetings in London. He was a lovable enthusiast who might have found final acceptance in the Church of England if he had not put himself beyond the pale when he requested priestly ordination from Vilatte, an *episcopus vagans*.

As we conclude our review of the different strands in the Benedictine fabric of the nineteenth century, we can marvel at the spontaneous generation of so many monastic organisms in an unfavourable ambient, at the strong-minded men who, though the future was so blank and even perilous, did not hesitate to commit the lives of themselves and others to an ideal their era had little room for. There were heavy limitations we can see to their achievement. Nearly everywhere they seemed more anxious to tap the riches of privileged moments in the past than to trust to the resources God had given to their own age and to the guidance of the Spirit. Those solitary eminences who were the fountainheads of the different streams of monastic revival seem to have acted as monarchs, with anonymous communities ranged behind them. The monasteries sought to develop into establishments that would impress by their size. Strictness of discipline and a literal interpretation of the Rule were thought to be the necessary ingredients of a self-evidently better form of Benedictinism. Nevertheless, in spite of all its woodenness, the Benedictinism of the last century became a living stock with its own power of self-transcendence, which would make a rich contribution to the life of the Church in the following era.

by Dom Daniel Rees

BIBLIOGRAPHY

Dizionario degli Istituti di Perfezione, 5 volumes so far. (Rome 1974–).

H. Tausch, *Bendiktinisches Monchtum in Oesterreich* (Vienna 1949).

Revue Bénédictine, 1973, Centenary Number for Maredsous' Founda tion in 1873.

Beuron 1863–1963 (Beuron 1963).

P. Wenzel, *Der Freunderkreis um Anton Gunther und die Grundung Beurons* (Essen 1965).

L. Soltner, *Solesmes et Dom Guéranger* (Solesmes 1974).

Abbot Delatte, *Dom Guéranger, Abbé de Solesmes* (Paris 1909).

D. Huerre, *J. B. Muard* (Pierre-qui-Vire 1950).

G. Penco, *Storia del Monachesimo in Italia*, Vol. 2 (Rome 1968).

P. Anson, *The Call of the Cloister* (London 1964).

L. Lekai, *The Cistercians, Ideals and Reality* (Kent State University 1977).

J. Oetgen, *An American Abbot, Boniface Wimmer O.S.B., 1809* (Latrobe, Pa., 1976).

C. J. Barry, *Worship and Work* (Collegeville 1956).

I Monasteri Italiani della Congregazione Sublacense (1843–1972).

Studia Monastica (1972) Fasc. 2. entirely given up to articles on Casaretto.

Justin McCann, *Annals of the English Benedictine Congregation* (Typescript).

Basil Whelan, *Annals of the English Benedictine Congregation* (Typescript).

Archbishop Ullathorne (1806–89)

'From the time Saint Benedict converted the peasants around his cave at Subiaco and on Mount Cassino, the Benedictine Order has been missionary as well as monastic'. So wrote William Bernard Ullathorne, the monk who became the first Roman Catholic bishop of Birmingham and grand old man of the Church in Victorian England. And well he might, for 'missionary as well as monastic' could aptly describe his life. He was and remained at heart a monk of the very strictest observance, one who had no other ambition or desire beyong leading the life of a simple Benedictine. His ideas on monasticism and the spiritual life were predominantly formed by his *lectio divina*, his extensive reading of Scripture, Cassian and the Desert Fathers, and have a marked primitive tinge. He bore the characteristic marks of a thorough and great monk, and Dom Cuthbert Butler, who wrote his major biography, considers his sermon 'On All Monks' the best analysis of Saint Benedict's Rule and the clearest and truest short exposition of Benedictine spirituality, principles and life. Stability in community and the *Opus Dei* are its great themes, which produce a temper of largeness of spirit or freedom, apt, he warns, to degenerate into laxity. The remarkable feature about Ullathorne the monk, however, is that he spent most of his life outside the cloister.

It was an exile that was keenly felt. In 1844 while spending Ascensiontide at his monastery, Downside, near Bath, he wrote: 'I attend choir, meditate and think over all that has passed since I left this peaceful and happy abode and would be glad to remain here always. Everything tells me how much I have lost, gaining in nothing but the poor world's wisdom and conceit, since I left the cloister some fourteen years ago'. Writing in *The Rambler* in 1856 he claims that 'a monk thrown into the conflicts of the world, even for the holiest of causes, is like a land bird blown abroad upon the wide sea, thirsting for its quiet nest in the woods'. He, if anyone, should have known about the conflicts of the world, as he spent eight years at most within his monastery and travelled more widely than probably any monk of his day. Ullathorne's life was packed with controversy. As Newman, his lifelong friend, commented, 'I have been indoors all my life whilst you have battled for the Church in the world'.

He was a dreamer who managed to get his feet very firmly on the ground, one whom Newman in his *Apologia* could instance as the exemplary 'straightforward Englishman'. His straightforwardness was often to cause offence. The British Government's agent in Rome described him as 'a very injudicious man, rough, violent, ill-mannered and prejudiced and likely to endanger the peace H.M. Government so much desired the Roman Church to enjoy in England'. Ullathorne was not the greatest, but was the most central and characteristic figure in nineteenth-century English Catholic history. He was the last of the Vicars Apostolic who had ruled the Church during the penal days, and was largely responsible for the re-establishment of the English hierarchy, for the reconciliation of the old Catholics with the new converts, and for the gradual public acceptance of the Catholic Church in England. Butler concludes: 'not only does he stand out as a good and strong and human man and churchman, but also his title has been made good to a place in the honourable band of Great Victorians'.

A descendant of Saint Thomas More, he was born at Polkington in Yorkshire in 1806, the son of a grocer, draper, spirit and coal merchant who did half the business of the town. He was a somewhat clumsy and withdrawn child and a voracious reader. A romantic, his imagination was fired by works like *Robinson Crusoe* which he considered the climax of his literary enjoyment, and York Minster, which left him ecstatic. It 'gave me an impression of awe and of grandeur, a sense of the power of religion, which to my childish mind was like a revelation; and many a long day did my imagination feed upon that wonderful recollection.' A classical statue on the other hand bored him. The peace of his childhood was overshadowed by the Methodist revival which split the village. Ullathorne was not the most ecumenical of clerics and had little time for this 'sour principle' and its 'fanatical accompaniments—much pious sentiment uttered with an unctious drawl'. It awakened his curiosity but was singularly unattractive to his youthful mind.

When William was nine or ten the family moved to Scarborough, where he first saw the sea which was to prove far more alluring to him than revivalism. His early education had been carried out at the village school at Burnby, near Polkington, where he lodged with the blacksmith. Now he was sent as a day boy to Mr Hornsey's school, also a Protestant establishment. As there was a Mass only once every six weeks in Scarborough, William's father led the weekly Catholic worship. The boy continued to read everything he could lay his hands on, often until late into the night. His preference for travel books soon aroused a desire to see the world, and at the age of thirteen, after a year in his father's business, he announced to his horrified parents his desire to go to sea. However, neither parents nor priest could dissuade him despite frequent

II

warnings on the dangers and humiliations of such a life, particularly for a boy as lonely and proud as William. Luckily, a new ship was about to be launched whose owners were personal friends of his parents and whose captain was a superior gentleman, the type of whom they approved. The crew, it appears, were also eminently respectable. As William had as yet received neither first communion nor confirmation, he was ordered by the local priest to present himself for instruction so that he could receive the sacraments before he went away. However, he resented this invasion of his privacy and liberty; consequently he went to sea without the sacraments.

As cabin boy on board the *Leghorn* he did not attend Mass but his religious instincts were far from dormant, for in his wanderings he discovered both the beauty of creation and the ugliness of man's sin. Despite his slowness and a good deal of teasing from the other sailors (who called him 'Lumpy'), he appears to have won popularity by his story-telling. Many a long evening was passed amusing the crew with tales from Sir Walter Scott. His prowess as a story teller did not prevent them putting tar in his mouth as he slept or setting dogs on him or dowsing him with wine as he lay in his hammock. The ship's first voyage, to the Mediterranean, opened up a strange new world and awakened many pleasant thoughts and feelings. At Tarragona the great cathedral loomed above city walls still crumbling after the assaults of the Peninsular War. At Gibraltar the cabin boy and the mate were the only members of the crew sober after a drunken orgy on Spanish rum. Storms dogged the voyage home so that the fresh water turned putrid, the bread soured with maggots and cobwebs, and the beef was veritable mahogany, except that the inside of it was green. The second voyage, across the Baltic to St Petersburg, was more tranquil: the northern skies and scenes proved even more enchanting than the South. The magnificent dawns, the Norwegian fiords, sailing through the Russian fleet, the impressive quays of St Petersburg glowing with its metal domes and spires, the profound Russian piety, stirred the young poet's imagination. The most beautiful aspect of the Creation which Ullathorne ever beheld was a sunrise in the Baltic—'colour expanding into colour over half the hemisphere, and the opposite half being a pale reflection of their hues upon the blue, whilst the deck itself was checkered with a verberation of their brilliancy'.

The gorgeous spectacles of this Baltic idyll were soon to fade, as the *Leghorn* was reduced to the 'Black Trade', ferrying coal from Newcastle to London, under a new and far from genteel captain. The latter, in one of his many less sober moods, gave William a kick which so wounded the boy's pride that he ran away back to dry land and stayed there for the winter studying navigation. Not wishing to lose face with his parents, he rather reluctantly took to the water again in the spring, not as a cabin boy but in the forecastle 'amongst a set of men whose conversation was the vilest imaginable'. Here, by the ears he learnt to know everything about every form of vice.

Against this sordid background he suddenly returned to the practice of his family religion. The story of his conversion is told in his autobiography. At Memel he was invited by the ship's mate to attend Mass and surprisingly accepted. When they entered the Church, Mass had already begun, and the intense devotion of the congregation, who were singing the Litany of the Blessed Virgin, was immediately striking. Ullathorne wrote: 'The moment I entered, so awestruck was I with the simplicity and fervour of what I beheld that it threw me into a cold shiver, and turned my heart completely round upon myself. I saw the claim of God upon me and felt a deep reproach within my soul. When we came out I gave what little money I had about me to the poor. No sooner were we on board than I asked Craythorne (the ship's mate) what religious books he had'. Two were produced and these were read alternately. The lives of the saints carried the young penitent into a new world, exalted his imagination and filled him with the sense of God, and of a life for God, which hitherto he had never realized. His conscience was awakened and he lived in what he describes as 'a sort of ecstasy of the imagination' until the ship reached London.

When he arrived back in England, his first act was to inform his parents that he wished to give up the sea and return home; he was duly re-employed in his father's business. Ullathorne's vocation was as remarkable as his conversion. A friend of his father's, who had a son studying for the church at Downside, was pressing Ullathorne's elder brother James, a fine singer, to join his son. James being none too impressed by this suggestion, Ullathorne promptly volunteered to go in his place. His father arranged matters immediately, and in February 1823 at the age of sixteen Ullathorne began his studies with the Benedictine monks at Downside.

Here his experience at sea stood him in good stead. He wrote: 'It gave me a deep insight into the natural hearts of men, and especially of man as he is isolated from the ordinary conditions of society; and when I had to deal with large classes of mankind in conditions still more exceptional, I found I had nothing to learn as to the working of such men's hearts which I did not already know. The heart of the sailor is the most open and unreserved of all hearts amidst his shipmates, and his manifestation of himself is like a continuous public confession, with this difference, that it is devoid of all that disguise and dressing with which self-love contrives to clothe the formal self-manifestations of other men'.

The first thing which struck Ullathorne about his new college was the friendliness and piety of the boys and the good relations which existed between them and the monks, very different to anything he had known before and revealing the practical benefits of his religion. He quickly discovered that he was as ignorant in matters of the spirit as the monks were in worldly affairs, and proceeded to make up for lost ground in the two areas which were to be his main concern in the monastery, his studies and his soul. Considered a somewhat rough specimen when he arrived as Downside, with his trousers a good deal too short for him revealing speckled stockings, his life now underwent a total and earnest change. The earliest of his many letters dates from 1824 and in it he tells his parents of his first Communion: 'I had the inexpressible happiness of approaching Holy Communion for the first time on Christmas day, and promised now to begin in earnest and serve God with all my heart, which indeed is a very poor return for all the mercies and blessings which he has vouchsafed to grant to such an unworthy being as myself. And now, my dear parents, I feel as if I were entering into a new being, so much happier am I than during my former course of life. . . . Much yet remains to be done; and now I humbly and sincerely, and from my heart, ask your pardon for all the uneasiness, troubles and disquietudes which I have caused you which I hope you will grant through the love you bear our Blessed Lord, and through the goodness of your own hearts. I must also ask pardon of my brothers for all the scandal which I have given them, when I ought to have set them a good example'.

Ullathorne's love of books and aptitude for study, which enabled him to pass with rapidity and distinction through the school, earned him another nickname. Lumpy became Old Plato. After a mere year in the school he joined the monastery, beginning his novitiate on 12 March 1824. He took the name of Bernard and made his solemn vows on 5 April of the following year. His novitiate, under the benign and much loved Fr Polding, was a happy one though it involved learning the spiritual chapters of the Rule and the entire Pauline epistles by heart. His passion for reading continued unabated and was to lead him astray. After lights-out he would lay under his bed reading by the light of a candle placed in a foot-pan, with the result that in the morning he frequently overslept. His reading of the Lives of the Desert Fathers and of St Bernard and the Abbot de Rancé drew him towards the Trappists and it was only with difficulty that he was dissuaded from plunging himself into the penitential austerity of La Trappe. As the priesthood and the duty of preaching drew near, he felt the need to cure himself of certain physical defects, namely a lisp and a limp. He stood for hours at his studies to strengthen his weaker leg and the lisp was dealt with by reciting aloud with pebbles in his mouth. Working through the exercises of Austen's *Cheiroania* with dumb-bells helped his general gaucherie.

Ullathorne loved the monastic life and was enlightened by the divine office, whose spirit was deepened in him by the Gregorian chants and the recurrence of the festivals which celebrated the mysteries of faith and the great saints of the Order. He loved to read the ascetical writings of the saints and to muse upon the ways of those who had sought God with all their soul. It was the Desert Fathers however who were his great inspiration. He considered that they had worked out the true maxims of the spiritual life. 'Their life was so completely spent between themselves and God, and was so fenced in by seclusion, labour and self-denial, God and the soul was so exclusively their aim, and their grace was so abundant, and their lives so simple, that they appear as the very prophets as well as the experts of the interior life'. The Fathers of the Church he read in depth: with Scripture their works constituted his main source for preaching. The closer he stuck to these, he claimed, the more effective was his preaching. St Augustine's *Confessions*, that marvellous book in which a great mind reveals a great heart, took him into the depths of the human soul and up into the heights of God's greatness, 'I do not think,' he wrote, 'that any book ever did so much in opening my intelligence and in setting before me the principles on which human life should move'.

His studies still uncompleted, Ullathorne was ordained deacon in 1830 and sent as headmaster to another monastic school, Ampleforth College near York, where he arrived to find the place totally deserted and the walls daubed with slogans to the effect that he was not welcome. When he eventually found his students he expressed his surprise at their manners, 'of a pothouse or kennel' and threatened to punish the entire school if the slogans were not speedily removed. The walls were clean by the next break, and the ringleaders thrashed and expelled. This incident unfortunately set the tone for the whole of his short stay. Suffice it to say that Ullathorne was not a very successful school teacher. As often happens, the good ruler of men could not cope with boys. To make matters worse, he did not get on with his new superior. Altogether his first major assignment was an unqualified disaster and he was soon ordered back to his own monastery by the shortest possible road.

The priesthood was conferred on him at Ushaw in 1831. Sacrifice was for Ullathorne its great theme and in this the ideals of monk and priest ran together into one. As a monk he was offering himself spontaneously to God through the grace of God's call; as a priest he was made one with Christ who lived again in him, to be offered openly in sacrifice for the souls of men. His reluctance to use his consecrated hands to punish boys earned him a sharp rebuke from the prior for his squeamishness. The sense of sacrifice kept him alert for ways of giving more and more to God, and made him prompt to respond to the needs of the Australian Mission. Bishop Morris, a Downside monk, was Vicar-Apostolic of Mauritius and its dependencies, which at that time included Australia, New Zealand, the South Sea Islands and parts of British India. Not surprisingly he desperately needed priests and Ullathorne duly became Vicar-General of his vast diocese to organize the young Church in Australia. The life with God alone was given up for the sake of souls. Once again Ullathorne was thrust into the midst of a highly problematic situation where again he was regarded as an intruder. The Benedictine President General considered him ambitious for accepting the post and sadly he replied: 'I do not think the situation one of honour but of labour, of trial and of never ceasing toil'. This proved a most accurate description. He spent the voyage to Australia as a hermit, studying canon law. His Majesty's Catholic chaplain in New South Wales reached Sydney in February 1833.

At 27 he found himself Vicar-General of the Church's largest diocese, 4,000 miles from his bishop and half the world away from Rome. The new and unknown continent was a mission in every sense of the word, a penal colony of bitter enemies of Catholicism with an interior population of 'naked wandering savages', simmering in corruption. The penal settlements formed the nucleus of the rough and ready population of immigrants who were pouring in. No writing better preserves the horrors of transportation than Ullathorne's autobiography. The realistic glimpses of the inhuman cruelties and agonies through which he stepped, like Dante through the Inferno, constitute a gloomy panorama, He found a nucleus of a Church in the Irish convicts, many of whom had been transported for political reasons alone, but the Catholic community had been treated with negligence and contempt. A few devoted pioneer-priests ministered to their scattered families and trampled souls, but there was disagreement among them and with the Governor. This Ullathorne remedied on his arrival in his usual blunt fashion, announcing that though there were two parties yesterday there are none today. 'They arose from the unfortunate want of some person carrying ecclesiastical authority. That is at an end. For the present in New South Wales, I am the Church'.

He began immediately working with the Australian government for the religious and social equality of his fellow-worshippers. The Catholics composed a strong minority, about a third of the population, about twenty thousand in all. The rule was military and severe. Desperate men ranged the distant bush and the lessons the unhappy aborigines were learning from civilization were truly awful. Ullathorne left a curtain drawn over the factory where 1500 transported women lived and stagnated, whose confessions made him physically sick. Man's inhumanity to man was everywhere in evidence. These were the conditions of the concentration camp. The convicts' needs were never-ending and dealing with them involved long and frequent journeys into the interior on horseback. They came with their papers to be signed when they were granted freedom or leave to marry; they asked for his interference when floggings were brutally illegal; they begged for his presence before they were hanged and received his last ministrations as he scattered the alien soil on their graves.

On Norfolk Island an unsuccessful convict revolt ended in the condemnation of thirty-one men and the governor summoned Ullathorne to prepare them for death. All but thirteen were reprieved but it was not those who were to die who wept. They fell on their knees and thanked God that their living hell was over. Ullathorne spent a week preparing them for the end and inquiring into the general condition of the other prisoners on the island. The condemned prayed throughout the night before their executions which took place before the entire prison population under a heavy guard. On the scaffold the condemned began to chant aloud, in a kind of solemn chorus, the prayer which the priest had taught them: 'Into Thy hands I commend my spirit. Lord Jesus receive my soul', repeating it until the fall and the ropes stopped their voices for ever. It made a great impression on all present. The sea extended around the island for a thousand miles before it reached another shore. No ship except the government vessel was allowed to approach: only criminals, military and officials were allowed on shore. Everything was on the alert, as in a state of siege. Ullathorne was the first priest ever to set foot there. His work among the convicts taught him that men are rarely what they appear to be and are frequently misjudged. He saw that there is much heroism and humanity in even the basest criminal; hence God's judgement is needed to rectify that of men.

On his return to England in 1836 to raise help for the Australian Church Ullathorne began a fierce campaign against the terrible system he had witnessed. The next two years were to be the most eventful in his life. He was constantly on the move to Ireland, to

Rome, to Westminster. In *The Catholic Mission in Australia*, published in 1837, he exposed the evils of transportation to an unsuspecting British public. 'Sixty thousand souls are festering in bondage. The iron which cankers their heel corrodes their heart; the scourge which drinks the blood of their flesh, devours the spirit of their manhood. They are cast out for purification, and they are infinitely worse than when their country threw them away. . . . We have been doing an ungracious and an ungodly thing. We have taken a vast portion of God's earth, and have made it a cesspool'. He describes Norfolk Island, starkly contrasting the beauty of creation with man's sin: 'Earth's most magnificent verdure waved over a putrid sink of vice and wickedness and misery such as can hardly have a parallel in the history of the human race'. The document is a classic indictment of the complacency of the British Government. Ceaselessly he campaigned for the abolition of the whole system. To this end he wrote a second pamphlet *The Horrors of Transportation* and gave important evidence to the Parliamentary Commission on the subject. This commission eventually decreed the abolition of the system, but Ullathorne's revelations at Westminster raised a storm of fury in the colony. He was dubbed 'Her Majesty's Agitator-General for New South Wales'.

Ullathorne returned to Australia with fifteen Irish priests, five Sister of Charity and five Church students, to find himself the object of universal hatred. He had offended both freemen and emancipists in two most vulnerable points, their pride and their pockets. They depended on convict labour for their prosperity, but there were to be no more convict ships after 1840. He was bitterly attacked on all fronts, and to make matters worse, he was left undefended by his new bishop, his former novice-master, Polding. The latter had been appointed first Bishop of Sidney in 1834 after Ullathorne had suggested the need for a Vicar-Apostolic for Australia. Ullathorne was also the driving force behind the establishment of an Australian hierarchy, in 1842. He found himself increasingly out of sympathy with the inadequacies of Poldings' administration, although Polding relied totally on him. Other disappointments were his failure to secure Australia as an English Benedictine mission and the increasing conflict with the Irish clergy. The latter considered him a snob. The situation deteriorated rapidly until Bishop Polding's chaplain was forced to spell out the truth. 'The fact is, Fr Ullathorne, we shall have no peace, so long as you are in the colony'. When Bishop Polding, after a grand send-off, left for Europe on Church business at the close of the 1830's, Ullathorne insisted on accompanying him, never to return.

The journey home took him via New Zealand and South America, and he arrived back in England a sick man. His health was broken and never fully recovered from the rigours of the Australian Mission and climate. This was among the reasons for his declining no fewer than five Australian bishoprics. Henceforth his mission was to be in England and he was sent to Coventry to run a small Catholic mission in the Midlands. A greater change in scale would be difficult to imagine, but the four years spent at Coventry proved the happiest and most fruitful in Ullathorne's life. In Australia he had failed to secure a mission which was both Benedictine and English, and at Coventry he sought for the realization of his frustrated hopes. Once again, the situation facing him was daunting. Coventry in 1841 was an old world provincial town of 30,000 inhabitants, of whom only 1,000 were Catholics. Ullathorne found the mission, which was situated in the poorest part of the town, in a desolate condition. His predecessor appears to have spent most of his time in prayer and in an asylum. The chapel was ruinous and many of the congregation lapsed.

In remedying this situation the new rector was assisted by an outstanding woman. On her death Ullathorne described her as 'the most remarkable religious woman of our age and country'. This was Margaret Hallahan, who acted as his housekeeper and sacristan. Like Newman, she was destined to be a great spiritual friend of his life. She was recommended to him by a friend who knew her worth. She was a London orphan who had worked as a servant in Bruges in Belgium for many years, enjoying its rich catholic life. When Ullathorne met her she was forty; all she asked was board and lodging in return for work among the poor.

Returning from a visit to Rome, where he disentangled himself from the new Australian hierarchy which he had planned, he found that she had already made a tremendous impact on the mission, founding a school for some 200 girls and singling out the sick and destitute. Sister Margaret, as she was known, had been accustomed at Bruges to all the practices of a full Catholic devotional life and deplored the fact that many of these popular devotions, the rosary, processions, Benediction, were hardly ever practised in England, as English Catholics had hardly emerged from the long depression of penal times. It was mainly owing to her influence that Coventry under Ullathorne was the first place in England where many of these practices were introduced.

Encouraged by Sister Margaret, Ullathorne determined to build a fine new gothic church. And not only a church would he build but a priory, to be the residence of a small community of five or six monks, living their monastic life and supplying the pastoral needs of Coventry. The establishment of such missionary priories was to be a lifelong ambition. Ullathorne felt that monasticism in England had lost its bearings and departed from the spirit of Saint Benedict. In the celebrated sermon 'On All Monks' he outlines his views on the subject. The spiritual directions of the Rule he considers 'the concentrated essence of the divine law and the blessed counsels in which our Lord himself showed us the way to peace and beatitude'. For him the heart of monastic life was the liturgy, the worship of God in community. Its three keys were stability, the choral office and the common life. These were the things which formed saints and civilized mankind. In England historical circumstances had dictated that monks lived alone on the mission like ordinary secular priests. Those circumstances now no longer existed : Ullathorne felt that it was time to return to a more authentic form of monasticism in which monks serving the mission lived in communities, worshipping together and preserving the essential features of monastic life. This he felt would provide a secure contemplative basis for apostolic activity. These views made him rather unpopular in the English Benedictine Congregation.

His plan for a missionary priory is one of the reasons for the size and splendour of the new church which Ullathorne built. In architecture as in music he was a purist and was determined that his church was to be a model of what church architecture should be, recalling, as far as possible, the glories of the pre-reformation parish churches. His architect was Charles Hansom, the town surveyor and the only member of his congregation to keep a servant, and Saint Osburg's was the first of many notable commissions. To study the best extant examples and to fill their minds with the proper ideals and ideas, priest and architect went on a tour of the Low Countries and North Germany. The new church was a reproduction of a thirteenth century model, a good example of the puginesque gothic revival. To finance its construction Sister Margaret organized weekly collections for the congregation whilst Ullathorne toured the country begging. They were criticized for building so large and expensive a church for so poor a mission. It was considered far too grand for a parish so lacking in 'respectable' people, but as Margaret Hallahan commented, 'the Coventry church has been built not for man but for God, and he is always respectable.' The church was consecrated on 9 September 1845 and all the bishops attended. For the occasion Ullathorne wore the Benedictine habit, the first time it had been worn in England since the sixteenth century. Henceforth he always wore it in the church and house and when preaching abroad.

The opening of the church led to a great burst of catholicism in Coventry. This activity was epitomized in the formation of the

Institute of Dominican Tertiary Nuns, which Ullathorne would probably have regarded as the great work of his life. Sister Margaret's work gave rise to the desire of giving a more regular and stable form to her apostolate of charity. Thus in the course of her weekly spiritual talk with Ullathorne, the project of founding a community devoted to educational and charitable works gradually developed. The Dominican provincial gave his permission and transferred his authority to Ullathorne, who became novice master and director. The small community of Sister Margaret and three others was then able to begin its period of probation in the rector of Coventry's presbytery. On 8 December 1845 the first profession took place in the new church; from this date the congregation dates its establishment. Ullathorne's stipend was their common purse and he shared their meals, They sang the Little Office of Our Lady together. It was the closest Ullathorne ever came to his missionary priory. Shortage of manpower and his elevation to the episcopate prevented the idea ever getting off the ground.

Before his consecration as bishop in 1846 Ullathorne declared that the episcopate is 'a state of life I feel not one attraction for of any kind'. Indeed, one of the advantages of Coventry for him was that here he felt safe from the mitre which loomed so large in Australia. His appointment as Vicar Apostolic for the Western District then came as a great blow. The only person he could turn to was Margaret Hallahan, who recognized his problem immediately —'I see by the look in your eyes that you are made a bishop'. Ullathorne remarks that 'she knew well that it was a summons from the only work to which I felt any attraction'. With a heavy heart he was persuaded to accept by his religious superior, the President-General. His consecration took place in the church he had built on Sunday 21 June 1846, the day on which Pius IX was crowned as pope. Newman, who had just been received into the Catholic Church, attended. Ullathorne's new Dominican community moved with him to the Western District. The sad parting from Coventry is described in the autobiography: 'I had next the trying task of parting with that good and pious flock which I loved so well. I knew them all so well . . . and seldom have pastor and flock understood each other better. But few of them gave me real trouble, and they were so much of one class, the industrious weavers and watchmakers, that they were like one family.' They presented him with a chalice which he used ever since at his daily Mass. He left Coventry with extreme regret and his lasting affection for the people is reflected in his description of a visitation he made to the parish in 1856 as bishop of Birmingham: 'It has been a feast to be among them'.

As bishop of Hetalona and Vicar Apostolic of the Western

District he was charged with the souls of Catholics living in the six south westerly counties of England. His immediate problem here was to form a missionary centre for the district at Bristol and to deal with the scandal of Prior Park. The latter was Bishop Baines' ambitious but ill-fated attempt to establish a great Catholic university near Bath. In this undertaking he had absorbed the whole resources of the district, and divided it into two parties, which stood in bitter antagonism. The college now had very few students and was dangerously short of money. The establishment was housed in a vast classical palace, to Ullathorne the apotheosis of pagan art, where the president lived in considerable state. Ullathorne declared war on the college and warned the president of an ensuing visitation. When the visitation took place, the bishop was refused access to the accounts, so Rome ordered the setting up of an official commission of enquiry. Ullathorne moved out of Prior Park, where he had been expected to live, and bought a small house in Bristol for himself and another for his nuns. While at Clifton he turned a derelict shell into a cathedral, assisted by his old friend Hansom, whom he instructed to bury his reputation as an architect in order to build a cathedral for £2,000. During the Irish famine he worked tirelessly to raise money for the suffering. He also worked ceaselessly for the restoration of the English hierarchy and was determined never to rest until this was accomplished. He became the leading protagonist of the cause in Rome. At his first meeting of the Vicars Apostolic in 1847 he was elected to go to Rome to press for restoration, and represent the English episcopate in the negotiations. The story of these transactions he afterwards minutely detailed in his *History of the Restoration of the Catholic Hierarchy in England*. One of the main difficulties to be settled was how the country was to be divided into twelve sees. This necessitated another journey to Rome the following year. On the way there, he passed through revolutionary Paris, where he witnessed most of the main events in the attempt to establish the Red Republic. Politically conservative, he was unimpressed by the rebels—the 'scum of the populace'. He was later to complain that Disraeli's reform bills would be the ruin of England. For nine weeks he laboured for the English cause in Rome, and came away with the affairs of the new hierarchy settled. He himself was transfered from the Western to the Central District, where the financial situation was even more desperate. Revolution broke out the night he left Rome. It was not until two years later, on 29 September 1850, that the Bill setting up the English hierarchy was published. Ullathorne was much fancied to become first archbishop of Westminster but in the event he was made bishop of Birmingham.

The bishopric of Birmingham was the only job which Ullathorne held long enough to see it bear much fruit. 'For the first time in my agitated life I found myself placed in a peaceful jurisdiction over a unified clergy, conspicuous for their devotion to the episcopal authority'. His tenure of the see extended over thirty-eight years, during which time the cause of Catholicism made great progress in the diocese. Finances were once again his main problem. The administration was in considerable debt. It took the entire forty years of his episcopate to establish the diocese on a permanently solid financial basis; but it was done. He repaid the debts, restored funds that had been alienated, and formed new and much needed funds for ecclesiastical education and diocesan administration. This was done by funding all benefactions, and never paying away capital, but only the proceeds of interest. Unfortunately, a fluke resulted in his spending a short period in Warwick Gaol for debt in 1853. An insolvent bank had made a claim on its shareholders, of which the diocese was one. £1,000 was paid out but a further demand for £3,500 resulted in the embarrassing spectacle of the bishop being sent to gaol. Ullathorne refused point blank to force the Catholic community to pay and eventually the bank withdrew its suit after the bishop handed over his meagre personal resources.

His predominant interest as a bishop was the sanctification of all those in his care, particularly his clergy and his nuns. He disliked the adjective 'secular' for his clergy: 'they are Christ's own pastoral order of His own Divine Foundation'. For their formation he opened a new seminary, St Bernard's, Olton. If there was anything in his life which might induce God to have mercy on him, Ullathorne felt that it was the fact that he had never forgotten to take care of His nuns. His chief joy in this regard was to see the Dominican Tertiaries established in a fine new mother house at Stone, Staffs. The two main assets which he inherited from his predecessor were Saint Chad's Cathedral and Oscott, the diocesan college. At the latter in 1852, the first Synod of Westminster was held at which Newman preached his renowned 'Second Spring' sermon. As a Benedictine bishop he was particularly concerned with the divine worship, especially at his own cathedral of St Chad. In his 'Discourse on Church Music' he wrote: 'It has always been my desire, as becomes the episcopal office, that this cathedral should be a school to the diocese of what is best, according to the spirit and law of the Church in parochial administration, in rubrical law and in ecclesiastical song. As such, I believe, it is generally recognized throughout the diocese.' He was determined that the congregation should learn to sing, the graver style of plainchant being the ideal. With regards to church music he was strongly opposed to two things: 'flash singing in churches and advertizing church exhibitions in newspapers'. One such advertizement, announcing that the organist was celebrating his birthday at a Mass with all his own compositions, resulted in the organist being forbidden to introduce his own compositions at any mass. The bishop also disliked women's voices in choirs. A nun's heartfelt rendering of a Sanctus provoked a gruff rebuke while the soloist was still in full flight. 'When a bishop sings mass in 'is own diocese 'e doesn't need a woman to show 'im 'ow'. It was not only when he was angry that Ullathorne failed to sound his h's. He never did, but always retained his Yorkshire accent.

The re-establishment of the hierarchy produced a violent reaction from the British public. During the fierce outburst against the 'papal aggression' Wiseman, archbishop of Westminster, was abroad, so it fell to Ullathorne to take the lead in answering this hostility. He wrote a scathing reply to Lord John Russell and attempted to smooth over Wiseman's imprudent 'Outside the Flaminian Gate' letter, for which he was dubbed by *Punch* with the singularly inappropriate title of 'His oiliness'. He made it clear that the measures of the pope were only spiritual, that in all temporal matters, Catholics were subject to, and guided by, the laws of the land, and were loyal subjects of the Queen. His speeches at public meetings in Birmingham Town Hall had a marked effect in abating the agitation. Once again, however, the strains of office were undermining his health. In 1857 Ullathorne was ordered to take a complete rest and it was not until 1860 that he fully recovered.

The bishop of Birmingham's correspondence during his attendance at the First Vatican Council has proved an important historical source for later researchers. In the conflict between Ultramontanes and Gallicans Ullathorne found himself at variance with his metropolitan, Manning. He was one of the few English bishops who was not afraid of Manning and ceaselessly defended Newman, who resided in his diocese, against him. He was also Newman's champion in Rome. When Manning suggested that the bishop was no match for the Oxford scholar, Ullathorne retorted that it was Manning who was no match for Newman. Another discussion was terminated by Ullathorne reminding Manning that 'I was teaching the catechism with the mitre on my 'ead while you were still an 'eretic'. Against Manning Ullathorne insisted that the infallible power of the Church resided in the head and body of the Church acting together rather than solely in the pope. He favoured 'a calm and moderate definition provided it was duly balanced and duly limited, and he desired a dogma which would not make the pope appear impeccable or capable of making decisions 'ex cathedra' without the bishops being in the position of a platform behind the chair rather than as an entirely docile audience in front. He wanted a good clear definition which left no room for misunderstanding. Unfortunately this stance made him suspect as a Gallican, which Ullathorne deeply resented. When another bishop at the council had the audacity to charge him as such, the ageing delegate from Birmingham leapt across several intervening benches to confront him. His friend Newman considered that in his heart he opposed any doctrinal definition, although as a monk his instinct of obedience was so strong that he would never go against the pope's known wishes. Despite his protestations of innocence Ullathorne felt the need to write to *The Times* to deny that he had joined the opposition to infallibility, later he sought an audience with the pope to assure him on this point. Although Ullathorne had wished to add a clarifying term to the great Definition and for this reason at first voted only conditionally, a week later he added his full *placet* to the dogma and stood for the Infallibility till his death. He brought to a successful conclusion the debate on the formula 'Holy Catholic Apostolic Roman Church' so that there was no possibility of the survival of the three-branch theory of Catholicism. Thus the opening words of the actual dogmatic decrees of the Council are due to Ullathorne's intervention. By July 1870 unanimity had been reached on Infallibility. 'How could it be otherwise,' wrote Ullathorne, 'seeing that everyone here offers the Holy Sacrifice each morning and assists at another Mass with his brethren in this place.'

The cross was at the very heart of Ullathorne's spirituality, which like his character was positive and straightforward. Humility is its key. In his *Groundwork of the Christian Virtues* Ullathorne comments that it is the least known and consequently the most misunderstood of the virtues, yet humility is the very groundwork of the Christian religion. 'What God accepts from man is humility and what he rejects is pride'. Humility for Ullathorne then, as for Saint Benedict, was the basis of all growth in the knowledge, likeness and love of God. It is a teaching which is profoundly scriptural, christological and traditional. Man's choice, for him, is between proud self enslavement or humble divine liberty. 'There is no master so large minded, so generous, or who is so well aquainted with you and your requirements, as God; no father so loving and bountiful; no friend so free from all jealousy; none who so completely loves you for your greater good. Whilst there is no tyrant so narrow-minded, so proud-hearted, so exacting, so suspicious, so utterly bent on keeping you to your own littleness, as the one we all know so well, of whose tyranny we have had such bitter experience and who goes by the name of Myself. Yet God or yourself you must choose for your master'. The fundamental efforts of christian virtue then are to leave our own selfish affections and to get as near to God with our will and affections as we can, and to act on principle rather then feeling. A humble and cheerful trust in the Divine Goodness are for Ullathorne the essence of the Gospel. Thus sadness is dismissed as totally selfish, anxiety as totally unspiritual. In this stress on the Love of God one can detect the influence of Saint Francis of Sales, who probably provided the model for his friendship with Margaret Hallahan, as well as that of the Fathers. God's love and humility could only be realized in prayer.

It was prayer which occupied most of his last years spent in retirement at Oscott. After frequent requests he was finally allowed to hand over the bulk of his diocesan duties to an auxiliary Bishop Ilsley in 1879. The old sailor listening for the winter gales in his great empty house enjoyed his loneliness. It was a solitude for which he had craved all his life. 'I am never less alone than when alone. It is this peopled world that makes solitude. I was made for a hermit'. The quiet gave him an opportunity to put his papers in order. His *Endowments of Man* was published in 1880 to stem the tide of materialistic and agnostic thought. *The Groundwork of Christian Virtues* followed two years later, and *Christian Patience* dedicated to Newman, in 1886. In the dedication he regretted 'It is the last work of any importance that I shall ever write, and I can only wish it were more worthy of your patronage'.

Thus the wild youth mellowed into the wise old man, to his contemporaries the epitome of sound common sense. It was a transformation due in no small measure to the influence of Benedictine spirituality opening him to the power of God which, as so many saints reassuringly prove, works on the most unlikely materials. Ullathorne was both a truly human and a truly spiritual man, like all great Christians; his gruff exterior hid a warm and sensitive heart with a deep capacity for friendship. Like his Order he was large of spirit and never small-minded. Bishop Hedley, who saw him above all as a man of prayer, describes him as 'a real man, rooted and founded in unmistakable solid earth, a man who might rebuff you but would never pass you false coin'. His sound practical grip of men and human affairs was rooted in his intense life of prayer instilled by his monastic training, which made him so much a man in, but not of, the world.

These were the qualities which made him such a great bishop, a real father of his clergy, his nuns and his people. He handed on to his successor his diocese of Birmingham, second to none in organization, equipment, vigorous life, corporate spirit, and above all, in its devoted body of clergy. The statistics of the diocese reflect his achievement. Under Ullathorne over forty new missions were founded, sixty-seven churches and more than a hundred elementary schools built. The number of priests grew from eighty-six to two hundred and of convents of women from seven to thirty-six. Most remarkable of all, instead of a single charitable institution there were many new orphanages, asylums and hospitals. Newman's tribute in an address of 1871 fittingly summarizes the greatness of Ullathorne's pastoral ministry:

> My Lord, we come before you with this address, young and old; but whatever be our age according to the years that we have had experience of your governance, we gratefully recognize in you a vigilant unwearied Pastor; a tender Father; a Friend in need; an upright, wise and equitable Ruler; a Superior who inspires confidence by bestowing it; the zealous Ruler of his people; the Champion by word and pen of Catholic interests, religious and social; the Defender of the defenceless; the Vindicator of our sacred ordinances amid the conflict of political parties and the violence of theological hostility; a faithful Servant of his Lord, who by his life and conduct claims that cheerful obedience which we hereby, with a full heart, offer to you.

In short, as Ullathorne wrote of Saint Benedict, 'He has the gift of ruling men in religion with a power that is divinely humane'.

Ullathorne was granted the honorary title of archbishop of Cabasa in his last year. After a stroke which left him half-paralysed, he faced death with complete tranquillity. He died on St Benedict's Day, 21 March 1889, and marked the historical nature of the occasion by murmuring: 'The last of the Vicars Apostolic is passing'. He was indeed one of the last links with the three centuries of persecution for English Catholics. During the prayers for the dying, the words of the Litany 'From the snares of the devil deliver him, o Lord' evoked from him the snorted comment 'The devil's a jackass'.

The Mass of St Benedict was celebrated in his room, after which he is said to have passed quite consciously into a vision of his great patron surrounded by angels. Often his sinking memories must have returned to the uttermost parts of the sea and the strange lands he had travelled. In his wanderings however he never for a second lost sight of his true goal. His stability was that of the pilgrim and, as such, profoundly monastic. For he reminds us that ultimate monastic stability is not about places but about a Person. As he wrote to a nun from the confines of Warwick Gaol: 'If only we look away from our own subjective existence and look straight towards

Our Lord, who is always with us even when we are not with Him, we shall find all places alike. For God is our true place'.

by Dom Alexander Austin

BIBLIOGRAPHY

W. B. Ullathorne, *Autobiography* (London 1943).
Letters of Archbishop Ullathorne (London 1892).
C. Butler, *The Life and Times of Bishop Ullathorne* (London 1926).
G. A. Beck (ed.), *The English Catholics* 1850–1950 (London 1950).
W. B. Ullathorne, *The Endowments of Man* (London 1880).
  The Groundwork of the Christian Virtues (London 1882).
  Christian Patience (London 1886).

Benedictines of Today

The twentieth has been a good century for Benedictines; when Mr Harold Macmillan announced in 1964 that we had never had it so good, he was unwittingly furnishing an accurate summary of seventy years of Black Monk history. Fifteen years later, in monasticism as in politics, the Prime Minister's glad tidings would need re-appraisal, but nevertheless they contain a truth. It has already been noted that the nineteenth century was a time of recovery after the all-time low of the early 1800's when there were fewer Benedictine monasteries in Europe than at any other period since the days of St Gregory the Great; this recovery continued, even galloped, into the following century: Abbot Cuthbert Butler of Downside, delighting in statistics, noted that between 1800 and 1910 the monasteries increased by fifty per cent and the number of monks doubled. This was no flash in the pan; the 1960 statistics showed that in the previous seventy years the Benedictines, and indeed almost all the monastic bodies, had increased more rapidly than at any time since the early seventeenth century; in 1880 there had been 107 monasteries and 2,765 monks; in 1960 there were respectively 237 and 12,131.

The increase is remarkable because, on the face of it, this century has not been conducive to a growth of monastic life. The two world wars brought recruitment virtually to a standstill, and during these wars individual houses suffered badly—everyone knows what happened to Monte Cassino in 1944. Hitler's government suppressed six monasteries of the Austrian Congregation before and during the war, not to mention a number of houses in Germany; a similar policy was in operation after 1945 in those European countries which fell under Communist control. In Hungary eleven houses were suppressed in 1950 and only two remain: Pannonhalma and Györ. Two houses of the Slav Congregation have survived—the priories of Lubin in Poland and Cokovac in Jugoslavia. The monks of the other three houses have been forced to live outside the cloister.

In the Far East the Communists suppressed the monastery of Yenki in North Korea, a house of the St Ottilien Congregation, in 1946, and the monastery of Tokwon, of the same Congregation, in 1949. Some of the monks were able to return to Germany, others managed with great difficulty to reach South Korea where they established a house at Waegwan; but the other monks were put in prison from which they never emerged; some were slaughtered outright and the rest died of starvation. To all these factors which should in theory have inhibited the growth of monastic life, must be added the phenomenon of materialism which is characteristic of the twentieth century and which, like a Trojan horse, is potentially far more dangerous than an enemy at the gates.

As long ago as the ninth century King Alfred's biographer, Asser, wrote: 'He [Alfred] had no noble or freeman of his own nation who would of his own accord enter the monastic life for, indeed, for many years past the desire for monastic life had been utterly lacking in all that people—I know not why; either on account of the onslaughts of foreigners, who very often invaded by land or sea, or on account of the nation's too great abundance of riches of every kind, which I am much more inclined to think the reason for that contempt of the monastic life.' When one reflects that there is little to choose between our materialism and, say, the materialism of the late Roman Empire (indeed, if the fifth-century Romans had published a magazine, it would surely have borne a considerable resemblance to our weekend Colour Supplements), then the progress made by the Benedictines in our times becomes truly surprising.

How, then, do we explain the growth? Not all the reasons are clear, but it is significant that the growth-rate was highest in the years following the two world wars, i.e. between 1919 and 1925 and also in the 1950's; for example, the Swiss-American Benedictines had only five monasteries between 1900 and 1945 but founded eight between 1950 and 1960. World-wide, the number of vocations to Benedictine monasteries in the 1950's was greater than in any decade since 1880; of the 237 monasteries listed in 1960, thirty-two had come into existence after 1955. We seem to have here an application of Newton's Third Law of Motion, namely, that 'to every action there is an equal and opposite reaction': from the horrors of modern warfare to the reaffirmation of God. This has happened many times in history: it was from the decadence of Roman society that St Benedict 'dropped out' and formulated a new way of life; in England, in the wake of the ninth-century Viking invasions, came the magnificent tenth-century revival under St Dunstan. The phoenix arises sooner or later. And if it is true that Newton's Law is valid not only in Physics but in the life of the Spirit, then materialism can be seen as a positive boon to monasticism. A little materialism may be a dangerous thing, but a lot of it is absolutely splendid; as with over-indulgence in marzipan, a reaction is sure to come.

The most noteworthy areas of growth in the first half of the century were the United States, France and Germany. In 1965 the biggest of the sixteen Benedictine Congregations was the American

Cassinese, with a total of 2,045 monks in twenty monasteries, the biggest of them being St John's, Collegeville, with a community of three hundred and ninety-one. The United States also contained the fifth largest Benedictine Congregation, the Swiss-American. This numbered five independent monasteries in 1945; it began the 1950's with seven and by 1965 there were four more. By 1975 another four independent monasteries had raised the total to fifteen. But the Americans had no monopoly of expansion; the French province of the Subiaco Congregation was equally active, especially the monastery of La Pierre-qui-Vire which in 1965 had a community of 174 monks, not to speak of foundations in Cambodia, Madagascar and the Congo, made in 1951, 1955 and 1958 respectively. Finally, the German missionary Congregation of St Ottilien could boast a community of 279 monks belonging to St Ottilien itself, 304 at Münsterschwarzach, and a string of other large and important houses, particularly in East Africa where, for example, the monastery of Peramiho, with its community of 172 monks, ran forty mission stations, a major and a minor seminary, two leper colonies, twenty-three medical stations and a whole variety of schools from industrial to catechetical. At the same time the diocese of Eshowe in Zululand was in the hands of this Congregation, and it has been estimated that St Ottilien's African Mission stations looked after 232,000 Catholics.

A distinctive feature of monastic growth in this century is that it has carried the Rule to the southern hemisphere and to the East. At the moment the Subiaco Congregation has houses in every continent save North America; its most recent foundations have been in Brazil, the Congo, Madagascar and Vietnam. The Belgian Congregation (now known as the Congregation of the Annunciation) has made foundations in Angola, Zaïre and India; the Olivetans in Brazil, Mexico and Guatemala; the Silvestrines in India and Ceylon; and, as we have seen, the St Ottilien Congregation has focused its interest on Africa and Korea. A second point to note is that growth has occurred in every sort of Benedictine life, contemplative as well as active: in the Trappist and 'common observance' branches of the Cistercians, in the more austere and cloistered Black Monk Congregations, such as the French Province of the Subiaco Congregation, and also in the 'out-going' Congregations such as St Ottilien and the two American Congregations.

Nothing has so far been said of the most ancient Benedictine Congregation of all, the English Congregation. In 1960 it, too, might have been pardoned a feeling of quiet satisfaction, since from a total of four monasteries in 1900 it had increased to eleven. Of these four houses, one, Belmont, founded in 1859 as a common novitiate, did not achieve full independence until 1917; a fifth, Fort Augustus, had been outside the Congregation from 1883 to 1910. In that year a dependency of Downside Abbey in West London, at Ealing, was constituted as a Priory. Three other dependent Priories were founded between the wars—Portsmouth, Rhode Island in 1918; Washington, D.C. in 1924; and Worth in 1933. In the years following the second World War all four of these became independent and were raised to the rank of Abbeys. A tenth monastery was added when Buckfast joined the Congregation from Subiaco in 1960. The eleventh was the Priory at St Louis, Mo., founded from Ampleforth in 1955, and which did not gain its independence till thirteen years after 1960. The two older American foundations were the result of initiatives on the part of Americans who wished to see the English Congregation's interpretation of monastic life established in their own country; St Louis was founded by Ampleforth in answer to an invitation. Downside founded Ealing and Worth at times when there had been some increase of vocations. All these foundations were in their different ways characteristic of what we may call Benedictine expansionism. In 1960 there were six hundred and six monks in the Congregation, of which Ampleforth in Yorkshire had the largest share with a community of 145.

Also in England there was a remarkable growth in the Congregation of Subiaco. The senior house of its English province, Ramsgate, currently comprises thirty monks and usually provides an Abbot Visitor to the other houses. These consist of Prinknash and its foundations, now independent, at Farnborough and Pluscarden (Moray), which together number eighty monks. The Prinknash community began life in the Church of England in the late nineteenth century and gained celebrity when most of its members, then at Caldy Island, joined the Roman Catholic Church in 1914. Sixty-five years later, not a little modified, it offers a distinctive way of life, but one more traditionally Black Benedictine than its white habit suggests.

It is worth returning to the year 1960 to prod the anthill, so to speak, in an effort to see what was being done by Benedictines at that time. The metaphor is less facetious than it sounds, because Benedictine organization and activity defy simple description. For example, many people speak of the 'Benedictine Order', but they are wrong. An Order, in Abbot Cuthbert Butler's definition, is 'an organized corporate body composed of several houses, diffused through various lands, with centralized government and objects and methods of its own'; an Order such as this the Benedictines manifestly are not. For one thing, there is no central government;

for another, Benedictine monks of different houses would hotly deny that their aims and objects were identical. The correct description of the Benedictines is that they are a Confederation of Congregations. As we have seen, there were fifteen such Congregations in 1960.

These Congregations, however, constitute a trap for the unwary. One would assume that the Belgian Congregation operated in Belgium, the Swiss in Switzerland, the English in England. Wrong again: there are English Benedictines in America, Swiss in Brazil, Belgians in Peru, not to mention French in Vietnam, Italians in Guatemala and Germans in Korea. The only safe path through this luxuriant jungle is to think of Benedictines in terms of the work they do. Broadly speaking—very broadly speaking—some Congregations are 'active' while others are 'contemplative', i.e. reducing external works to a minimum and laying the stress on seclusion and prayer. Thus, within the compass of the British Isles, the monastery of Quarr on the Isle of Wight, which belongs to the French Solesmes Congregation, is 'contemplative', as are the Cistercians and the Prinknash houses, while all the monasteries of the English Congregation are 'active'—for example, they administer schools and parishes. Any Benedictine reader will writhe at the use of the terms 'active' and 'contemplative'; they so easily suggest that active monks are given to no contemplation and contemplative monks are given to no action; but, *faute de mieux*, the labels may be allowed. A far more serious snag about using work as a criterion is that it can insidiously and falsely become *the* criterion, with the implication that only those monasteries which are 'active' are useful. Such a view is wholly alien to the Benedictine mentality; as Abbot Cuthbert Butler wrote, 'the real use of a monastic house lies not in activities and usefulness. It lies rather in things that cannot be counted by statistics or estimated by results'. Monks exist primarily for the direct adoration of the unseen God; good works and utilities will surely follow, but they are by-products. This point cannot be made too forcibly.

Given these important qualifications, we can examine the visible activities of the Benedictines in the years before the Second Vatican Council. Like all things Benedictine, they are not easy to categorize: one handbook gives ten headings: academic study, fine arts, printing and publishing; schools and institutes; parishes; hospitality; missions; ecumenism; periodicals; other publications. These ten may legitimately be reduced to three: scholarly work, pastoral work and education.

a. *Scholarly work*. St Benedict made no specific provision in his Rule for scholars, but his stipulation that several hours a day should be set aside for reading has meant that it has always been possible for Benedictine monasteries to be places of erudition. The first real

monastic scholar was the Venerable Bede, and his 'delight in learning, teaching and writing' has been a characteristic of at least some
Benedictines from that day to this. In the twentieth century certain
Congregations have been justly renowned for their scholarship: for
example the Solesmes and Beuron Congregations. Solesmes itself
has reconstructed and made available the ancient monastic chant,
and has also produced, among other publications, a critical edition
of the works of John of St Thomas. Ligugé, which since 1905 has
produced the scholarly *Revue Mabillon*, is important for its work on
monastic history. Clervaux, also of the Solesmes Congregation,
supplied a community in 1933 for the Pontifical Abbey of San
Girolamo in Rome, with the task (recently completed) of working on
a critical text of the Latin Vulgate. Dom Jean Leclercq is perhaps its
most widely known scholar of to-day. The Beuronese Congregation
has made itself equally famous in this century: the houses of Beuron
and Maria Laach were leading lights in the liturgical movement
before the Second Vatican Council, Maria Laach being a focal
point for liturgical and historical research under Abbot Herwegen
and Dom Odo Casel. More recently Beuron has produced a critical
edition of the Old Latin Bible. Perhaps the most distinguished abbey
of the Congregation in this century has been Maredsous in Belgium
(it now belongs to the Belgian 'Congregation of the Annunciation').
The second abbot of this house was an Irishman, Dom Columba
Marmion, one of the most widely read spiritual writers of the last
seventy years. He was influential in the founding of Glenstal, in
Ireland, now an abbey. He also presided over a galaxy of scholarly
talent: the historians Dom Ursmer Berlière, Dom Germain Morin
and Dom Philibert Schmitz; also the English patristic and scriptural
scholar, Dom John Chapman, who was later to become abbot of
Downside. Since 1881 Maredsous has edited and produced the
Revue Bénédictine, the leading periodical on patristic literature and
monastic history. Famous herself, Maredsous has also been honoured
in her children: Mont-César at Louvain excelled in historical and
patristic studies and carried out a liturgical apostolate among the
clergy, while Saint-André at Bruges was known for the more popular
liturgical work of Dom Gaspar Lefèbvre and its scriptural scholarship. Mention should also be made of the monastery of Steenbrugge
in Belgium, of the Subiaco Congregation; though small (thirty-three
monks in 1960) it had undertaken the vast enterprise of editing the
Corpus Christianorum, which aims at presenting in 120 volumes a new
critical text of the writers printed in Migne's great collection,
together with works of these and other authors omitted by Migne.

Most of these scholars belong to 'contemplative' houses, but to put
matters in perspective, to show that scholarship is not incompatible

with life in an 'active' monastery, and also to speak of things nearer home, it is worth recording that the English Congregation has not been without its great names in this century. Dom John Chapman belongs at least as much to Downside as to Maredsous; Dom David Knowles acquired at Downside his interest in history which would eventually lead him to the Regius Professorship at Cambridge. Dom Hugh Connolly is regarded as having demonstrated that the 'Egyptian Church Order' is to be regarded as the same as the 'Apostolic Tradition' of St Hippolytus. Two other Downside monks, Dom Cuthbert Butler and Dom Thomas Symons, are rightly honoured for their work in monastic history: Cuthbert Butler's *Benedictine Monachism* (which is more than a work of history) is a classic, and Dom Thomas's name is a household word to those medievalists who interest themselves in anything to do with the reform movement of the tenth-century Church. And a later Abbot Butler of Downside, Christopher Butler, now auxiliary bishop in Westminster diocese, has been an author of consequence in the field of New Testament studies. The first Abbot Butler was accustomed to say that there were only two-and-a-half learned Benedictine abbeys—Maredsous, Farnborough and Downside (the half)—but he did allow Downside the half.

b. *Pastoral work*. Apostolic work by Benedictines has a long and illustrious tradition behind it. The Rule itself makes no provision for any activity that has an end or purpose outside the monastic precincts: 'The monastery should, if possible, be so arranged that all necessary things . . . may be within the enclosure, so that monks may not be compelled to wander outside it, for that is not at all expedient for their souls' (Ch. 66); but the conditions of the times after St Benedict's death soon involved the monks in external activities. There was the whole of northern Europe to convert to Christianity and this work could not and would not have been carried out by others. Thus, between about 700 and 1000 Benedictines were very active in the missionary field; as evidence of this, the titles Apostle of the English, Apostle of Holland, Apostle of Germany, Apostle of Sweden, Apostle of the Wends and Apostle of the Prussians all belong to Benedictine monks. Much later, in the seventeenth century, English Benedictines took part in the dangerous mission to Protestant England and eight of them were executed for their trouble. In the nineteenth century two Benedictines, Dom Bernard Ullathorne, later to be a bishop, and Bishop Polding, launched a mission to Australia.

It is unsurprising therefore to find twentieth-century Benedictines still heavily involved in missionary work. The St Ottilien Congregation was founded in 1884 specifically for this purpose; to Germans, remembering the conversion of their country by the Benedictine St Boniface (*c.* 675–775), it seemed natural to adopt the Rule as an effective and traditional means of spreading the Gospel. Before the colonial upsets of the 1950's the St Ottilien Congregation had founded numerous abbeys or priories in Korea, East Africa, Zulu- land and Venezuela, with the three German houses of St Ottilien, Münsterschwarzach and Schweiklberg acting as recruiting abbeys. The two abbeys in East Africa, Peramiho and Ndanda, both abbeys *nullius* (i.e. where the abbot has full jurisdiction over a territory which is outside all diocesan control) contained more than two hundred monks, and before the Korean War the monks had charge of two 'apostolic vicariates' (i.e. missionary administrative districts) in Korea and Manchuria. It was for missionary reasons that the monastery of La Pierre-qui-vire (of the French province of the Subiaco Congregation) made foundations in Vietnam, Cambodia, Madagascar and Morocco. Before the upheavals of the 1960's in Africa, the Belgian Congregation controlled the Apostolic Vicariate of Elizabethville (Katanga) and it also made foundations in China, India and Angola. It would seem that twentieth-century Benedic- tines had begun to rival the missionary activities of St Boniface and St Anscar eleven hundred years earlier.

Apart from mission—the work of evangelization—Benedictines have also been heavily involved in maintenance—the work of fostering the faith already planted. Of the 237 houses listed in 1960, 115 were involved in parish work. In St Benedict's day this situation could not arise, since there were no parishes and very few of his monks were priests, but the ordained monk became common very early in Benedictine history, and ever since Benedictines have been called upon to make up a shortage of pastoral clergy. This shortage has been particularly marked in our own times, which explains why the English Congregation is, and always has been, heavily involved in parish work. Ampleforth Abbey administered twenty-three parishes in the 1960's, and they were spread over South Wales, Cheshire, Lancashire, Yorkshire and Cumbria, absorbing the energies of one-third of the monastery's large community.

c. *Education.* St Gregory the Great tells us that St Benedict received boys into the monastery and there are several references in the Rule to *pueri* and *infantes.* These boys were intended to be monks, dedicated to the service of God from their infancy by their parents (in those days 'vocations', like marriages, were often arranged, with no consultation with the parties concerned. The modern concept of a 'vocation' would have been as incomprehensible then as the idea of marrying for love). Thus, there were 'children of the cloister' and claustral schools from the earliest times. Later on, 'external' schools

were established, in which monks taught a few boys destined, not for
monastic life, but for careers in the world, either as clerics or laymen.
Such schools, always comparatively small, were envisaged by St
Boniface and were opened in the various monasteries he established
in an overwhelmingly illiterate society. The legislation of Charlemagne, though often unfulfilled, endorsed this initiative. The great
Benedictine family of Cluny, which made the prayer of the liturgy,
as it were, the *raison d'être* of monasticism, was hostile to these
schools; for this and other reasons, such as the growth of the
cathedral schools and the later arrival of the Friars, education
gradually passed from the hands of the Benedictines.

The schools were revived after the Reformation—partly because
the age of copying and illumination of manuscripts, the traditional
work of monks, had come to an end, partly because Catholic education was at a premium—since then external schools have become
common in Benedictine monasteries. In the twentieth century
secondary education, whether in boarding schools or in day-schools,
became one of the commonest forms of Benedictine external work,
particularly in the Austrian, Swiss, Bavarian, English, Swiss-
American and American Cassinese Congregations. 100 of the 237
houses listed in 1965 were concerned with the running of schools,
some of them as small as thirty pupils, and others as large as 800.
All eleven houses of the English Congregation run schools, catering
for a total of about 4,200 pupils. The biggest of these are Ealing
(750), Ampleforth (700) and Downside (560). Growth has been the
keynote in the twentieth century; for example, St Louis Priory in
America, founded from Ampleforth in 1955, opened a school in
1956 with thirty pupils; by 1973 there were well over 300.

It is not often that a Benedictine house can have a finger in each
of the activities mentioned, scholarship, pastoral work and education, but a few of them do so and one of these, St John's Abbey,
Collegeville, Minnesota, may serve as an example. St John's, of the
American-Cassinese Congregation, was founded in 1856; by 1960 it
had a community of 391 monks—the nearest thing in modern times,
perhaps, to the great monasteries of the Middle Ages. An official
(1973) list of its activities runs as follows:

1. *Academic study:* Monastic Manuscript Microfilm Library. Founded 1965 to safeguard ancient manuscripts, and to make them
   available to American scholars. More than 20,000 codices of
   pre-1600 material in Austria, and some 300 others in Italy,
   Hungary and Poland have been microfilmed. This amounts to an
   estimated 140,000 treatises, essays, chronicles and poems,
   covering some 8,000,000 pages. The work is continuing in Austria

at the present time and will be taken up in other countries as
time goes on.

2. *Printing and publishing:* The Liturgical Press, Collegeville,
Minnesota 56311, publishes liturgical texts and books on Liturgy,
Scripture and Theology.

3. *Schools and Institutes:* Schools conducted by monks of St John's
Abbey:

At Collegeville: St John's University, 1500 College students.
St John's School of Divinity, 48 students. St John's Graduate
School of Theology, 33 students. St John's Preparatory School
(High School), 272 students.

At Minneapolis: Benilde Benedictine High School for boys,
600 students.

Institute for Mental Health: Founded 1953. Deals with problems
of youth, marriage counselling, the aged, retirement and the
psychology of death.

Center for the Study of Local Government: Founded 1967. Research
institute for studying the problems of society with special emphasis
on the non-metropolitan areas.

Hill Program for Tutorial Learning: Founded 1971. A special
program for a limited number of college students who wish to
specialize in subjects of their personal choice.

Minnesota Educational Radio: An educational FM Radio broadcasting program over KSJR-FM (90.1 kc, 150,000 watts), with
three broadcasting towers, one at Collegeville, another in
Minneapolis, and a third in the Fargo-Moorhead area. Founded
1966. The station also broadcasts programs for the blind over a
special wave-length.

4. *Parishes in charge of monks of St John's Abbey:* 33 parishes in the
State of Minnesota, with 11 mission churches affiliated. Two large
parishes with 40,000 souls each in New York City, N.Y.

Chaplaincies at convents, hospitals, nursing homes and State
Institutions: 18.

Military Chaplaincies: 3.

5. *Missions:* in Nassau, Bahamas; Humacao, Puerto Rico; Tokyo,
Japan.

6. *Ecumenism: Institute for Ecumenical and cultural Research:* Founded
1968. Ten competent scholars from all parts of the world are
selected each year to live in residence at the Institute for one year.
One of the Fathers of the abbey is the Director of the Institute.
The resident scholars do research in ecumenism and form a center
of concern for the unity of the churches.

*Interdenominational Continuing Education Program for Clergy in
Minnesota.* A program designed to aid ministers, rabbis and

priests in the continuing process of personal learning, deepening of their ministerial vocations, so that they may serve the Church more effectively and meaningfully in its contemporary needs.

7. *Publications: Worship*—A Review concerned with the problems of liturgical renewal. Founded 1926. Published ten times a year.

Sisters Today—A Review to explore the role of the religious woman in the Church in our time. Founded 1929. Published ten times a year.

The Bible Today—A Periodical promoting popular appreciation of the Word of God. Founded 1961. Published six times a year.

And so to the sixties, a decade of turmoil in every area of life, and therefore in monasticism as well. Perhaps the quickest way to see what happened in the sixties is to open a booklet published in 1969 by the American-Cassinese Congregation, of which St John's, Collegeville, is a conspicuous member; the booklet, entitled 'Renew and Create' is a statement on the American-Cassinese Benedictine monastic life, and it makes it clear from the beginning that the halcyon days of the fifties are over. Here are some extracts from its second chapter:

No one who reads the signs of the times can be surprised that our monasteries to-day should be experiencing unusual tensions and strain. For our communities mirror the ferment that pervades the whole of society and the Church itself, in what the Second Vatican Council in hope has called a crisis in growth . . . we are taking part in a cultural evolution so rapid and so profound that to many it appears to be a revolution . . . our communities are facing a critical time, a decisive turning point in their history. (pp. 10, 15, 23)

In the same year, 1969, David Knowles published his *Christian Monasticism*, in which he wrote:

In the past four or five years, a sudden and unforeseen change has come about. Throughout the Church there has been a profound movement of sentiment and a strange division of mind. On the one hand, there has been the enthusiasm of forces released from bondage and springing forward to action, and on the other a profound malaise and questioning. Nowhere is this more apparent than in the monastic sector of the Church's life, where, for the moment at least, there is a keen sense of landmarks lost and of low visibility on the road ahead. (p. 224)

Periods of rapid and dramatic change are at once the delight and the despair of historians; it is exhilarating to write of crucibles and melting-pots and watersheds, but very difficult to say exactly what happened. Usually we are left with a partially completed jigsaw, of which some of the pieces can seem bizarre indeed. To give a parallel from medieval monastic history: in the second half of the eleventh century there occurred an extraordinary flowering and diversification of the religious life—this was the period which saw the foundation of the Carthusians, the Cistercians and the Augustinian Canons, and other new religious institutions; Black Benedictines lost their monopoly in the religious life of Europe, never to regain it.

These religious developments reflected and were a part of a rapid process of growth in every sector of European society, a growth so striking that it has been called 'the most striking fact in medieval history'. The whole mood of Europe changed: the men who went on the First Crusade at the end of the eleventh century were aggresive, assertive, self-confident, superior, brash; this was very different from the fear and insecurity of, say, the ninth and tenth centuries. Behind this psychological change lay a profound economic change: for the first time Europe was becoming an area of surplus population and surplus productivity; urban life was reviving, waste land was being reclaimed, colonization was beginning. This economic change was itself partly dependent—and here come some of the bizarre pieces of the jigsaw—on an improvement in the climate of Europe about the year 1000 and on the much wider use of a more efficient type of plough. The present chapter is not intended to be a history lesson but the example of the eleventh century is instructive: we see economic, social and technological change bearing down on and altering everyday life and monastic life alike; there is a corresponding alteration of psychological and spiritual attitudes; in particular, the old, traditional way of Benedictine life was felt by some to be not good enough. St Anselm (1033–1109), seeking the monastic life in the 1050's, considered Cluny but looked elsewhere; the life there, he felt, gave too much time to the liturgy and too little to study and reading. The Cistercians, who were founded in 1098, broke away from traditional Benedictine life because they wanted greater seclusion, simplicity and poverty, with more opportunity for personal, private prayer. The same desire for personal rather than corporate religious experience lay behind the foundation of the Carthusian Order by St Bruno in the 1080's.

Nine hundred years later, in the 1960's, the feeling that 'this will not do' reappeared in our society. While students rioted in Paris and hippies and flower-people 'dropped out' in San Francisco, monks of every sort of monastic observance began to question the very fundamentals of monastic life. There have been tensions in

Christian monasticism throughout history, but previously the struggle had been between laxity and zeal, between mediocrity and strict observance, and the end to be attained had been clear— greater fidelity to the Rule; in short, there had always been general agreement as to the ideal. In the 1960's, however, monastic ideals themselves were brought into question; the prevailing mood was captured in everyday speech, where it became fashionable to give our nouns the prefix 'a crisis of'. There was no longer authority but 'a crisis of authority', not obedience but a 'crisis of obedience'. Certain words became 'hurrah' words, others became 'boo' words. Thus freedom, authenticity, honesty, conscience became 'hurrah' words, while tradition, celibacy, obedience and authority were well up in the 'boo' category.

If the parallel of the eleventh century is a valid one, then the ultimate causes of the turmoil of the sixties will indeed be far to seek, and the volcano must have been grumbling for many years before; the chain reaction began with technological change and passed through psychology to religion. Thus, for example, advances in technology certainly led to a pre-occupation with the wonders of this world which in turn led to a lack of interest in 'ultimate' questions and to secularization, i.e. a loss of the sense of the sacred. It was then only a question of time before the whole concept underlying monasticism, which is a kingdom not of this world, was challenged. Or let us pick out another strand in the tangled skein: we now have a heightened sense of history; i.e., we are now more aware that human thought and human institutions are historically conditioned, that doctrines and structures come to birth, grow and then die. It will soon be seen that in such a climate of thought an appeal to a venerable past might not carry much weight. In the 1960's people, monks included, insisted that they wanted, not custom and tradition but truth and authenticity. 'Relevance' became the slogan that one so often heard; against a background of horrific modern wars, the massacre of the Jews, persistent racial discrimination and other attacks on humanity, ethical systems of the past were seen as being both irrelevant and futile. Thus those in authority who appealed to a past which had been good enough for them were politely or impolitely ignored. This is a classic case of history repeating itself: St Anselm, whom we have already mentioned, tried to persuade his monks at Bec and Canterbury in the eleventh century that their personal religion was by no means hindered by a mass of customary regulations:

> If a monk thinks he could achieve better and greater things with more spiritual fervour than the customs of his present monastery

allow, he should consider that he may be mistaken, or at least let him think that he doesn't deserve what he desires. Let him patiently bear the divine judgement, which doesn't deny anything unjustly to any man.

Anselm was no more successful in his century than many another religious superior in ours.

It was not just a question of disruptive attitudes and ideas breaking in on the Church from outside, attitudes one could repulse as from a stronghold; these attitudes were becoming part of Christian thinking itself. In some cases the very action of the Church contributed to the sense of uneasiness. For example, the introduction of the new liturgy in the Roman Catholic Church, for whatever excellent reasons, had some disturbing implications: if the Church was willing to set aside the ancient liturgy, hallowed by hundreds of years of use, then nothing was safe. For some, this feeling that 'anything (or everything) goes' was a matter for rejoicing; for others, it was cause for deep disquiet. In this way developments inside and outside the Church conspired to discredit the past.

Again, there can be little doubt that the introduction of the new liturgy contributed, however unwittingly, to an erosion of the sense of the sacred. The old Mass certainly could give a sense of otherness, of mystery, of the numinous, whereas the new Mass is often innocent of all three. The same criticism could be made of the abolition of the old law which demanded fasting from midnight before receiving Communion, of the introduction of the practice of receiving Communion standing and in the hand, and of many other similar changes. The reader may object that these are very small matters, but unfortunately nothing is calculated to generate more heat, particularly among the clergy, than liturgical change. To this day there are Catholics who refuse point-blank to attend a vernacular Mass, who say that attendance would be sinful, and that the validity of such a Mass is extremely doubtful. Unjustifiable as this may be, it highlights an attitude that was common among Catholics, namely, that the Church is and should be beyond change. When this view was undermined in the sixties, the implications were profound. It was not merely the unchangeable liturgy that changed: theological opinions which had previously been accepted as though they were practically defined doctrines of faith were set aside, attacked, discarded or re-expressed; an example would be the attempt in the sixties to re-formulate the doctrine of the Eucharist using terms such as 'transignification' or 'transfinalisation'. Theologies came and went, implying that nothing was certain, nothing safe.

An interesting and far less perceptible development was the

emergence of what may be termed a new theology of the world. Which way the wind was blowing was perhaps first indicated by Teilhard de Chardin when he dedicated his *Milieu Divin* to 'those who love the world'. Such a dedication would have been quite impossible in an earlier climate of Catholic thought; any reader of the 'Imitation of Christ' will know that in the author's view the world is the very last thing one should love. The author of the 'Imitation' had good scriptural backing: 'You must not love this passing world', says St John, 'or anything that is in the world. The love of the Father cannot be in any man who loves the world, because nothing the world has to offer—the sensual body, the lustful eye, pride in possessions—could ever come from God the Father, but only from the world; and the world, with all its craves for, is coming to an end' (I Jn ii, 15–16). Teilhard, of course, could claim the authority of another text, also from St John: 'God loved the world so much that he gave his only Son . . . God sent his Son into the world not to condemn the world, but so that through him the world might be saved' (Jn iii, 16, 17). This is not a matter of a slanging match using biblical texts; what it really showed was that a new attitude could be taken to 'the world', and in recent years the Church has taken it. The Second Vatican Council made it quite clear that the Church is and should be deeply concerned with the world, with what used to called, somewhat disparagingly, 'the merely human' or 'merely natural'. The Church looked at the world and saw, like God somewhat earlier, that it was good, indeed, very good. But this new attitude had important ramifications for monks who are, by definition, people who are in some sense separated from the world. For many centuries *fuga mundi*, flight from the world, had been advocated as a good move because the world was well worth flying from. But, by re-instating the world, the Church implicitly made the whole notion of *fuga mundi* problematical: should monks be separated from the world? Separated in what sense and to what extent? As we shall see, this question of separation from the world is one of the most hotly debated topics among monks; the whole question of monastic work—what monks should or shouldn't do—depends on it.

What has been said makes no pretence of giving a comprehensive analysis of what happened in the sixties; if ever that becomes possible it will require a sort of hindsight which we are not yet able to achieve. It is sufficient to note that there was considerable upset in that decade and that the monastic body suffered as a result. From all the religious Orders there was an exodus of individuals of all ages; at the same time there was a shortage of recruits which was without recent parallel as a universal phenomenon except in times

12

of war. This is reflected in official statistics: in 1960, as already noted, there were 12,131 Benedictines in sixteen Congregations and 237 monasteries. Fifteen years later, in 1975, although the number of Congregations had risen to twenty-one, the number of monks had fallen to 10,324; this represents a decrease of almost fifteen per cent. Statistics for individual Congregations have the same tale to tell: comparing the 1960 and 1975 figures, the American-Cassinese Congregation went from 1,998 to 1,638; the Subiaco Congregation from 1,846 to 1,468; St Ottilien from 1,250 to 1,182; the French Congregation, which had meanwhile given birth to the new Dutch Congregation, from 1,066 to 783.

Interpretation of these figures is a matter for disagreement among Benedictines; for some they are a warning of impending doom; for others they represent a hopeful and healthy sign of growing pains leading to a renewed form of Benedictine life. But such divergent interpretations share a common ground: each in its own way is an admission that Benedictine communities are facing a time of crisis, using 'crisis' in its limited sense of turning point, a moment when development must move in one direction or another. It is time to examine Benedictine monasticism in the 1970's.

There is still considerable turmoil in our world—one thinks of the wars and rumours of wars in Africa, the Middle East, the Far East and Northern Ireland, for example. And yet in many ways the 1970's have been a much more quiet and peaceful decade in the West that the 1960's. Young people, for instance, are far more positive, conservative and amenable than they were ten years ago; drugs and student riots have not made so many headlines as they used to. In monasteries, too, life is more peaceful; those who wanted to leave have left, and there are signs that monastic recruitment is recovering. We seem to be in a period of relative stability, and monks are using this time to examine critically their structures, their way of life and their external works. They seem to be far more aware now than ever before of developments in the outside world and more attentive to what Benedictine life means or ought to mean. Reappraisal and renewal are the keywords in our days; this was demanded of monks by the Second Vatican Council and is also required by common sense after the upheavals of the sixties; considerable self-examination is being carried out by monks. As we have seen, the American-Cassinese monks issued *Renew and Create* in June 1969; at about the same time the Swiss-American Congregation produced *Covenant of Peace*; finally, in 1978, the English Benedictine Congregation published *Consider your Call*, a theology of monastic life today, which had been eight years in the making. Monasteries and Congregations throughout the world have held endless community meetings, discussions, congresses and seminars. The criteria for renewal of the monastic life have been described by the Second Vatican Council as follows: a return to the sources (i.e. the Gospels, the spirit of St Benedict and the sound traditions of the past), followed by adaptation to the changed conditions of our times. We are asked to revise our Constitutions (general laws, interpreting the Rule for each Congregation) and these revisions should contain 'an apt and accurate formulation in which the spirit and aims of the founder shall be clearly recognised and faithfully preserved'. Expressed more succinctly, Benedictine monks today have to work out what St Benedict would do if he were alive now.

At this point the general reader will need to be made aware that Benedictine monks disagree, and have always disagreed, about the nature of Benedictinism. Differences of opinion usually begin over two allied topics—separation from the world and work. Some Benedictines, as we have seen, are very separated from the world and lead what we have called a 'contemplative' life; others are deeply immersed in external activities—for example, apostolic work and education, and these are the so-called 'active' houses. Thus Martha and Mary are alive and well in modern Benedictinism, and their wrangling in the Gospel is still with us. Sometimes the disagreement has been acrimonious and then one is more inclined to think of the two harlots before King Solomon. Given that there are several different interpretations of the Rule, one must perforce adopt one of three propositions: all interpretations are right; some are right and some are wrong; all are wrong. The third view was sometimes heard in the sixties, but presumably those who held it have made other arrangements, so we are left with the first two; and it is the second, the view that certain interpretations are definitely wrong, that has been most common in history.

Let the reader not imagine that such discussions are purely academic; the very life of a monastery, the whole 'success' of its work, depends on finding the correct solution to this intellectual problem. For example, some would say that the Benedictines suffered in the 1960's because they deserved to suffer; they were not faithful to the Rule and therefore they paid the penalty: 'since you have rejected the word of Yahweh, he has rejected you'. This is precisely the view taken of an earlier cataclysm by David Knowles at the end of his magnificent survey of religious life in England up to the Dissolution of the monasteries by Henry VIII; his ultimate paragraph contains the following:

At the end of this long review of monastic history, with its splendours and its miseries, and with its rhythm of recurring rise and fall, a monk cannot but ask what message for himself and for his brethren the long story may convey. It is the old and simple one; only in fidelity to the Rule can a monk or a monastery find security. A Rule is a safe path, and it is for the religious the only safe path . . . it comes as a sure guide to one who seeks God, and who seeks that he may indeed find. When a religious house or a religious Order ceases to direct its sons to the abandonment of all that is not God . . . it sinks to the level of a purely human institution, and whatever its works may be, they are the works of time and not of eternity.

Quarrels about the correct interpretation of the Rule go back at least to the twelfth century when St Bernard, abbot of the Cistercian monastery of Clairvaux, clashed famously with Peter the Venerable, abbot of Cluny. St Bernard said quite flatly, as was his wont, that Cluny was unfaithful to the Rule; life there left no time for manual labour or *lectio divina* which St Benedict had clearly intended for his monks; the Cluniacs transgressed the Rule in matters of food, drink and clothing, etc. etc. Notice the burden of St Bernard's argument: Cluny is unfaithful to the Rule because it has chosen the wrong work, the wrong activity—Cluniacs spend, and should not spend, too much of their time on the liturgy (some years earlier Peter Damian had remarked that he did not see how a Cluniac monk had time to commit any sin, save possibly one of thought). If we move forward to the twentieth century, we find that the topic of work is still at the centre of Benedictine discussion; two quotations will make clear the extent of the disagreement. First, Abbot Cuthbert Butler in *Benedictine Monachism*, which he published in 1919:

> The advantages they (schools) afford are very great. The work is compatible with living in community; it complies with St Benedict's admonition that monks ought to live on their own labour. Lastly, teaching stands the test of true work, both as a serious monotonous grind, involving very real physical fatigue, and as a useful contribution to the work of the world. Indeed it may be thought that the work in modern times which is most conformable in character to St Benedict's agriculture is the cultivation of the minds and characters of the young, the eradication of faults, and the implanting of virtues and of knowledge. (pp. 375-6)

The second quotation is from David Knowles's *Christian Monasticism*, which appeared in 1969:

> It is difficult to see how the running of a large school can be reconciled in the modern world with the monastic vocation . . .

in Europe and America, and nowhere more than in England, the whole conception and scope of education have changed. The schools are large, and a number of monks must be regularly absent from many conventual duties, unless the monastic time-table is dislocated and to a certain extent deformed. The masters must immerse themselves in the subjects taught to the higher classes, they must take an interest in athletics of all kinds, and in the political and cultural interests of the world, in order to be able to meet their pupils on an equality to influence their educa-tion. Moreover, a schoolmaster's life, with its alternation of absorbing and exhausting duties in term time, and reaction and lack of mental and spiritual energy in vacations, is at variance with monastic tranquillity. (pp. 242–3)

A parallel to all this can be found in the history of the Protestant Reformation in the sixteenth century: the Reformers appealed to *sola Scriptura*, the Bible and nothing but the Bible, while the Catholics insisted that correct belief was determined by both Scripture and tradition. Education and apostolic work, David Knowles would argue (with the Cistercians), should find no place in monastic life, because they have no place in the Rule, and the Rule is the only sure guide. Not granted, others would say, because although not found *tel quel* in the Rule, these activities are sanctioned by tradition; the Vatican Council says that renewal will be achieved by a return to the sources and also to the 'sound traditions' of the religious body: *ergo* . . . It would also doubtless be pointed out by those who oppose David Knowles's view that there are plenty of examples of 'legitimate development' in other sectors of the Church's life; doctrine develops, as any Catholic knows, even though Revelation ended with Christ, God's last word. The Last Supper is still recognizable in the Roman Catholic Pontifical High Mass. We have been instructed to re-capture the spirit and aims of St Benedict, but it is clear that these aims changed within his own lifetime; at first he felt called to 'drop out' and be a hermit but then, because he was asked to, he organized and legislated for a type of communal life 'in association with many brethren'. There was a need, and he supplied it. He was, as the Vatican Council document would put it, 'adapting to the changed conditions' of his times.

One way not to answer the question is to leave the world out of monastic reckoning: 'The world forgetting, by the world forgot' is an old definition of the monk, and often used; but it is a bad defini-tion; it is, and always has been, untrue. Those familiar with Tolkien's *Lord of the Rings* may remember the words of Gildor to Frodo, hobbit of the Shire: ' "It is not you own Shire", said Gildor.

"Others dwelt here before hobbits were; and others will dwell here again when hobbits are no more. The wide world is all about you; you can fence yourselves in, but you cannot for ever fence it out".' Whether they like it or not, monks must cultivate the quality of relevance; the danger of irrelevance is one for which English monks have paid dearly in the past. Describing the twilight that gathered round English monasticism in the century leading up to the Dissolution, David Knowles wrote:

> The tide of English social and economic life was running very strongly out to the new and the unknown, whilst the monasteries, like hulks embedded in the mud far up among the meadows of a creek of the Tamar or the Fal, whither the spring tides had borne them so long ago, saw the ebb falling past them without a thought that they were losing any hope they might have had of riding the flood across the bar and out to sea.

Too often relevance to the world has been derided as a quality inapplicable to, or unworthy of, monks and monasteries, but such derision betrays an imperfect knowledge of monastic history. Even the Cistercians, who made 'flight from the world' one of their loudest slogans in the twelfth century and who tried so hard to be as irrelevant as possible, were unwittingly answering one of the most deeply felt needs of their time, the need for deep, personal communion with God. They gave the 'customer' what he wanted and needed; hence, and because their juridical and economic arrangements were so appropriate, the astonishing growth of the Cistercian Order between 1115 and 1153. St Benedict, too, as we have seen, gave just what was needed in his own day. It will be noted that 'relevance' does not mean 'fashionable' or 'gimmicky'; nor does it mean providing material goods and nothing more. In the two cases of St Benedict and the Cistercians, relevance consisted in satisfying the deepest aspirations and needs of their contemporaries. In our own day, perhaps more urgently than at any time before, it is important for monks to concentrate on, and to assess, what is going on outside; partly because contemporary developments are fast-moving and complicated and therefore require concentration; partly because the needs of our contemporaries are very great. From monks, to whom a great deal has been given, much will be expected. Renewal, therefore, certainly means attentiveness to 'what the Spirit is saying to the Churches', and the Spirit works in human events that surround us.

What form a Benedictine contribution to the world might take in our times cannot be determined by a decision at 'Headquarters' because the Benedictines, not being an Order, have no Headquarters. This is an enormous asset and gives each monastery a wonderful opportunity to do what is best in circumstances which are thoroughly familiar to the community concerned. Sometimes the contribution might be on the spiritual level, sometimes on the spiritual and material together. The phrase 'the spiritual level' may sound anaemic on paper; in practice it involves what might be called 'hospitality of the soul'. St Benedict gave a high priority to guests in his Rule—'Let all guests that come be received like Christ, for he will say: "I was a stranger and you took me in".'—and he made detailed provision for their comfort and well-being. In our own time the guests that come, or who need to come, are more often than not already well provided for materially; their poverty is of another sort: they look for rest, peace, counsel, reassurance, compassion, a meaning to their lives, a way to God. This spiritual level is one on which every sort of monastery, active or contemplative, can and should operate. In other places and other circumstances the spiritual will not be enough: for example, in Peru, where one house of the English Congregation has a foundation, it is unrealistic to attempt to evangelize the people unless one is also prepared to ensure that they have food to eat, a roof over their heads and medicine to heal their diseases. As St John says: 'If a man who was rich enough in this world's goods saw that one of his brothers was in need, but closed his heart to him, how could the love of God be living in him? Our love is not to be just words or mere talk, but something real and active' (I Jn iii, 17–18). The aim, of course, is to cater for the whole man, spiritual and material, but one must put first things first; it is not only armies that march on their stomachs; grace builds on nature.

Assuming that Benedictines are willing to read the signs of the times and to act on their insights, there is no reason why their contribution to the world should not be very substantial. At the same time, it must be a specifically Benedictine contribution. This for two reasons: Benedictines are, or should be, proud enough to think that they have something special to contribute; and secondly, for their own peace of mind, Benedictines must be convinced that they are correctly interpreting the mind of their founder. Putting it another way, no monastery can make a specifically Benedictine contribution to our society unless that monastery is faithful to the Rule. The fact that there is controversy about how to interpret the Rule has already been noted; the present writer, by inclination and by conviction, would hold that both the 'contemplative' and 'active' interpretations are legitimate because both safeguard the essentials of St Benedict's teaching.

These essentials can be more easily sensed than defined; first, anyone familiar with several monasteries, even of the same Congregation, will have been struck by the differences between them; not differences in detail or in horarium but palpable differences in atmosphere and ethos; each has its own 'flavour'; there is a distinctive 'feel' about each. The same is true of human families and the parallel is made deliberately because St Benedict's intention was, precisely, to found a family; that each monastery, therefore, should have its own distinctive atmosphere, attitude, allegiance, traditions, even its own brand of humour, is a healthy sign, a mark of authenticity. The monastic family is created by the vows, and this in several ways. First, Benedictines take their vows not to 'the Order' or to the Congregation but to a particular house; by taking the vows, a monk throws in his lot with a relatively small group of people. Secondly, since each monastery is autonomous, left to sink or swim by itself, the taking of vows creates a very close bond between the members of the community—somewhat like, but far deeper than, the affinity felt by the occupants of the same First World War trench. Thirdly, the vows themselves have a family intention: obedience, binding a monk to his abbot and to his brethren, is the virtue by which he puts others first. Stability (a vow invented by St Benedict) gives the monk roots, geographical and psychological; without this vow, a monastery might be a hotel but never a home. The third vow, *conversio morum*, which involves celibacy and common ownership of goods, ensures that the monk's belonging to and involvement in the family is complete; there is no-one and nothing (time, for example) that he can call his own.

The monastery is to be a family not merely theoretically or juridically but in fact; in other words the monks must be palpably committed to each other. One monk must show courtesy to another, have time for him, be concerned for him, not because they might happen to be 'on the same wavelength' but because they are both members of the same family. As St Benedict would say, the brethren must love one another. Being a Benedictine does not absolve a monk from being a Christian.

This family, like any other, must live together; it must eat together, work together, relax together. Most important of all, it must pray together. Prayer is the most important work of the monastic family and should be the distinctive mark of any monastery. In St Benedict's thinking, the first criterion of a monastic vocation is that a man 'truly seeks God' and prayer is the way *par excellence* by which God is found. Therefore a monastery which does not put prayer first has no right to call itself Benedictine. What other work should be undertaken by the monastery can be determined by two criteria, one negative and one positive. The negative criterion is that the work should not be destructive of either the prayer life or the family life of the house. The positive criterion is that the work should answer a genuine need, in the sense already defined; e.g. it might mean enriching the morally bankrupt or feeding those who are spiritually starved; but in any case the world must not be forgotten. Thus a monastery must be a family, a praying family, a family which is constantly attentive to God and alert for signs of his will concerning the world. We are all asked to be 'open to the Spirit', but Benedictine organization, or lack of it, gives Benedictine monks a wonderful opportunity to react quickly and flexibly to what the Spirit is saying to the churches in our society.

For David Knowles, writing in 1969, the future of monasticism appeared bleak:

> Those who live a stable, cloistered, liturgical life, in an age which has been shedding its traditions and its conventions, along with its sense of security and (on another level) its sense of mystery, are assailed with doubts as to the value, or indeed the psychological feasibility, of a liturgical secluded monastic life at the present day.

As for the active Benedictines, he remarks that

> it is very clear that their daily life is not precisely that of the Rule of St Benedict to which they have taken their vows. (*Christian Monasticism*, p. 238)

This is gloomy indeed; its author could only hope that 'a remnant of Israel' would be left:

> (Monastic life) has for more than seventeen centuries had a notable place in the life of the Church. So far as we can judge it will not attain . . . to a religious, economic and social influence of the first importance in the life of both Church and society. But it will remain as a Christian way of life for a greater or smaller number of individuals, with a significance greater than its numerical strength, and if a particular generation (even though it be our own) destroys it or disfigures it, it will return again when saints arise to show its nobility to the modern world. (*Christian Monasticism*, p. 244)

To quarrel with David Knowles the historian would be foolhardy, but when it comes to prophecy one may be allowed to chance one's arm. There is no doubt that the Benedictines have reached an interesting and important (some would say dangerous) crossroads in their history. The future is not certain, and the existence of many problems will demand as much reflection in the 1980's as they have received in the 1970's. For example, those monasteries involved in external works realize that the whole approach to the parish apostolate may have to be altered because the validity and viability of the parish in our society is seriously questioned. In education the desirability of Catholic schools is under review, and the future of English public schools, for example, is by no means clear. Congregations involved in missionary work face the problem of survival in countries which are suspicious of colonialism; it is also pertinent to ask whether Benedictinism will 'take' among non-Europeans.

Apart from these problems, questions need answering which are posed by the very nature of Benedictinism: are some of our monasteries too big, making family life in a real sense unattainable? Does the possession of parishes far from the monastery square with the vow of stability? Are Benedictine monasteries too wedded to the past, still geared to needs which were real in years gone by but which are no longer pressing? Has the possession of large buildings and much plant deprived Benedictines of the willingness to experiment with fresh work in new areas? Have we put too many eggs into too few baskets?

There is no room for complacency but equally, there is no reason to be despondent. Real as the questions are which we have listed, they concern the application of principles rather than principles themselves, and there is every reason to think that these principles will be as valid in the future as they have been in the past.

Benedictines stand for the priority of God and of prayer in human existence; for life lived in a group or family; and for compassion and attentiveness to the needs of others. To survive, monasteries need recruits; humanly speaking, therefore, the present mood of young people is of the greatest significance.

In the 1960's we were told that God was dead, and there was widespread impatience with organized, institutional religion. The impatience still exists but the 1970's have shown that God is not quite as dead as the American theologians thought. Inside the Church the 1970's have been noteworthy for the charismatic movement which has renewed the virtue of faith in Christians of all denominations; outside the Church the resurgence of interest, not perhaps in religion but certainly in Christ, has been equally remarkable: witness the success of 'Son of Man', 'Godspell', 'Jesus Christ Superstar' and 'Jesus of Nazareth'. At the same time there has been a tremendous interest in the practice of prayer and meditation; many Eastern religions have attracted Western followers by offering them the secret of communion with the Infinite. All the signs, therefore, show that there is a distinct 'market', if the word be allowed, for God and for prayer. There is also a desire for life in communes, groups and associations: the hippie groups and the Israeli *kibbutzim* are merely two examples of this. Finally, young people today are remarkable for their awareness and compassion; much more than an earlier generation, they are deeply conscious of the suffering, injustice and exploitation in the world, and are concerned to help. This is quite clear to anyone who has seen young people helping the old, the handicapped and those who are mentally or physically sick.

This desire for God, for life with others and for a context in which a contribution of value can be made to the world in which we live is met at every point by the life which St Benedict proposed. As in the twelfth century, so in the twentieth: the Rule contains that which can appeal to the aspirations of our society. The opportunities open to Benedictines today are manifold and the means necessary to realize them have already been summarized by Abbot Cuthbert Butler:

> Benedictines will do well to realise that the value, religious and other, of our contribution to the New Era unfolding itself before us will be proportionate to the fulness with which we receive those first words our Holy Father speaks to us:
> 'Hearken, my son, to the precepts of the master; freely accept and faithfully fulfil the instructions of a loving father'.

by Dom Stephen Ortiger

BIBLIOGRAPHY

C. Butler, *Benedictine Monachism* (London 1919).
D. Knowles, *The Benedictines* (London 1929).
——, *Christian Monasticism* (London 1969).
Renew and Create (Collegeville 1969).
D. Rees and others, *Consider Your Call* (London 1978).
A. Morey, *David Knowles: a memoir* (London 1979).
Statistical information can be found in:
SS. Patriarchae Benedicti Familiae Confoederatae Catalogus Monasteriorum O.S.B. (Rome 1975: new edition due in 1980).
J. P. Muller, *Atlas O.S.B.: Index Monasteriorum* (Editiones Anselmianae, Rome 1973).

Appendix: Medieval and Modern Statistics

Note. The medieval statistics concern England and Wales only; they are based on those in D. Knowles and R. N. Hadcock, *Medieval Religious Houses; England and Wales*. These are *approximate*. Here the Black Benedictine totals represent the addition of Cluniacs, Tironian and Grandmontine monks to the estimated numbers in houses of English origin. The totals for the Cistercians include those of the Order of Savigny, aggregated to the Cistercians in 1147. They do not include Cistercian laybrothers, estimated at about 3,200 in *c.* 1200, but whose numbers had diminished to very few by *c.* 1400. The totals for the nuns include those of Sempringham as well as those of Benedictine and Cistercian houses. They exclude those of canonesses, of the Mendicant Orders and of the Bridgettines.

The modern statistics are world-wide and the most recent available.

MEDIEVAL STATISTICS

	I. Black Benedictines		II. Cistercians		III. Nuns	
Date	Houses	Monks	Houses	Monks	Houses	Nuns
1066	48	844	nil	nil	12	206
1100	133	2136	nil	nil	18	337
1154	245	4150	51	1405	67	1300
1216	266	4066	68	2112	116	2648
1350	269	3464	75	1956	119	2622
1422	246	2508	75	1078	117	1657
1500	182	2499	76	1311	115	1639
1534	170	2292	76	1230	113	1532

MODERN STATISTICS

1. THE BENEDICTINE CONFEDERATION OF MONKS

Congregation	Date of Formation	Abbeys	Priories	Dep. Houses	Monks
Cassinese	1408	10	—	2	167
English	1300	10	1	3	514
Hungarian	1514	1	2	1	209
Swiss	1602	6	—	5	482
Bavarian	1684	10	—	3	355
Brasilian	1835	4	—	7	155
Solesmes	1837	14	3	3	783
American Cassinese	1855	18	4	10	1638
Subiaco	1851 (1872)	34	13	15	1468
Beuronese	1868	9	—	2	490
Pan American	1881	14	1	8	873
Austrian	1889	12	—	2	438
Ottilien	1884 (1904)	10	3	21	1182
Annunciation (Belgian)	1920	6	5	8	574
Slavonic	1945	3	—	3	43
Olivetan	1344 (1960)	6	7	11	226
Vallumbrosian	1090 (1966)	2	4	3	56
Camaldolese	1074 (1966)	—	4	3	97
Dutch	1969	3	—	—	113
Sylvestrine	1250 (1973)	1	5	17	195
S. American 'Cono-Sur'	1970 (1973)	2	4	1	99
Single Monasteries		4	3	6	167
21 Congregations	372 Houses-	179	59	134	10324

(. . . .) = Date of entry into the Confederation   (1975 figures)

II. BENEDICTINE NUNS (MONIALES)

Countries	Monasteries	Nuns
Austria	2	107
Belgium	14	403
Denmark	1	23
W. Germany	23	1128
E. Germany	1	36
Eire	1	25
Spain	28	809
France	39	1694
Great Britain	13	316
Holland	6	243
Italy	123	2768
Jugoslavia	8	107
Luxembourg	1	29
Poland	13	308
Switzerland	7	192
Africa	8	75
N. America	7	243
S. America	14	272
Asia	4	166
Australia	1	35
	314	8979

III. BENEDICTINE SISTERS AND OBLATES

These had (in 1975) 526 houses and 11,992 members.